Turning the Tables:

How the Third World Overthrew the West

Rupert Hodder

Turning the Tables:
How the Third World Overthrew the West

Rupert Hodder

Academica Press
Washington~London

Library of Congress Cataloging-in-Publication Data

Names: Hodder, Rupert, author.
Title: Turning the tables : how the third world overthrew the west | Rupert Hodder
Description: Washington : Academica Press, 2023.
Identifiers: LCCN 2023934308 | ISBN 9781680537239 (hardcover) | ISBN 9781680537246 (ebook)

For when you are a little bit older, Xavier.
From one old man to another, with love.

Contents

Introduction:

Notes for the reader

Human societies advance materially through redistribution. Third World countries live by this truth. The West, meanwhile, is too confident in its belief that markets, democracy, and rules bring stability and economic development. Certainty also contributes to a penchant for splitting the world into narrow, ordered, and specialized fragments, limiting possibility in thought and practice.

Why is the Third World rising and the West declining? The explanation offered here is straightforward. Social transfers, patronage, dense and mobile populations, and informal behavior are critical for effective organization and economic development. Market exchange, stagnant population, formalized behavior, and democratic ideals help push societies into decline.

Underlying this argument are what I take to be two facts. One is that improvements in material living standards depend upon society's arrangements for redistribution. The other is that society's mood changes prompt shifts back and forth amongst those qualities responsible for progress and regress. These oscillating and interdependent moods – one I describe as puritan and the other affective - are inherent in all human societies. Puritan means treating relationships as substantial, material, and phenomenal. Affective means thinking and acting *as if* relationships are substantial and separate things. Puritanism helps characterize societies in the West. Those societies where the affective prevails, we call the Third World. The division is far from perfect, but it is serviceable, at least for now.

Who is this book for?

Readers turning over these pages in a shop, or swiping through its preliminaries on their 'phones, are probably asking themselves, what kind of book is this? If it is about Third World development, why is there no mention of urbanization, globalization, colonialism, institutions, civil society, or the environment in its table of contents?

There are no dedicated sections on geopolitics, military capabilities, soft power, diplomacy, climate, or natural resources in its discussion on the West's decline. A single volume that combines 'development of the Third World' and 'decline of the West' might also raise eyebrows.

Is it for philosophers, perhaps? Readers familiar with Hans Vaihinger (b.1852) might think of his book *The Philosophy of As If*,[1] written in Kant's wake. Or is it for political scientists, specialists in international relationships, or geographers and historians? Economists will ask if growth *really* favors a society centered on redistribution rather than one focused on manufacturing and saving? There are long queues of people from all walks of life ready to say just the opposite. Sociologists and social theorists might wonder if moods really exist. What is the provenance of these assertions? They are reminiscent of Sorokin's [2] cultural mentalities or Polanyi's's[3] types of exchange - ideas which, though influential in their time, have long since dropped out from mainstream thought. What precisely is the accumulated body of literature, evidence, theories, methods, and assumptions from which this book emerges? What is its perspective or approach? Or is this book all idiosyncrasy and opinion? Just who is it for, then? A direct answer such as 'the general reader,' 'people,' or 'you' is likely to sound facetious or maudlin. So let me explain with an indirect one.

Keeping it simple

One difficulty with social theory is that it requires people to conform to its demands, whereas human behavior runs its own course. In my view, one must attempt to divine and summarise fundamental patterns of thought and practice without involving extraneous factors or elements. There are only aspects of mind and interactions with one another (relationships) and the natural world. No other conveniences can be invoked to compel or explain behavior. That is what I mean by keeping it simple.

I suppose (see chapter 5) that the social world comprises a single material (human relationships) fused with 'me' (that sense of being we each possess). I say 'me' is *fused* because it arises from our relationships and our interactions with the natural world. Thus, it allows us to behave in ways familiar to everyone else, which others can recognize as signifying a conscious presence. Since we are each of these materials, we directly perceive the world and its organic-like complexity. And we intuitively work relationships into societies' myriad features and practices - from the business, family, or government department to trade routes, economic exchange, and political transactions. This often involves creating the *appearance* of something other than relationships, and this is where society's moods come in. I say more about these moods in chapter 5.

Readers who have spent time in a classroom teaching - especially if they have also read Holt's[4] *How Children Fail* - will probably 'get' what I mean instantly when I say we each directly perceive the world. They will recognize my meaning in the similarity and sameness of ideas constantly whirling off their students who, without degrees or decades of study under their belts, arrive at conclusions and make observations already generated by earlier thinkers of whom they have no prior knowledge. It's a quality we often ignore unless incorporated into forms that professional academics approve of and state education rewards. Yet even in its raw condition, it ought to be learned from and encouraged. The most accurate rendition of the social world rests in spontaneous knowledge of it, for the simple reason that such knowledge is the prime material from which that world is in fact made.

Being cautious about disciplines

I am, therefore, cautious about a willingness to fragment the world into specialisms and the disciplines and intellectualisms that result. Such practices assume that each bailiwick supplies us with a glass without which we would be unable to analyze and understand the world as effectively as we do.

I am also wary of the premise that the regularities in behavior that help define a discipline's boundaries (and make their analysis of society possible) reflect otherwise invisible structures or are the product of agency (countless individual decisions). 'Structure' is a perennial explanatory device of the social sciences. 'Agency,' on the other hand, tends to fall in and out of fashion. This is because the aggregate effect of individuals' decisions may differ radically from the local impact of those decisions. And because 'agency' is equated (unfairly in my view) with political bias (by which is meant neo-liberal ideology and anti-Marxist rhetoric) and an inability to handle abstract thought. The compromise arrived at is that structure shapes the individual's actions, and individuals incrementally re-shape structure through minor adjustments and modifications. The settlement is entirely plausible to many writers but does not resolve any doubts about the reality of structure and agency.

My other reason for wariness about these concepts is that they are an unnecessary complication. 'Me' and relationships are organically fused such that one cannot talk of them as separate entities or 'individuals.' As for 'structure,' we can easily do without this if we accept variations in the psychological treatment of relationships that I describe as moods.

I am not saying we should discard the West's disciplinary outlook entirely. The more ideas, the better. But it is not enough and is certainly not the only way of looking at the world. We must also recognize *why* breaking the world into disciplinary and explanatory fragments dominates our thinking.

Habit is one reason. From that awful moment we are handed over at the nursery or left at the school gates for the first time, we are taught to look at the world through a kaleidoscope or as Rubik's cube.[5] We learn about geography, history, writing, reading, art, music, maths, and science. And we are introduced to many other divisions as we get older.

The other reason is that teachers are often remarkably loyal to their discipline. This is all very well as long as we remember what we are being faithful to - a nineteenth-century bureaucratic convenience. Their subject is their living, profession, and framework for instruction. Theories are seized on to establish identities and boundaries for expertise. Knowledge of these ideas and their further development help establish conditions for entry, the award of qualifications, and career progression. A geographer, for instance, might tell us that to comprehend marketplaces and their role in settlement formation, we must know about the theories of Christaller. Since the early 1960s, these have dominated thinking by American scholars on marketplaces and settlement evolution in China. Or the economist might insist that firms are explained by a need to reduce transaction costs.

These professional considerations drive the proliferation of disciplines. New people enter the profession, take up the flag, and look to establish themselves. This helps universities, colleges, and schools expand or fuse existing departments, create new ones, split them into finer specialisms, or bridge them through establishing interdisciplinary, cross-disciplinary, or trans-disciplinary centers. Being multidisciplinary might appear like a solution to the limitations and defensiveness of intellectual silos. In practice, however, it means taking a kaleidoscopic outlook in principle and stitching together accepted interpretations from various fields to throw what is believed to be new light on a given question. Sometimes, those interdisciplinary studies lay the groundwork for a new discipline so that yet another silo is dug.

Two examples of obvious relevance are development studies and declinism. In the 1950s, an introduction to development comprising 6 square meters (about 270 pages, each measuring 5x7 inches) was thought ample. It covered everything from practical difficulties with measurements and collating statistics to natural resources, population (size and quality), capital, government, and policy. An introductory text published fifty years later covers 550 pages, each measuring 7 X 9.5 inches, or about 24 square meters in all. That's about four times larger than the book printed fifty years earlier. The modern version includes concepts, colonialism, theories, globalization, people, resources and environment, institutions (the role of state and civil society), movement and flows, and urban and rural spaces. These are matters that include, amongst many others, empowerment, human capabilities, institutional change, adaption to changing climates, and government by discussion. Any one of these topics is a specialism in its own right. One recent volume on institutions, for instance, stretches to 35m2. Universities have flourished over that same period, as have development journals, specialized research organizations, international organizations involved in development practice, and courses on development.

The decline of the West is not yet a fiefdom, but it is getting there. Courses on the West's decline are run in universities. Scholars list it as one of their research interests. Articles and books on the question have become a staple, and a respectable lineage is often traced back to Kohn's 1957 book *Is the Liberal West in Decline?*[6] or Spengler's *The Decline of the West*[7] published in 1918. And it is said[8] that its emphasis has shifted from descriptions of broad social change to causal explanations. It has undoubtedly become more self-conscious. What is declinism concerned with, its scholars ask? What should its remit be? It has also acquired a history that is re-interpreted and re-written. The British Empire's decline was predicted and fretted over even before it had reached its height and long before Kohn's and Spengler's publications. Others suggest that declinism is probably closer to 300 years old. Adam Smith argues that a society that consumes more than it produces reflects or induces decline. Excessively high profits of stock, constraints on the free circulation of labor, or unfavorable laws and institutions (such as those which led China to neglect or despise foreign commerce, are indicative of this condition.

The meaning of the Third World and the West

My third note to the reader concerns the term 'Third World.' The phrase entered common usage after WWII. It referred to those countries that belonged neither to the West nor the communist bloc (centered on the Soviet Union and China). Subsequently, it became a byword for poor, backward, chaotic, and hopeless.

Today the term is widely thought of as unhelpful and tired. Many countries that were once poor are now rich or at least a good deal wealthier, the communist bloc has dissolved, and there are enclaves of poverty in the West. The Third World is also extraordinarily diverse. Some countries are enormous, densely populated, and were commercialized many centuries ago. Others are sparsely populated and dominated by agriculture. Some were colonized by America, Europe, Russia, or Japan. Many retained western forms of government even after independence. Some nations were cobbled together from disparate peoples and languages. In many instances, their officials were educated in the West or received a western-style education, unlike the general populace. The West also pressures these countries to adopt principles and policies it favors and bind them into international organizations such as World Bank, IMF, and WTO. Some commentators even question whether the Third World was ever more than a half-baked idea cooked up by colonial rulers and 'scholars of coloniality,' which, in any case, is being superseded by 'the rise of the rest.'[9]

'The West' is no less vague. 'The West,' like the 'Third World,' also contains countries large and small, more and less crowded, and divided by language, religion, ideology, interests, identity, and historical experience. And since its development has been interlaced with other parts of the world, why not include, say, Turkey, Syria, Israel or Palestine, Iraq or India, Ukraine or Belarus, or Russia? Why not China, South Africa or Latin America? Or even Japan or South Korea or Singapore or Nigeria, or Ghana?

Despite all this, I have elected to keep both terms. I define the West as North America, Europe, Australia, and New Zealand. And I expand the Third World to include every territory – even those such as Japan, South Korea, Singapore, China, Hong Kong, Singapore, and Taiwan - outside the West. This, to my mind, reminds us just how far the status of the West has changed.

The meaning of the West's decline

My final note to the readers is about the meaning of the West's 'decline.' All societies and civilizations resemble Trigger's broom (or Theseus's ship). Trigger, a road sweeper, received a medal from local government for using the same broom for twenty years and saving his employer money. He later revealed that it had had only seven new brushes and fourteen new handles during that time. Nothing lasts, yet everything remains. But when there is no one to maintain the broom (or the ship) or no one who can or wants to do the job, it falls apart or is replaced by something else entirely different in content and looks. That is what is happening in the West. By the end of the century, it will have become a memory. Its societies, to survive, will have already become distinctly Third World-ish.

Part I

Perspective

Chapter 1

Economic Growth

An understanding of economic growth has changed little even after two centuries. It describes the production of more things more efficiently through re-arrangements of land, labor, and capital. Because changes in these arrangements and growth itself set in motion imbalances in the apportionment of the factors of production, the real trick is to raise production without throwing those arrangements out of kilter. Some feel this is better left to the market; others believe that governments make growth faster and less painful. The compromise arrived at in the West is a mixed economy.

The existence of complex human society presupposes arrangements to produce, collect, move, store, and distribute materials and goods. It also suggests the presence of ideas characterized as 'economic.' Trade and the centralization of food and its subsequent redistribution precede the appearance of agriculture and the first states by a long way. Both were common practices among early modern humans by around 150,000 BP and possibly among archaic human groups by 1.5 million BP. By the third or second millennium BC, economic advice and pronouncements had been written down in the Rig-Veda. By the 4th century BC, counsel on price, interest, tax, property rights, public finance, redistribution, and public infrastructure was offered in The Arthashastr[10] and the Mahabharata. At about the same time, the Greeks discussed oikonomia (the laws or norms of the household), the division and specialization of labor, and the advantages and disbenefits of private and public ownership. A little later, around the second or third centuries BC,[11] arguments to stimulate markets and production through state spending and to control the supply of grain by manipulating the amount of coinage in circulation were set out in 'Guanzi'- a series of essays offering advice on statecraft in China. Sometime after, Rome built up a repertoire of accounting, credit, logistical, and monetary techniques for the practical management of the economy.[12]

Nevertheless, how society raises living standards and does so reasonably consistently through the generations is treated as a modern concern. 'Modern' because it emerged with economics as a distinct science in the late eighteenth century. Until then, or so it is believed today, thinking about economic matters was neither focused, specialized, rational, or systematic enough to be considered a science. Growth took place over decades rather than monthly quarters if it happened at all. 'Modern,' too, because of a wish to present as current a central tenet that has not changed for nearly a quarter of a millennium - that producing more things lies at the heart of economic growth.[13]

To produce more things requires more of those elements used to make those things in the first place. These elements (or factors of production) are land, labor, and capital. The more factors commanded, the more produced and the higher the income. However, there are limits: after a certain point, each additional unit of land, labor, or capital yields fewer and fewer things and less and less income until, eventually, the returns stop. The reason for these diminishing returns depends on circumstances. It might be that extra workers have progressively smaller plots of land to cultivate or that each new worker makes the production shop more crowded and less efficient. To get around these diminishing returns, something else has to change. That often means the introduction of new technology. But it does not have to be. A simple organizational change of great importance is the division of labor: the breakup of manufacturing into a series of clearly defined tasks each worker concentrates on. This improves agility, saves time, and, by delineating specific actions, makes it easier to imagine and formulate new technology. It is not enough to rely on more land, labor, or capital to grow production: productivity must be raised.

The significance of trade in all this was recognized from the start. It allows a single worker, household, company, region, or country to specialize. This is because they can always buy what they don't produce on the market. Trade also enables smaller economies to sidestep the problem of diminishing returns. In a small economy, an increase in production causes prices to drop and diminishing returns to set in early, limiting the production of specialized items. But if that country produces for a vast global market, that limit is, in effect, removed or pushed back quite some distance.

If capital is to be accumulated and used sensibly, inequalities must be tolerated. The pursuit of self-interest, Adam Smith[14] (d.1790) declared confidently, benefits society as a whole: all boats are lifted with time. But what about the problem of demand? Who do businesses sell their goods to if there is no widespread market at the start? How do they generate an income? The answer, believed Say (d.1832), is plain. Since production earns an income (which is then spent), production is the source of demand.[15] The more produced, the more revenue there is to consume subsequent manufactures. It is, therefore, impossible to produce too much, and other entrepreneurs will fix any breaks in the process quickly as shortages bite. Those who only consume hold the economy back. It behooves everyone to produce.

These arguments did not convince everyone. As populations grew, increased demand for food pushed up rent and the price of food. Wages rose, and profits squeezed. It is unlikely diminishing returns could be overcome. Mill (d.1873) thought this was no bad thing: once a reasonably comfortable standard of living was realized, it would be better if people concentrated on the Art of Life rather than chase material wealth.[16] Malthus (d.1834) was less sanguine: it was only a matter of time before population growth outstripped agriculture's capacity to feed everyone.[17] Marx (d.1883) thought the whole edifice was doomed. Since the owners of capital and land extracted their income (profit) from the difference between their total revenues and the sum paid out in wages, the latter was kept as low as possible. Workers could not form the necessary market for the goods they manufactured. Profits would fall, and wages would sink even further. Eventually, labor would rebel and end this miserable downward spiral.

Time, though, favored the market. The agricultural revolution turned into an industrial one. Continuing growth showed that diminishing returns could be overcome, especially by technology. Production really is the source of demand. Everybody's material well-being can be raised, if not at the same moment and to the same extent. By the middle of the nineteenth century, many felt that an understanding of growth was firmly established. Attention now shifted to the nuts and bolts of an economy. Credit, price, value, supply, rent, surplus, demand, income, utility, profit, spending, and cost, as well as institutions and human behavior, were as wheels, springs, pinions, trains, and balances whose movements could be revealed and elucidated. The elaborate mechanism they believed they saw occupied economists for the next seventy years, and the best exemplar of its study is Marshall's (d.1924) *Principles of Economics*, published in 1890.[18]

However, by the time of his death, it was evident that a good deal about economies and their development was still not understood. War and revolution had thrown up the Soviet Union and sent waves of Marxist influence rolling across Europe and its colonies in Africa, India, the Far East, and Latin America. Depression gripped both Europe and North America. Economists needed to respond.

Keynes (d.1946) took the view that depression arose out of success. When incomes rise, savings increase, and when savings increase, expenditure falls. This can lead to a depression that becomes long-lasting: long-lasting because the more people hold onto their cash, the more interest rates climb (as an incentive to part with it and extend loans). In the expectation that rates will increase still further, people only tighten their grip. This pushes investment rates down even further. It falls to the state to spend, increasing demand.

Economists subsequently concluded that it is possible to grow an economy steadily without upsetting the delicate balance at its heart with careful thought and planning. The amount invested and the amount saved must be poised exactly, such that the production equipment available and the goods produced are in equilibrium. The trick is knowing where this point is and getting predictions spot-on. Too much investment beyond a plant's capacity to meet expected production levels causes entrepreneurs to feel they have not done enough and to pour in additional money and effort and prolong inflation. Too little investment and it will seem that capital and stock are in excess, leading to further cuts, unemployment, and depression.[19]

Others took quite a different view. Economies do not need to walk a tightrope. Assuming full employment, a rise in investment (and so in demand) will lift prices and profits and reduce consumption. Conversely, a fall in investment (and so in demand) lowers prices and increases consumption.[20] Alternatively, stability can be explained by diminishing returns. Economies tend naturally to equilibria or stasis because additions of land, labor, and capital yield less growth. One inference is that poorer countries will inevitably catch up with richer countries, given the same technological levels. This is because incomes rise faster in developing countries where diminishing returns have not yet set in.

In practice, technological standards rarely stay the same. Education, research in wealthy countries, and technological spillovers from trade led to improvements. Advantages might be conferred on the producer by introducing new technology, new goods, networks of production, or new organizational forms; or discovering additional markets or sources of raw materials or semi-finished goods. But improvements can also create downturns. As other businesses see mounting rewards derived from some new technology or method, they swarm in with the hope that they can also make money. Production expands quickly, too much credit is handed out, prices fall, and a slump follows.[21]

Kaldor[22] went further: it cannot be assumed that capital accumulation or technical progress has much to do with growth. Ultimately, output and profit earned by each unit of capital depend upon human attitudes to risk and money-making. It is this stock that brings about productivity increases.

On the other hand, Kuznets was sure growth was rooted in technological progress. He drew his conclusion from a mass of empirical material on national incomes in different parts of the world, including Asia and Latin America. To him, it demonstrated that as growth proceeds, inequalities initially widen (as people leave their farms and migrate to cities) before they close again (as the welfare state comes into being).

Kuznets' view of technology as the source of growth pre-empts a more recent suggestion that ideas, once formed, do not have to be reinvented and go on giving as other people take them up. Since they do not wear out, each idea adds to the aggregate stock of knowledge. And since this stock of knowledge is constantly expanding, it has increasing returns. It is this stock that brings about productivity increases.

Political economy was born alongside economics. The accumulation and effective use of land, labor, and capital must be protected if rising income is to be generated. Property rights and, more broadly, the rule of law must be placed within an armature of courts, rulings, legislation, enforcement, and punishment. Only then can one rely on contracts and measures to curtail rulers' power to interfere and sequester goods and income. It follows that inequalities need to be defended as well as accepted. These patterns of organizations, practices, behavior, and values within which growth occurs are just as important as the economic formula for growth. They are the 'development' part of 'economic growth and development.'

Explanations for the rise of the West frequently identify the seventeenth and eighteenth centuries as pivotal. Within the networks of markets, towns, cities, and ports already laid down by then, something ignited capitalism and then an industrial revolution. That 'something' was competition, property rights, science, and moral and ethical beliefs sympathetic to money-making.

Competition, sometimes rephrased as decentralization or political weakness,[23] is evident in that no empire to match Rome's was established in Europe between the fifth century and the industrial revolution. Many ambitious rulers tried to do so, but none succeeded. Political and economic authority remained fragmented. This kept thought and practice flexible. Friction amongst the competing polities in Europe turned commerce into Fortunatus's purse. Merchants acquired considerable power when permitted to found independent towns and cities where they were free to produce, sell, and make money. In England, by the seventeenth century, they had secured the measure of political authority necessary to establish the rule of law. Parliament met with greater frequency and passed more legislation, a good part of which affected property rights.[24] Ownership, and the right to use and dispose of property and income as desired, brought an incentive to work, save, and invest, reduced transaction costs, and allowed owners to focus their efforts and money on putting land to good use rather than on its protection. The seventeenth and eighteenth centuries also saw the rise of science. This required a shift in outlook – one in which the natural world is understood in its own terms and worked to advantage. This only strengthened once it became clear that its application brought phenomenal increases in production and other advantages over large parts of humanity. One other ingredient in this brew was Protestantism. It separated thought and practice from the Catholic Church. Outside the cloisters - profiting from hard work in the ordinary world and spending wisely and modestly - was where and how Christians should live life.

How reliable are such explanations? Competition, political weakness, or commercial networks stretched over miles and centuries are not peculiar to Europe. It isn't clear when property rights were established and what effect they had. And there is no certainty about the importance of Protestantism: was it a cause or a tonic?[25] As for explanations of the rise of science, these are mostly descriptive. It is unclear why the modes of thought and corpus of discoveries called science emerged where and when they did. There is good reason to think that aspects of scientific study evolved first outside Europe. And there is no question that all kinds of technological inventions were devised in the Middle East, India, China, and elsewhere long before the West's industrial revolution.

Nevertheless, it is widely assumed that the West's formula for growth and development is being followed and applied in the rest of the world. To all intents and purposes, the world economic system is western. The market sets prices and determines the flow of trade and division of labor. Governments play a role closer to that envisaged by Keynes. And patterns of organization and practice, from the rule of law to notions of hard work, thrift, and the righteousness of profit, bear an uncanny resemblance to Protestantism, even if sometimes described as Confucian, Asian, Igbo, Botswanian, African, or Islamic values.

Our understanding of economic growth has changed little, even after two centuries. It describes the production of more things more efficiently through re-arrangements of land, labor, and capital. (We can, perhaps, add technology to these factors of production, or maybe not if 'technology' is understood as the reorganization of materials supported by capital.) Because changes in arrangements for growth, and growth itself, set in motion imbalances in the apportionment of the factors of production, the real trick is to raise production without throwing it all out of kilter.[26] In this way, improvements in production would remain constant. Is this matter so complex that it is best left to the market? Or do theory, science, and experience allow governments to make growth faster and less painful? Or can we go so far as to suggest that government redistribution, more care over taxation, and universalism (keeping transfer costs down and the population healthier and happier) would more than compensate for any reduction in GDP?[27]

Chapter 2

Development

With the question of growth already settled long before 1949, the debate was not about what to do but how. At first, many governments and their advisors believed they should school the Third World in values and behavior conducive to growth. But events quickly outpaced study and theory. Seventy years on, there is little or no agreement on whether the study of development was necessary or possible in any objective sense.

By the time Truman spoke of 'the underdeveloped' areas of the world, an understanding of economic growth had required neither reinvention nor serious revision. Growth was (and, to this day, remains) about a constant rise in the production of goods and services, which necessitates productivity improvements. The question was not what to do but how to do it. The West felt that outside its borders, traditional values dominated. Profit and capital were, more often than not, treated with disdain. Effective contracts and economic transactions depended on trust. Social and economic life were not adequately separated from one another. Given that the West had already industrialized and, on this matter, possessed an enormous back catalog of ideas, it seemed evident that populations in other parts of the world should be schooled in behavior conducive to growth and development. One immediate step, taken just after the War, was to reestablish a framework for international trade. An agreement on a foreign exchange system was reached at Bretton Woods in New Hampshire. Two new institutions were created in support - the International Monetary Fund and the World Bank.

There was, however, a wide gap between good intentions and practice. Japan's economic competitors in Europe and America did not expect the enormous physical destruction that the country had suffered to get in the way of a swift recovery.[28] Yet American policies to reform Japan – such as imposing reparations, purging business leaders, dissolving the zaibatsu, limiting trade with the outside world, and restricting strategically important industries - succeeded only in prolonging economic distress. Not until America's fear of communism supplanted its concern that Japan was still harboring imperial ambitions were those policies tossed aside. And not until War broke out on the Korean peninsula did Japan's economy fire up.

In Europe, colonial offices dreamt up vast development projects with only slender knowledge of the places on which they were to be imposed thousands of miles away, with predictable consequences. Decolonization energized communism: what was needed, said the revolutionaries, was a willingness to throw off dependency on the West and its controlling ways. A sense that the socialist's day had come was at least as strong in the West as in its former colonies. After two world wars and millions of dead, words like 'freedom' and 'democracy' sounded more like palliates than a rousing call to reconstruct and modernize. The Korean War only reinforced that cynicism. A war in Vietnam only added to the feeling that behind all the bluster and bumptiousness lay weakness, indecision, and nescience. Few political or military leaders in America thought they could win it. Their determination to conduct it as though an exercise in quantitative business management was hopelessly blinkered. And the draft was blatantly unfair.

By the end of the 1960s, modernization was giving way to 'dependency.' Its focus was not on growth but on the process of underdevelopment in the Third World. People and territories were being sucked dry and used up. Only by avoiding unequal exchange with the West could the world's poor hope to raise their incomes and better themselves materially. Richly colored by dependency and socialist thought, one state after another, from Latin America to Asia and Africa, implemented centralized planning and 'bottom-up' or 'alternative' methods (characterized by self-sufficiency and an emphasis on local industry, local production, and local employment).

Criticisms of these practices quickly mounted, however. Governments were restricting markets, spending too much money, and distorting the price system directly or through attempts to control incomes and subsidize essential goods such as electricity, petrol, and rice. At worst, national markets were erased, fragmenting societies into thousands of tiny self-sufficient cells. Economies grew either very slowly or slipped into humanitarian crises.

In the West, too, enthusiasm for socialist and Keynesian-style practice and thought was, by the 1970s, on the wane. Its economies had stagnated, and both unemployment and inflation were high. This was not supposed to be possible: measures that lowered inflation were bound to increase unemployment, and spending to reduce unemployment would lead to inflation, or so Keynes had argued.

Economists and governments decided once again to entrust the future to the market. Cut taxes, cut regulation, cut away the dead hand of the state, allow capital to accumulate in the hands of those who will create firms and employ others, and watch the newly created wealth trickle down through the rest of society.

Multinational companies had already concluded that to be successful, they had to shape themselves into 'global corporations.' National boundaries were only as significant to overall corporate objectives as the reality of time and place required.[29] Countries linked to these flows did extraordinarily well, and even governments at first hesitant to join eventually opened their doors.

The East Asian 'dragons' were red meat for what was rapidly becoming the new orthodoxy. They began their rise by participating in world trade in the 1960s and 1970s. They used revenue from exports to buy investment goods. They controlled borrowing and spending and left price systems intact. And they intervened only to the extent they built infrastructure and legal systems which, above all, defended property rights. Japan owed its success to private entrepreneurs responding to the free market, or so many economists claimed.

Communist regimes offered the most dramatic illustration of the strategy. After Mao died in 1976, China lowered the drawbridge to initiate its extraordinary recovery. Within a few years, Vietnam started to do what America had failed to do with all its firepower: turn the country into a market economy or something very much like it. Then the Soviet Union dissolved, and its republics converted.

In the early 1990s, the World Bank[30] granted another dimension to this story by recognizing the state's role. Its duty was not just to stand back and let the market rip. Governments had to take a market-friendly approach to development for the simple reason that state and market are complementary. The best way to organize production and distribution, and unleash entrepreneurship and technology, is through competitive markets; and only governments can provide the legal and regulatory frameworks that markets need. The specific formula for success included: a stable macroeconomic environment; high rates of savings and investment; a literate, well-educated, and well-trained population; a merit-based bureaucracy; low inequalities such that the new wealth finds its way into a broad section of the people, and that meant less social tension and bigger markets; the promotion of exports; flexible and thoughtful industrialization policies; and foreign direct investment, which also involved technological transfers.

States were not simply market-friendly facilitators or *animateurs*. They treated development as a long-term state project. In Brunei and Indonesia - both heavily dependent upon oil and vulnerable to changes in world demand and price - governments drove the diversification of their economies. Taiwan's administrations periodically instigated radical changes in direction. In the 1950s, the country switched from import-substituting industrialization to export-oriented industrialization. By the 1970s, when Taiwan was classified as a newly industrialized country, it emphasized capital-intensive industries. The government then adjusted the economy to higher energy costs and pushed forward the petrochemical industry. In the 1980s, it turned its attention to the computer and electronics industry. Singapore's government also intervened thoughtfully and pragmatically. It adjusted, guided, and directed as necessary. It responded quickly to changing circumstances. Soon, countries throughout southeast Asia were being used as examples of what the state was capable of.

Two events soon outpaced the debate on economic success in the Third World. The first, the Asian crisis, struck in 1997. Many people saw in this vindication of their belief that the free market, the rule of law, and transparency were necessary after all. Governments were not as strong as thought. Nor as committed to the national interest. Nor as insulated from vested interests. The developmental state was just another name for collusion, corruption, and crony capitalism. Other commentators were more circumspect. The crux of the matter was deregulation in the financial markets internationally; and too much openness from Asian governments. The state was essential. In Asia, countries once known and often praised for providing only a basic safety net or services – including Singapore, Malaysia, Thailand, Indonesia, Laos, the Philippines, Vietnam, and Cambodia – became more heavily engaged in welfare. The second event, the Great Financial Crisis, placed the boot firmly on the other foot, or so the statists felt. The new crisis showed what happens when the market has too much freedom. The truth is that equality and economic performance complement rather than antagonize each other. Inequality weakens aggregate demand, wastes human potential, undermines growth prospects, and makes public investment less likely.

From the 1980s to the Great Crisis, Marxist criticism of neo-liberalism did not disappear altogether, though it did weaken. Taking up the slack was a feeling that America and Europe (and especially their political and business elites) were manipulating world events, pushing their agendas, and imposing their model of 'what should be,' a sameness, on the rest of humanity. Development had become nothing less than 'an attempt by the West to produce societies in its own image' or, less delicately, an expression of the colonizing ambitions and ethnocentrism of white

Anglo-Saxons.[31] Development implies change, and all change can be for better or worse. What is subjectively termed 'good' development can equally be 'bad.' Economic growth, national progress, and modernization along Western lines might successfully meet basic needs and improve governance; yet involves a dependent and subordinate process, creates and widens spatial inequalities, harms local cultures and values, perpetuates poverty and poor working and living conditions, produces unsustainable environments, and infringes human rights and democracy. The response should be to protect and advance the vernacular and the traditional. The non-western is intrinsically and unremittingly different, and its development should follow its path at its own pace, measured against its own criteria.

A diverse collection of 'new' strands of thought grew and entangled themselves around one another: an emphasis on grassroots movements, non-governmental organizations, gender, justice, democracy, citizenship, environment, climate, resilience, empowerment of the poor, and people rather than place. Also included were updated versions of 'development from below' and 'basic needs' that had accompanied dependency theory in the sixties and seventies.

One further reaction to perceived oppression by western ideas and practices was to turn modernization on its head: indigenous cultures, not western values, determine economic success. Of this belief, 'the Chinese' became the most important symbol. It did so for good reasons: three of the economies of East and Southeast Asia (excluding mainland China) were populated mainly by Chinese; two were thought to be heavily influenced by Confucianism; and, in most of the remainder, the Chinese were believed to dominate some or all economic sectors despite the fact they were in the minority and, in some cases, made up just one or two percent of the population.

Even the relevance of development studies and theory and practice came to be questioned.[32] The allegation is that it has become an industry, a profession, with its own criteria for excellence and advancement. It turns people into mere carriers of intellectualized and technical constructs. Development professionals view these constructs as a better way of understanding and explaining the world. Facts need theory, just as theory needs facts. Knowledge must be worked at, uncovered, and made sense of in rational, technical, objective, and ethical ways. These criteria matter because the world must be accurately understood before it can be changed. It is only the professional who can do this effectively. The knowledge 'produced' is of a kind and quality very different from the local beliefs and ideas held by the people who are being studied and helped. The best development professionals are aware of these criticisms, it is said. In fact, it is they who are most likely to draw up the charge sheet: irrelevance, esotericism, abstruseness, and elitism! But the worst of them peddle snake oil and forms of words designed to baffle and dazzle and distract from the emptiness of what is offered. The rest take no stance. They act like phagocytes, absorbing ideas, facts, observations, and methods, only to disgorge them as agency initiatives or items on the student timetable.

Chapter 3

Explaining the rise of the Third World

The rise of the Third World caught the West by surprise. But extant understandings of growth meant that ready and familiar accounts in the form of the market and globalization were soon forthcoming.

A generation grew up between 1960 and the early 1990s with the idea that to study development was to study poverty, squalor, hunger, misery, inequality, corruption, ineptitude, exploitation, and their causes. Hopelessness was baked into the idea of 'the Third World.' The phrase was synonymous with cheap, throwaway electronics from Taiwan; gimcrack and shoddy plastic toys from Hong Kong and Japan; tinpot government; mountains of rubbish; endless slums; faces and hands scarred by leprosy; and the bloated stomachs of underfed children. Development was about explaining stagnation and regression.

But when practitioners and academics documenting these failures looked up from the grindstone, wiped their brows, and caught their breath, they found that economies across the Third World had progressed. Japan, Hong Kong, South Korea, Singapore, Taiwan, Indonesia, and Malaysia had by 1993 been growing by around 7% a year for a quarter of a century. Fifteen years later, China, Botswana, Brazil, Malta, Oman, India, and Vietnam had all matched that performance.[33] Between the mid-1990s and 2015, real GDP in the Third World *in toto* had been increasing at some 4%-7% a year, and at around 3% per person; and its share of GDP rose from 37% in 1960 to 50% in 2019.

Even in Africa south of the Sahara, GDP growth after 1995 hit around 5% a year – a rate last experienced in the 1960s and early 1970s before the oil crisis. Over the first decade-and-a-half of the twenty-first century, nearly two-thirds of countries on the continent saw rates of around 4%, and more than a dozen states experienced 5% or more. Angola, Chad, Equatorial Guinea, Ethiopia, Ghana, Liberia, Sierra Leone,

Tanzania, Uganda, and Zambia logged rates closer to those of the larger, emerging economies.[34]

The Third World's involvement in mergers and acquisitions pushed the US, UK, Germany, and France down UNCTAD's rankings.[35] Its share of global inward FDI rose from a quarter or so in the early 1970s to 55% by 2019, while its outward share grew from 10% to nearly half. India, China, and Brazil were the primary destinations for FDI, though the quantity of investment in Africa also increased. Most of this originated in other Third World countries, including China which became properly engaged in Africa after 2000. Its direct investment into the continent rose from less than 100 million dollars to 2.7 billion within twenty years. China extended another 143 billion dollars of loans to construct roads, seaports, railways, and airports[36] - infrastructure vital in a continent that can swallow the United States, China, and Europe combined. Next to large state companies such as China Bridge and Road, thousands of small, privately-owned Chinese concerns were working in Africa, taking advantage of cheaper labor and tariff-free exports to the USA.[37] They comprised the bulk of Chinese operations. Turkey, India, Brazil, and the Gulf states followed China's lead. The UAE and India overtook Japan's growing, if restrained, involvement in Kenya, Egypt, and the Ivory Coast, amongst other countries on the continent. One reason for the comparatively reserved participation from Japan is the reluctance of its businesses to grant autonomy to Japanese suppliers whom African start-ups have consequently outmaneuvered.[38]

Patterns of global trade have also been on the move. The Third World's share of exports rose to 53% during the second decade of the twenty-first century, from 30% in the 1970s. These countries are also more likely to trade with each other. In 2000, a little over 60% of bilateral trade took place with the West.[39] Today, as dependency on the West dissolves, a little over half of bilateral trade involves Third World countries. China now buys around 29% of Latin America's agricultural exports. Three-quarters of the remainder of such exports from Brazil and Argentina are destined for other emerging markets. China, India, Botswana, and Mozambique absorb more than half of South Africa's metals and gems. India and Vietnam procure 28% of China's largest category of exports – electronics. Nearly half of OPEC's crude exports go to emerging markets: India is behind only the US as OPEC's largest customer. The Third World has also consolidated its share of foreign exchange reserves. These rose from around 30% in the 1970s to 66% in 1997 and 80% in 2019.

Improvements in health are also marked. By the turn of the century, HIV, tuberculosis, and malaria were coming under control in countries as diverse as

Uganda, Thailand, Senegal, India, China, Nepal, Peru, Kenya, Ethiopia, and Vietnam.[40] Across the Third World, child infant mortality rates fell, and life expectancy had by 2016 reached the minimum levels achieved by developed countries on or shortly after 1990. This has tremendous significance for the future. In sub-Saharan Africa, fewer people die from infectious diseases. More are succumbing to non-communicable ones such as diabetes, hypertension, and cancer. This brings with it financial challenges. But it is a remarkable turnaround and, together with the growth in infrastructure and investment, leaves Africa with considerable potential. With a GDP equal to India's, and with some of the world's fastest-growing economies (such as Ghana, Ivory Coast, Senegal, Djibouti, Ethiopia, and Tanzania), Africa will double its population by 2 billion by 2050[41] and double it again by the end of the century. Once desperately underpopulated, there is now every reason to think that the African market will continue to expand for at least the next century.

Another striking change across the Third World has been poverty reduction. Numbers fell by 1% annually between 1981 and 2005, so the proportion of indigents dropped to 25% from 52%.[42] As the average income of the bottom 50% of earners doubled, those in extreme poverty fell from 2 billion to 700 million after 1990.[43] Today, a little over half of the world's population lives in households with enough disposable income to be called middle class.[44] China accounts for a good part of this improvement. The number of poor in Brazil was cut by half, while their per capita income rose by 68%. India brought down the number of people in extreme poverty from 476 million in 2002 to 268 million by 2011 and around 50 million in 2018. The poverty rate in its towns and cities dropped sharply from 13.7% in 2014 to 3.8% in 2018.[45] And while the number of people living in slums rose from 52 to 65 million between 2001 and 2011, this amounted to a fall in the share of the total population from 18.3% to 17%. That figure saw a further reduction to around 10% by 2021.[46]

Most of the world's poor (nearly three-quarters) are now found in Africa. Yet even here, more people are escaping extreme poverty than falling into it. If this continues, less than a quarter of Africa's population will still be in poverty by 2030. Several countries already have poverty rates below 3% - Equatorial Guinea, Gabon, Mauritius, and Seychelles. Mauritania and Gambia should fall to 3% by 2030, and Ethiopia, Ghana, Kenya, Angola, Cote D'Ivoire, and Djibouti should be close to that rate.

One related observation is that although wages in the Third World are low (which has helped to attract business from the West), those wages can buy more things. For example, it will take a person on minimum wage in the UK three months (assuming no holidays or deductions) before their accumulated pay equals the purchasing power of the average yearly minimum wage across the Third World. It can take twelve months or longer compared with South Korea, Japan, and Mauritania.

How was this to be explained? Many wondered if the improvements experienced in the Third World were real and permanent. Could the West's financial houses be over-egging the pudding to drum up business? They might well have seen an opportunity to bring in money on the back of China's rise, high commodity prices, and expanding volumes of cross-border trade by putting together attractive investment packages with exciting labels: Emerging Markets, BRICS (Brazil, Russia, India, China, and South Africa), MINT (Mexico, Indonesia, Nigeria, and Turkey), and the N11 (the Next Eleven Emerging Economies (Bangladesh, Egypt, Indonesia, Iran, South Korea, Mexico, Nigeria, Pakistan, the Philippines, Turkey, and Vietnam). Yet all this growth is built on sand. There are no shortages of statistics to indicate that the conditions thought to have propelled growth are changing. The long-term effects of COVID, rising energy costs, and inflation on the world economy have yet to be seen. Economists in the West have long predicted the collapse of China. Its debt-fuelled growth cannot continue much longer, or so many argue. And China is not the only one struggling with debt. More countries in the Third World are borrowing in their own currency and from bond markets (rather than short-term bank funding), but that doesn't eliminate risk.[47] Rates of growth are simply too low to sweep away extreme poverty by 2030 as hoped.[48]

For those commentators less despondent about Third World growth, firmer explanations of some kind are needed. The most obvious place to start is East and Southeast Asia. Culture is a popular and understandable rationale, given what is thought to be the influence of Confucianism in Japan, Korea, and China and the economic significance of Chinese communities throughout Southeast Asia. But it poses obvious limitations.

State capitalism and authoritarian regimes are other possibilities. They are effective clubs to wield in the short term as they allow non-western governments to minimize political risks and political goals by generating large amounts of wealth.[49] But do they lead to more efficient, equitable, or nimble economies in the longer term? The market and market-friendly governments, or arrangements very similar to Asia's developmental state, are, for many analysts, surely the only serious answer. In 2008 the World Bank determined that China, Botswana, Brazil, Malta, Oman, and India had maintained the necessary growth rate over the required duration to gain entry to the elite club of miracle economies. They had done so by following a familiar prescription: they exploited world markets, preserved macroeconomic stability and high rates of savings and investment, let the market allocate resources, and had credible and competent governments. They kept inflation low, were fiscally responsible, and made sure that firms and entrepreneurs had enough claim on assets to invest in them. The removal of ineffective regimes once tolerated because they opposed communism, which had faded away, was crucial to reform across the Third World. More capable national leaders came to the fore, determined to educate and train their people. This, in turn, established benign global conditions, which spurred further national growth. The expansion of China, Brazil, Indonesia, India, and Turkey created a boom in commodities such as oil and gas, building materials, and timber which favored poorer countries that could now generate the wherewithal to grow their economies.

The explanation for Asia's miracle back in the 1980s and 1990s has thus proved exceptionally resilient and is now applied to the rest of the Third World. *The Great Surge*,[50] as one writer calls it, is explained by the end of communism, the spread of capitalism and democracy, effective legal systems, pragmatic management and leadership, and globalization. Included in this package for growth are solutions to the problems it creates. Globalization can be disruptive. Democracy is its salve. Globalization weakens the capacity of states, making democracy more difficult.[51] So people in the developing world have become frustrated with it in recent years. But democracy is slow and difficult because of its complex decision-making and power-sharing arrangements. It evolves in fits and starts: it has always been that way. It's designed that way. A little patience and thought will only make developing countries stronger. The real dangers to progress are, firstly, overpopulation and the strain this puts on the environment; and, secondly, China's unwillingness to integrate into the international community's rules-based system.

To scholars inclined to a mixture of economic and social theory, 'institutions' provide the only convincing account of development in the global south. Institutions describe any form of constraint that people devise to guide and shape their interactions with each other, reduce uncertainties, lower costs, and bring structure to everyday life.[52] In practice, institutions are rules - formal and informal, written and unwritten, spoken and unspoken. Organizations (such as political, economic, social, and educational bodies) are consequences of the institutional framework. Understand institutions and how they evolve and interact with organizations, and one can understand society and how it changes. The rules which become engrained are generally those created to favor people with the most power and influence. Only sometimes do these rules also favor increases in national production and productivity. When they do, it is the result of centuries of evolution. This, anyway, is the experience of the West, whose societies are no longer recognizable. Exchange is highly impersonal, the division and specialization of labor are finely calibrated, information costs are low, interdependence has become worldwide, and political and economic institutions and organizations have taken over some aspects of the family's role. The details of development vary with a society's starting point. But those which grow materially exhibit common principles and features, namely property rights, the rule of law, and the protection of civil and political freedoms. These ensure adaptive efficiencies, enabling allocative efficiencies, political stability, and economic growth.[53]

Institutionalism offers explanation or justification for the rule of law and property rights and political freedom and for why, over decades and centuries, economies seem to diverge and converge. Different parts of Europe suffered decline and benefitted from pulses of expansion at different times. The Italian central and northern states saw rises in per capita income of around 0.8% between 1350 and 1420; Holland followed with growth rates of around 1.3% between 1505 and 1595; Sweden and Portugal followed suit during the first half of the seventeenth century, and England during the second half of the seventeenth century. And as each experienced growth, other countries went into decline. As Holland rose, Italy and Portugal fell. Portugal would see expansion again in the sixteenth century but Italy would struggle for the next four centuries. As Sweden grew, Holland declined, and as Sweden devolved, England rose. These pulses occurred within a broader pattern of overall sustained growth, which accelerated after 1800. There were fewer short-term downturns, and Britain's industrial gathered pace. By 1870 the gap between Britain and other European countries began to shrink, and by 1914 America's per capita income exceeded that of Britain.[54]

This upward trend in Europe was itself but a section of peaks and valleys in a much longer wavelength only visible globally. A few years before the industrial revolution began during the first half of the eighteenth century, the world's biggest economy and leading cotton producer was India, with a population of 165 million, followed by China with 138 million. Britain's tiny population of 8.6 million produced less than 3% of the world's output. Even in 1820, as the industrial revolution gathered pace, India and China still accounted for half the world's GDP. Past success could explain recent success.[55]

The Asian economies might have seemed like 'miracles' when attention was finally paid to them. But if there had been any miracles, these had occurred more than a century earlier. Japan remade itself in the latter half of the nineteenth century, throwing aside feudalism in 1868 and effecting a revolution in agriculture and industry, all in one fell swoop. Nearly a decade later, Korea began to follow suit more grudgingly and slowly under duress from European powers, Russia, China, and Japan. The kingdom was compelled to open itself to foreign trade, investment, and industry, and when annexed by Japan in 1910, Korea found itself transformed into a relatively efficient colonial state. China saw its ancient imperial regime swept away the following year, having been prized open and carved up by the same cabal of powers. In all three cases – Japan, Korea, and China – the changes adopted, willingly or not, had come after many centuries during which commerce expanded, agriculture intensified, manufacturing thrived, and towns and cities and the connections amongst them matured.

That Africa has a long history of markets, towns, cities, and commercial networks stretched over distances that at least equaled those of China and exceeded those of Europe, is also intriguing in the light of growth rates between 5% and 8% exhibited by many African countries in the1960s and 1970s, and more recently. No less eye-catching is the fact that the per capita GDP of Latin American countries had by the late 1970s and 1980s reached or surpassed that of Spain in 1960. Argentina managed this as early as 1895.[56]

These developments can also be read as transfers of income and wealth to new centers of accumulation. The shift in capital from the Netherlands to London brought about the industrial revolution in the eighteenth century. Its migration from London to America preceded the rise of the United States. The current pulse in the global south describes its shift from the US. It is complicated and prolonged by counterflows of capital back to the US from China, Japan, India, OPEC, and others because their domestic markets could not absorb it effectively.[57] But this is temporary. As Third World countries become more closely integrated[58] and establish large-scale production and trade zones, southward capital movements are evident. At the same time, the West's ability to rig the new markets through protectionism, gunboats, and drug trafficking has weakened.[59]

Chapter 4

Explaining the Decline of the West

Since the market and its handmaiden (the rule of law) explained the rise of the Third World, it follows that the West has lost its edge because it has lost its faith in the market and relies too much on state involvement and mixed economies. An alternative diagnosis is that the market is given too much rein. Governments are enjoined to 'level up,' spend on welfare and intervene in all aspects of life more extensively. Others declare that too much or too little social conservatism, and excessive materialism, weaken social cohesion.

A corollary of the rise of the Third World is the relative and real decline of the West. Europe was the dominant power in international affairs for at least four centuries. It controlled the oceans, drew large parts of the world into its hands, and industrialized. America took command during the early twentieth century and saved Europe from itself on two occasions within thirty years.

The West peaked with the fall of the Berlin Wall. America's wish to lead, its reasons for doing so, and its ability to do so, dissipated. Today, political rights and civil liberties are fraying. The US election in 2016 was marred by interference, violations of basic ethical standards, and left in its wake more cloistered government. In Hungary and Poland, new governments are working to consolidate power, curb civil society, and control the judiciary. Xenophobic parties have gained electoral ground in France, Germany, the Netherlands, and Austria. In Serbia, the opposition is being side-lined by the Serbian Progressive Party, and what remains of the country's independent media is being undermined. England, too, has shifted to the right; and politicians who make a point of being popular and ostentatiously maverick (even if that means sorely incompetent) find ready and widespread support. Everywhere private and public news conglomerates who treat political preference and fake news as fact are on the rise. Politicians and their advisers have become savvy in using social media: win the support of small but strategic groups in particular constituencies, and one can ignore whatever the rest of the country might think. Wading into all this are committed lobbyists working for corporations and other groups determined to have an 'influence.' Just as politicians target small strategic groups, niche groups of special interests work to target strategically emplaced politician. Governments are more like royal courts made up of socialites, attention seekers, merchants, activists, and lawyers vying for support, rewards, and influence. As for European organizations,[60] one does not have to be a Brexiter or right-wing zealot to doubt their legitimacy. Preserving the euro seemed to require actions that many felt to be anti-democratic. If anything, splits amongst countries are widening. Germany is constantly resentful of the rest of Europe and frequently distances itself from American foreign policy.[61] The costs of unification and its export vulnerabilities have added to its woes. Italy appears irredeemably dysfunctional, factionalized, corrupt, and unable to sort out tax and spending. France is also unable to make the economy competitive.

The West's economic power has also withered. Its share of global GDP stood at 62% in 2000 (a figure which had held steady since 1960) and had fallen to 50% by 2019. Its share of foreign exchange reserves has also fallen to just over 20% from about 70% in the early 1960s. This leaves it less able to influence exchange rates and trade, and more thinly insulated from economic shocks. A country that can buy and sell the dollar in sufficient quantities to affect its value can increase its share of exports or reduce its expenditure on imports and make it harder or easier to pay off dollar loans.

The West has also been losing jobs and whole industries to the Third World, where pay is often lower. This does not matter too much if the West can summon up new industries and services that other countries want. There is much chatter about 'unicorn' businesses, innovation clusters, leaders, and shifting to networked-based practices, smart grids, self-drive cars, clean energy, robotics, bioproducts, and digital platforms. But it is not clear that a genuinely new revolution comparable to that initiated by the steam engine, electricity, the internal combustion engine, flight, the jet engine, nuclear power, or electronics is likely anytime soon, nor any compelling reason why it should emerge in the West.

Living standards in the West have either ground to a halt for most people or are improving only slowly and unevenly, especially amongst those on the lowest wages. In 2015, almost 119 million people, or 23.7% of the EU population, were deprived materially and excluded socially. These levels of poverty are entrenched. They stretch back decades and the poverty experienced is not only relative but, in many cases, absolute. One reflection of this is that the low-paid in the West have to work longer and longer hours to realize an income with the same buying power as their counterparts in many Third World countries. Another is that of the 769 million people globally who existed on $1.90 or less a day in 2013, 5.5 million live in the West. Life for these people is often as hard as, or worse than, it is for the poor in the Third World. There are ways of mitigating poverty in the Third World that are often not open to people in the West: squatting on land, building one's own permanent shelter, drawing support from extensive networks of kinship and fictive kinship, tapping into water and electricity supplies, or throwing up a small business without licenses of any kind.

Agriculture in the West is also suffering. It employs fewer people on a shrinking number of expanding farms. The trend is often interpreted as economies of scale working their way through, and an inevitable feature of economic development. And levels of production are indeed either stable or growing. But the West's declining share of global production has been dramatic, such that now China, India, Brazil, and 'the rest' now dominate. This matters for various reasons. As far as possible, supplies need to be reliable and the food itself safe to eat. Where and how crops and livestock is raised also matters because this strongly influences or determines how it tastes. It is difficult if not impossible to replicate 'here' the taste and texture of food produced 'there.' Food influences not only physical health but psychological well-being. Agriculture and the rhythms of agricultural life shape landscapes, how people feel and think, their sense of who they are and what matters, and their attachment to place. It keeps us spiritually tied to the land, and without it, the bucoliasts lament, we are lost and empty.[62] It is, their more conservative partisans assert, a crucial aspect of the content of tradition, along with citizenship, neighborliness, a common language, custom, and common cause. Through tradition, we pass on knowledge and connect with society as a whole. Discard tradition and we discard the cement that keeps society together.[63]

Feminism, its antagonists believe, is busy ridiculing another facet of tradition and cohesion - the family - and offering itself as an alternative source of moral authority, or so many believe.[64] Even the law of the land – the local judgments (or common law) built up over time, protecting the individual and community from the diktats of the sovereign power – are being eroded, complains Scruton. Everything that holds western societies together, and makes them successful, is being demeaned and destroyed. This is one of Fergusson's points, too.[65] The West has given up on the qualities that made it great – competition, science, property rights, medicine, the consumer society, and the work ethic - just as other societies have been taking them on board. The sooner the West understands that these are its discoveries, the product of its history and culture, and explain its past successes, the better it will be.

One response to these analyses is that they reflect precisely the kind of social conservatism frustrating necessary change and bringing decline about. Reformists today accept the market but require government work to alleviate poverty. The owners of capital must also treat their workers more fairly and generously and adjust their activities to favor the environment, not destroy it. Education and health must be more inclusive, and equal opportunities available to everyone. Welfare should be less judgmental and parsimonious. Greater latitude in behavior must be given and expected so that individuals can live their lives as they wish. Greater protections for the weak and vulnerable must be established, which means closer monitoring of public and private sectors and government. The reformists strive for an economy and society that is both mixed and kinder. Social conservatives block these ambitions.

The strength with which these positions are adumbrated and defended indicates another weakness: failing trust. Without faith in the motives of people who hold views different from ours, we can have no confidence in society, and society can have no sense of purpose.[66] Liberals and conservatives both see each other as the problem. Both become more entrenched and rigid in their own beliefs. Accusations are thrown back and forth between reformers and social conservatives – moss backs and fogeys versus chronically disgruntled and change-obsessed reformers – until one cannot bear even to look at the other.

It is ironic, then, (and says much about the influence of economists) that their belief in 'the market' as the origin of wealth is one of the few points that liberals and conservatives can agree on. Social conservatives want more of it. Watered-down socialists wish to share out its fruits more evenly. While true radicals like Berman,[67] who has a deep moral antipathy to the pursuit of wealth, prefer to do without capitalism and would probably be happiest living in a countryside populated by monastic communities reminiscent of seventh-century Europe.

A common view is that inequality and division are a natural manifestation of how society works. Each social group, whomever it represents (businesses or workers, civil-rights activists, or professionals), will do what it can to get as much as possible for itself, whether this works against the interest of society or not. These interest groups are numerous. Each is factionalized, and each heave with desires and ambitions. It is not always clear what each one wants, and each arrives at its decisions slowly. Government finds it difficult to negotiate with them and impossible to fashion a clear course for the country. And once these groups acquire influence over government, they reshape bureaucracy and regulations to secure their standing and remove constraints on their operations.[68] These networks of interests become 'the establishment.'

Might the apparent inevitability of these fault lines explain deep-seated feelings of powerlessness and frustration in Western societies and a desire to rob those responsible for that condition? It is from this well of *ressentiment* that political opportunists draw energy. Opportunists are, first and foremost, outsiders. They feel the establishment has rejected them, so they reject it in return. They do not obey the conventions of speech, dress, behavior, and values. They are deliberately contrary and go out of their way to taunt and poke fun at their opponents. The more incensed their opponent is, the happier they feel. If their opponent is complex and intellectual, they will be anti-intellectual and deliberately simplistic. If their opponent gives a serious and considered answer, they will throw out a ridiculous one. If their opponent is careful to marshal facts and figures, they will make up flagrantly ludicrous ones. The joke is on the establishment. They are at one with their supporters, who are also outsiders. They aim to bring the old house down and build a new one in which they are the master.

Entwined around *ressentiment* is narcissism. The condition, many think, is rooted in the fact that so many parents have given up their responsibility to raise children or had it taken from them. Welfare, health, and legal services, radio and television, magazines, the advertising industry, schools, and universities have assumed those responsibilities. These surrogates - professionals, educators, the media, publishers, game designers, entertainers, sports stars, and filmmakers - work to tailor dreams for the young. Children are brought into a world where everything is just 'there.' They are not challenged but kept safe, protected, and encouraged. They expect to be successful. They can be what they want to be: the driven industrialist, the policeman, the young and successful politician, the FBI or MI5 agent, the lawyer, the actor, the scientist, the surgeon, the great artist, writer, or intellectual, the Nobel Prize laureate; the odd-ball, whizz-kid programmer; the singer, the footballer, or basketball player; the adviser and policy-maker, the opinion-making journalist, the social media or climate warrior, or the rough and ready seen-it-all, done-it-all anti-hero. But when others do not follow the script and the soundtrack fails, they become sensitive, manipulative, self-pitying, quick to deny any fault, and retreat into a dream-like state. Society has become so entitled it is failing to meet the expectations it creates for its members.[69]

Strategic errors are another part of the explanation for the West's decline and, for some writers, the crux of the matter. Whatever benefits it reaps from its geography, the West is always at a disadvantage. Mackinder's world island, once in Russian hands, is now Chinese as roads, railways, pipelines, cities, and economic regions are laid down between Shanghai and Madrid. The West has relied upon tying up either end of the heartland, establishing alliances in the crescent, and building large navies. But if Mackinder is correct, and whoever controls the heartland controls the world, then the collapse of the Soviet Union was a momentary reprieve for the West. Whatever one thinks of Mackinder, the harsh fact is that the more America tries to extend its power, diminishing returns set in, and the less it gets in return for each penny spent. The same happened to Spain, France, England, and Germany.[70]

Tactical errors by the US have not helped. One unnecessary war after another has gnawed away the nation's confidence and capability, weakening the resolve and trust of the people from whose ranks its army draws its volunteers and draftees. Frequent warfare also means a heavy emphasis on minimizing casualties at any cost. Combat units are quickly rendered ineffective on the ground as they try to get the wounded medical care. It's a risky obligation when the adversary is determined to fight to the death. The alternative is to rely on airpower, automation, and such overwhelming force that any encounter looks more like mass execution than warfare.

Nor has the military helped itself by absorbing business models of leadership. William Westmoreland, who graduated from the Harvard Business School and commanded forces in Vietnam, embraced operations research, systems analysis, and economic theory. He and his commanders used those disciplines to manage institutions and formulate policy. Waging war became about process, programming, putting numbers in, and getting numbers out. The result was that strategy as a central focus for the armed forces shriveled. Even today, vast sums are spent on technologies and techniques that do not match the threats facing the country. Technically advanced and complex military power is not an especially advisable response to terrorism, economic instability, the collapse of states, resource scarcity, pandemics, climate change, piracy, smuggling, and narcotics. Unable to graduate its responses to threats, the West might lash out and bring the world crashing down around it, the inevitable consequence of the bargain between machine and military.[71]

Poor economic management and deregulation have also smoothed the West's downward path. By making it easier for goods, materials, money, and people to cross national boundaries, it became easier for businesses to play one country off against another. Keep wages and costs low and unions weak, and make sure the regulatory environment favors us, or we shall move to another jurisdiction and take investments and jobs with us. A version of the medieval guilds - those groups of merchants who once established monopoly rights over urban territories across Europe – have returned. In thrall to their wealth and lifestyles, politicians hand authority to them. Regulations and purse strings are loosened, taxes lowered, and tax avoidance and evasion ignored. The financial crisis made favoritism blatant. Financiers traded in brightly colored papers wrapped around debt and chased profits until the pile collapsed under its own weight. They justified their earnings by claiming extraordinary abilities and a willingness to take risks but, in practice, lumped every member of society into the 'greater good' in whose name the financiers were bailed out. Whether the routine was called vampire capitalism or financialization, profits were diverted from long-term production improvements into a deregulated financial industry. Meantime, symptoms of decay are everywhere, from crumbling infrastructure and falling education standards to cultural wars against science, 'hot' wars overseas, excessive bureaucracy and debt, and ineffective governance.[72]

Even a rejection of decline can be interpreted as a manifestation of what propels it. The West's decay is a myth, insists Joffe.[73] There have been at least five waves of panic since the last war. Doom sells copies and movies, and that's good for publishers and writers, including academics with at least one eye on their careers. It also helps politicians rouse people and convince them of the need for policy changes. There is, argues Homer-Dixon, an upside to down.[74]

Yet surely, cries the pessimist, this tells us something about ourselves? – that everyone and every society faces an end. No matter how often we predict it or studiously ignore it, the end will come eventually. Herman[75] thinks society's collapse is a form of rebellion against individualism. It's a promise and threat, a reality we bring down upon ourselves if we don't remain part of a social whole. Be an individual, tinker with the environment, ignore tradition, and reject multicultural truths, and you guarantee a sticky end for all of us. Nor will recognition of this truth necessarily save us. Society doesn't always make the right choices and we don't always learn from experience.[76] Plenty of people blame social democracy, poor economic management, the failure of industrial policy, a failure to control incomes and inflation, an anti-enterprise culture, and laborers who are mesmerized by the unions and work too little.[77]

There is little new in these 'modern' diagnoses and explanations of decline. An unrestrained drive for wealth, infighting, inequality, polarization, a collapse in confidence, and social breakdown are observations made of the West time and time again. A long struggle between religious and secular ways of life, and the eventual subordination of spiritual and ethical values to commerce and trade, turned society's priorities upside down. Man devolved himself into an economic animal. Whereas the Puritans idealized wealth, observed Tawney,[78] the West today worships it; whereas the Puritans treated the poor as sinners, the West treats them as criminals or, at the very least, with disdain. A plaint often heard is why should some people pay for others? Why shouldn't each of us be responsible for ourselves and our families? Are the poor really deserving? Are the ill *really* ill or just feigning it? Aren't these unfortunates just life's failures? Can the state afford redistribution? Is state-run welfare as efficient as it could be? Wouldn't it be best to encourage the private sector to run hospitals, schools, and benefits and secure 'value for money.'

Greed, factionalism, inequality, intolerance, and rigidity: their repetitiveness suggests that decline is part of a sequence - almost biological - of birth, growth, senescence, decay, and collapse. As such, it is natural and inevitable. In Italy, Vico[79] (d.1744) envisaged a succession of ages punctuated by war, inequality, and revolution. Even the third and final age, characterized by fully developed human and rational knowledge, was consumed by corruption as individuals sought power and put their selfish interests first. Barbarism would then return, marking the end of one cycle and the start of another.

Spengler[80] thought he detected the culmination of patterns when he looked out across a Europe exhausted by the Great War. He saw the end in buildings and cities, literature and arts, and technologies familiar and characteristic enough to define a particular civilization distinct from any other. It is the inevitable expression of human behavior. Parents and children, bound by blood into families, clans, and tribes, move from pre-cultural forms (such as speech) to a higher culture (such as a script) and thence to civilization. They move inexorably through morphologies or modes of comprehending the world, from the apollonian (or systematic) to the physiognomic (or Faustian). The first concerns causal relationships and natural laws and describes the contours of the world as it appears to be. The second mode envisages an organic world, a world with direction and destiny but without limits or center, of uncertain form, and described by light and shade. Civilization emerges from apollonian, petrifies during the Faustian, and then terminates. The evolution from culture to civilization is obligatory, inevitable, and insusceptible to modification. It is a process limited in duration to a few centuries. Its metamorphosis from the Faustian to the systematic is shorter still and more datable. Classical civilization transitioned in the 4th century. The West began to do so in the nineteenth century and should have completed its transformation by around 2000. Upon its bones, another culture might emerge and, in its turn, evolve from a lower form to a higher one before it, too, dies.

Do these cycles indicate a mentalité, a zeitgeist, a mood of some kind? There are such proposals.[81] Over the last 2500 years, a triad of mental states has cycled through western societies more than once: the ideational (a focus on God); the sensate (the satisfaction of human needs through the use of the environment); and idealistic (which recognizes both spiritual and material demands). Because the idealistic state is inclusive and blends with the sensory, it encourages more original, intuitive, and perceptive understandings of the social and natural worlds. The idealistic, which predominated from the eighth to fifth centuries BC, gave way to the sensate at the end of the fourth century BC. The sensate, in its turn, gave way around the fifth century AD to the ideational, which lasted some seven to eight hundred years. It was superseded by the idealistic in the thirteenth and fourteenth centuries. This was replaced in the fifteenth century by the sensate, which dominated for the next five centuries. By the mid-twentieth century, the sensate was decaying as the West morphed into its idealistic form.

Chapter 5

Re-explaining Growth, Development, and Decline

The rise of the Third World is an object lesson in unriddling the true nature of economic growth and development. Third World states defy western prescriptions for population control, put society before the market and the person before the rule, and emphasize redistribution rather than the vote. A more general story of growth and decline is derived from this.

A basic pattern of human society is the hierarchical fractal – the arrangement of people into clients and patrons or followers and leaders. It derives from the extreme dependency of the child, who must heed and obey the adult who must protect and nurture the child. Kinship merges with political formulations and, eventually, the creation of the state.

Reciprocity is another recurring principle or theme. From one of the earliest surviving 'handbooks' for government mentioned in chapter 1 comes this:

> '*Success in government lies in following the hearts of the people. Failure lies in opposing them. If the Prince can provide them with leisure and freedom from care, the people will be willing to endure trouble and toil for him. If he can provide them with riches and honor, they will be willing to endure poverty and a low position for him. If he can ensure their existence and provide them with security, they will be willing to endure danger and disaster for him. If he enables them to live and propagate, they will be willing to endure death and annihilation for him.... Thus knowing that "to give is to receive" is the most precious thing in government.*'[82]

The attention paid to the ruler's duties to his followers was widely noted in societies not yet shaped by colonial rule. And it remains a notable feature in the Third World today. This *quid pro quo*, and the fact that a larger population means a bigger labor force and army, provide the conditions for subsequent population growth. This, in turn, is likely to set groups of patrons and clients in competition with each other. Growing competition and density oblige each patron to deliver perpetual improvements in the supply of materials and opportunities to their clients.

At first, patrons can meet these demands by leading their clients away to greener pastures. At some point, however, when this is no longer possible, patrons and clients are confined to a given area. This is especially true if environmental boundaries exist or firm social borders are established. Once their territory is delineated and all available land reclaimed and occupied, patrons face an intractable problem. Each patron's growing band of followers entails an increase in population, which supplies more labor to work the land more intensively and defend it more effectively. More followers also mean higher demand for food, cloth, weapons, and shelter. When land productivity reaches its limits and expansion is no longer feasible, patrons must choose. They must either subjugate themselves and their followers to an even stronger patron or become strong men and take other territories.

To avoid conflicts, competing patrons must find ways to generate more goods and materials and share and distribute these resources and the political power this implies. Another solution is to alter the group's basis of wealth from land to commerce. This releases the group from its dependency on the productivity and area of land, provides the wherewithal to support their followers, allows a far greater density of population, and has the potential to channel military conflict into economic competition, at least in the first instance. This arrangement reflects what I describe as functional political logic.

Functional economic logic

Imagine the economy as a plate resting on a series of jacks around its rim. And upon the plate stands society. Resources are transferred first to one jack, then another, and then another. The plate is lifted gradually at angles shallow enough to let society keep itself upright. The market, or capitalism, merely describes one mode of transfer. Privately-owned businesses, motivated by profit and aided by freely moving prices, are sensitive to demand and an effective means of directing resources. For this reason, they are licensed by the community. Private business helps generate growth as part of broader arrangements for social transfers.

The observation that commerce is a response to growing and increasingly dense populations is important. It suggests that society already knows that commerce is an effective mode of distribution. And it knows this because trade originates as a consequence of external contact. One reason for this is that other societies are more likely to have goods that are different and, sometimes for that quality alone, desirable. Another reason is that exchange appears unequal: it is easier for someone to gain at the expense of another if that other person is an outsider and not part of the mutual obligations that an insider bears. Trade, then, tends to be external. And when the domestic population is not yet of sufficient size and density, trade occurs amongst communities either separated by long distances or living in different ecological zones (such as mountain and lowlands or desert and tropical). For this reason, immigrant groups often become economically influential in their host society and, as merchants, are assigned a low and dependent social status. It also seems highly likely that trade preceded settled life and agriculture by a very long way.

Why the market is not a source of growth.

Commerce, however, brings its own problems. From the perspective of merchants who successfully convince others to buy their wares, there is no question that commerce generates wealth. Yet from the standpoint of society, it cannot do so. The reason is straightforward and has long been apparent. A business must ensure its income exceeds the cost of materials and labor to secure a profit. Since a laborer's wages are less than the price of goods sold, fewer and fewer laborers can afford the goods produced. (This difficulty, tied up with Marx's notion of the 'realization of profit,' we shall call the wage-profit problem). As demand shrinks, so do the companies' profits. Eventually, the economy will grind to a halt. Attempts to get around this problem are unsuccessful and describe the course of the market in the West.

One method is mechanization and changes in the organization of a business. These allow it to produce more goods more cheaply so that workers can afford more things (and so their standard of living improves), profits will fall. But wages must remain lower than the price of goods sold if the company is to make a profit.

A second method is to encourage business owners (the capitalists) to spend more.[83] Like everyone else, they must buy things to live (wage goods). They also need to purchase equipment, parts, services, and buildings to set up their operations and keep them going (capital goods). The workers producing 'capital goods' are being paid wages, which will also contribute to the profits of those businesses producing wage goods. With capitalists and workers from both wage-good and capital-goods sectors buying wage goods, demand (and profits) can be kept buoyant. However, this puts the cart before the horse in that financing the capital goods sector and its workers depend on a thriving wage-goods sector.

A third method is to create a so-called mixed economy in which the state makes transfers to the general populace. These are half measures in the absence of a coherent national system designed to move resources and raise the economy and society. Delivered as handouts when thought necessary, the mixed economy serves only to keep the market hobbling along and cannot avoid society's material degeneration.

A fourth is to develop a financial market. A business must bring cash in through the shop front to keep the organization working, meet its financial obligations (especially wages or purchases of stock), and survive. It must maintain this flow and build up a sound reputation or what accountants call 'goodwill and intangible assets.' Doing so allows the business to make and receive investments, take on loans, and trade real estate, shares, and financial instruments. These 'products' - which are notionally secured by cash and sometimes redeemed after days, weeks, months, or years – help the business draw in more cash to sustain its growing operations. Financialization, however, only stores up a series of problems for the future.

The growth and concentration of notional cash in these financial markets are more than can be met with real cash either by the business or by society. If reputations are damaged, faith evaporates, loans are called, investments are sold, and a crash quickly follows.

Notional profits and remuneration in the financial sector (so long as there is no reason to meet them in full) whisk up prices and a luxury goods market. Businesses focus their interests and energies here because this is where they can make large profits. Wages stagnate or fall in the real economy, increasing the importance of the financial sector. Individual workers are compelled to take on loans, again favoring the financial sector. Businesses also look to draw in more resources from outside the system. This is often described as the extraction of surplus, exploitation, or under-development. Subsidization on a massive scale is another description of what is happening.

Growth and decline

To compete, survive, and flourish, a group must be serviced and attract followers, and its numbers must grow. Large and dense populations require the organization of complex social transfers, and this drives growth. For this to work, organizations must remain effective, and leaders must concentrate on ensuring transfers are made such that all boats are raised. These features are a logical consequence of the organization of society, and while not in any one instance inevitable, they will emerge at some stage. The question is not why the Third World is developing: that is built-in to society and expected. It is what human societies do. What we see in the Third World is no miracle.

The rise of the West followed a similar path. In Europe and America, industrialization was preceded by long periods of commercialization and growing populations arranged into clumps of dense settlements. Markets were licensed and harnessed for their revenue. Materials, labor, and money were collected, stored, and redistributed officially and unofficially by Church, secular authorities, and communities. Transfers were regularized and put on a national footing, laying the basis for growth.

That the West was the first to industrialize is no great mystery. It was going to happen somewhere at some time. Europe was as likely a candidate as any because of its geography. Japan can absorb everything from southern Spain to northern Germany. India can gobble up the whole of western Europe. China can do the same to western and eastern Europe, parts of the middle east, and the western fringes of Russia. Africa can swallow China three times over and do so with ease. The essential fact is that western Europe is compact and well-defined by its physical features. This is also true of divisions within it - especially the Italian and Greek peninsulas and the English isles. There is room enough for a large population to build up and physical restrictions strong enough to limit expansion, such that densities can rise quickly. There is also the fact that western Europe lies to the north of a crossroads where arose a complex of civilizations linked with Africa, India, and China, whose histories of migration, conquest, trade, and empire are entwined. Initially centered at the confluence of the African, European, and Asian continental landmasses, this complex gradually expanded as its center of power shifted from Mesopotamia to the Mediterranean.

The real question, as far as the West is concerned, is not why it developed but why it abandoned that path, wedded itself to the market, and remains bound despite its consequent decline.

An important part of the answer is that the West industrialized first. This made it easier to subsidize its market by drawing in resources and people from the rest of the world. Colonialism, empire, war, globalization, and financialization gave the impression that the West's star was still rising. In the mid-twentieth century, the justification for one war helped bring together the market and democracy. The West also had to define itself self-consciously in opposition to the communist bloc: command economy versus market, authoritarianism versus democracy, arbitrary power versus the rule of law, and opaqueness versus the transparency of formal processes.

Thus the West mistakenly attributed its success to a market braced with principles and practices. The market traduced redistribution. The notion that the state must serve the people came to be thought facile and naïve. Society was transformed into a lattice of rules-based processes and organizations. And now that the market determines redistribution, depriving politicians of their essential role, the process of selecting leaders – the vote - was idolized. Geographic proximity between America and Canada, Australia and New Zealand, and among European countries, and the rise of English as the primary lingua franca contributed to synchronicity in thought and practice. So did the presence of supranational organizations such as the EU, NATO, and the Commonwealth.

Another part of the answer is the West's determination to perfect its qualities in itself and the rest of the world. The more it tries to perfect this facade – the rules-based, market-dominated democracy – the more inflexible and ineffective it becomes. Aberrant behavior is incubated. People try to circumvent the clumsy and rigid procedural frameworks and cover up gross imperfections or try to get out of it what they can for themselves. As they do so, organizations, and the systems they are arranged into, weaken. Alienation grows, and a return to a more affective atmosphere is set. The only question is whether this is preceded by collapse.

Why does the West insist on perfecting these qualities in itself and others? And why has the Third World done what it can to resist? The answer lies in the 'moods' that grip societies from time to time.

Moods

By mood, we are apt to mean that general feeling that colors how we look at the world and our place within it. A mood is contentment felt as we set out one morning when the sun is bright, the sky a perfect blue, and leaves and grass shaking gently in a warm breeze. In this state of mind, we are generous interpreting every other aspect of our world. We may be less constructive when we slip into a low mood. The clouds gather, and a heavy gloom settles over us. Colors fade, and the air is stagnant and oppressive. We feel there is little to be done because we are sure little can be done.

Our moods are public and easily read by others. They can also be intensely private and personal. Sometimes it passes quickly over us like a shadow. Sometimes it clings to the inside of our skulls. But it is transient and does not seem to be part of our personalities. If we cannot free ourselves from it, then other people may begin to think something is wrong, and a psychologist might even say we are suffering from a disorder of the mind.

I use moods or states of mind or *mentalité* somewhat differently. I use these terms to describe how we think and feel about 'me' or the 'self,' other people, and my relationships with everyone else. Are other people, the self, and their relationships with others important in themselves? Are they treated as if they matter in their own right? If so, then it is described as an affective mood. Or are people, self, and self's relationships, thought of and treated as instruments, as a means to an end? This is an instrumental mood. Or do we think of other people, self, and relationships as absolutes comprising independent beings whose thoughts and actions are, or should be, pure, discrete, and untainted by any ulterior motive? This I describe as absolute or as a Puritanical mood. These moods are almost tangible in that they constantly shape how we look at the world in general (both animate and inanimate), the events within it, and how we formulate our behavior.

These moods pervade our minds because 'I,' 'self,' or 'me' arises from interactions with other people and the wider world. From the moment of birth, the child makes one connection after another. This thing or action leads to this or that. There is a connection between the ball sailing through the air and the splash of water. Early in life, an extraordinary conclusion is reached – that of a link between these connections and their observation, between, say, the observation of the splash as the ball hits the water and the event itself. There is a 'me.' Small children, gaping at their new world, are putting together a new 'me.'

Let us call this the intellectual 'me': to which things were done, which did things, around which things happen, and a story can be told. This me has another dimension - the here-and-now me. The me who feels air moving in and out of his lungs, the sun on his shoulders, the ground beneath him, and his feet slipping in his shoes. The me who smells magnolia drifting on a breeze past his face and pinpricks of sweat on his back. This is the emotional me. What do I mean by that?

Emotions

We tend to think of emotion as distinct and different from thought. Emotions, it is believed, are specific and immediate and intuitive and spontaneous and autonomous. Some people claim there are discrete types of emotions. Thought, on the other hand, is more deliberate, controlled, reasoned, and rational. We warn each other not to let our emotions run away with us or get the better of us.

My contention, however, is that the experience of emotion (such as a sense of loss or longing or fear), and the physical sensations that go with it, are thoughts or conclusions that we reach in and of themselves. I would go so far as to reinforce an implicit point just made – that physical sensations, such as the sun's warmth, the scent of magnolia, the draw of breath, or the bite of a mosquito - are emotions. They are the conclusions we reach from the signals our minds receive and in the context in which we find ourselves, and it is the process of arriving at those conclusions which gives them their immediacy.

Emotion, then, is the experience of reaching a thought or conclusion by oneself. For instance, as I read a book, look at a painting, or listen to a piece of music, I experience a sense of elation, sadness, or relief. I do so because I have concluded that, in this context, it is entirely reasonable I should do so. It is, I have said, the difference between being told a piece of music conveys desperate loneliness and longing and realizing that for oneself. It is the difference between being told a bear is frightening and coming across a bear in a forest at night. Perhaps this marks out a good book or painting or music: the fashioning of words and forms and colors and sounds such that the listener, reader, or viewer can, by arriving at a conclusion for themselves, realize an experience. The emotional self - all the here-and-now sensations of being, a kind of authentic first-hand thought - is quickly integrated into the intellectual self.

In this understanding, the self emerges from and is utterly dependent upon interaction with the world. Cutting those interactions is bound to have far-reaching effects. Its primary consequence is to leave us with a sense of alienation as the self disintegrates. We become more instrumental and treat others as a means to an end, as temporary conveniences, deepening alienation. The eventual and only solution is to return to a more affective mood in which we recognize that other people are significant in their own right. In this light, one can understand the importance of organizations, which have a crucial bearing on our states of mind.

Organizations influence moods

As the population grows in size and density, so does the need for arrangements of people with particular tasks to perform in specific ways at a certain time and place. Thus, collectively, a given function is performed and repeated. These demands interrupt social relationships. To perform tasks in a certain way at a particular time and place, and to repeat these actions, compels people to break or reshape their relationships with others who are not of the organization. It also requires them to behave towards others in the organization in ways at odds with accepted practices outside the organization. In other words, the organization's members must become highly instrumental in their behavior. This would erode the basis of what sustains them as a person. To avoid this, psychological adjustments that amount to an exercise in self-delusion and pretense are required. These include the denial that behavior within the organization can be construed as social. Instead, behavior is treated *as if* it comprises rules, procedures, and processes. The choreography that *is* the organization is thought of, designed, and presented *as if* it is separate from relationships.

To all intents and purposes, relationships are treated as the technical structure of the organization, and people go about their business as if this is so. Yet there remains a doubt and an unspoken realization that it is not, in fact, so and that the organization is, in truth, a collaboration of social relationships. The organization seems to be something else merely because there is a choice to treat those relationships as technicalities. This doubt, this recognition that there is a choice, brings a degree of flexibility essential to the organization.

Self-delusion enables the organization to operate more effectively, but its essential purpose is to protect the social nature of relationships outside the organization. In other words, the organization is a side effect of the desire to preserve social relationships. These adjustments, however, are not perfect solutions. Once people get used to the idea that the organization is, conceptually at least, distinct from relationships, it becomes not just an idea but something real and separate with its own independent, almost organic presence. Similarly, the social sphere where relationships are confined conceptually becomes real and idealized.

Thus, the mind drifts into an absolute or puritanical state. Rules and relationships are treated no longer *as if* important in themselves but fetishized. Alienation deepens, and rigidity encourages instrumentalism as people try to get around the rules and processes in the way of their interests. This incites further rigidity and monitoring, creating a vicious downward spiral until the organization seizes up or falls apart.

The nature and interdependency of moods

While the practice of organization influences moods, moods derive from seminal qualities that enable human societies to cohere and organize. The most fundamental of these is 'Me' or what we experience as awareness or consciousness. This, I have asserted, evolves from our interaction with the natural world and other people during the first months and years of life.

Another way of looking at 'me' (and awareness) is as emotion. Emotion, I have asserted, is what we experience when the mind reaches what is, in the context it creates, an undeniable conclusion. It is a moment of realization. It is the difference between being told a passage of music or a combination of form and colors is moving, or that the water splashing on one's hand is hot, and putting the sounds, sights, and sensations together and experiencing this for oneself. There is, therefore, no fundamental distinction between a physical sensation and what we experience as emotion. 'Me' is simply an emotional experience that is constantly being registered.

The mind's predominant atmosphere or mood is affective. Realizing something for oneself – that a piece of music is beautiful, that coming face to face with a bear in the forest is frightening, or the water is cold, or that I am here – implies choice. Choice implies doubt. And doubt means we treat our thoughts about the world, and the world itself, *as if* significant in themselves.

This sense of 'me' allows us to infer that every other person reaches the same conclusion. At the same time, other people's recognition of 'me' would not be possible unless I behaved in ways that were, to them, familiar. 'Me' allows us to envisage others and compels coordination in that I must behave in ways familiar to others if I am to be recognized. 'Me' is a shared experience fused with our biological and social interdependence. Because of this, we are bound to arrive at similar responses in similar circumstances, and we can adapt on the fly and reach common solutions even when circumstances change.

Conditions that interfere with our interactions and realizations dull our emotions and induce alienation and other pathologies, leading to a mixture of rigidity and instrumentalism that erode society's coherence. These conditions are manifold. They include the routine that organizations enable, relative social isolation, or the imposition of broad measures to insist on given patterns of practice and thought. A puritanical state of mind is more comfortable with certainty. It shaves away possibility, dimensions, and doubt. Something is or is not, does or does not, or should or should not be. Yet, in the end, this stirs a craving for a return to an affective state.

Moods are not abstractions. We can feel their presence in ourselves and see their effects around us all the time. Every day we do things that are real and true. They make up the facts of our lives. I get out of bed. I get dressed. I go to the shop and buy a bottle of milk. I go back home and make porridge and coffee. Each of these actions is objective. They really happen. They are like a stone in my shoe, the tree I must walk around, or the river I must cross by the bridge. Our actions also comprise thoughts and feelings, involve other people, and tend to be arranged into patterns. Together these patterned relationships make up the social world. For instance, a government department, non-governmental organization, business, family, or credit association all comprise relationships stretching beyond each organization's nominal boundaries. How relationships and patterns are treated enables them to cohere or retain form over time and take on very different qualities.

Part II

The Rise of the Third World

Chapter 6

Resisting the Population Problem

The enthusiasm with which population control was initially pursued soon dissipated. Population growth, increasing density, and vigorous competition encourage political organization centered on collection, storage, and redistribution. The arrangement is essentially democratic in that the leadership's right to rule depends upon the effective and fair redistribution of goods, materials, and services to the populace. Technical advances and the creation of new ideas are necessary and made possible in these population concentrations. A virtuous and upward spiral is set in motion between population growth and density on the one hand and material and organizational development on the other.

If development and economic growth are not about people, then the exercise is meaningless. That might sound like a dreadful cliché, but it is astonishing just how quickly simple truths are lost and how easily development becomes about ideas, bureaucracy, careers, ambition, status, opportunity, legacy, and anything else other than people. In the immediate post-war decades, coteries of academics, journalists, politicians, and practitioners convinced one another that only a decline in fertility and slower growth or, better still, a fall in population would reduce poverty. If the rise in population were not halted or reversed, then food shortages, hunger, and political unrest on a global scale would surely follow. Terms such as population bomb, population explosion, overpopulation, and Malthusian Specter encapsulated these predictions

In 1983 a report entitled *A Program for Survival* was published by the Independent Commission on International Development Issues chaired by Willy Brandt, a former chancellor of West Germany. The *Brandt Report* was highly regarded, not least because it reflected views already widely held by academics, governments, and policymakers. In the Commission's view, the population bomb had gone off, and while 'the explosion seemed to be abating,' people in the developing world were now so young that even if couples limited themselves to just two children, populations would continue to grow by over a third over the next seventeen years. Cities were growing even faster, and there was no question that the developing world would soon be over-urbanized. Shelter, cultivable land, food production, health services, and jobs would fail to keep pace. The effects of population on rates of ecological change were already dire. Early in the twenty-first century, the earth would become unmanageable. '*Whether the nightmarish vision of a hopelessly overcrowded planet in the next century can be averted depends gravely on what is done now to stabilize the population.*'[84] Ending poverty and limiting population went hand in hand.

The publication was one of many in a similar vein produced since the 1960s.[85] It closely follows Malthus in his *Essay on the Principles of Population,* written nearly two hundred years earlier.[86] His concern, too, was the 'future improvement of society,' and his starting point was the certainty that '*the power of population is indefinitely greater than the power in the earth to produce sustenance for man. Population, when unchecked, increases in a geometrical ratio. Subsistence increases only in an arithmetical ratio.*'[87] Consequently, worries about sustaining one's family could never be removed, and there was no hope of perfecting society. But it could be bettered if prepared through foresight (preventative checks) to avoid the difficulties and distress (positive checks) that would otherwise materialize.

> '*The laborer who earns eighteen pence a day and lives with some degree of comfort as a single man, will hesitate a little before he divides that pittance among four or five, which seems to be but just sufficient for one. Harder fare and harder labor he would submit to for the sake of living with the woman that he loves, but he must feel conscious, if he thinks at all, that should he have a large family, and any ill luck whatever, no degree of frugality, no possible exertion of his manual strength could preserve him from the heart-rending sensation of seeing his children starve, or of forfeiting his independence, and being obliged to the parish for their support.*'[88]

Writing styles have changed, but the argument and belief in arithmetic have not. In poorer countries with limited human capital, rudimentary technology, and large agricultural sectors, the advantages brought by each additional person are said to diminish pretty rapidly: bigger populations mean lower per capita income.[89] Even in somewhat more advanced economies, writes Orbeta, there is an enduring link between family size and the incidence of poverty and vulnerability to poverty.[90]

Larger families mean poorer families. Children are more likely to die in infancy and, if they survive, will be smaller and weaker physically, less healthy, and fair less well at their studies. Larger families also mean fewer savings, less investment in industry, and less of the wherewithal required to compete effectively.

It says much about the arguments and sentiments swirling about in the sixties and seventies that China and India – two of the most populous states – took radical actions to deal with overpopulation. India began a compulsory sterilization program in 1974; China launched its one-child policy in 1978. Reactions amongst Malthusians to these policies were also telling. China had shown its commitment to Deng's 'wise policy.'[91] There was a little more humming and hawing from different quarters over Gandhi's program. Compulsory sterilization might be unfortunate (this seemed to depend on just how zealous one felt), but it was certainly necessary. The view was put in more restrained way by others who understood the need to acknowledge political realities. The extent to which sterilization was forced was admittedly a controversial question – controversial enough to help bring down the government. But voluntary sterilization - as well as information, services, and constant exhortation - would still be needed if the birth rate was to be lowered. Compulsory sterilization, argued one philosopher,[92] was conceivably a moral enterprise under four conditions: that the people selected had first exercised their procreative power (which he put at about 3-4 children in India); that there was sufficient welfare in place to make up for the support that would have been forthcoming from the additional children; that no group was singled out; and that those selected for sterilization should receive no further punishment should they opt for imprisonment rather than undergo sterilization.[93]

Professionals in the family planning establishment were at once dismayed and relieved by Gandhi's decision. Dismayed because India had not yet successfully provided voluntary services on a mass scale: compulsory sterilization would only make that more difficult. Relieved because the month before the decision was taken, India's Minister for Health and Family Planning, Karan Singh had said publicly: '*Population policy ... cannot be effective unless certain concomitant economic policies and social programs succeed in changing the basic determinants of high fertility. It has...been said that the best contraceptive is development.*'[94] If an accurate indication of the government's intentions, this statement ran against 'the vigorous furtherance of fertility reduction' and suggested that India had given up the fight. Gandhi had now clearly settled the matter of intention and direction, though whether the government would deliver the budgets to realize its policy remained to be seen.

Even little Singapore thought its population too great a burden. Two children were quite enough, the government decided. Singaporeans, it turned out, were more than willing to comply and brought the total fertility rate down to 1.42 in 1986, well below the 2.1 needed to keep the population stable. The government then enjoined its people to have more than two children if they could afford it[95] and claimed somewhat disingenuously that its change of heart was not a crude way of linking family size to education. Graduates in Singapore's highly competitive education system bagged an inordinate amount of status. They earned many times more than non-graduates and twice as much as graduates in the rest of the world. The government even set up a dating service to encourage its graduates to mate.

In more recent years, the Malthusian argument has had to be adjusted. Improvements in living standards in heavily populated countries demanded this. The explanation provided was that as fertility levels drop, working-age people grow in proportion to the very young and very old. This window of opportunity or 'demographic dividend'[96] allowed the state to spend more on education, health, and infrastructure and make everyone more prosperous. But it doesn't stay open for long. The fundamental problem of too many people remains.

The emphasis placed on climate and the degradation of the environment demanded a second adjustment. The responsibility of the North to deal with the problem had to be driven home. Otherwise, the West's anxieties will seem like an excuse to keep developing countries in their place. *The Brandt Report* had argued for massive transfers to the South. A little over a decade earlier, *Limits to Growth*[97] had made similar warnings about the fate of humanity and presented an even more radical solution. Written and published under the auspices of the Club of Rome as part of its 'project on the predicament of mankind,' *Limits* had insisted that the world's future depended on trends in population, industrialization, pollution, food production, and resource depletion. At some point before 2072, the planet would no longer support continuing growth: a sudden and uncontrollable decline in population and industrial capacity would follow. Action was needed today. People everywhere, including the rich, must get used to having enough rather than always demanding more. Nations must stop their restless drive for growth, establish an equilibrium with the natural environment, and learn to be content with that. Forty years later, one of the authors of *Limits to Growth*, in his assessment of how the world should look in 2052, upped the ante: population will peak at about 8 billion in 2040 before stabilizing. Productivity and economic growth will fall because society has not yet found a way to deal with poverty, unemployment, and pensions other than to press for still more productivity and growth. And the more spent on infrastructure or getting oil out of the ground while simultaneously avoiding climate change, the lower the returns. Water is bound to become more scarce and more expensive. Other resources will become pricier as cheaper varieties and alternatives run out. The rich might have enough food, but the poor won't, and the climate crisis will continue to build until it reaches its zenith sometime during the second half of this century. To avoid or mitigate impending catastrophe, the rich will have 'to have fewer children.' The point is made with Abrahamic fervor. "*I'll repeat this: my daughter, who is 29 and Norwegian, is the most dangerous animal on the surface of the earth. She consumes between 10–30 times as many resources and generates 10–30 times as much pollution as an Indian child. So, it's much more important to have one less rich kid than it is to have 10–30 fewer Indians. I'm serious. Population control in the rich world should be the prime focus.*"[98]

Doubts

Despite the enthusiasm for alarm bells in the West, populations in developing regions doubled between 1950 and 1985. Since then, the global population has reached 6.5 billion. And many countries have raised their living standards and done so dramatically. The most successful countries are also the most populous and have some of the highest densities in the world. None of this surprises critics of the 'population problem.'

One reason the warning issued by Malthus and those who broadly accepted his thesis has come to little is improvements in technology and productivity. Another is that a growing number of people does not have to cause poverty. Such a link ignores that poverty is also characteristic of lightly populated countries. The notion that the poor are a problem, and their willingness to forgo children a solution, also shuffles off responsibility for asking other questions. Is society working properly? Is it stacked in favor of some and not others? Is it badly organized and operated incompetently? How much of the poverty witnessed is down to a government's unwise and insensible economic arrangements? The idea that people are not just unwanted but dangerous once allocated a number above some notional limit is uncomfortable and even has something nasty about it.

The view that the poor should have fewer children is restrictive in another sense. More children can improve a family's lot because they represent more streams of income and an opportunity to operate at economies of scale. The social influence (and the potential material benefits) flowing in from each grown child's friendships are often considerable and sometimes critical. Dividing a family's income by the number of people in the family is not always helpful because it does not consider the sophistication of everyday life.

A final and obvious point is that an aging society is dying. The fact that a society's GDP per capita grows faster, and members of that society are getting wealthier, if there are progressively fewer people amongst whom to divide that wealth, is not in the least comforting, except from a purely selfish and very short-term perspective.

However, the Third World's primary motivation for rejecting the population problem has a far more significant and direct influence on economic growth and development. More people and a growing density mean that interactions and exchanges, discussions and arguments, are more intense. And so, therefore, is the adjustment and alteration of existing ideas and the creation of new ones. There is also a greater volume and velocity in behavioral, organizational, and emotional changes and how people treat ideas about self, others, and the wider world. More people crowded together encourages technological changes. City walls, storeyed buildings, and water supplies are needed. Sewerage must be contained, taken away, and re-used as new ways to meet the demand for food and materials are sought. Crowded living encourages specialization because clustering the same activities is a more effective use of space. It is also easier to distribute goods and materials, find and arrange labor, and educate people. These benefits are magnified when one clump of people is proximate and in contact with another. And competition, cooperation, exchange, and movement make it more difficult for communities to become set in their ways.

These advantages are magnified again when these dense clumps find themselves in contact with other such groupings, whether or not they exist in the same political unit. So important is the presence of these communities to each other that it may be difficult, perhaps impossible, for a single clump of any size to emerge by itself; or for a single group to sustain itself in isolation for any length of time. Growth in the size and density of the population is most effective as a stimulus for the emergence of new ideas and technologies when it occurs in more than one place at a time.

A concomitant of density is the mobility and churning of people. Natural increase and migration often contribute in broadly equal proportions to the growth of urban populations. In Brazil in the 1970s, in-migration accounted for 2.2 percent per annum out of a total urban growth rate of 4.4 percent per year.[99] Elsewhere, migration's share of urban growth in the 1980s varied from 35 percent in Argentina to 64 percent in Nigeria and Tanzania. Migration can aggravate problems that characterize the Third World City - disease, unemployment, pollution, poverty, crime, overloaded services, and gimcrack housing. But it also helps spread ideas and nurture rural communities, blending even the remotest into urban life as migrants return home. These threads are beaten in, and the weave made tighter still by the import of rural beliefs and practices into the city, by mutual aid associations formed there around common language or kinship or hometown, and by remittances from migrants and associations in the city to families and communities in the countryside. This movement and the knitting of people and settlements help explain the recent physical expansion and density of urban centers.

Chapter 7

Society over Market: transfers I

As populations grow and become more densely packed, shunting goods and services and funds and people to where they are needed becomes more pressing and complex. Transfers enable improvements in the material basis evenly over long periods and, when conducted deliberately, at astonishing speeds.

In chapter 5 we supposed the economy is a plate on which society rests, and business sectors are jacks supporting the plate's rim. Concentrations of wealth in one sector, accorded by temporary sacrifices in others, allow the plate's edges to rise in turn and at angles gentle enough to leave society upright. This present chapter considers how transfers are made in the Third World.

Economic data should come with loud cautionary statements rather than quiet little notes tucked out of sight. So much can go wrong between the collection of data and its publication and broadcast. Such problems – from a desire to conceal or exaggerate figures, make them up or leave them opaque, to sloppiness and overwork and shortcuts - are often more significant than governments and central banks are willing to admit. There is also the question of definition. Just what is a subsidy? A tax change, new tariff, or welfare payment can subsidize businesses just as effectively as a direct payment labeled 'subsidy.' 'Depreciation' is usually thought of as that part of a machine's value that automatically fixes itself to the products it churns out. Depreciation is treated as an objective economic phenomenon to all intents and purposes. Yet, it emerged in the United States during the 1830s and 1840s to even out spending on expensive assets. It was popular neither with the railway companies, as it reduced their reported earnings, nor with the supreme court, who objected to it because funds allocated for depreciation on paper were not in fact spent during the reported period. Not until the start of the twentieth century was it made a requirement. Not until the first world war did its use become more widespread.

Depreciation also attracted criticism in the UK, Canada, Australia, India, Pakistan, and Sweden, and in the Netherlands, where allowances were liberalized to encourage private investment.[100] Back in the US, depreciation allowances were either tightened up to increase tax revenue or loosened during periods of conflict or low growth. After World War II and the Korean War, labor and consumer groups thought corporate profits were unconscionably high; corporations argued their gains only seemed high because their depreciation allowances were too low.[101]

Defining and delimiting 'profit' is also fraught with difficulties. Adam Smith proposes that profit is the surplus over wages (set at a subsistence level). Ricardo similarly treats profit as a form of income allotted to the owners of capital or stocks, just as labor earns wages and rents accrue to landowners. Marx sees profit as the value added by labor to its produce. Mill thinks profit is rooted in the farmers' ability to grow more than they and their families need for themselves. Robinson believes that profit stems from technological change. It is this which allows workers to produce more than they consume as well as cover the amortization to maintain capital. It is, at the same time, the source of technological change. Profit is also a reward for monitoring others in the firm,[102] delaying spending one's own income, or bearing uncertainty and making decisions. Others say it derives from a natural equilibrium upset by new markets, materials, and technology. Or from the difference between income and production costs or a good's price and capital costs. It is whatever revenue there is after deducting all expenses. And it is the result of being able to sell goods at a value greater than the aggregate contractual costs for production.[103] Is profit qualitatively different from any other form of income? Von Thunen thinks so because it is uncertain and, therefore, uninsurable.

With these kinds of problems in mind, it is better to treat figures on the volumes and value of goods, materials, and people merely as indicative. Subsidies worldwide during the last half of the twentieth century exceeded 4% of national GDP for only three countries – Norway (for much of the period), Sweden (1980s), and Switzerland (1990-2004). The WTO estimates these numbers from its members' notifications, government finance statistics, and national accounts. Most other developed countries' subsidies have been well under 4% and, during the 1998-2002 period, usually no more than one or two percent. Figure 7.1 shows that probably all countries are involved in subsidies.[104] Other sources provide figures which vary from 4.2% of GDP for China, 0.112% for Japan, and 0.33% for South Korea.

The caution the WTO presents these estimates with is well advised. Even for just one industry in one country, subsidies are impressive. Accumulated subsidies of around 4.5 billion

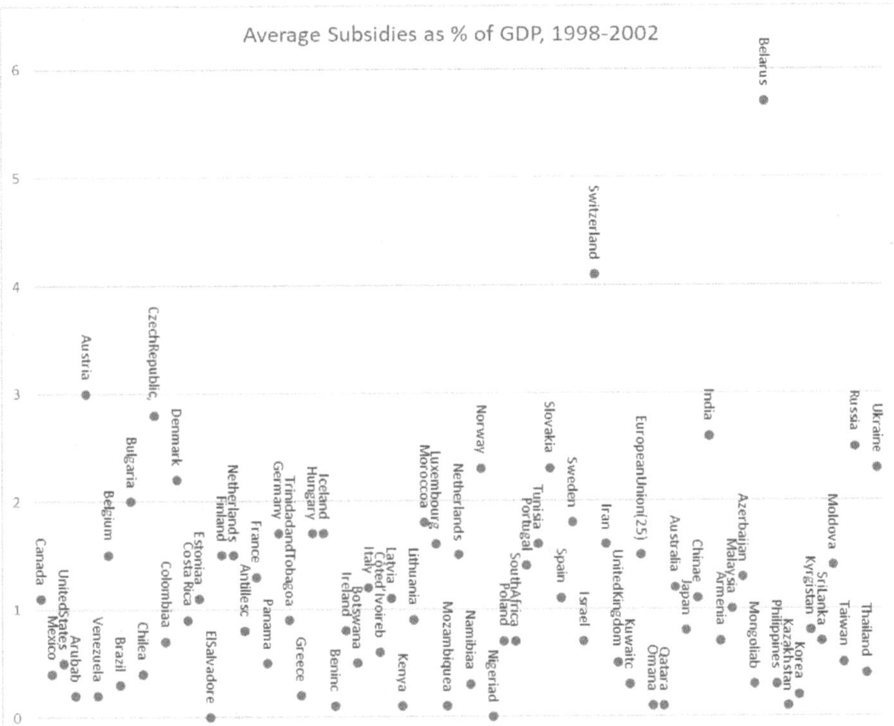

Figure 7.1

dollars for the years 2006-2012 helped China double its share of shipbuilding globally from 25% at the start of that period to 50% by the end of it, leaving Japan, South Korea, and Europe trailing.[105] Aluminum is firmly in China's hands as well. By 2019 nine of the seventeen largest firms internationally were Chinese and responsible for about 50% of primary aluminum and semi-finished products. Chinese firms benefitted from 85% of subsidies worth 70 billion dollars paid to producers the world over. Chinese companies received the largest non-financial subsidies, mainly for energy and other raw materials. China imposed taxes on the export of primary aluminum and provided VAT rebates on aluminum products.[106] China also subsidizes its semiconductor industry. The value of these subsidies is unknown, but hundreds of millions of dollars is a standard estimate. Indirect subsidies are used to acquire technology companies overseas. These were valued at 49 billion dollars in 2016 for purchases in just one country - the US.

These figures are dwarfed by subsidies in the petrochemical and coal industries. These amounted to 149.3 billion dollars in 2012 for exploration alone.[107] To this can be added loans from the China Development Bank, which by 2012 stood at 766 billion. The IEA puts total energy subsidies in China at 2.3 trillion dollars two years later, equivalent to more than twice the combined GDP of all low-income countries.

Smaller but hefty energy subventions are disbursed in many other Third World countries. In Indonesia, between 2014 and 2015, subsidies for electricity and fuel rose from 6.1 to 6.2 billion dollars and from 18.1 to 25 billion dollars, respectively.[108] Together, these two subsidies amounted to around a quarter of central government's total expenditure. India's subsidies on fossil fuel consumption reached 21 billion. Russia's amounted to 355 billion (for 2015), while in Thailand, figures vary from 6.9 billion in 2012 to 16.363 billion, the latter being a post-tax estimate.[109] In Algeria, Iran, Kuwait, Saudi Arabia, and Venezuela, fossil fuel subsidies amount to about 20% of each country's GDP.[110] In Egypt, Jordan, and Yemen, energy subsidies exceeded expenditure on health and education. They amounted to somewhere between 13% and 30% of the GDP in Asia, the Middle East, North Africa, Pakistan, and the Commonwealth of Independent States.[111]

Agricultural subsidies are also extensive. In Thailand, for example, rice farmers number some 15 million – about a fifth of the entire population – making up an important constituency. Pledges to buy rice have been made and honored by successive governments. The most dramatic came from Yinglook, who bought rice 40-50% above the market price, resulting in a stockpile of 18.2 million tonnes, about a quarter of which rotted away in warehouses.

Welfare is not easy to define, nor are these forms of payments easy to estimate or track. Nevertheless, there has been a noticeable rise in expenditure over the last twenty years as more East and Southeast Asian governments expand social assistance programs. Coverage has also increased elsewhere in the Third World. Data are patchy, and the quality of programs varies. But, as a percentage of GDP, states were spending at least 5% on social protection throughout much of south and central America, Russia, East Asia, South Asia, the Middle East, and parts of north and south Africa.[112]

This expansion is often explained by modernization, evolving democratic politics, and a desire to balance economic growth. It is also thought of as a response to growing inequality or economic shocks, notably the 1997 Asian crisis. There is truth in this, but any implication that welfare is antithetical to growth and affordable only once it is well underway is misleading. Welfare precedes capitalism and does so a long way. It exists as patron-clientelism – transfers made to clients by patriarchs – whether kings or emperors or the heads of families and local 'big men.' It is central to accords struck amongst leaders and followers at any level. Expanding alliances from small nests of supporters to large segments of entire societies is a political necessity, for it is a means of forestalling political opponents. Politics and governance are about the distribution of resources.

Welfare manifests itself in many ways: as burial and funeral organizations; as benefit organizations established around occupation, kinship, place of origin, or some other kernel of association such as freed slave (as in Jamaica) or caste (as in India); as churches, temples, mosques, and religious, charitable organizations; and as rotating credit organizations from the *arisan* of Indonesia and the *stokvels* of South Africa to the *tontines* of west Africa, and the *cesta* in Mexico.[113] It is indistinguishable from the give and take and mutual aid of everyday social relationships, kinship, friendship, and community. Keeping demand buoyant and goods and services flowing through society gives capitalism a lease of life that it would not otherwise enjoy.

Government efforts to dispense welfare are often integrated with, or modeled on, earlier welfare arrangements, as in the case of the *bazis* and *lazis* of Indonesia. Legislation, too, is used to compel or encourage businesses to arrange welfare functions such as pensions. Official arrangements in some countries date back to colonial or even pre-colonial times. Ghana had had rudimentary welfare arrangements in place before independence in 1957. The Department of Social Welfare and Housing was set up in 1946. The Workman's Compensation Act (1963), the Social Security Act and the Industrial Relations Act (both in 1965), and the Labor Decree (1967), and the Social Security Decree of 1972,[114] all followed. Thailand, which was spared colonization, established its department of welfare in 1940 and brought in a social security act in 1954.

At first, state welfare organizations targeted defined groups. In South Korea, this meant government employees, soldiers, teachers, and those working in core industries. These segments of the population were thought essential to economic and political stability. The medical protection law of 1976 was followed quickly by a medical aid program in 1977 and, eleven years later, by the Universal Care Act. By the late 1990s, pension employment insurance and livelihood security covered South

Korea's entire population.[115] On the face of it, social security became less productivist (aimed at improving the economic efficiency of people) and more about helping people simply because they are poor or ill. But 'adaptable' is probably a more accurate description. As the chaebols' sales as a percentage of GDP fall or rise (and in 2012, that share peaked at around 80%), social security became less or more productivist.

In Taiwan, it was also soldiers, teachers, and government employees who benefitted at the start. The old and the poor received only meager aid. However, indirect payments in the form of subsidies already existed, and later direct welfare subventions became more inclusive. Taiwan's benefits were extended to manual workers and fishermen and made universal by the turn of the new millennium. In 1995, universal access to health care was financed through tax revenue (28%) and premiums (72%). That ratio (tax to premium) rose to 100/0 for military and government personnel and fell to 10/90 for private-sector employees. Thailand also greatly expanded coverage through two universal non-contributory programs. Meanwhile, at least in theory and often in practice, China's citizens have enjoyed broad protections since the 1950s as part and parcel of an economy owned and managed by the state (central authorities) and collectives (sub-state government units). Retirement, medical care, injury, birth, illness, death, sick pay, education, transport, housing, energy, heating, meals, and essential goods (such as grain, vegetables, and clothing) have been the responsibility of collectives or state. Much has depended on political stability and the extent to which the population became caught up in factional infighting, which led to poor decisions, weak organization, and a breakdown in logistical operations and supplies. Welfare, though, has remained part and parcel of the reforms enacted since 1978 despite the rise of the private sector. The state has often had to take the strain by maintaining and improving food subsidies, energy subsidies, medical care, education, and benefits through its companies or administrative bureaucracy.

Tax is another essential mode of transfer. In large parts of the Third World, corporation tax and taxes on general goods and services (including goods and services moved in and out of the country) comprise the bulk of government revenues. In contrast, the West's tax on personal income supplies the leading share. Tax in developing countries is also somewhat different in that benefits are mostly tax-free, unlike those in developed countries where they are often taxable. Indeed, the overall tax burden tends to be lower in developing countries and does not lie primarily with the general populace. More wealth is left in the hands of citizens.

The Third World's reliance on corporation tax and taxes on goods and services is often viewed as a consequence of underdevelopment. Governments, it is said, do not have the organizations or money to run an effective tax system. They do not have the control over revenue to formulate and implement good economic policy. Pakistan's slow development is sometimes explained in such terms. The government does not have the tax system necessary to collect enough revenue. Consequently, it cannot fulfill its basic functions and is forced to borrow overseas. Debt and repayments grow, taking cash away from services that must be forfeited or continued with further loans and more debt. Nigeria, too, has a revenue - not a debt – problem, or so it is said. The solution is a more effective system that broadens the tax base to include personal income.

The ability to collect revenue is essential to management but does not equate with a dependence on personal tax. Large parts of East Asia have effective tax systems but emphasize corporations, goods, and services. This keeps demand and resources flowing. In fact, an attempt to 'broaden' the tax base is unhelpful. The model emulated is inherently flawed. It cuts away at demand and makes life for much of the populace more difficult.

Maintaining tight control over the financial system - the banks and other financial organizations - means that government can order money directly to flow wherever it feels is best rather than try to influence its movement. For instance, altering the exchange rate can help stimulate exports generally. But ordering loans to a specific sector or company can be far more effective, sensitive, and quicker. A rise in interest rates may suck money out of a population and slow down investments. But it is easier and less damaging to order a ban on loans. Decisions and orders become easier if large industries are owned or directly controlled and, in many cases, run by government officials – the state-owned organizations. Management of these also means the management of debt and sources of foreign revenue.

Blurring ownership boundaries, as in China and Japan, also reflects a willingness to shunt goods, materials, people, and subsidies around the economy. It enables domestic liabilities to be moved off the books, either to the central bank outside the economy or into companies whose sole function is to retire bad debt. If ownership boundaries were sacrosanct, and if there was a determination to enforce rights over loans and bankruptcies, the transfer of resources in ways benefitting society would be impossible.

Deficit and debt, then, is another important mode of transfer. Government deficit refers to the shortfall of revenue over spending from one year to the next.

Debt refers to the accumulated deficit – how much the government owes. Developing countries treat debt and deficit pragmatically – as a way to drive economic growth.

A deficit does little more than reflect economic activity if a country borrows from itself. That might appear to be the solution to all problems because the sums borrowed can be limitless: why even bother with external sources of revenue (exports) or taxation? Unfortunately, matters are not so straightforward. While a government can issue as much currency as it wants, the size of an economy and its inequalities will restrict what can be absorbed. Imagine a small, isolated community of a thousand people growing food and managing a few basic crafts (such as cloth and pottery). Its king might issue billions in the local currency, creating unimaginable wealth. But this society has neither the population nor the technology or knowledge to do much with all that currency. If it is spread about evenly, life continues much as before, though now the price of goods is higher. If concentrated in just a few hands, the market will be cornered, creating an elite who buy and sell at inflated prices. Everyone else is rendered destitute, and society collapses. Nor can domestic debt substitute for foreign revenue. No matter how much is issued, an isolated community's currency is worthless overseas if other states do not recognize it. Only when that community sells goods overseas and earns foreign exchange can it buy imports, set up new businesses, stimulate new wants, and grow its economy much faster than if it had relied on domestic liabilities alone. Only then might other countries be willing to accept its currency. Exports do not just provide an alternative to increases in local debt. Exports also allow increases in domestic debt. More importantly, exports bring in additional capital to invest.

Export-oriented industrialization is a popular explanation for the success of East Asia's tiger economies - Taiwan, South Korea, Hong Kong, and Singapore. The tactic relied on cheap labor and low exchange rates, ensuring that goods produced for export found orders more quickly. Imports also became more expensive, but this had the advantage of protecting domestic industries. Thus, countries followed a mixture of import-substitution and export-oriented industrialization, shifting emphasis towards the latter over time. Early export-oriented industrialization is unavoidable in some cases because import substitution can only work when supported by growing domestic demand. And the domestic market was limited, either by the population size or low purchasing power. Some commentators added Japan, Malaysia, Thailand, and China to the list of East and Southeast Asian countries that relied upon a remarkably similar export-manufacturing model.

Indonesia, Vietnam, and Burma also sought to replicate the strategy. While there are differences in state involvement and intervention, all these countries exported products for consumers in the West cheaper, faster, and more reliably than anyone else.

The question, though, remains. How does one develop exports without racking up external debts, given that the domestic economy, and the amount of debt tolerated, are small? One way is to encourage savings. Another is aid. In Taiwan, foreign assistance provided around 28% of capital between 1951 and 1965, while domestic savings rose from about 7% in 1960 to 28% in 1976.[116] War reparations demanded by Korea from Japan can be helpful. So are remittances, as in the Philippines. A government can also encourage foreign companies to invest, employ, and manufacture for export and often for export *only*. In this way, governments can control the domestic economy's direction and limit multinational corporations' influence on local incomes and consumer behavior. Once domestic firms are strong enough, they can establish companies overseas, adding to the state's earnings.

Another method is to exchange strategic advantage for loans or, better still, grants and aid on favorable terms. Many countries in East Asia did with the US. After the last war, the US took up Japan's interests; Japan became dependent upon the US economically for post-war rebuilding and trading opportunities and protection against threats from the Asian mainland. The logic of the US argument was clear: build up a strong economy in Japan through aid and a policy of liberal trade as a means of deterring the Soviet Union from spreading its power and influence into the pacific. To make the policy work, the US encouraged triangular trade between the US (which provided the capital and technology), Japan (which provided mass consumer and capital goods), and southeast Asia (providing the raw materials). And as the Japanese economy grew, capital, know-how, and markets were diffused to the rest of the region, including China. This effectively knitted together the region's economies and turned it into one of the powerhouses of the world economy with growth rates twice that of other parts of the world. A case often made, then, is that the US regarded the region's countries as vital to its own geopolitical interests and provided the catalyst and the motive power for their rapid economic advance. After Japan's defeat, the US nurtured the country back to economic health and sponsored the country's return to prominence through open international markets and military security. That provided the crucial context for an alliance within Japan between the conservative party, bureaucracy, and big business, which concentrated on leading the economy to high export volumes and technical sophistication. China, in its turn, is now offering that route to many Third World countries.

Domestic debt, then, is not necessarily a bad thing, especially when married to expanding sources of foreign revenue. Take, for instance, Japan's domestic or internal debt. It is extremely high - equivalent to around two-and-a-half times the GDP. However, the country's *niip* (or net international investment position) is favorable. It describes the sum of a country's (government, business, and citizens)' assets and liabilities overseas. If, say, Japan was to repatriate all its interests back home and dispose of all its liabilities, and if other countries were to do the same with their interest and liabilities in Japan, then the *niip* is the gap between the two piles of wealth. If your pile is higher than everyone else's, then you are a creditor nation. Japan's *niip* is the highest in the world. Thus, whilst Japan's domestic debt is high relative to its GDP, this merely reflects the activity that has led it to become a robust economic presence internationally. China also has high domestic debt, equivalent to about 300 percent of its GDP. Many observers believe this portends imminent economic collapse. But its external debt is only 7% of its exports, and its *niip* is very favorable. It is a creditor nation of some import. Its debt pile reflects activities that make it strong economically.

The picture is not too dissimilar in many parts of Southeast Asia. Thailand is a net debtor nation. If its assets and liabilities overseas are counted up, the sum is about 45 billion less than foreign assets and liabilities in Thailand. And Thailand's internal debt is a little higher at 40% of GDP. But its external debt is only 8.3% of its exports. We can even find creditor nations in Africa. Botswana is a tiny, land-locked country of around two million people on a vast continent. It is a creditor nation by about 7.5 billion dollars, with a small domestic debt of just 12% of its GDP and external debt of just 12% of exports.

Provided wealth flowing in and out of the country is balanced or, better still, the country's assets outdo its liabilities, domestic debt remains an indication of activity and economic expansion. External debt is a different matter. It is a problem because the creditor is entirely separate and likely to demand an income from the loan and the return of the original amount. The accumulation of external debt is the start of a slippery slope. As debt grows, more revenue has to be used to service it, and it becomes more expensive to take on new debt if needed. The currency's value may well depreciate, and imports become more expensive. Eventually, the government may lose control of the economy to its creditors, who demand that it cut spending and raise income. This has happened in many Third World countries and keeps them in poverty. Some countries, especially in Africa, have been left with large external debts they cannot repay.

The role of the market and private business in all this is fraught with tension. Profit-making attracts opprobrium and obliges merchants to be outsiders not because of some base and irrational prejudice but because private businesses create damaging inequalities and undermine the material foundations of society. Ambiguous relationships between government and industry, and a desire of the former to control and absorb the latter, have long been a feature of many complex societies. The real question is not why the Third World exhibits this tension but why the West does its best to let the market dominate. But that is for later.

Chapter 8

Society over Market: transfers II

Profits and wages are ways of directing money and resources to industry and the general population. Ultimately, profit stems from exports, overseas remittances, aid, grants, and debt (both external and domestic) channeled to businesses through workers' purchases of their products. As profits accrue, industries are built. Better technology, better designs, more efficient production, access to cheaper materials, or cheaper labor enable some businesses to eliminate others. Wages are a vital counterflow that the Third World keeps relatively open, leaving resources in the hands of the general population.

Collective bargaining, union action, bringing informal pressure to bear on companies to raise wages, legislation on minimum wages, or building up large and well-paid public sectors (which compel private enterprises to pay more) are a few of the methods used to funnel resources to the general population. Subsidies to firms to improve training and hire workers from certain sections of the population (such as the unemployed, younger or older workers, or women) are also common. Although these measures are more about reducing the pool of unemployed, if practiced widely enough, the effect can be to encourage businesses to raise wages.

Another set of methods aims to control inflation. This is needed because, when left up to business, wages are usually funded by pushing up prices for goods that those workers will buy and who will ask for additional raises. Controlling inflation often involves price management or altering the broad economic context. In China, to keep the *yuan's* value low against other currencies (especially the dollar) so that its exports remain competitive, the government buys up dollars earned through exports and issues yuan. Taking the dollar out of circulation this way increases its value while the yuan's value is lowered. This keeps Chinese exports competitive and the wages and salaries of workers in China buoyant. Dollars are also sold if the yuan's value falls too far. The issuance of yuan in China raises inflation risks, so the domestic currency is also controlled. The government sells bonds to absorb the excess. It increases the quantity of currency that banks can hold in reserve. And it alters the discount rate (the rate bank use to lend to each other). It can also increase or decrease subsidies. It may also control prices directly – a practice held over from the days of central planning.

Wages are just one way of keeping counterflows open. (Restrictions on executives' pay, a relatively high tax on corporations, and a lower tax on wages, subsidies, and welfare are mentioned above.) Important back channels through patronage and corruption also exist between private businesses, the government, and the public sector on the one hand and the general population on the other. The following chapters discuss these. The combined effect is that more resources are left with the general population, which has experienced real wage growth, unlike its counterparts in the West.

Government or public procurement is another form of transfer. It describes the state's use of its organizations and infrastructure or the private sector to move goods and materials. Countries have come under pressure from the West and organizations such as the UN, World Bank, IMF, ADB, and WTO to rely more upon the private sector and be as transparent as possible. Subsequent efforts to remedy poor governance and improve organizational capacity have attracted much attention. The problem of procurement, though, is an old one.

As America drew up its plans for the administration of the Philippines at the end of the nineteenth century, Taft, the chair of the Philippine Commission, inveighed against the corrupt management of public funds. The Commission thought that putting an honest and efficient man at the head of a financial system and giving him firm control over his deputies was part of the solution. So was establishing a civil service based on merit. This was the intention of the fifth law enacted by the Commission in 1900. The civil service was to include treasurers and auditors with clear duties and responsibilities. Methods for keeping and rendering accounts of their receipts and disbursements were required under separate legislation. Procedures for bidding and awarding contracts were attached to various other pieces of legislation defining types of construction projects from ports to warehouses. Other related items of legislation were added during the Commonwealth era, creating cities such as Cebu complete with a Quartermaster Service. Not until 1976, under Marcos, were these strands picked up and knitted together into something like a system. A trial procurement scheme to furnish supplies and materials to the national government was begun that year and expanded over the next two years. Attached to the Office of the President, it became known as the Procurement Service. Presidential Decree 1594 (which focused on supplies for infrastructure and construction projects) was signed in 1978. The implementing rules and regulations were released to national agencies in 1980. Local governments, meanwhile, would have to wait until 1991 for their system to be shaped under the Local Governments Code.

Amendments and changes to both local and national systems continued to be made, most notably in 1996, 2000, and 2001 under the Ramos and Estrada Presidencies. The reforms and measures contained in another act (RA 9184) passed in 2003 ticked all the right boxes for western governments, international banks, and aid agencies. The new bill aimed to establish a transparent, efficient, and integrity-based procurement system that engaged the public and CSO, used the latest information technology and was insulated from political interference and collusion amongst businesses. It was a world-class piece of legislation, declared a World Bank official.

In practice, however, scandals continued. Further adjustments and amendments were made, and performance indicators were defined and measured. 'Institutional frameworks' and management 'capacities' were to be improved. Procurement would have to be integrated with the Public Sector Government program and harmonized with systems used by the Philippines' development partners. More effective staff evaluations and action plans were expounded. Thus the system became heavier, thicker, and more laborious and cumbersome than it had ever been. It was just as prone to all the 'crying evils' of which Taft had complained more than a century earlier and, worse still, prevented the government from spending money on anything and everything from medicines and roads to schools and housing. Terms such as 'fiscal wastage,' 'underspend,' and a 'failure to meet obligations' were convenient anesthetics. Compliance with procurement rules and regulations (an amended version of which runs to 45 pages) became, for many agencies, their raison d'etre and any deviation subject to investigation and analysis by the Commission on Audit.

Rules and the pressure to follow them were not the only difficulties. Rules must be interpreted and communicated, and there are many different interpretations and failures of communication amongst thousands of national, regional, provincial, and local governments and agencies. Added to this is the sprawling, ill-defined nature of planning and coordination involving 5,000 local government units facing widely different circumstances, conflicting ambitions, and varying technical capabilities.

In an attempt to absorb and speed up the more essential procurement items – especially IT projects, medicines, medical equipment, and large infrastructure projects (such as airports and bridges) in this archipelago of 7,000 islands - the Department of Budget and Management's own procurement service (established originally to buy paper and office supplies for the national government) was conscripted. But it, too, was tangled up in its own procedures. Each item took, on average, four years to clear. The value of procurement items caught up in this mess amounted to over 90 billion dollars.

The total value of underspending each year over the last decade has only increased with the money available to the government. Over seven years, the national budget doubled from 1.54 trillion pesos in 2010 to 3.35 trillion in 2017, while official figures for underspending rose from 78 billion to 276 billion (somewhere between 5 and 10% of available funds). Strip out funds labeled 'obligated' (the bureaucratic and accounting methods used to earmark funds without spending them), and the true figure rises to over 20% of the budget. For some departments, the figure is as high as 30%. In some years, the figure is closer to 40% in some agencies. These numbers do not include underspending in LGUs.

The damaging effects of officialism in the Philippines demanded by the West are thrown into sharp relief by countries where it is resisted. To whatever extent the three decades after 1949 limited China's economic growth, those years also gave the leadership, bureaucracy, and people unparalleled experience in state-organized commerce. Goods and materials, from rice and vegetable to steel and concrete, were produced, procured, and distributed according to administrative commands. Trade was periodically encouraged and banned as political and ideological battles raged. Only after 1978 were trade and markets allowed a greater role. The number of private trade organizations (businesses with less than eight employees) rose from 100,000 in 1978 to over 14 million by the late 1980s. Over the same period, their share of total retail sales increased from about 0.5% to around twenty-five percent. Private trade organizations also grew into private enterprises (entities with eight or more employees). They numbered about 40,000 by the end of 1988, 66,500 by the end of June 1989, and 90,790 by the end of that year. The growth in small businesses surprised many in government and bureaucracy. The all-weather, omnipresent state procurement and distribution system was supposed to remain the primary channel. In theory, new administrative organization and contracts would enable appendages of state administrative organs to be more responsive, flexible, and efficient and, in this sense, imitate private commerce. Small private businesses would remain complementary, delivering agricultural goods (especially perishable commodities) and everyday industrial consumables and catering, repair, construction, transport, and other services. A party report published in 1988 predicted that private business was never likely to capture a share of more than 10% of China's economy. It was hopelessly off the mark. By 2014 they numbered 50 million and were responsible for around 60% of industrial output value, 75% of employment, and 70% of exports. By the start of 2018, they numbered a little over 65 million. As they grew in number, some grew in size. More than eight million were classified as corporate entities. A few became very large indeed, ranking alongside China's state-owned leviathans.

Despite its expansion, the private sector is integrated with and ultimately dependent upon state decisions and control. The merchant is only a surrogate. In the end, the enterprise belongs to the state. When a business gets big enough (as did Alibaba, Ant Financial, and Didi), or their command of a sector (such as education) becomes too great, the state reaches in. Every conceivable combination of state and private commercial interests is continually evolving, forming an extraordinarily varied, sophisticated, and flexible system that allows China to shift resources around in ways that permit very rapid growth.

China has undoubtedly moved towards what is expected and often demanded by the West in its organizational arrangements for government procurement. A bidding law was established in 2000, followed in 2003 by a government procurement law. In between, at the end of 2001, China joined the WTO. Since then, China has proffered terms for its accession to the GPA in 2008, 2010, 2011, 2013, 2014, and 2019, all of which were rejected. It has also updated its procurement system and made it more transparent. Foreign companies are supposed to have a fighting chance at securing bids. In practice, China has, for obvious reasons, been reluctant to see its people lose out to foreigners. Unwritten quotas are passed down; unwritten understandings dominate.

From the West's point of view, it was plain why China should join the GPA. It would gain access to other countries' procurement markets and vice versa. Competition amongst bidders for contracts would intensify, driving up quality and reducing costs. And domestic firms would have to become more efficient and innovative. China has only to deal with conflicts and confusion in the country's legal framework to reap these benefits. China's preference for its own companies particularly irked the West. In 2018, PPPs - which numbered about 10,000 and were valued at 15 trillion RMB - were awarded mainly to state-owned companies. Uncertainty over the size of China's public procurement market was also frustrating. Official procurement figures for 2017 are 3.21 trillion, or 12% of official expenditure, or 3.9% of GDP. These are said to be too low. More accurate estimates are probably closer to 30% and 15%, respectively. Innovation is hindered by contracts detailing the products needed rather than the problem for which a solution is required. Criticisms are also made of the small number of bidders and, paradoxically, the overly transparent nature of the process: competitors are allowed to see the details of each other's bids so they can learn from each other.

But to grumble there is no fair and rules-based system is to complain against a feature that helps explain the efficacy of China's approach. Rules, laws, and organizations are treated in practice as affective in nature rather than objective facts. The Party supplies broad plans (informed by details on the ground). But these have no legal power. The Party, state council, and the national development committee then formulate more detailed plans together with implementing rules and regulations. This provides a mixture of guidance and detail into which local units (such as city mayors) integrate theirs. Legislation follows practice and provides a record, a set of minutes, of what was agreed upon and done. A good deal of debate precedes it. A broad goal and set of problems are defined. It is up to governments (local and central) to find effective and acceptable solutions. Decisions are made, action is taken, and paperwork follows and legitimizes what is done.

This might be thought a roundabout way of saying China is authoritarian. But that would be a mistake. Decisions and actions emerge collectively. The leader depends upon the support of others, including subordinates. He cannot wield punishment at will if he is to last. He must consult. What do others in the organization feel about this or that course of action? Is it practical, will it work, will it be supported, will they agree, will they complain, will it seem too high-handed? The subordinate is respectful, yet arguments are had, and points are scored behind closed doors. Different views are necessary, and different ways of operating are needed.

What is true for him is true for those further down the hierarchy. None is their own man or woman. Each works as the leader does, uncovering what others think. The collective's parts move together but not as one. They try this or that tactic or strategy. If it fails, then it is revised, and something else is tried. The collective's parts move in the same general direction but not along the same exact path and not at the same time or in the same way. Reform and experimentation are constant. Practice is contingent upon circumstances. It is as though the collective is feeling its way in the dark, creeping forward, occasionally making a leap (and sometimes regretting it), taking stock, and moving on again.

All the while, one makes do. This person might not be particularly suited to this task, but so what? They might turn out to be suited to another. One also makes do with equipment, methods, and rules. It's enough if a machine or technique works. Sometimes rules matter. Sometimes they don't. If something doesn't work, then put it to one side and replace it later. The organization comprises people, and what matters, in the end, is that they have each other at heart.

Chapter 9

Build-up

Population growth, increasing density, and transfers set the scene for more intense competition with other societies. Increased pressure on agriculture and other resources compels the leadership to cultivate and emphasize a specific form of transfer – commerce. Commerce – or exchange for profit conducted by nominally private entities – is a flexible and sensitive mode of transfer. It enables society to swell and compress further and compete more effectively. This further heightens the need for commerce. Thus, a virtuous upward spiral is initiated. Large, dense, and commercially experienced populations laid the foundation for substantial economic growth and development after 1945 in territories as diverse as Japan, South Asia, West Africa, and Central America.

Between 2000 and 2014 Tokyo generated about 37% of Japan's GDP. Osaka, Kobe (an old port and former capital), and Kyoto accounted for about 19% of Japan's GDP in 2016: that's equivalent to a little more than Switzerland's entire GDP and a little less than Australia's that same year. The significance of the area stretching from Tokyo to Fukuoka in the south and Sendai in the north is also evident when tax contributions to central government are measured. The commercial and urban network this portrays was laid out during the seven centuries before the Meiji Restoration in 1868. Steam was applied to Japan's existing and new industries, from mining (1859) and metal production (1861) to cotton spinning, silk-reeling, railways, and iron and steel in the 1870s and 1880s. By 1890, steam engines and turbines generated 87% of the country's horsepower. Not every growing industrial center had preindustrial origins. Sapporo, for instance, was an administrative creation of the Colonization Bureau in the later nineteenth century. But most did. Niigata, a center for oil production, had been a port for rice. Gumma, where silk mills flourished, had long produced silk. Kaimaishi, where iron ore was discovered in the late eighteenth century, concentrated on iron and steel. Tokyo, Osaka, and Kyoto remained closely linked centers of commerce and finance.

A notable increase in population and density took place immediately before industrialization began and just after the culmination of a steady rise in population from the start of the sixteenth century. The urban population grew from 1.4 to 5 million during the seventeenth century. Edo (or Tokyo) held about 1 million people by the end of that century, packed in at somewhere between 49000 and 60,000/km2. [117] Osaka, Japan's commercial and financial center, hit 400,000, as did Kyoto, its former imperial city and center for arts and handicrafts. Outside these three cities, the castle towns (the seats of the daimyos) spread across the archipelago and grew in size. Some contained only a few thousand people. Others, such as Sendai, Okagama, Kagoshima, Hiroshima, and Nagasaki, held around 60,000 each. A few, such as Kanazawa and Nagoya, approached 100,000. Densities amongst the commoners could reach 58,000/km2, some four times that of the Samurai and ten times that of the temples. Many other settlements - postal way stations, ports, local markets, religious centers, and mines - were scattered over the archipelago. These were usually smaller in size,

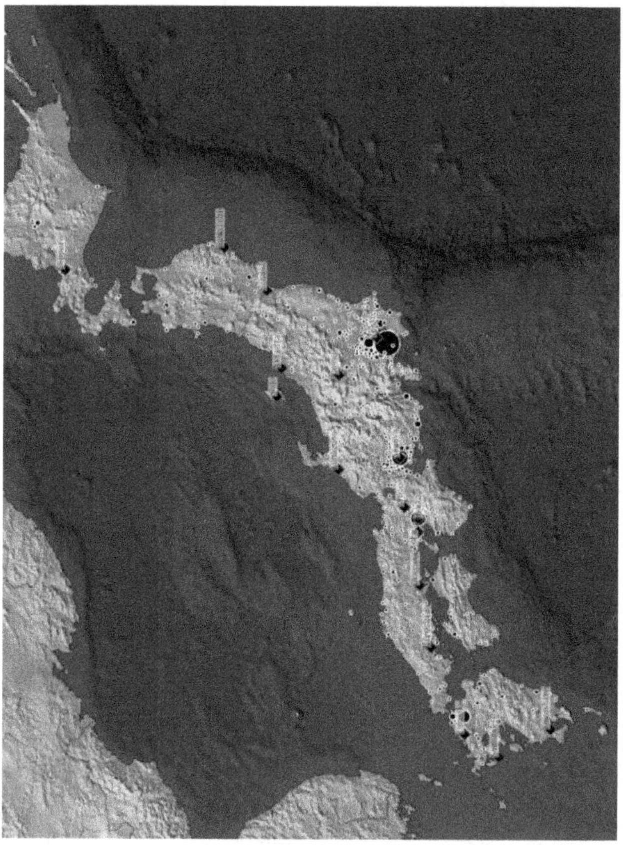

(Left) Figure 9.1. Japan Settlement Patterns (arranged by tax contributions).

though some matched the castle towns. Aikawa's populace - who mined gold and silver on Sado Island - numbered 100,000 by the middle of the seventeenth century. All in all, Japan's population rose from around 18 million to about 30 million between 1600 and 1721. It leveled off for the next eighty years before rising to 37 million by the Meiji Restoration.

The dispersal of people throughout Japan was driven partly by 'putting out' manufacturing from the cities and larger towns to the rural districts. This practice, which led at first to mild de-urbanization during the eighteenth and early nineteenth centuries, helped bind rural and urban areas. It also reflected political realities. The stability of the Tokugawa depended upon meting out men and resources. Merchants contributed by selling, buying, transporting, and distributing goods, transforming rice into cash, lending to the Daimyos and Samurai, and paying taxes. Thus, they kept government viable and officials living in style: functions important enough to ensure that merchants stayed at the bottom of the social hierarchy in Confucian cosmology.

West Africa

Wherever land capable of bearing people in large numbers is hemmed in by the sea, a harsher environment, or by other populations unwilling to give way, there lies the potential for densities to rise, groups to compete, and states to emerge. One of the largest kingdoms to appear in west Africa by the eighth century was the Wagadu (Koumbi Saleh), or Ghana. It arose more than 450 miles northwest of modern Ghana's northern border. There it occupied several basins on the northern and eastern fringes of the Senegal river basin, spilled out onto a sliver of the Niger basin, and fell just short of Djenne and Timbuktu.

At Wagadu's heart lay markets – way stations linking trade routes north across the Sahara with those driving south to the gold-producing areas of west Africa.[118] The Kingdom came under pressure from Berber warriors of the Mauritanian Sahara. But it was not they who benefitted from Wagadu's collapse when that came in the thirteenth century. It was the Mandinka who hitherto had been middlemen in the gold trade. They established an even larger Empire - Mali. It engulfed the entire Senegal basin, its western, northern, and eastern fringes, and much of the upper and middle Niger, stretching from Tukrur in the West to Niani in the south, Tichit in the north, and Timbuktu and Gao in the east. In its turn, Mali was replaced by the Songhay, which, at its height, reached the salt pans of Taghaza. It also took in the Senegal and Gambia basins. And it spanned most of the Niger, including Agadez on the basin's eastern rim and, further south, the Hausa states on the edge of the Chad basins. The Hausa looked to Kano, whose origins date to around the eleventh century when towns and cities were beginning to appear in England. Then, as now, Kano is a center of manufacturing and dyeing textiles. Katina and Zaria were important marts; Gobir state, whose capital was Alkalawa, was a defense outpost to the north; and the southernmost city Zaria was a nexus for the slave trade.

Neither the Wagadu, Mali, nor Songhay extended far enough into the Chad basin to disturb the Kanem Empire, which, from around the twelfth century, expanded to Darfur in the east and Bilma and Djado in the north and, beyond, to the city of Murzuk. Nor did the Songhay to its immediate south breach the Volta basin where the Mossi and the Gonja lived and (around the lower reaches of that basin) the Asante and Ga. And while the Songhay touched upon the Hausa for a short time, it did not impinge upon the Yoruba and Igbo, who occupied the lowest section of the Niger basin. The Igbo, who dominated the region just east of the Niger, comprised looser political assemblages. To the west, the Yoruba prevailed. Reliance on oral traditions makes it difficult to be sure about the origins of these settlements before the early nineteenth century, but the oldest appears to be Oyo. War amongst the Yoruba kingdoms in the mid-nineteenth century, and invasion from the north by the Hausa, put an end to the older realms from whose wreckage new ones sprung up, including new Oyo, Ilorin, Abeokuta, Ibadan, and Iyara. Lagos, established by the Awori Yoruba in the south before the seventeenth century, survived these irruptions despite being one of the smallest and weakest entities; and it would see the slave trade give way to palm oil and other legitimate goods. So did Calabar, further to the west. So did Benin, which sat between the Igbo and Yoruba.

Few settlements were constructed in response to European contact and colonization. New colonial cities were established along the railways from Port Harcourt, Enugu, Jos, and Kaduna, though some had pre-colonial antecedents. Talemo, in northern Ghana, was a collection of villages of the Dagoma before the British made it an administrative town. But most were indigenous creations and would remain sites for growth after independence in 1961. Lagos, Ibadan, Abeokuta, Benin, and Kano were the largest and most densely populated manufacturing centers. They remain so today and account for a large share of GDP.

It was the same story elsewhere in west Africa. The original, pre-colonial settlements formed the basis for colonial control and subsequent industrialization, which began at the turn of the twentieth and proceeded slowly. The old settlement patterns along the upper and middle Niger became Mali's heart. A river basin in that strip of land known as Gambia *is* Gambia. The settlements along the Senegal River, which once formed the soul of the Mali and Songhay empires, *are* Senegal. Ghana *is* centered on the Asante and Ga in the south and the Tamale in the north. Burkino Faso *is* Ougadougu and the Mossi.

Central America

On the other side of the Atlantic, large parts of the area now called Mexico were occupied by competing groups who had arranged themselves into a complex of small city-states by the time the Spanish arrived in the early 16th century. These states frequently patterned themselves through alliances into confederations. Three of these confederations introduced another level of complexity by establishing a grand triple alliance that came to be known as the Aztecs. They controlled the basin of Mexico and most of Meso-America. To the north were patchworks of other competing groups. Populations in and around what are today known as Sinaloa and Michoaloa were comparatively dense, but there were no urban settlements. To the south, on the border of the Aztecs, lay Oaxaca - the home of the Zapotecs. They fell under the Aztecs for a short period in the fifteenth century. Beyond them lay the Yucatan peninsula, occupied by the Maya.

Figure 9.2 Markets and towns of the Western Sahel.

Figure 9.3 Mexico settlement patterns (arranged by contribution to GDP)

The Spanish ended the Aztecs through trade, the force of arms, and disease, but indigenous settlements remained the basis for colonial control. The Spanish built on or near the existing settlements and often did so with materials taken from them. Drawn by their interest in silver mining and their concern about British and later American encroachment, it was mainly in the north that new towns – San Luis Potosi, Monterrey, Torres, Durango, and others - appeared where none had existed before. These grew in importance over the following centuries. Yet, the distribution and concentration of the population remained focused on areas of pre-colonial settlement in the south. Today, Mexico City (the basin of Mexico), Toluca, Oaxaca, and Merida together account for more than half of the country's GDP.

India

By the time the Europeans arrived in the early fifteenth century, India was a macédoine of kingdoms replete with cities that were places of administration, trade, art, and politics. Seven of the ten most economically influential cities today are from this stock. A Rajput clan founded Dehli in the eighth century, which, following Arab invasions, became the most important of the northern sultanates. Visakhapatnam dates to the sixth century BC, Pune to around the sixth century AD. The Sultan of Gujarat established Ahmedabad as a new capital in 1411. Bangalore and Surat were laid out early in the sixteenth century. Hyderabad was begun in 1589 by the Qutb Shahi dynasty, rulers of Golconda. The three others, Mumbai, Kolkata, and Chennai are colonial edifices but have pre-colonial antecedents.

The growth of settlements and commerce followed a train of events similar to those occurring in Japan, west Africa, and Meso-America. Harappan civilization had petered out by the middle of the second millennium BC, worn down by one invasion after another. But even as it dissolved, new states arose. Families engaged in agriculture and pastoralism organized themselves into villages, clans (led by a chief), and confederations. During the first half of the first millennium BC, these arrangements began to approximate states. Kinship weakened a little, while a sense of caste also evolved. As competition amongst groups intensified, commerce, though socially despised, became more important for practical reasons. Newly formed Kingdoms attempted to incorporate one another. None ever unified India. But a few, such as the Magadha, Maurya, Asoka, Gupta, Harsa, Cola, and Visakh, held on to their empires for 200-300 years. Matters were further complicated by the Arabs, who controlled much of northern India after the twelfth century, following in the footsteps of the Greeks, Kusana, Saka, Hunas, and others.

China

China's modern economic and urban geography is also rooted in an urban and commercial network that long predates its recent industrialization. Commerce and growth were more vibrant here than in eighteenth-century Europe. Living standards were high and still rising such that even ordinary people had increased their consumption of "non-essentials" between 1500 and 1750. Many of these were the same as those found in Europe: tobacco, sugar, more and better clothes, eating utensils, and so on. Most estimates of caloric intake in eighteenth-century China compare well with Europe, and that's true whether we are talking about averages for the whole population or figures for the hardest-working laborers. Indeed, the poor in China reached these nutritional standards without spending more of their incomes on basic foodstuffs than poor Europeans. Rural life expectancies in China around 1750 also suggest nutrition levels equal to those of Britain at the time and higher than most of continental Europe. Chinese birth rates were similar to those in Europe between 1550 and 1850. China's overall population growth rate was either faster than (1550-1750) or equal to rates found in Europe (1750-1850). Chinese death rates were lower. Chinese per capita consumption and production were comparable to Europe's at the same or later date, not only for tea and silk but also for sugar and cloth. And despite numerous data problems, per-capita cloth output for the Yangzi Delta in 1750 appears close to that for England in 1800.

With their arrival in Hong Kong, the British stumbled upon China's commercial expansion, which had been underway since the sixteenth century. In Jiangnan, near Shanghai, specialized market towns helped funnel goods - such as cotton textiles, silks, rice, salt, fish, bamboo, wood, pottery, metals, embroidery, tobacco, vegetable oils, writing brushes, carts, and much else besides - across the empire. Factor markets – markets in labor, land, and credit – had developed so that farms could adapt to family life cycles and changes in demand, season, and climate. And financial organizations made it easier for merchants to trade over long distances. These were less evident in Jiangnan - where the density of transactions made it easier for merchants to carry around cash – than elsewhere. One kind of organization - the *zhangju* - acted as a bank for deposits and made loans to facilitate Chinese-Russian trade. Another type, the *piaohao*, which had been in operation at least since 1683, facilitated merchants' transactions between the northern half of the empire and Jiangnan. The remittance drafts guaranteed that merchants who traveled to a different part of the empire could pay for goods there.

This commercial revolution had not been the first. From the tenth century onwards, developments in agricultural technology, water transport, metallurgy, diversification, handicraft production, and commercialization brought almost an industrial quality to parts of the state.[119] Money penetrated even the backcountry villages, and many different types of credit were used. Cities grew in numbers and size. Textile manufacturing had already transformed itself into an efficient industry of mass production. Machine technology matched that used to spin flax and silk in Europe in 1700. China's iron and steel industry had expanded from south Hebei to northern Jiangsu. As early as the fourteenth century, China's industrial technology, productivity, literacy, and numeracy levels already equaled Europe's in the mid-eighteenth century.[120]

Chapter 10

Marketplaces, Towns, and Cities

The marketplace is a locus around which dense clumps of population sometimes grow. It is where commerce is literally and figuratively assigned a place in society, generally subordinate to society's redistributive efforts. It is often owned and controlled by a religious order, powerful lineage, or another influential group. Outsiders come to the marketplace because profit-making is easier for outsiders, who also spend much of their lives traveling the long distances necessary to secure exotic goods. It is, therefore, a place of contact with a much larger world - a place that often predates the settlement gathering around it. As trade insinuates itself throughout society alongside redistribution, the marketplace becomes the settlement rather than just an attachment to it.

Limited bursts of urbanism took place in Japan during the fourteenth and early fifteenth centuries, mainly along the coast where flatter land and most of the population were found. Towns were places for administration or defense or belonged to temples. They might allow a market or possess one. Commerce was a means of acquiring wealth over and above whatever agriculture could offer and supplied exotic status symbols. But there was not yet any great urge to create multiple and linked pockets of commercial freedom. That would come later.

At the start of the sixteenth century, a new leadership ordered more accurate and detailed information on what each plot of agricultural land could produce and how much tax it could realistically bear. And those who cultivated the land were designated as taxpayers and given security over it. A body of independent family cultivators with more say over village affairs coalesced. At the same time, the Samurai (warrior farmers) had to choose: either stay on the land as farmers or remain warriors and move to the castle towns of their lord. But they could not do both. Some chose to farm; many went to the castle towns under the patronage of their daimyo and at great cost to him (for they were accustomed to a fine lifestyle and now had no other means of support). Each daimyo had other expenses, not the least of which was housing his own family and retainers in estates in Edo as a demonstration and guarantee of his loyalty to the Shogun. These fiscal demands - and the freedom that cultivators now had to keep more of their produce - were met with forest clearance, irrigation, water conservancy, land reclamation from bays and tidal marshes, and a drive to extract more from existing agricultural land.[121]

But commerce was a more obvious way of generating wealth quickly. The towns were already swollen by the Samurai - around a million of them together with their families and retainers. An immediate burden, they also constituted a new market for artisans and merchants. The marketplaces, once mere attachments to the castle towns, now frequently *became* the town. Initially, the daimyos, like the patrons of ancient Greece, minted their own coins.[122] In response, the Shogunate, anxious to ensure free-flowing commercial networks, issued its own national currency and restricted monopolies such that towns became interconnected islands. Here, merchants could ply their trade. They could not work in rural areas or change professions. But neither farmers nor Samurai could become merchants. And when demands for a share of their wealth grew, and taxation increased, the merchants nevertheless roamed well beyond the confines of the towns, commercializing the countryside. By the latter part of the seventeenth century, commerce was the most vigorously growing part of the economy.

As domestic and international competition grew more febrile, Japan's ruling club became ever more dependent upon commerce and towns. The club maintained continuity and stability by ensuring that the 'first' among all these 'equals' held the largest share of land and commerce. An enormous bureaucracy evolved through which the Tokugawa family managed its extensive land holdings, mines, and forests scattered throughout Japan; levied taxes on industry and commerce in those cities under its direct authority; and, thus, controlled the wherewithal to forestall any challenge from the daimyo.[123]

Hong Kong

Transforming the marketplace from appendage into settlement took far longer in Hong Kong. Around the ninth and tenth centuries, a small village on the southern shore of Hong Kong island was the sole exporting agent for incense grown in Dongguan, Shatin, and Lantau. Before being shipped to Canton, the fragrance was bulked and processed at Tsimshatsui, the main port of call for Chinese and foreign ships, arriving from Arabia, Persia, India, and Indochina with the summer's southwest monsoon before sailing up the Pearl River. They called again as they departed with the northeast monsoon at their backs. On the east side of the peninsula, Kowloon Bay served as a shelter and thoroughfare for ships navigating the coast from Jiangsu, Shejiang, and Fujian. Remnants of the Sung court also established a residence on or near the site of what would become Kowloon city. On the land routes from there to Shenzhen (an important mart in the seventeenth century) and Canton, other markets grew, including Taipo and Yuenlong. As elsewhere, markets were often associated with clans and lineages to whom they were who treated them as a source of revenue and symbol of power and status.[124]

In 1841 the British military first established themselves at Saiyingpun and West Point and at Shungwan (Central) on the east side of a nullah, which later became Garden Road. Most of the European merchants settled in Shungwan, the Chinese at Saiyingpun.[125] A bazaar was set up on a beachhead between the two groups, which later became part of Jervois street. That same year, work began on a road that followed a well-marked track along the Island's north shore. The road (named Queen's Road) was completed in mid-1842 when there were some 12,000 Chinese on the Island. Markets sprang up so quickly after the first bazaar opened that the British authorities stepped in to regulate and relocate them. Shops quickly clustered around the bazaar and then spilled out along the seaward side of Queen's Road. The areas between Saiyingpun and Shungwan formed the heart of Chinese business and the center of trade links with China and Southeast Asia until after the second world war.

Urban growth remained concentrated at Saiyingpun and Shungwan throughout the nineteenth century, but odd clumps of buildings gathered here and there along the north coast up to Shaukiwan. One such gathering was at East Point. To its east, on the shore of Causeway Bay, lay the small village of Sokenpoo. To the west, set about half a mile back from the coast at the head of a valley of paddy fields (which later became the Happy Valley racecourse), lay the village of Wongnaichun on a path through the gap to Stanley and Aberdeen on the south side of the Island. The existence of all three settlements preceded the arrival of the British. Indeed, it may have been the presence of a settlement at East Point which attracted Jardine, Matheson, and Co. They established the company village there in 1841, expecting it to become the Island's main focus of growth. Many Chinese preferred Saiyingpun: malaria, which infected the whole territory, was severe at East Point around the paddy fields' still waters. Even so, enough laborers, artisans, and shopkeepers followed the company, and a bazaar was opened just to the west of Sokenpoo village, a little way behind the go-downs. From Jardine's Bazaar, the settlement spread over the next fifty years along Irving Street and Keswick Street to the east and westwards along Yeewo Street, which later became the business heart of Causeway Bay. Over that same period, shops, industries, and services fanned out from two additional foci, a little further to the west of East Point and Jardine's Bazaar. One was Canal Road East which ran along Bowring canal - a channel cut through land reclaimed from the sea at the mouth of the Wongnaichun valley. Here junks loaded and unloaded their cargoes. The other was Wanchai market, which lay still further west at the foot of Morrison Hill, where Queen's Road East meets Wanchai Road.

The uncertainty created by the Taiping Rebellion was sufficient to encourage the British to secure the Kowloon Peninsular and for the military and colonial civil authorities to argue over its use, such that growth was slow and constrained.[126] The main settlements lay on the peninsula's west side. These comprised a few small villages and industries (primarily incense and salt), and an assortment of forts and smaller military outposts built during the seventeenth century to protect against piracy and uncontrolled foreign trading vessels. They included Shamshuipo and, to its south, Fuktsun and Taikotsui. To the northeast of the latter two settlements lay Kowloon Tong. Immediately east of Taikoktsui, across an inlet later reclaimed from the sea, was Mongkok village and, to its south, Mongkoktsui and Mati. On the west side lay the administrative center of Kowloon City. To the south of Kowloon City lay Matou and Matouwei, To Kwa Wan, Hunghom, Tsimshatsui, and Chopae (where incense was processed).

The main foci of growth were Taikoktsui, Mongkoktsui, and Yaumatei, where the water was shallow enough for reclamation and deep enough for ships. The Cosmopolitan Docks were built at Taikoktsui in 1875, by which time go-downs, wharves, and boatyards had begun to scatter along the coastline. A market was sandwiched between Shanghai Street (then known as station road) and Temple Street. To the north, immediately opposite the marketplace and across Market Street, was a public square. A temple sat on the square's east side and a police station on the west. To the north of the square was a small, haphazard collection of buildings - a group of hovels associated with the shipping trades. A little to the north of the police station was a pier. Shops, services, and industries spread from the market southwards along Shanghai Street, Temple Street, and adjacent roads, gradually filling the street grids. Mongkoktsui's expansion also followed a grid, dicing the villages of Taikoktsui and Fuktsun, which operated several lime kilns. Squatters collected around these villages such that they began to merge with Shamshuipo just across the Kowloon-China boundary immediately to the north.

Shamshuipo lay on the junction of three land routes. One followed the coast northwest via Tsuen Wan to Tuen Mun and ran northeast through a valley to the Yuen Long plain and the market at Yuen Long. Another ran a little to the northwest of Shamshuipo and then struck northeast through the Kowloon hills via butterfly valley to Shatin, Taipo, and beyond. The third ran straight across the peninsula to Kowloon city on the eastern fringe, where development remained straggled and beaded until the 1930s. The market which appeared here, as at Yaumatei, lay at the entrance to a pier and was initially held periodically. By the 1870s, shops had gathered around the marketplace and stretched along adjacent streets, forming Shamshuipo's commercial center.[127]

With the leasing of the New Territories to Britain in 1898, Yaumatei, Mongkok, Shamshuipo, and, a little further along the coast to the northwest, Tsuen Wan, found themselves at the junction between the newly acquired land and the business heart of Hong Kong island. The next twenty years saw existing routes through this junction upgraded. The road through Butterfly Valley was improved, and another to Taipo was completed. In 1910, the railway was run along the peninsula's eastern side, through the Kowloon hills, and on to Taipo and China. The road to Tuen Mun was finished in 1919, and extensions from the peninsula's western side to Kowloon City followed.[128]

Tsuen Wan was already an established mart at the time of the cession. A century earlier, shops had already collected in and around the old marketplace and had begun to spread along adjacent streets to merge with a new market that was still operating twenty years after cession. By 1920 Tsuen Wan's long-established handicraft and processing workshops were being replaced by small factories manufacturing all kinds of goods, including soy sauce, ginger, and joss sticks.

Immigrants followed in the wake of the communist victory in 1949, trade embargos imposed by the UN and USA, and other economic and political ructions. Places had to be found for them, and manufacturing industries developed. During the 1950s and 1960s, when immigration peaked, government housing was sited mostly on the periphery of existing settlements or in the New Territories. In 1973 a start was made decentralizing population and industry to the old settlements of Tuen Mun, Shatin, Taipo, Fanling, Sheungshui, and Yuenlong. But the markets did not die out. Old markets continued to operate, and there were demands for new ones. Markets such as Shewuhui and Luenwohui still exhibited vestiges of periodicity in the early 1990s. In Kwai Chung, the stained, muddy green blocks of the estate, completed in the early 1960s looked much older than their 30 or so years. They were scheduled to be demolished, but a few shops lining the ground floors remained open. Some of the tiny flats were still occupied: birdcages, pot plants, and clothes hung from grimy and peeling window grills. On the ground floor of one building, a children's nursery, its windows still covered with brightly colored paper animals, had closed. Running between these monuments were wooden stalls and street restaurants. At dawn, these thoroughfares were filled with the smells of freshly brewed tea, deep-frying dough, coarse cigarettes, fish gutted by blood-soaked hands, spices and tamarind from shops selling dried groceries, and mothballs from old winter coats brought out of storage for the cold November morning. Behind the blocks were factories with blackened windows and dirty, streaked walls draped with thick webs of piping. And behind the factories were rough, steep hills, their ridges and boulders precisely defined and rust-reddened by the early morning sun. The market was one of three which operated in the same place. The first was a legal market comprising stalls to which illegal traders had become permanently attached. The second was a small, illicit weekday market. And the third was an illegal weekend periodic market with around 200 traders that broke up by 8.45 am.

Davao City, the Philippines

Seven years after the British claimed Hong Kong, the Spanish established the city of Davao on the Philippines' southern Island of Mindanao. As in Hong Kong, markets and ports formed the core of the city's physical growth. In Davao, though, the city's expansion has been much slower. Under Spanish rule, the outpost comprising about 4,000 missionaries, soldiers, and their families was connected to the outside world only by a long and arduous journey to Manila. The settlement lay a little to the west of Landing and Trading (a place that still bears the same name today) near the mouth of the Davao River. By the late 1850s, three streets ran parallel from north to south. A church marked the northern end; two streets running east-west marked the southern end. When the Americans took over from the Spanish in 1899, they encouraged discharged American soldiers to cultivate coconuts and abaca; and Japanese manual laborers were brought in. Professionals, homesteaders, small businesses, and Chinese merchants also made their way from the central Philippines and Luzon.

Over the next forty years, the city's growth focused on Trading and a market at the junction of Bolton (a street that ran north-south) and Magallanes (running east-west). About two kilometers to the northeast of Trading, a small wharf (named Santa Ana) was built. The one was separated from the other by a mix of agricultural land and swamp. In 1928 a public market (Acacia) stood at the north end of the main settlement at Recto and Uyanguren (now Magsaysay Avenue), connected to Santa Ana. A decade later, another market was operating at Bangkerohan, marking the western end of a triangle, with Acaia at its northern point and Trading at its southern end. Growth remained within this triangle until after the Second World War. A second adjacent triangle, formed by Santa Ana, Acacia, and Trading saw even less progress.

During the 1950s and 1960s, new waves of immigrants were attracted by logging concessions and the availability of large tracts of land for plantation crops. In 1954, another market – Agdao - was established just to the north of Santa Ana on agricultural land. Seven kilometers or so to the southwest along the coast from Trading is Toril - a market town, which, before the road was built in the early twentieth century, could be reached from Davao by walking along the beach at low tide. It was a permanent market that swelled on Sundays when farmers came down to buy and sell from the rolling hills and valleys to the north and west, and from mountains three kilometres further to the south and southwest. Even in the mid-1960s, Toril comprised little more than a church and a few nipa huts scattered along streets that radiated from the marketplace. Around the market and along these tracks, shops, commercial buildings, and residences gradually appeared, forming the heart of Toril. In the mid-1970s, the market was relocated to the northern edge of town, where goods were bulked up and loaded onto trucks destined for Bangkerohan. By the early 1990s, the original marketplace was just a small empty square, overgrown with grass and palm trees, surrounded by nipa huts and, along the roadside, a handful of wood stalls selling meat, fruits, and vegetables.

The main foci of Davao's growth, then, have been markets. The most important of these were: Trading (the original landing place of the Spanish) and its attached market; Bangkerohan, the main point of entry for goods from the hills and valleys and mountains to the south and the west; Toril; Acacia; Santa Ana; and Agdao where marine products were landed and agricultural goods from the north and the south were bulked up.

Chapter 11

Mobile Cities

Like the marketplaces they often form around, towns and cities are akin to relay stations. They are temporary gatherings of itinerants at designated sites. The site and its buildings only seem permanent because they are constantly being reused and re-populated.

Commercial networks studded with densely packed clumps of people are crucial for economic growth and development. Marketplaces are important physical expressions of those networks. So are the buildings that grow up in and around the market. So are the settlements and great cities into which the market evolves. But how and why does this happen?

Any scenario begins with a landscape thinly populated by small groups of hunter-gatherers. As movements are regularised and migratory routes established, way stations appear at intervals – common places, such as wells or patches of vegetation easily harvested - to victual people on the move. These way stations are often coincident: with meeting places between different groups, especially those whose circuits lie across or touch on different environmental zones (such as forest and savannah, highland and lowland, and coast and interior); or with mineral deposits; or with the raw materials for making tools; or with points to navigate by or to measure time and changes in the seasons; or with places that offer animals water or pasture.

In and around these places to victual, exchange, navigate, measure, shelter, mine, or hunt, wild crops are cultivated, livestock reared, minerals extracted, and tools made. This happens in a desultory fashion but, for the first time, in a fixed location. The people who 'settle' here do so only temporarily: that is, they include this place in their own circuits and return to it only occasionally. As the population grows and knowledge of the place spreads, so does the frequency of visits. Permanent structures are thrown up and periodically renovated by groups who move separately through them. Thus, a population larger than the physical structures can accommodate at any one time is rotated through the settlement.

These nascent production centers take on greater significance as people are compelled to settle for extended and lengthening periods or even permanently. This is because other lands are occupied or because these peripatetic groups of cultivators, herders, miners, and artisans are too large to move en masse. Or it is because the place attracts so many other dedicated itinerants that the rewards from servicing them outweigh the drawbacks of permanent settlement and cultivation. They become production centers linked to redistribution networks.

Commerce's significance grows as competition amongst swelling groups of patrons and clients intensifies. Where there is more opportunity and need for exchange, there is also a need for surplus, specialization, more complex forms of organization, and places where people can meet. As streams of people and things are focussed on particular places, way stations evolve into settlements.

An assortment of evidence points to this scenario. First, trade and the centralization of food and its subsequent redistribution precede agriculture and the first states by a very long way. Both were common practices among early modern humans by around 150,000 BP and possibly among archaic human groups by 1.5 million BP. [129] The reason for the centralization of food speaks for itself. The motivation for trade at such an early time is not difficult to understand either.Trade supplies exotic goods that serve as symbols of authority and unity. A physical place for exchange may become a symbol of status and, even without physical structures, a place of some importance amongst others. More importantly, trade mitigates tension and conflict amongst competing groups by supplying goods in addition to those each group alone can produce. And it provides an entrée to other groups and mating networks. In this regard, it is worth noting the lack of genetic diversity amongst humans and the strong likelihood that, some 120,000 years ago, modern humans around the Mediterranean basin lived in small and highly dispersed groups.[130] For sedentary groups to remain viable, long-distance mating networks must have been in place. Population expansion in the millennia immediately after the Last Glacial Maximum and before the emergence of agriculture in Europe, Africa, and North America [131] also indicates effective mating networks, possibly encouraging peripatetic cultivators and hunter-gatherers to settle permanently.

Second is the presence of sedentary villages before full-scale settled agriculture. In China, for instance, village settlements appeared 'before cultivated plants make a significant contribution to diet and several millennia before agricultural systems with domesticated plants and prepared fields are in place.'[132] Indeed, groups that formed different cultural areas seem to have emerged as part of shared and extensive networks of information and social exchange whose roots were interactions among Late Paleolithic hunter-gatherer societies.

The third is the coexistence of hunter-gatherers, farmers, foragers, farmer-foragers, pastoralists, and permanently settled agriculturalists.[133] That such a mix characterized the Levant, a critical section of the route from Africa to Asia and Europe, is undoubtedly significant. That this region is one of the earliest places for the appearance of permanently settled agriculture and states also speaks volumes. It is possible that in a world otherwise sparsely populated, cultivators, herders, and artisans servicing other itinerant populations emerged first in the Levant precisely because of the heavy traffic through it. The manufacture of composite tools, decorated items, and figurines, and the presence of silos among Natufian groups who were not yet entirely sedentary between 15,000 and 12,000 BP is also suggestive. In Japan which, comparatively speaking, laid off the beaten track, hunter-gatherers persisted much longer than in the Levant. Not until about 2000 BP did the Jomon (hunter-gatherers) finally merge with Yayoi (agriculturalists).[134]

Fourth are places dedicated to tool cutting by anatomically modern humans scattered along routes from East Africa to northeast Africa, the Levant, and the Arabian Peninsula. One cannot rule out these places as way stations. For instance, *Station One* is set on an inselberg overlooking 'the pre-Neolithic peneplain,' suggesting that its inhabitants 'employed a subsistence strategy tied to game moving through the savannah.'[135] Another likely way station is found on Iran's Shir Plateau at Maqta, where the permanent availability of spring water made it an important resting place for nomads and their herds and probably on millennia-old trade routes from the Omani coast inland.[136] The tombs found immediately above Maqta date back to around 5,000 BP and likely mark the place and the route, a common practice throughout the rest of the Arabian peninsula. Natufian cemeteries dating back to about 12,000 BP might also be cast in this light.

The fifth reason to think that settlements originate as way stations are the ubiquity and significance of 'empty' places – places where activities of one kind or another, usually commercial, occur at regular intervals but are otherwise unused and unpopulated. Permanent structures can appear here, often as the intensity of movement and exchanges through it increases. At first a seasonal camp, Timbuktu was one of many trade centers running along the rivers and trans-Saharan trade routes from West Africa to North Africa, including Morocco, Taouadny, and

Bamako Ouagadougou, Fada-n-Gourma, Gaya, Jega, Kano, and Dikwa.[137] All occupy West Sudan, a region separating savannah and forest, and all were entrepots linking the two ecological zones.

Empty places do not have to evolve into permanent urban agglomerations, nor, if they do so, do they have to do so through 'stages.' At first, mobility and empty places may even render fixed towns unnecessary. In Morocco, for example, periodic markets made the existence of market towns superfluous. Only with Spanish occupation did buildings of importance signal marketplaces. Formerly they were left unmarked or found near a well or spring or a few stone booths unoccupied except for a few hours once a week when goods 'from live animals to grain, and from Oriental spices to North African medicines and charms, changed hands…'[138] Similar places existed in China and Japan.[139]

Wherever found, 'empty' places are often abandoned in the end. About 12 miles West of Mombasa in 1884 stood Kisimani, which Gissing called a 'market village because no one lives in it' where the Wa-nika bring their produce to sell and make a market on the spot; the place itself consists of a few grass huts.'[140] Today it is just the name of a road junction in the suburbs, just off a highway that runs north from Mombasa along the east coast. Yet other 'empty' places may survive for centuries. Berbera in Somalia in 1876 was no more than a space deserted except when a market was held and somewhere between 20,000 and 60,000 people attended. Here '*there is no fixed town, no resident population, and consequently, no merchants to make purchases from natives at all seasons of the year. It is simply a place for commercial assignations: a place to which buyers and sellers come and meet to transact business, by mutual consent, at certain seasons of the year.*'[141] From April to the early part of October, it was utterly deserted. Then with the northerly monsoon in November, the inland tribes began moving in and small crafts from the ports of Yemen, followed by merchants from Muscat Soor and Ras el Kyma. '*During the height of the fair Berbera is a perfect Babel, in confusion as in languages….Long strings of camels are arriving and departing day and night….By the end of March, the fair is nearly at a close…. And…in April, Berbera is again deserted, nothing being left to mark the site of a town lately containing 20,000 inhabitants…except the framework of a few huts… carefully piled up on the beach in readiness for the ensuing year.*'[142] Odd as it may sound, this 'empty' place was known to the Egyptians in 1450BC. And to the Greeks and Romans 1200 years later.[143] The Portuguese reportedly intended to loot it in 1518, but a storm prevented them from doing so, or they found nothing. Not until the late nineteenth century did a settlement of mud huts appear, sheltering around 8,000 -10,000 people. More substantial buildings, marking the start of the modern city of Berbera, were not constructed until 1893.

Alternatively, empty places may see erected buildings intended for occupation for years rather than just months or weeks. Mbanza Kongo, the capital of the Kongo Kingdom, held anything from 10,000-100,000 people, with most estimates at 50,000 or more. It was spacious and richly decorated, built of earth, straw, wood, palms, and bamboo. Yet, it looked delicate, felt like a garden city, and occasionally moved, usually when a new king ascended the throne. A new ruler of the Lunda and the Luba did likewise; and, in the case of the Luba, turned the abandoned center into a ritual site.[144]

Function had a say over the stability of these places. The Lunda empire or commonwealth, which covered parts of central Africa between present-day Angola and Tanzania during the sixteenth, seventeenth, and early eighteenth centuries, was a federation or alliance of states crisscrossed with tributary and exchange networks. Redistribution was the primary duty of its rulers and of the urban agglomerations that housed them. The paramount chief accepted salt, copper, slaves, and ivory tribute and returned gifts of imported cloth and other goods.[145] He mediated between the ordinary and the exotic, and on this, his legitimacy rested.

Function, though, d not necessarily determine whether empty places are built on and occupied permanently. The Igbo and Ibibo east of the Niger successfully coordinated their activities at scales and distances usually associated with urban settlements. Yet, the rustic appearance of the landscape did not alter. In other cases, towns appeared even though the economy remained distinctly agricultural. An example is the Yoruba town of Fiditi, where empty places (way stations and markets) became permanently occupied (and closer in size to towns than villages). A good proportion of its population was farmers,[146] while the rest comprised itinerants on the way to somewhere else.

Settlements on the other side of the continent, too, were often precarious. Egyptian influence on northern Sudan left scattered tombs, temples, and palaces constructed between 300BC and 350AD. These were solid and imposing structures but isolated. Whether they were ever more than ceremonial centers is uncertain.[147] Further south, cities connected by long caravan routes looked more like glorified camps: quarters were well defined, but within those broad guidelines, one-story buildings cast from mud and straw and reeds were laid down any old how.[148] At Dongla's center in 1699 stood a large and spacious castle. Its fortifications were modest to European eyes but were just enough 'to keep in awe the Arabs – the masters of the open country.' But the surrounding streets were half-deserted and filled with heaps of sand. A little further on the way to Gondar, Sennar was a collection of poorly constructed, one-storeyed buildings and wretched cottages encased in reeds. And the palace, a confused heap, was richly furnished with carpets and protected by a high wall made of sun-dried bricks. Seke, the capital of Ethiopia, was a gathering of houses made of Indian cane. Gondar itself had no shops. But at its heart, as in Sennar and many other settlements, a large market gathered daily.[149]

The sense of impermanence was no illusion. Most settlements lasted no more than a few decades, their lifespan dependent upon the religious leader or change in religious fashions. When he died or moved on, or loyalties switched, the settlement dissolved and moved elsewhere. When European travelers arrived at the end of the seventeenth century, Gondar existed for about sixty years. It was a place of relative stability and had had time enough for a few more solid buildings, churches mostly, to be built. But before 1636, the settlement had been in constant motion for two hundred years, and it would resume its wanderings[150] in just another thirty years.

People stick to their migratory rhythms even when buildings are made of stone. Delhi has arisen at different locations within a triangular-shaped area of 180 square kilometers at least a dozen times since the fifth century BC and has been given other names on each occasion. One incarnation, constructed between 1639 and 1648, was occupied by the Mughal emperor and was called Shajahanabad. It was built to last with a defensive stone wall nearly four miles long, 27 feet high, 12 feet thick, and studded with watchtowers and massive gates.[151] Outside the walls lay the suburbs covering another five square miles. Yet the whole edifice was a shell. When the emperor and his army left, so did more than four-fifths of the city's population of 450,000 who lived cheek by jowl (with about 49000 souls to every square kilometer),[152] leaving the place deserted and lifeless. For thirty years after 1679, it was left in this state. The emperor's successor returned in 1707 only to go off for another five years before his vast entourage finally re-occupied and revived the city. The Mughal capital declined over the next one-and-a-half centuries as British influence grew. They destroyed many of its buildings in 1858 and moved the capital first to Calcutta and then back to Raisena (a little to the north of Shahjahanabad), which they called New Delhi.

Shah Jahana was not the only roving emperor, nor was Delhi the only wandering capital. The court moved frequently, and so did the capital, not only within its triangle. Agra, Fakegur, Sikri, and Lahore also served as the capital between the early sixteenth century and the early eighteenth century, and sometimes two places functioned as capital simultaneously.[153] Massive tent cities were established as emperors toured their empires or fought for them.

The court, its armies, and the population who sustained it were not medieval India's only itinerants. The Banjara people were vital to the movement of goods and trade and allotted spaces or *tanda* around Mughal cities while they carried out business. They specialized in bulk over long distances with animals and carts and by rivers and coastal waters, hauling food grains, pulses, ghee, and salt as well as luxuries and silk. These bands were huge, with tens of thousands, perhaps as many as 100,000, on the move at any time. They carried at least 2820 million metric ton-miles a year, equivalent to about a third of the goods shipped on Indian Railways in 1882.[154]

All too often, migration is treated as a problem and one that threatens to overwhelm a country's physical infrastructure and financial reserves. Figures vary a good deal but are always daunting. In the Philippines, for example, about 44% of migration occurs amongst cities. That figure rises to 53% in Brazil. In India, over half takes place within rural areas. The proportion is a little over two-thirds in Tanzania.[155] Probably around 700 million people are on the move within their respective countries (thirty-one of them) in Asia (excluding India and China), Latin America, and Africa south of the Sahara at any moment. About a third of these movements occur within rural areas and 28% in urban areas. If India and China are included, the number on the move to cities grows to over a billion.[156]

These figures should not surprise us if we think of population churn as part of the redistribution of goods, services, and people necessary for growth. Today's modern cities are relay points or way stations through which people move. Commerce is but a mode of transfer, as are gift-giving and centralized procurement and distribution. Marketplaces are streams of transfers and people focused on a specific place and time. The buildings gathered at a marketplace are temporary and fragile expressions of those activities and together form a shell through which people and things constantly pass. However paradoxical it might seem, the settlement reflects mobility, and the more urban that settlement, the more intense that movement.

Chapter 12

Society over Market: strategy

Commerce is a logistical technique that helps funnel wealth to those who manufacture things or bring in items and services in demand. Other modes of transfer keep wealth in the hands of the populace from whom it can be redirected as needed. Blending and integrating these techniques so that all boats are raised describes the purpose of economic strategies.

The modes of redistribution sketched in the last five chapters allow resources to be switched amongst sectors and particular units. Efforts are frequently concentrated on agriculture and mining first. Materials are delivered for export, generating foreign exchange and domestic capital for industry. At the same time, the population continues to be fed, and skills such as financing, banking, and marketing are practiced and honed. It is a more self-conscious extension of what has already been happening for decades or centuries in more populous societies with long experience in these forms of organization and transfer. Perhaps the best-documented example of agriculture and its commercialization outside Europe is Japan. As noted in earlier chapters, agriculture changed dramatically even before the country's early industrialization during the late 19th century. Rural areas were producing commercial crops for markets in the cities; agriculture had already begun to specialize; craft producers of silks and high-grade textiles in urban areas were 'putting out' work into the countryside. These trends stimulated rural incomes and required changes in labor organization: businesses brought in non-family workers and new technology.

Raising factories, crops, and minerals from the soil demands heavy and direct subsidies for physical infrastructure, education, health, and welfare, as well as constant adjustments. To this extent, strategies and tactics are always *sui generis*. I want to illustrate this with two examples: Korea and India.

South Korea

Figure 12.1 depicts a shift in profitability from manufacturing and heavy and chemical industries to a more diverse range of activities in South Korea. It picks up the story of the country's development nearly forty years after its war with the North between 1950 and 1953. The remainder of that decade was devoted to reconstruction, land reform, and agricultural modernization in a country of farmers. In 1961 attention shifted to industry. This meant cement, fertilizers, chemicals, machinery, and oil refineries. It meant generating electrical power and laying down other forms of infrastructure. Developing exports and becoming competitive was also on the agenda, which meant using what Korea had in abundance – cheap labor to man low-technology light manufactories. In 1973 the country re-focussed on heavy and chemical industries. A decade later, it turned to electronics. By the early twenty-first century, the government was favoring information technology, biotechnology, nanotechnology, intelligent business systems, biomedicine, next-generation batteries and semi-conductors, green growth, and creative economies.

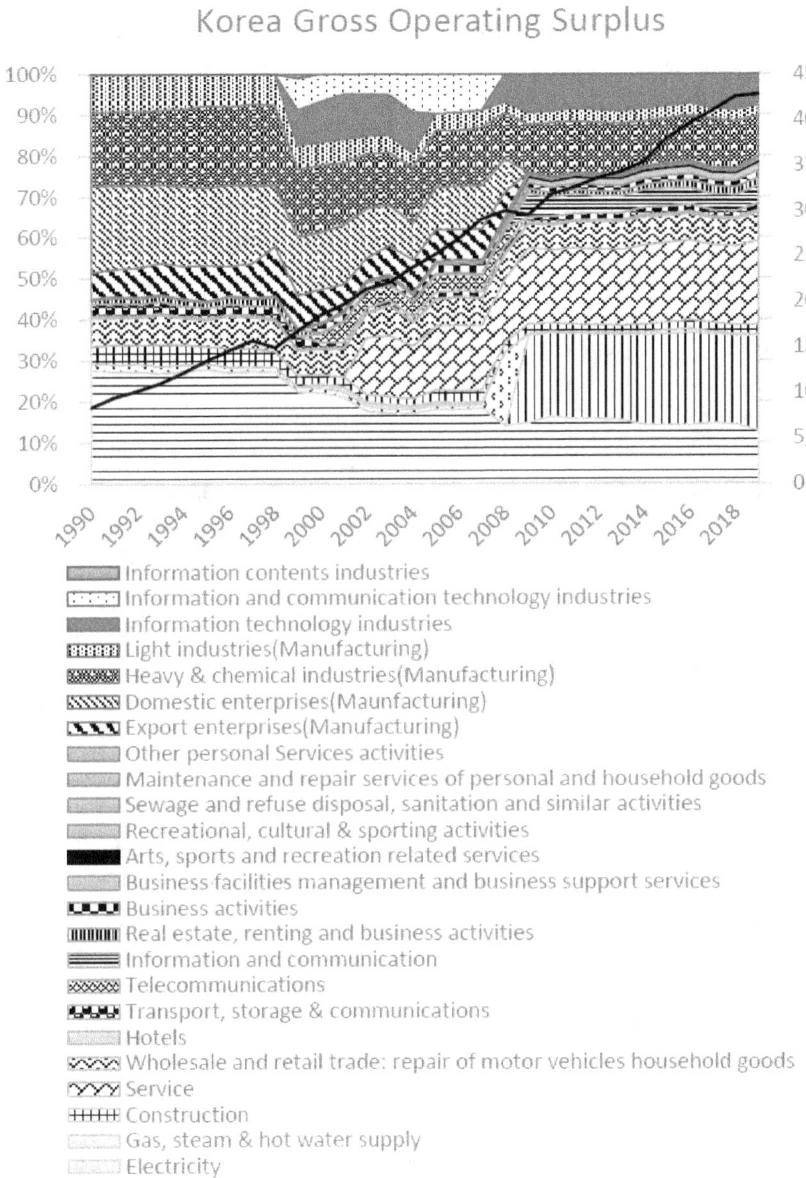
Korea Gross Operating Surplus
100%
90%
80%
70%
60%
50%
40%
30%
20%
10%
0%
45,000
40,000
35,000
30,000
25,000
20,000
15,000
10,000
5,000
0
1990
1992
1994
1996
1998
2000
2002
2004
2006
2008
2010
2012
2014
2016
2018
Information contents industries
Information and communication technology industries
Information technology industries
Light industries(Manufacturing)
Heavy & chemical industries(Manufacturing)
Domestic enterprises(Maunfacturing)
Export enterprises(Manufacturing)
Other personal Services activities
Maintenance and repair services of personal and household goods
Sewage and refuse disposal, sanitation and similar activities
Recreational, cultural & sporting activities
Arts, sports and recreation related services
Business facilities management and business support services
Business activities
Real estate, renting and business activities
Information and communication
Telecommunications
Transport, storage & communications
Hotels
Wholesale and retail trade: repair of motor vehicles household goods
Service
Construction
Gas, steam & hot water supply
Electricity

These switches entailed the intentional redirection of materials, goods, funds, and people and were marked by three features. One was a good deal of overlap: even as attention shifted from one sector or industry to another, the once-favored continued to receive support and develop. The second was long-term planning. The cornerstones of favored sectors were often laid several years in advance. Elements of heavy industry and chemicals were already in place when in 1973 government targeted steel, non-ferrous metals, machinery, shipbuilding, electronics, and chemical engineering. An oil refinery built in 1964 preceded the Pohang Iron and Steel Company and the Ulsan Petrochemical complex, both completed by the early 1970s. A legislative framework, too, had been laid by then to provide financial and tax incentives and exemptions to promote machinery (1967), shipbuilding and textile modernization (1967), petrochemicals (1970), non-ferrous metals (1971), and the steel industry (1969). The emphasis on exports accompanying this drive reached back to a 1964 Act on the Development and Creation of Industrial Complexes for Export. It was reinforced in 1973 by additional legislation (an Act for the Promotion of Industrial Complexes) and by the Electronics Exporters Association and Kaisit University, established in 1973 and 1971.

The government did not stop there. Currency devaluation in 1960 was vital to exports. To bring greater control sensitivity, a new exchange rate system was set up in 1964. Exemptions provided channels through the wall of tariffs and import licenses thrown up around the country – a wall strengthened with buy-national policies. Through the Foreign Capital Inducement Law of 1962, the government also took powers to approve the acquisition of foreign technology. It also took control of the banking system and established a series of specialized funds – The Korean Development Investment Company, the Technological Development Fund, and the National Investment Fund. This allowed the government to manage credit, direct funds, and loans with preferential rates (frequently negative) and target chosen businesses, projects, and sectors. By the end of the 1970s, interest subsidies alone were worth around 10% of GNP.

Specialized agencies to plan, direct and implement the nation's strategies were a third feature of Korea's redistributive efforts. Chief amongst these was the Economic Planning Board in 1961 and the Ministry of Science and Technology in 1963, whose remit was to coordinate science-related policies. The Korean Institute of Science and Technology was established in 1966 to organize contract research with universities to absorb foreign technology. This was just one part of a broader science and technology education system integrated into development efforts. New corporations were also conjured up, including the Korean Electrical and Communication Corp (which later became KT Corporation) in 1981 and Korea Data Telecommunications in 1982 (which became LG Dacom Corporation).

As it transferred its attention from one set of activities to another, the government formed new agencies and assigned new responsibilities to existing ones. The establishment of the Ministry of Knowledge Economy and the Korean Communications Commission in 2008 was part of an effort to stimulate a creative economy. ICT and planning were handed to the Ministry of Science; the Ministry of Trade and Energy took on industrial policy, SME administration, and intellectual property. The Ministry of Strategy and Finance dealt with budgeting, and the Ministry of Culture, Sports, and Tourism handled cultural policy.

Wages and welfare were lynchpins of the nation's campaigns. Enormous sacrifices made by cheap and disciplined labor in the 1960s were repaid, if only modestly, with rising wages and savings in the 1970s. Rather than thwart these increases and keep existing businesses competitive, a decision was made to move into higher-wage, capital-intensive, high-productivity manufacturing and services and enable their share of employment to grow. An inescapable part of this was social policy and public spending on health and education. The quality of labor and the general standard of living of the people went hand-in-hand with a shift into higher productivity manufacturing and services.

The second decade of the twenty-first century saw a concomitant change in living and employment conditions. The knowledge economy and creative networks envisaged demanded a different and decentralized approach. It meant loosening up the spread and flow of resources through society. It meant redirecting resources away from the chaebols – the giant corporations, once essential for Korea's presence on the world market, and that still offered the highest salaries and best opportunities for personal advancement. The question was how to change. Import licenses and tariffs had tailed off through the 1970s and, by the 1980s, had a much smaller role. Governments had also relaxed their control over finance. A deal of pressure on Korea to open up and reduce its trade surplus was having its effect.

The energy for liberalization – a short-hand for adopting western-style, rules-based, political and economic practices and policies – had come from two directions. One was American concerns over its long-standing trade deficit with South Korea (averaging some 17.5 billion) and the cost (around 4.5 billion annually) of shielding the country with its defense umbrella. The WTO's launch and Korea's membership in the OECD also required the government to modify or axe many of its techniques.

And the 1997 crisis forced Korea to accept an IMF loan and the stringent conditions that came with it. Korea quickly paid it off following a whip-round amongst the population for gold. But the country was well on the road to a market economy.

The other was from Korean society itself. Rule by the Generals did not end until 1992, five years after direct presential elections had been instituted in 1987, marking the formal start of democratization. Korea should congratulate itself on its progress so far, the West declared encouragingly. But solutions to the remaining challenges were still more economic freedom and democracy, as Americans quickly pointed out. The two went hand-in-hand. The chaebols were on board. They had long wanted greater freedom to pursue their own interests rather than the people's. Given that they formed the backbone of the economy, what else could the government do but ensure that macroeconomic policies favored them? Their informal connections, not least through kinship to different branches of government, also protected them. Serious attempts at redistribution would look like socialism. With the shadow of the North looming over the country, that would look like treason.

But the issue was not cut and dried. The 1997 and 2008 crises showed that the market was scarcely infallible. If there had been any doubt, both had taught Korea that its basic instincts about development were right and that handing responsibility and decisions over to 'the market' was perilous. Redistributive techniques would have to be more subtle than they had been - or blatant. 'Buy national' could be as effective as any tariff wall. There is also the fact that trade with the Third World is becoming increasingly important. Perhaps Korea does not have to mimic the West's economic model. The country's democracy is in trouble, too, believe some.[157] The old ways might return. If so, the West must learn to live with that or change itself.

India

Figure 12.2 takes up the story twenty years or so into India's post-war development. Here, as in many other countries, the emphasis was on agriculture. In the first five-year plan (1951-56), efforts were made to increase the area of land under cultivation, mechanize irrigation, and encourage wider use of chemical fertilizer. At the end of the plan, there followed a rapid shift in emphasis and resources to heavy industry: chemicals, machinery, tools, locomotives, and, above all, steel and power. Gigantic state-owned corporations were the vehicles through which governments poured money, efforts, resources, and people. The manufacture of commercial goods was left to small, private enterprises whose activities and size were limited and controlled through a maze of government licenses.

The sudden change in direction was a shock to agriculture, now left hanging in the wind. It had expanded but not deepened. The fact hit home when dry weather became a drought, and food supplies were reduced to a trickle in some parts of the country. Government had little choice but to change tack again, back to agriculture. But dry weather and then war, first with China and then with Pakistan, meant that agriculture could do little better than limp along until another drought struck in 1965-66. Foreign exchange leaked to pay for food imports, bringing about a balance of payments crisis that took three years to stabilize. During that period, the government did not have enough confidence to commit resources for more than a year at any one time. Not until 1969 was the fifth five-year plan finally launched.

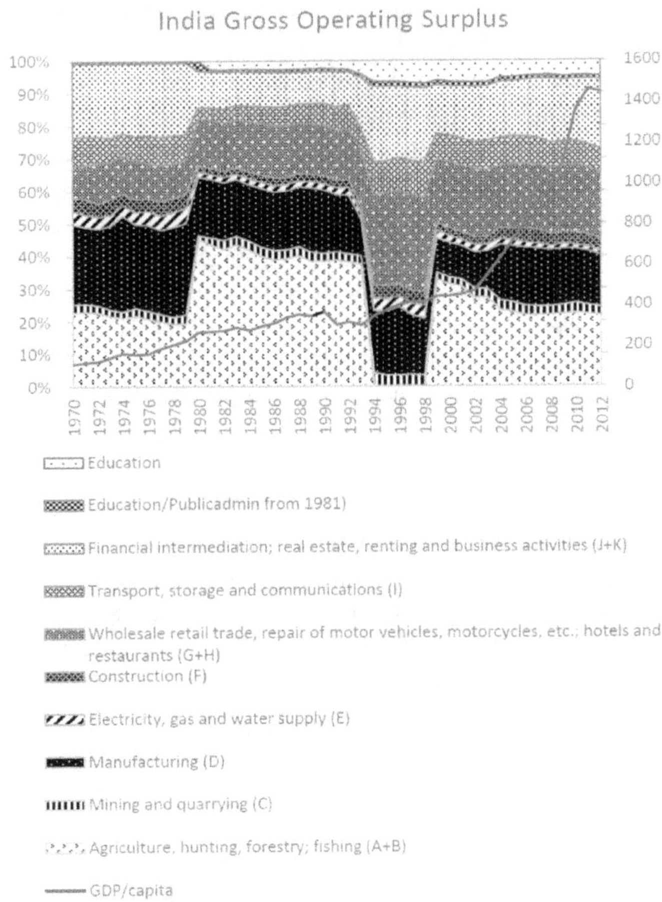

The new plan determined to fix agriculture once and for all. Banks were nationalized, and branches were opened in rural areas so that farmers had somewhere to put their savings. Credit and technology were systematically channeled into agriculture in what became known as the Green Revolution. But the plan's objectives were nebulous and left any gains and successes disconnected. Soon the country was facing another balance of payments crisis.

At the end of the decade, an IMF loan was secured. In return, the government dismantled the license system, slashed tax and import duties, removed price control, put state companies up for sale, and encouraged foreign investment. Compelled to stand back more than it had been, the government now had to watch resources go where they would. Smaller businesses and services about which it had had no concerns - except that they might grow too quickly and take away resources from agriculture and manufacturing - flourished as never before. The chart reflects this shift as profits flow into more diverse activities.

Throughout this period, India's economy grew as it continues to do so today. It established a complex repertoire of techniques to move resources around. It created large state organizations to focus investment and use economies of scale. It set up agencies to direct efforts. It constructed intricate walls of licenses and import duties behind which its businesses could grow. It eventually took control of credit. It issued subsidies as and when it thought necessary. But it did not provide a clear framework to arrange those techniques. The government's worst foible, though, and one which allowed liberalization to take credit for the bust of growth from the 1990s, was its hostility to exports. It thus denied itself the room and means for expansion.

Government, government, government!

In the years following World War II, when most colonial territories gained their independence, the new states' governments placed themselves front and center in development efforts. Throughout the 1960s, the state became involved in 'virtually every aspect of the economy, administering prices and regulating labor, foreign exchange, and financial markets.'[158] They nationalized public utility, mining, and agricultural enterprises and created large state concerns.

These practices were not a consequence of some ethereal religious, cultural, or philosophical construct or some Asian, African, Confucian, or even 'Third World' vision. Nor is state intervention just a matter of tinkering so that economies are more or less mixed. It was supremely practical. It was about what worked. It *is* about what works. Transfers are neither a luxury nor a drag on the economy, whatever mode they take. They keep wealth in the hands of the populace from whom it can be redirected if needed and whose claim to business fortunes is entirely legitimate because profit is merely one expression of transfers. The alternative is ruinous. The state hollows itself out if it abrogates its responsibilities to arrange and determine who gets what. It becomes a shell in which few will have much faith. If it transmutes economics into highly abstract and theoretical phenomena, then society becomes its navvy with little say over those phenomena or those who claim to understand them.

By the end of the 1980s, Third World states were having to rearrange transfers and put society first in the teeth of opposition from the West, the IMF, the World Bank, and a legion of consultants. Neoliberalism was du jour. The state was to be a coordinator and enabler. Prescriptions for institutional change and debt reduction were issued. Government spending had to be cut, and state activities and decision-making devolved. Public monopolies in education, health, and other services were carved up into private and voluntary sectors, and demand was pared down through fees and other cost mitigation and recovery methods. Without these conditions, rescheduling debts and securing additional funds from creditors were impossible. It was nothing less than blackmail.

A strong pro-market and anti-state theme also ran through universities. Governments in East Asia, it was said, had begun to allow market forces to operate; and progressive liberalization and opening up to outside markets ensured success.[159] Friedman's view on this was categorical. He claimed that Malaysia, Singapore, Korea, Taiwan, Hong Kong, and Japan, relying extensively on private markets, were thriving. By contrast, India, Indonesia, and China, relying heavily on central planning, experienced economic stagnation. It did not matter that it was all fiction.

Chapter 13

Breaking the Rules

As well as resisting attempts to reduce population and facilitate the market's domination, Third World societies have also opposed the West's persistent and relentless attempts to formalize them.

A mess of cables slithers and seethes between crooked posts and leaning walls. Tangles of cars, buses, trucks, and motorbikes edge forward around ramshackle buildings and through massed, squirming bodies. Children play with scraps of cardboard and ragged strips of tin and whatever else comes to hand, school only an occasional excursion, a place of bare rooms and corridors echoing with yells and screams and laughter and demands for money to pay for books and pencils. Hospitals are grubby and always crowded, noisy, and restless. Jaded government buildings, fronted by listless officials, seem unresponsive, leaving fixers promising this or that document for a price. In the worst parts of town, the only difference between path and sewer is a trace left by others in the midden. On a good day, the sun rises quickly through a clear sky and hovers directly overhead for an hour or so, bleaching out colors and shadows and burning away the stench. Amongst this littering of shanties, streets, and stores, making a living and living life are the same.

It is impossible to say how many people cling to this uncertain and hand-to-mouth existence. It blends with officialdom and yet goes unrecorded. It generates about 30% of GDP on average, with highs of around 65% in Africa and 63% in Bolivia and lows of around 7% in Switzerland and North America. Its share of employment is higher still – up to about 90% of non-agricultural work in parts of Sub-Saharan Africa.[160]

'It' - the precariat - became known as the informal sector in the 1970s and subsequently as the 'shadow,' 'underground,' 'hidden,' 'disorganized,' 'unorganized,' 'concealed,' and just plain 'illegal' economy. Up to that point, over the previous twenty years or so, it was described variously as subsistence, agricultural, rural, unskilled, surplus, casual, jobbing, unemployed, disguised unemployed, traditional, and petty. It was said to have a vital role in economic development, supplying what was, in effect, an unlimited quantity of labor for capitalists in towns and cities.[161] The fact that it was unlimited meant that wages did not have to exceed the prevailing rate in the subsistence or informal sector by more than 30 percent. (This took care of the higher cost of urban living, the more rigorous practices workers had to endure, and their changing tastes induced by life in a more sophisticated urban society). Assuming that all profits were either invested in the capitalist's existing businesses or new ones, the formal sector would continue to expand until the reservoir of surplus labor dried up, or so economists believed. It was always possible that the formal sector might stop growing. If shadow incomes rose, then wages paid by capitalists would also have to rise. This would hit profits, lower investment, and reduce the rate at which surplus labor is absorbed. On the other hand, immigration or the export of capital might push wages down. Many variables complicate the informal and formal sectors' effects on each other. But the general picture was clear: what later became known as the informal sector facilitates both development and its own demise.

Some experts retain that hope. A casual, jobbing, hand-to-mouth existence merely expresses poverty and will evaporate with development. Though it is taking longer than thought, the informal sector has declined by about 6% since 1991. Other authorities believe that it is not just an expression of poverty: it is a cause, which is why it takes so long to eradicate. Informality's rulelessness permeates everything and explains so much for many development professionals. Development is about being focused, logical, organized, and rational. It is about ending uncertainty. It is about better use of people and their energy and labor. It is about training and allocating them efficiently so that society can compete. It is about the rule of law, contracts, and predictability. It is about getting rid of informal businesses.

The charge sheet is a long one. With little capital and inferior labor, dependent upon simple technology, and turning out inferior products, informal businesses are inefficient, poorly managed, have low employment rates, and seldom evolve into anything bigger or better. They close down opportunities, suppress motivation, discourage freedom and creativity, and inhibit and distort communications. And they become less cost-effective as markets expand, the division of labor sharpens, and the number, scale, and complexity of transactions increase.[162]

The informal sector is hidden from regulation and tax authorities and so competes unfairly with the official economy. It leaves the state with lower revenues while simultaneously demanding infrastructure and public services and putting further pressure on state expenditure. It may be a refuge for the poor and, in this sense, keeps the welfare bill down, which might be helpful in the long run (though the jury is still out on this).[163] But add up its contributions and subtract its costs, and there is little question that it enfeebles the formal sector.[164]

All of this - the informal sector - is amateurish, wasteful, inefficient, and incompetent. It attracts more of the same from the countryside, aggravating unemployment in the city and adding tons of pollution to the air, water, and streets. It clogs up the roads and crushes public services. Its denizens do what they can to evade regulators; when they cannot, they corrupt them. They have no license and pay little or no tax because it is cheaper to pay off the official. If caught dumping rubbish and blocking a street, they will bribe the policeman rather than pay the government's fine. They have no electricity, telephone, or water bill; it costs them little to tap into the cables above them or the pipes beneath their feet.

Just look at the cities in sub-Saharan Africa. They grow and change informally.[165] Three-quarters of homes in Kinshasa, for instance, are slums.[166] In Nigeria, somewhere between 25% and 40% of the country's cities are constructed without formal government approval.[167] Cities throughout the continent are crowded, unplanned, unregulated, and chaotic. Few areas are truly specialized. Zoning laws are ineffective. Industrial, residential, developed, and undeveloped plots of land are thrown together. Valuations are little more than guesswork. Packed informal dwellings are scattered here and there. Transport infrastructure is fragmented. Vehicles are owned by patchworks of unregulated and inefficient companies. And the land on which all this stands is frequently unregistered. The result is a mess of local economies called a city but dominated by goods and services, unable to find markets beyond their immediate neighborhood, and quite unable to attract investment.

Development is about sweeping away the hawkers, the letter-writers, the pedicab drivers, the hairdressers, the photo-copier stalls, the scavengers, and all the rest eking out a living on the pavements or in the slums. It is about sweeping away the slums, too, the shanty towns, the squatter settlements, the *barriadas*, the *colonias proletarias*, the *favelas*, the *bidonvilles*, and *bustees*: call them what you will - that vast collection of tiny shelters, tottering on someone else's land, patched together from metal sheets, concrete blocks, old tarpaulins, and slats of wood, cardboard, and plastic.

It dawned on the development community that local and national governments could seize on an unguarded flash of impatience from international agencies towards the informal sector to justify harsher tactics such as slum clearances. From the 1990s onwards, there was a deal of talk about enablement, decentralization, partnership, and creating the right environment in which training could be upgraded, land tenure systems rationalized, and forced evictions ended. Sustainable and healthy settlements that were 'broad-based, 'inclusive,' 'accountable,' and provided 'adequate shelter for all' should be established. High-sounding programs were launched, such as the WHOs Healthy City Programme, the Global Campaign on Urban Governance, and the Global Campaign for Secure Tenure, involving the World Bank, UNDP, UN-Habitat, WHO, ICLEI, cities, and NGOs. There was also talk about restoring connections between indigenous and transplanted formal institutions. Yet the intention behind these anodyne platitudes was the same: to formalize urban life, not through compulsion but through mass action. Large international development agencies would lay down a framework of exemplary projects and help local communities and organizations build up their 'capacity' until they were ready to take over and finish the job. Government would serve as a facilitator. The International Labour Organization assigned itself a special place in this movement. Its mission in the 1980s was to save people from the informal sector,[168] having coined the term in the 1970s. Poor governance was to blame when market reforms pushed by the West did not work as expected. Local and city governments felt this as pressure to formulate solutions to the problems created by people who contributed little or no tax revenue. Streets were cluttered, building patterns haphazard, and piracy was interfering with globalization and the profits of western companies. From the 1990s onwards, its mission was to formalize the sector by improving its productivity, establishing proper social protection for those working in it, and confecting a regulatory framework with which groups could help each other through collective action.[169] Thus, was open hostility to informality joined by Janus-faced do-gooding.

The Third World was presented with a new dimension to informality during the opening decades of the twenty-first century. A stony-faced West set about rebuilding societies it had just undone through military force in its battle with ghost-like and deadly networks of terror and fear. Accusatory and gimlet-eyed, it pointed out that informality was responsible for poor governance, market failures, and war-like acts. Just what was going to be done about it?

All kinds of taxonomies were on hand to describe and analyze subversive behavior: patrimonialism, clientelism, sultanism, bossism, hierarchical, centralized, decentralized, and unsystematic. Each tells how the procurement and supply of goods, services, revenues, and funds are cornered and accessed. How decisions about who gets hired and fired, promoted or demoted, or left in the wings, are influenced. How disbursements and processes, and the means for reward and punishment, are controlled. How cliques and cabals - fashioned around ethnicity, kinship, friendship, language, educational and professional background, religion, or hometown - are shaped into networks and stretched throughout society. How the moment at which favors and friendships end and corruption and criminality begins is left deliberately vague. How struggles to secure personal advantage consume energy. How a vision for society and the governed dissolves. How a meritocratic and independent bureaucracy, if it exists, is distorted, and distrust in government deepens.

The specific effects of corruption are felt everywhere. Corruption worsens or creates market imperfections. By extracting direct payments - and by compelling merchants to spend their time (and a deal of their money) working networks of officials and politicians - corruption increases costs to businesses in much the same way as an arbitrary tax. Corruption also favors well-connected businesses, encourages rent-seeking behavior, and, by distorting incentives, misdirects the merchant's energy and talent. For all these reasons, corruption discourages foreign investment.

Corruption encumbers national consolidation. It does so partly by undermining government control: authority cannot be delegated effectively; the efficiency of government and other agencies weakens; meritocracies are destroyed or prevented from emerging; faith in public services erodes; and politicians, bureaucrats, and citizens are encouraged to treat each other with suspicion and cynicism. And now that it is believed, rightly or wrongly, that corruption is endemic, there is little incentive or reason to remain uncorrupted oneself. Factions multiply through society, producing intense cleavages. In extreme cases, the legitimacy of the public sector is called into question, and governments face violence, political instability, or collapse. Third World states have been involved in 70% of the intra-state conflicts recorded since the early nineteenth century, and most of these broke out after 1945.[170]

Corruption distorts government priorities, policies, and planning. It raises the costs to businesses, reduces public revenues, and increases the burden on government procurements. In Thailand and Indonesia, procurement costs during the 1960s and 1970s were somewhere between 20% and 100% higher than they would otherwise have been.[171] Corruption also shifts public expenditure towards those items (such as defense) that attract larger and more easily concealed bribes and away from those items (such as education) that do not.[172] Direction is lost as bureaucrats spin labyrinthine processes to attract 'speed' money. Misdirection of public finances damages not just the occasional project or sector but an entire political economy. In the Philippines, from the late 1970s until the late 1990s, $48 billion was misappropriated, surpassing the country's total foreign debt. Aid donations are diverted, too. Once aid to a given country reaches 1% of its GDP, holdings in its off-shore accounts (which, on average, amount to 2.2% of that country's GDP) increase by around 3.4%. In other words, something like 5 - 15% of donations make their way into the pockets of government officials and their cronies. About 3 billion dollars were skimmed off between 1990 and 2010 by Kenya's leaders; 0.58 billion in Tanzania; 0.27 in Uganda; 0.19 billion in Rwanda; and 0.122 in Burundi. As a whole, as much as $30 billion of aid to Africa ended up in the foreign bank accounts of African leaders during this period.

Chapter 14

The Philippines

The Philippines is one of many countries scattered throughout Asia, Africa, and Latin America thought to be rendered soft, messy, and desperately ineffectual by informality. Indigenous practices and values, it is widely claimed, infiltrate and undermine necessary formal western arrangements leaving them corrupted and unworkable.

Explanations for informality across the Third World rely heavily on what is sometimes called, rather grandly, historical contingency or, in other words, the passage of time and events. Circumstances - namely the imposition of Western-style bureaucracies on non-western societies in which reciprocal exchange dominates - generate informal and corrupt behavior which becomes engrained over time. Informality is enhanced wherever there is a heavy churning of people, creating a patchwork of insiders and outsiders.

Philippine society, well known for high levels of corruption, is extensively creolized and seems to absorb new influences and ideas as simply as drawing breath. Indian, Arab, Chinese, and Southeast Asian traders operated in the islands long before Magellan arrived in Cebu in 1521 - the same year the Portuguese took control of the Moloccus. Colonization had to wait until Spain had control of Mexico, which gave the Spanish a base on America's pacific shore and a route (via Guam and Marianas) to the archipelago. That was easier than sailing around the cape and India and through the intricate channels of Southeast Asia where other powers and pirates were active. Not until 1565 was the first permanent settlement in Cebu established. A year later, the Spanish attacked and defeated the sultans who had founded settlements on the shore of Manila Bay.

Spanish rule was harsh or ignored and alienated the local chiefdoms, which consequently found themselves relying on kinship more than ever. The Spanish also bequeathed an unequal land tenure system, creating an exploitable class of tenants (clients) dependent upon landowners (patrons).

The revolt of the American colonies and the declaration of independence spelled the end of Spanish interests in the Philippines. The colony's only remaining link to Spain was a long, tortuous journey running west through waters controlled by hostile European powers. When the Americans destroyed a Spanish squadron in Manila Bay in 1898, three years after the start of the Spanish-American War over Cuba, an action to keep the Spanish squadron pinned down in Asia turned into the messy acquisition of a colony. Almost as soon as its decision was taken, America was anxious to free itself of the archipelago. In 1935, America promised the newly labeled Commonwealth of the Philippines independence within ten years. The deadline was only just missed following Japan's invasion and occupation of the islands during world war II.

The Bell Act and Tydings Act accompanied the Philippines' declaration of independence on July 4, 1946. The first ensured free trade between the Philippines and the US, while the second guaranteed financial aid to the former colony. From then until the early 1970s, the Liberal Party and the Nacionalistas dominated politics. It was not the two countries' only similarity. The Philippines replicated the US constitutional model almost in its entirety. It had an elected presidential system of government constrained by congressional and judicial checks and balances. Executive power was vested with the president of the Philippines, who was elected for a maximum of two terms. (This changed to just one six-year term in 1987.) And, like the US president, the Philippines' president is the commander-in-chief of the armed forces. As in America, the power of the president (the executive) is separate from the legislature and judiciary. Legislative powers lie with congress. The upper house comprises around 24 senators (the Senate), with two senators representing each senatorial district. The lower house (the House of Representatives) comprises members elected in smaller congressional districts. There are about 250 or so congressmen (and now women too). The upper house is supposed to include mature, able, and experienced people who serve as a check against the passing of hasty, ill-prepared, and ill-considered legislation and take a broader view of national events and interests. Members of Congress will likely focus narrowly on their own small districts. The third branch of government, the judiciary, applies and interprets the law. Judicial power lies in the supreme court, comprising a chief justice and 14 associate justices. The president chooses them from a list provided by the Judicial and Bar Council, which operates independently from the executive or legislature. Once appointed, each judge can hold office until the age of 70.

Below the executive, legislature, and judiciary sits a complex of local governments. The most important of these are the municipal and city governments and, beneath these, the barangays. Above the municipalities are the provinces and regions. The barangay and its subdivisions (the *puroks*) are intended as planning and delivery units. They also work as mediators, settling local disputes before they escalate and require the courts' intervention. The difference between city and municipality is determined by a formula that includes income and population. But they both run the settlements – planning land use, maintaining roads, buying medicines for local government hospitals, running state schools, and setting and collecting local taxes. Each has its council and mayor.

The province's main function is to coordinate development efforts among cities and between cities and rural areas within the province. And just as a city sits within the province, a province sits within a region. Except in one instance, regions only have coordinating functions executed through the regional development councils, whose job is to filter plans from the cities to the national government and filter demands and decisions passed down from the national government to the cities. The Autonomous Region of Muslim Mindanao is the exception. It has legislative and tax-raising powers. The configuration allows for recognizing and implementing various aspects of Islamic law and more local control over administration, development, and education in this Muslim-dominated part of the southern Philippines.

American rule and an American-style system of government did not bring much improvement. Elite landed families merely extended their influence and interests over the new, outwardly Western, and seemingly democratic organizations left by the Americans and turned them to their advantage. Ultimately dependent upon vertical patron-client relationships, neither leader nor follower could afford a sense of national policy or party loyalty. The fiefdom – comprising the politician willing to keep his clients in the barangays and congressional districts happy through the distribution of local and national resources – was the basis of Philippine politics. These fiefdoms, and the alliances amongst them, are what presidents depend upon and must reward.

At the core of these alliances is kinship. Ambitious politicians regularly maneuver children, brothers, cousins, wives, parents, and in-laws into office to consolidate their political bases. For example, President Estrada's son became mayor of Estrada's home town San Juan. President Ramos's sister Shahani was a senator. Duterte's daughter, who ran Davao while her father was president, is now vice president and hopes to succeed Marcos's son when his term of office finishes.

But there are also close non-kin alliances at work, such that political office is handed to favored allies through courtly succession. These relationships are frequently organized around social kernels or points of commonality, including place of origin and language. For instance, the Nationalist Party was strong in the Tagalog-speaking parts of the northern Philippines (because this is where their leaders and their families came from). On the other hand, the Liberal Party drew strong support further north in central and northern Luzon, where Pampanga is spoken. And when leaders change, the support base of the Party alters. So, for example, when Marcos switched from the Liberal Party to the National Party and became its leader, the Party's regional base switched from southern Luzon and Cebu to the north of the Philippines, especially the Ilocano-speaking areas of Ilocos.

In 1972, Ferdinand Marcos, who had been elected president twice in 1965 and in 1969 and was prevented under the constitution from serving any further terms, declared Marital law. Elections were suspended, and leading opposition politicians were harassed and bullied out of the country or tortured and thrown in prison. Congress was padlocked at first and then replaced by a People's Assembly through which he could, in theory, tap directly into local communities. The economy seemed to benefit at first; law and order improved, and the administration became more efficient. But there then followed a long period of economic mismanagement, abuses of power, and stifling corruption.

Martial law ended in 1981 but without significant political change. The KBL (*Kilusang Bagong Lipunan*) still dominated politics and subsumed members of other parties so long as they supported Marcos. It won nearly all seats (165 out of 178) in the revived congress. Small fledgling parties were permitted so long as they provided only token opposition. These included *Lakas ng Bayan* or *Laban*, formed by Benigno Aquino shortly before fleeing to the US. In 1983 Aquino, who was now Marcos's principal opponent, returned to the Philippines only to be shot dead as he stepped off the plane at Manila airport. Popular defiance in the Philippines, drawing energy from Reagan's evident frustration with the regime, pushed Marcos into a snap election in 1986 'so that the people could pass judgment,' he said, on his government. Both he and Aquino's widow, Cory Aquino, declared victory. She launched a disobedience campaign which ended when Regan advised Marcos to leave the country. With more armed forces siding with the rebels, Marcos took that advice and left. Cory Aquino became president.

A great many political parties have emerged and faded away since Marcos left. The more important of these serve as the colors for a president or presidential candidate. Around it, politicians, businesses, financiers, and other interests congregate and prepare to pry their runner into office. Cory Aquino's jack was *Laban ng Demokratikong Pilipino* (LDP). Her successor, Ramos, ran up *Lakas NUCD*, and Estrada the *Laban ng Makabayang Masang Pilipino* (LAMMP). Arroyo's pennant was *Kampi*, established in 1998. It then merged with *Lakas* in 2009, shortly before the 2010 elections. *Kampi* was abolished three years later. Its members created the National Unity Party, forming a loose coalition with Benigno Aquino's Liberal Party. Duterte's flag, the *PDP-Laban*, was stitched together by two older parties – the *PDP* launched in 1982 and Aquino's *Laban*. The two merged in 1986 and nominated Cory Aquino as their candidate, who instead joined UNDO (United Nationalist Democratic Organization). She subsequently ran up her own colors – the LDP.

The instability of parties is generally lamented because it reflects moneyed interests rather than the broader and deeper concerns of the electorate. Those who finance one Party and breathe life into it are often former members of earlier cabals who sponsored previous, often defunct parties. In the run-up to Aquino's election in 2010, two competing cliques, poorly defined and chameleonlike, supported Aquino's campaign, though each had preferred different candidates for the vice presidency. The *Balay* cheered on Roxas (who stepped aside in favor of Aquino) while the *Samar* stood behind Binay.

Corruption tainted each new administration. Despite her initial popularity, Cory Aquino was mired in allegations and besieged by her own army. Repeated coup attempts reminded her to spend on military hardware and salaries and dish out political influence to officers. Ramos brought some order to the government and economy initially. It was said that corruption fell 70% from the levels seen under Marcos. But cabinet ministers became embroiled, as did Ramos himself, in a series of scandals - Centennial Expo, PEA-Amari, and the Benpres-North Luzon Expressway. Estrada fared worse, and Vice President Arroyo removed him not quite halfway through his allotted six years. She, in her turn, was beset by scandal after scandal, from election rigging in 2004 to North Rail, South Rail, fertilizers, and a kickback worth 130 million dollars from ZTE. She was still facing charges after she left office. Cory Aquino's son was next up. He had, the Ombudsman declared, disbursed a billion dollars in state funds without the approval of congress. And it was his negligence that was responsible for a botched counter-insurgency operation in 2015 and the deaths of 44 police commandos.

Then came Duterte. His political base was Davao city on the island of Mindanao in the south of the Philippines. He had been the city's fiscal prosecutor when he met Juan – a former churchman and official terrorist. A tall, languorous, and diffident man with the sheen of flint in his large, soft eyes, Juan began his adult life studying in a seminary in Cebu. He then entered the priesthood. His ideas and ideals were too radical for a church that he found too conservative. He left the church for the National Democratic Front and the New People's Army. In the NPA, he was responsible for imbuing its members with political ideals and, later, for operations and strategy. He was captured in South Cotabato and imprisoned in Davao. But Duterte saw in him a valuable political ally, and during his three years in prison, the two men came to know each other well.

With Marcos's fall and Aquino's accession, Juan was released. He became Duterte's political consultant. Together he and Duterte developed what proved to be a valuable and distinctive mix of policies for social welfare, crime, and disorder, a blend quite literally of milk and blood. They gave milk to poor mothers and sanctioned the ex-judicial killing of persistent criminals. In city hall, he or his vice-mayor would sit at a heavy Nara wood desk with two rows of chairs at right angles. Supplicants would move down each row until it was their turn to petition. Around the office and throughout the rest of the building, quiet men sat expressionless, sporting cowboy boots, cigarettes between their fingers, and keys and mobile phones hanging from ostentatious belts around their ample waists. He took his populism and his quiet men with him to Manila when he rose to congressman, then senator, and finally president.

A question often asked through all this is why poor, ordinary voters support wealthy elite families? Why do they tolerate inequities, and why don't they vote for candidates from their class who share their interests? The answer often given is that they cannot afford to vote for the left if they are to share in this distribution of benefits. So instead, they have to vote for the monied who control resources and are willing to use violence more often is usually recognized. The populists - men such as Estrada and Duterte - who take on the facade of the straight-talking, hard-drinking, and fast-living Filipino are imposters. But they strike a pose that poorer Filipinos think they can live with.

Chapter 15

Understanding Informality: creating businesses

The informal sector isn't easy to delineate and enumerate, and so figures that purport to quantify it don't tell us much. Molded from relationships, the organizations are blurred and nebulous, and their external links are seemingly inexhaustible. These arrangements and qualities are both extensive and necessary for development.

The case against informality, and explanations for it, are nevertheless far from conclusive. To begin with, is informality all bad? Clearly not: look at the sheer number of people employed in the informal sector. Look at its share of GDP. Look at the training and experience it affords so many people. Look also at the importance of casual behavior within the formal organization. Rules and routines cannot accommodate every detail and eventuality: organizations seize up without personal judgment and discretion. And look at *who* is attacking the informal sector: western academics, western governments, and western agencies. They only 'see' problems such as 'corruption,' 'underdeveloped,' 'poor,' 'transitional,' 'developing,' and 'filling the gaps' left by weak states because they have an arbitrary 'cultural category' (formalism) locked into their heads. When this category is imposed and practiced in developing countries, difficulties arise.

Suppose observers can free themselves of this category. In that case, they will see that officials do not distinguish between their behavior as public servants and private citizens.[173] They will begin to appreciate complex and nuanced 'rituals,' 'conversation,' 'poems,' 'narratives,' 'forms of exchange,' or - as in the practice of Chinese *guanxi* - the 'art' which ties individuals and states together.[174] There is a clear choice between a Western mindset (and domineering bureaucracies) and a moral life amongst non-western local people. Those able to shrug off the West's psychological grip will apprehend informality's truth: it lies between the formal and the immoral and criminal. Informality might be illegal from the bureaucrat's perspective, but it does not offend moral conventions. It expresses creativity and entrepreneurial drive and is the key to survival.[175] It is nothing less than an expression of popular development.

One countercriticism of these more friendly, 'anthropological' commentaries is they are excessively optimistic and romantic. More severely, they are the work of apologists or 'ideologists of kleptocracy.'[176] I agree with this in that claims of exclusiveness are bound to feel contrived and intellectualized. But the 'anthropological approach' does sense something wrong with the distinction between informality and formality. Whereas 'the West' thinks that formal and informal are different from one another (and that the former is good and the latter is terrible), the anthropologist thinks they are just different.

I argue there is no actual difference between informal and formal, but that people do create conceptual or psychological distinctions. All organizations comprise relationships. The most effective organizations – whether they are described as formal or informal – treat relationships *as if* they are significant in themselves. In other words, people think and act as though relationships, on the one hand, and rules and processes, on the other, are distinct but understand they are not. In the least effective organizations, members treat rules and procedures as objective facts independent of relationships or dissolve the distinction entirely so that instrumentalism takes over.

Business

However uncertain and confusing the putative informal sector might be, and however difficult to measure, it is not in any sense rule-less. Food has to be prepared and cooked; clothes and bodies washed. Children must be fed, dressed, and watched over, and, in most parts of the world today, got to school and brought home. Life has to be arranged, patterned, organized and blended with attempts to bring in some money. Here lies the ubiquitous family business. '*I wake up early morning around 4:00 am. I need to prepare Bea's breakfast. I want to be sure that before she goes to school, she eats her breakfast. Then, after that, I prepare my ingredients and start cooking because I need to put the food outside in the morning. My clients come to me every morning. Some eat breakfast. Some take the food with them to eat at work. By midday, I am sold out. Then I rest for a while before Bea comes back from school. Then, when she arrives, I prepare her lunch. Once she's finished her lunch, we both take a nap. Then Bea helps me to look after the business. She helps me wash all the plates and cooking utensils and helps me with all the other household chores. Then, later in the afternoon, we will go together in the market; and, when we get back home, I start cooking dinner. After dinner, I help her with her homework and, after we've done her assignments, we pray together. At 11 pm, as long as I've done everything, I sleep.*'

The business reworked a pancake stall she had run while pregnant with her daughter several years earlier. It required very little capital and gave her an income sufficient to cover her daily needs. Her new venture offered a greater variety of cooked food. '*I started to cook a few dishes. They were sold out every day. I thought to myself, this business is good. I use only a little capital, but if everything is eaten, the profit is double, and our food is also free every day. So I cooked more dishes and cooked more food, and always they were finished. Lots of people are now buying my food. I already have regular customers who buy from me every day. At 10 am, I have to be sure their orders are ready so they can just pick them up. Now, all our expenses are met by the business. It pays the rent for our house, the electricity, water, and my daughter's schooling. I can also save a little money - in case of emergencies and for her future studies. Our life isn't luxurious. It's very simple. What's on the table is enough for us. This kind of business is hard work, but we are happy.*'

The business was primarily a solution to the complexities of being a single mother whose daughter, now aged seven, was to start school. School costs had to be met, and who would look after Bea when the school day ended, usually around mid-day? Liberty was already worried that Bea might come under the damaging influences of other youths in the community – the '*tambay*.' '*They don't go to school; they are noisy, especially at night; they bring in strangers; they drink wine or Red Horse; and when they are drunk, they make even more noise even in the middle of the night and don't care if they disturb us and wake us up. Some of them use drugs; they get high; they try to push the drugs on others, and they fight.*'

The sense of disorder they brought was aggravated by the barangay's failure to clear garbage from the streets. Both problems she laid squarely at the feet of the barangay captain who, she said, spent all his time overseas attending seminars. Then there was the gossip that went along with being a single mother. This concerned Liberty the most. If neighbors wanted to talk about her behind her back, that was up to them. '*I am the one who made the decision to raise my daughter by myself. I want this kind of life.*' But '*I don't want my daughter to see that I have a problem with the neighbors. She's young, and she might be affected and feel that she is the problem. To be an unwed mother isn't at all easy - I can say that for sure. I know that I can handle it. As long as my daughter is with me, my life is full of joy. She gives me all my happiness, and I do everything for her. And the most important thing is she and I are happy.*' However, making sure Bea felt this would be impossible if Liberty were just not there for most of the day.

Around three hours after Liberty prepares Bea's breakfast, Zenaida begins her own adamantine routine. '*I wash my face in the morning, drink coffee, and open my sari-sari store. After that, I start washing clothes. When I've finished, I start cooking lunch for when the children get back from school. Then I take a rest while they look after the store. Then I prepare food for dinner and attend the store. The evenings are the busiest time, and most nights, I will not close until 3 am.*'

She left school at sixteen, married at nineteen, and had her first child that same year. Neither she nor her husband finished secondary school, and neither had money. He worked as a room boy at a hotel in Quiapo. At the end of each six-month contract, he had to wait several weeks or months before the hotel considered him for another term. So she, too, found work at the hotel, washing and ironing clothes. Life became a little easier when her husband took a permanent job as a waiter. The salary, though small, was regular, and tips could make a big difference. But when the restaurant closed, they were back where they had started, only this time with no work and three children.

Her parents suggested she run the sari-sari stall her father had opened after he gave up driving altogether. She felt uncomfortable depending on them but accepted '*because at least we have an income to feed ourselves.*' She was also determined to ensure that her children would not experience the continuing unease, uncertainty, and fear poverty brings. Those same feelings pushed her to set up a tricycle business for her husband. She bought the motorcycle over three years. Repayments were calculated according to a fixed 'boundary': a portion of the income earned, determined by the distance covered each day, was handed to the lender every night. The remainder she left with her husband. She also set up a hamburger stall to cover daily expenses and fund her money-lending. The stall did not require much capital, and the burgers sold quickly. Even in the early days, it brought in five hundred pesos above costs.

The unspoken and unwritten rules that underlie these routines are just part of many others that extend into all spheres of life. '*I didn't ask for any help from my family. It's not nice to go there and ask for help, especially when they already have their own problems, and I need to show them that I can stand by myself.*' Nor did her parents and siblings ask much of her. If she had any money beyond the amount she was determined to save, she would send that. But it was never much. '*I also tell my daughter that we can only spend money on what we need, and she understands. I thank God that my daughter isn't spoiled, that she understands my situation.*' To be nurtured, friendships also had to be distanced. '*Friends are part of our lives. Not all my friends ask me for help. Some of them have a better income than me. Some of them, though poor, are content with what they have. Some come to me to borrow money. If I have anything spare, I will give it to them; but if I don't have anything, I will tell them straight – I only have enough for me and Bea. They understand, and that's why they are not insistent. Anyway, they are more likely to come to me for advice on other kinds of problems. Sometimes we go out together and eat, or take a walk with our children.*' For these reasons, she had scraped together capital for the business from her own savings and a moneylender – someone quite separate from her circle of family and friends. The loan was short-term and, she said, low-interest. Every day for two months, the lender would appear to collect payments on the principal and interest. She could then take out another loan if she wished. It was necessary and far better than the alternative: '*If you go to a bank to borrow money, there's a lot of papers to produce and process before they lend you the money. The moneylender is easy – there are no documents that you need to submit. Only the rich become very rich, but the poor are always poor.*'

What is evident here is the presence of rules and the behavior involved in their creation. People creating organizations have to make changes to their relationships. They have to turn up at a specific place and time, perform certain roles in a certain way, and yet cannot excise their relationships from the organization. All that is happening is that relationships are being re-modeled and re-presented. This requires those involved to take part in something of a pretense. They pretend, first, that the activities they participate in within the organization do not constitute relationships. They pretend, second, that they are not weakening their relationships with friends and family outside the organization by giving their time, allegiance, and loyalty to the organization. Instead, they regard conduct within the organization as technical and separate from their relationships. And third, they pretend that relationships are confined and concentrated in a social sphere that exists elsewhere and at another time. As a result, they have psychologically distanced their relationships. That is to say, they treat rules and organization *as if* absolute - *as if* important in themselves, *as if* independent and separate from relationships. And relationships are treated similarly. They are treated this way because to treat them as absolute would turn them into mutually exclusive dictates.

Focussing authority (especially over finances) was a lesson that Susan brought to her marriage from the start. Her mother was single, and her father, a security guard, had had five children with another woman to whom he was married. They had had little money from him, though, from time to time, he did help her mother, a laundrywoman, to collect, wash, and iron uniforms for staff and students (in midwifery) at Fabella Hospital. The income was irregular as it depended on customers who often had to wait until the middle or end of the month when they received their wages before paying. Susan and her mother sometimes went for a day or two or longer without food to eat and soap to wash. '*I promised myself, she said, that I would study very hard so that if I had a family, they would not have to live like this.*'

After graduating with a degree in commerce, Susan's father introduced her to his cousin, who owned a small art gallery. He appointed her as its accountant. The Gallery, which sold paintings, books, antiques, and general bric-a-brac, was small, and so was her salary. But she took a commission if she sold a painting or collected money from customers who had bought on credit. So she earned enough to live on. Moreover, her boss trusted her. During her father's illness and after his death, he helped with medical bills, taking some of the strain off her mother, who was still washing clothes. Not long after this, she found herself the de facto manager of the Gallery. She oversaw sales and collections, prepared salaries and assigned duties, and had a say on who was hired and fired.

The company grew, and so did her savings. When she married, she was clear that '*I am the decision-maker in the family, about financial or any other matter. When it comes to my family, I am the decision-maker. My husband gives his salary to me. As a wife, it's my right to know where he put his money – every single cent. If he sends money to his family without telling me, I will be angry because I don't like him keeping secrets.*' Shortly after the birth of their first child, her mother gave up her work as a washerwoman and came to live with them and look after her grandchild. Susan also began to lend money commercially. These were short-term, high-interest loans. A loan of 1,000 pesos would earn her 200 pesos over thirty days. She also used her credit card to buy goods – such as fridges or jewelry – on behalf of her customers, who would pay her back over an agreed term, usually between 6 and 12 months. After their second child in 1998, the business her husband worked for collapsed. He received a payout of 80,000 pesos. Some of this extended and improved their house (which now towered above their neighbors). The rest he used to set up a carpentry, welding, and driving business under his wife's firm control.

After their third child, Susan bought a jeepney. The income earned from this she split between herself and the driver. The 'boundary' (the minimum income remitted to the owner each day) was 500 pesos, though she also took on responsibility for maintaining the jeepney. A year later, they bought a second jeepney and a third operating on the same terms the year after.

The couple was now prosperous, especially in comparison to the rest of the community. They had various sources of income: the Gallery, money lending, carpentry and welding, and jeepneys. She controlled them entirely, and they operated as one, each supporting the other, each contributing to the family's expenses which she tightly regulated. Her husband's money, whether he used it to drink or play cards or mahjong, came from his allowance, which she gave to him. Occasionally he lent part of it out to his friends to earn a little extra, but unlike his wife, he found it difficult to recover the debts, and he never succeeded in making the enterprise work.

Their children's education accounted for the lion's share of the family's expenses. She rotated her two sons between private and public schools so that one was in a private school at any time. This arrangement continued until her second son asked to remain at public school (which he found easier and where he had a set of friends), allowing his sister to take his place and flourish.

In 2010, they ran into trouble. Susan was the de facto manager of the Gallery but not the owner. When the owner (her father's cousin) died, his sons took over, and the atmosphere changed. Neither was prepared to cede control over the business to the other. She was in an invidious position: if one son asked her to buy in stock, make a collection, or remit the sale of a painting, the other would be offended and become suspicious. She resigned, plowing her retirement trust from the Gallery back into money lending and her children's education. Then she fell ill and underwent a series of operations and treatments on her gallbladder. The effect on their finances was ruinous. Their savings and cash disappeared, and their businesses collapsed. And with her businesses, she felt, went her reputation and her networks in the community. '*Because I can't lend them money anymore, some of my friends became cold. It seemed that nobody knew me anymore. The politicians, including the barangay captain, didn't want to know me either. It's very hard to find real friends though at least now I can balance them with my family because we all understand each other and support each other.*'

But she remained determined that her children would finish school: '*if they have a good education, they won't have to go through the poverty I suffered. If all my children finish their school, I can say I have fulfilled my duty as a parent, and my dreams will have come true.'* To this end, she set up a small food store, a *carrinderia*, with the remainder of her savings. Her husband returned to work as an employee in someone else's business; and Susan now borrowed (from her husband's cousin) for her children's schooling. Their days were long. She woke up at '*four in the morning to prepare the food for the store and for her children before they set off for school. After that, I start cooking. My mother helps me. Then, when we've finished cooking, we take the food outside to sell. It's usually all sold by midday. If so, I take a nap, and then I prepare for the next day. If I have spare time, I'll play bingo and then go back to my house and prepare food for our dinner. I'll usually be in bed by 8 pm.*'

The business, the decision-making, and the control over expenses all remained centralized; the distinction between family and business remained clear. But there was a change in two respects. First, whereas she had been less careful about separating friendships from her business dealings before the collapse, she was now fastidious in doing so. Secondly, she was now more inclusive and trusting, unlike before when she had executed the separation of family and business so completely that she took on the burden of responsibility alone. She now assumed that other family members could distinguish between family and business just as she did. Her mother was involved in the cooking, her husband would help in other aspects of the business, and so would her children. Indeed, she wanted them to know how to manage a business. '*Who knows?*' she said, '*Someday, one of my children will decide to put up a business.*'

Chapter 16

Understanding informality: creating government bureaucracy

Government bureaucracy, or at least its most potent elements, is similarly and necessarily vague, though the formal box within which it operates is more sharply defined.

A business organization educes its own rules and regulations. The struggle is harder for bureaucrats and politicians. They live in an intricate framework made from imported rules, regulations, procedures, identities, ideologies, and ranks bolted together according to instructions from Western advisors and governments. Here they must stay. Relationships are raised within this cumbersome frame and shaped into the actual organization. Each of these organizations within the organization is different, molded by the people it comprises in the light of the circumstances in which they find themselves.

Throughout the bureaucracy, new or altered arrangements are constantly emerging. 'That is how it evolves - informality first, before formality.'[177] For some officials, it is a cardinal principle of management. '*Again, I have to talk from experience - whenever you [create] put people [in] a formal structure, there is a tendency for people to resist initially. I would rather have it evolve organically..... because then... people... feel that they are part of the decision-making itself, and it is not something imposed primarily because you have an expert or consultant who is supposed to know everything, who says this would be the best structure for you......Sometimes it [the evolution] [takes] longer, but sometimes it's....fast, because people see: "Yes we need to do that, so [they] form a committee, [then] a task force, [then] let's make that now a permanent organization."*'[178]

A small illustration is the redundancy of older, formal procedures for handling grievances and the emergence of new practices. While the older, formal machinery – that of written complaints, hearings, and resolutions – still exist, it is, in many agencies, rarely used. The Civil Service Commission had not dealt with internal cases in this way for more than two years at least. And even where, in other agencies, disputes are elevated to USECs or ASECs, informal means are preferred: '*I call their boss and I say "Okay, you better go and finish your conversation somewhere else"...*'[179] *The next obvious step has been taken in the Central Bank - to encourage and regularize existing informal practices and formalize them. In this instance, it means* '*dialogue*' *or, in other words,* '*...making people understand that they are not actually in a contest here - they have just misunderstood each other. So it is a way of making people realize that there is a way of doing things where you need not really file cases against each other because there is really no case to speak about.*'

The Bureau of Internal Revenue supplies a further example. Fifteen years ago, any member of staff who happened to be present in a district office when members of the public found their way in would find themselves having to deal with queries and requests for advice. An Officer-of-the-Day was assigned to deal with these matters, and the traffic in questions grew. Around this newly created position, a small group of assistants gathered to handle computations, supply the necessary forms, and advise on their completion. The arrangement was subsequently designated as the tax-payer assistance section.

Still another illustration was the emergence of a semi-permanent corps within the senate (and separate from its secretariat) whose members are often passed on from one senator to the next as elections are lost or as terms of office expire. They provide a continuity of experience and legislation; they train, steer, and, sometimes, carry new senators. Critically, they alleviate a little of the tension during fierce disagreements and personal disputes among politicians. At these moments, adherence to the protocols and conventions (such as being an 'honorable member') that make up the rituals of debate enables senators to distance their animosity from senate business, if only symbolically. To expect more than this would be to expect superhuman effort from them. And even when 'honorable members' could not stand the sight of each other, their staff were cordial to each other and continued to operate behind the scenes. This, at least, was the atmosphere and practice before the Estrada and Arroyo presidencies. '*But with ERAP and Gloria you could almost see the line of division, and it even came to a point that was pretty petty - that if you worked for an opposition senator, and you are administration, you were just civil, but that's all. It was that stupid. Osmena said that this is the first time that he felt that the chamber was so polarized, that there was this distinct line between opposition and administration. ....It came to a point that you wouldn't choose somebody who worked with the opposing team. Before it was never a problem. It was only competence that mattered. It became silly.'* [180]

Amongst the senators, meanwhile, *'you can't really say [of people in the Senate]: "he's my friend, I'll talk to him." I can say that in the [Lower] House, not with everybody, but with a good number. But I can't really say that in the senate with regard to a single senator. For example you say "Look, this senator he's been doing this and he's been doing that - he's been bothering me. But I am not in a position (I don't think anyone is in a position) to say, that's ok, I'll help, he's a good friend of mine, I'll take care of it."'* [181] Not all were quite so bleak. The atmosphere had improved toward the end of the Arroyo administration, some thought, '*to a point that now that they are no longer polarised by personality, but by issues, and they (the senators) will work together as a collegial body, whether opposition or administration. They are more ready to do it now than in the past.*' Certainly, the soon-to-be president Aquino was now taking '*a lot of people from previous senators. It is very useful. I have never worked in the senate before, so I know absolutely nothing about the ins and outs in - who we talk to about this or that. So it is [good] to have that institutional knowledge.*' [182] The surfacing of informal relationships and the strengthening of their affective dimensions are essential in many other respects. The breakdown of hierarchy, which is often implicit, encourages creativity and exchanges of ideas. It is a way to bring on subordinates and help superiors stimulate and clarify their thoughts and improve the quality of decisions. Policies, the analysis of problems, the solutions recommended, and the mode of implementation are unlikely to be either imaginative or effective if formulated through a mechanical process and by staff reluctant to speak their minds. It is when gatherings are primarily social that discussions are most creative.

The cultivation of these clusters is regarded as a moral duty, not a formal one. It is also a means of fashioning effective and reliable allies who may follow their mentor through the ranks and across offices and departments. While it may be said (and not without good reason) that mentoring gives expression to patronage, these relationships are also often largely about an interest in others, about affection, and about perpetuating the office, its competencies, its values, and its direction. More extensive networks are also valuable in countering a common problem within many organizations, particularly the larger ones: delayed and distorted communications between central and regional offices through the downward flow of memos and circulars and the upward flow of reports.

One way to elicit more accurate information is to place one's people covertly in those offices '*so that we can get the true situation.*' This also forestalls the need to issue memoranda, signed by an undersecretary, stating the data to be provided by regional offices in painful detail. Another way is to establish a rapport with those offices. This is especially important when the information is sensitive. For instance, in the Department of Education, letters complaining about improper appointments or the distortion of an election by teachers are funneled through records at central office to the secretary and back down to the undersecretary concerned. The undersecretary may deal with this directly through his own support networks. Or the case is passed on to personnel where it eventually lands on the desk of a division chief or section chief - staffs who, over the years, as part of their responsibilities, have nurtured relationships with regional officials. These relationships are cultivated through various forums, though more to smooth the general prosecution of business with the regions rather than seed informants. For instance, '*we conduct...workshops, and we see to it that [regional officials] are invited. Also we have the HRM [Human Resource Management] plan....The initial step taken [in making the plan] was to form the founder's group; and the founder's group is those who are considered expert in the field of human resource management; and they consist of...regional directors, superintendents, chief administrative officers - those AOs [Administrative Officers] who head the entire regions in terms of administrative service records officers, planning officers. So, you see...it is a mix of people coming from different levels and positions.*'[183] The management committee is another forum. This calls together all regional and bureau directors in one place and so provides an opportunity to select those regional directors most likely to prove willing and able to disseminate information and policies.

Relationships established by permanent civil servants amongst themselves as a counterpoise to political appointees can be tiresome to manage: '*... they have groups that have been there quite a time and they are very close. So if you make some mention against a particular person you spur the whole [network]...*'[184] It is also nigh impossible to neutralize the various motivations fuelling resistance. Subordinates may object to an appointee's ideas, ideals, or personal interests, or it may be that their priorities and responsibilities clash. Or they may be critical of an appointee's appetite for work. Or they may object to one aspect of their personality and the simple fact that their boss is a political appointee. Appointees may also find that permanent civil servants call on their political godfathers and are well-versed in many other techniques to make life difficult for political appointees. One is the use of '*white papers*'[185] *which* '*can really hit you hard with all their statements.... You* *don't know who they are, and they say....you're not performing a job....'*[186] A second is to withdraw cooperation, reducing the efficacy of the political appointee and adding to their workload. A third is to circumvent the authority of the appointee altogether. A fourth is to encourage a sense of exclusion in political appointees through a studied coldness. A fifth method is to prevaricate.

But permanent civil servants do not have a monopoly on constructive informal practice. Some political appointees see more defensiveness than professionalism in the permanent civil servants' emphasis on credentials; and who, as a corollary, are frustrated '*with all those schools and universities*' which, rather than treat education and students as matters of intrinsic significance, '*just give all these degrees so they can satisfy the standard [for appointment and promotion]...*' From the executive's point of view, the displacement of personnel within an agency when a new head brings in a slew of new people may ruffle feathers (especially if career civil servants find their promotions blocked). But it is also a necessary part of well-intentioned change.

There is no question that there are high-quality political appointees, and many of those who appoint them undoubtedly want the best for the nation. They genuinely believe their authority to overcome inertia and entrenched habits within a department is woefully inadequate. They have only a short time to turn a department around and are visibly champing at the bit. They must ease out some officials and bring in those they know and trust. It is also churlish to deny that there are members of the House who believe that public service is in itself worthwhile and who feel that the legal, procedural, organizational, and political framework in which they operate leaves them unable to meet the needs of their constituents. They, too, must attempt to influence appointments in the bureaucracy and adopt other practices (such as switching parties) they might otherwise prefer to shun. It is also the case that politicians will support civil servants vying for promotion and candidates hoping to enter the bureaucracy for a host of reasons free of ulterior motives. Political appointees - whose selection is less constrained by the processes, criteria, and detailed standards that govern the selection of permanent civil servants - bring a deal of varied experience from many different walks of life. They swim in the same waters. Over many years, they have come to know each other as they move among sectors, branches, and agencies and learn to cohere and coordinate quickly. These are precious qualities given frequent policy changes and political life's comparative brevity. The informal selection of political appointees also admits qualities and personalities that a more technical process might exclude or leave unrecognized but have their time and place. Political appointees often feel obliged to those who recommended them to the president. But this is by no means always the case. The sheer number of political appointees means that most are hardly likely to be at the forefront of the president's mind except those with the highest profiles. Some positions have fixed terms that exceed the president. Political appointees take on a post knowing that their life expectancy is limited and, therefore, do what they feel is best regardless of what the politicians think of them or want them to do. Others feel their choice is not between subservience and resistance but idealism and realism.

The search committee is one final illustration of relationships pulled and molded into an organization. The committee is not a constitutional requirement despite the importance of getting appointments right (and the repercussions of getting these wrong). It relies on personal knowledge and assurances spread by word of mouth to function. It is a nexus through which knowledge and assurances about potential appointees are broadcast, posts offered, and appointments made. Its existence as a discrete organization is uncertain. Under Cory Aquino, it could hardly be said to have any shape at all. The administration was put together quickly. '*You needed to set up a cabinet to show the public, and then you needed to set up the rest of the infrastructure for that cabinet. So there was no formal system. Cory asked some of her advisors - I mean the people she really trusted, politicians who had started out with their principles and did not want positions. They were asked for names, and these people gave names. And I think the other people in the various groups who formed parts of the coalition were asked [for names]....She asked the leaders of each of these groups who represented ordinary people – the social democratic bloc, the business bloc, the independent democrats of which I was part, the more religious groups, and the Aquino family-related groups. And so, apart from the people she [already] knew, she necessarily looked at these recommendations; and...if the names that came up also happened to be people that she had met, or people that she had somehow worked with, and she felt comfortable with them, then people were called in. That was it.*'[187]

The search committee was given more definition under Ramos. A series of clusters drew from academe, business, and other sectors, and the cabinet scrutinized applications and nominations. But membership was not fixed, so people floated between ad hoc groups. '*We had the Monday, Tuesday, Wednesday, Thursday and Friday groups, which covered all sectors. The Monday group was composed of senior members of the cabinet who looked at all of the applications.... at the whole range of qualified people we know who we can ask to fill up certain positions. So [then it] goes into a process. I belonged to the cluster E, which is national defence, security, and foreign affairs. So I took care of all appointments of ambassadors, consuls. Of course, you have to look first at the career foreign service, to see who is qualified, to look at who is qualified to be promoted, to be posted; and then we also look at....the political appointees, the political ambassadors, who come from the private sector - from business, from the military, from wherever. I guess our friends are first posted because that's how you get discipline. So we start looking at that. And before the president even considers talking to them, we already really have a complete picture of who you are, what you are. Because we don't want to put the president in the position in which he will be embarrassed later. And then from fifty people, we narrowed it to ten, you narrowed to five, and finally you say "Okay, those three people." And then you're able to go to the president and say "Okay, these are the three guys...Choose one to fill an ambassador position in the Court of St James." That's how we did it.'* [188] 'The president' to whom the final list was sent was often short-hand for '*a small circle of confidents who probably understood what the president wants. Some candidates' names went straight from the search committee [to the president]... but normally he would have an advisor or two to bounce ideas off... For example, when selecting people for the government's financial institutions, the secretary of finance would say whether or not that's the right choice. But the ultimate decision falls on the president.*' [189] Once selected, 'names' would usually be '*given a choice. So in my case... it was either government corporations - like PNOC, or Philippine airlines, or other corporations – or a choice between three banks; and since the PNB was being privatized at the time, and I came from the private sector, that was my choice rather than the Land Bank or the Development Bank of the Philippines.*' [190]

Similar arrangements were adopted by Angara (on whom the search committee focussed during the short-lived Estrada presidency) and subsequently by Arroyo. As the sense of haste permeating Aquino's election campaign seeped into government, the committee again became somewhat nebulous. '*I have to be honest... the problem with this administration is....I think it happened so fast: the death of the mother, the sudden decision to run; the switch from Ma Roxas to him; and then all of a sudden he found himself to be president. In other words there was no thinking process beforehand: Ah, if I become president, if I'm elected president who will be my [government]? Unless you do a lot of thinking in advance, you later find yourself really overwhelmed in the number of appointments you have to make.*' [191] Five months into the Noynoy Aquino administration, around 1,000 applications or nominations were received each month for what were estimated by the secretariat to be 1,000 vacancies. These were, on the secretariat's admission, probably conservative figures. '*The president hasn't even appointed 1000.... I think he still has a long way to go....five thousand is what [the number of posts to be filled] was announced by the palace.*' Meanwhile, the Career Executive Service Board put the number of vacancies at around 1,500 and the number of applications and nominations at many times that. Just how much greater can only be guessed. But the numbers of formal applications for a single (and attractive) post in, say, the Foreign Service can be as high as 2,000 - 3,000. The scramble grew with '*the "walk-ins"- the people who walk in to an agency and say they would like this or that [post], or try to get close to the president one way or another. For example....in the first month there were lines trying to see the president's uncle, Butch Aquino. He just had to tell them "I'm not the guy to see" but still ....people would not listen to him.*'[192]

By September 2010, 'the president....said "Go, convene!"' [193] the Search Committee. The response, however, was uncertain. '*For specific positions where the president already has an idea of who he wants to appoint, then that one doesn't go through the vetting process, although they were still required to provide their CV's. Then the others went through a vetting process..... First, they were recommended by a search committee, and when the search committee provided names, they provided their CV's and they say why they think this person will work; and also the other members of the search committee were allowed to voice why they think that person will not do.*'[194] Their vetting of candidates, too, quickly became informal. Early on, there was an attempt to professionalize selection by laying down firmer criteria and procedures, but events overtook this. There were so many candidates to consider, and so many who were applying off their own bat, that it became necessary to rely on heads of agencies who often had to rely on each other or friends and colleagues outside government to suggest names and provide recommendations. The danger was the committee would soon be acting as nothing more than a rubber stamp. '*There is a learning curve that the office of the executive secretary is going through, and the learning curve is slowing things down. I think a lot of people forget the high expectations...the sense that, you know, we should be doing more because, when you think about it, this is a really young government. Even if there are people who have been there before like me, it's a totally new government. We can pick the pace up a bit more but the desire to not make a mistake is holding it up. They need to go through an investigation, the background checks... That's the process that slows it down, because they're checking on many names, and they are checking on making sure that the information they have is correct. That causes a lot of difficulty. I think we should really have the search committee brought in [properly]...and we should have more people bringing their lists, and [we should] process the lists...The committee... is on and off... it [has] slowed down, and it's been meeting [only] intermittently.'* [195]

So uncertain was the response that the executive director of the Career Executive Service Board knew nothing about the committee. '*[There's] no committee constituted yet...and right now it is the presidential management staff and the office of the executive secretary which perform the staff work for the president. Since they don't have a [search] committee yet, we circulate, we openly share information with them. We have a blue book. It's like St Peter's list of names. It's our directory of all our CESOs and eligibles. It also has names of eligibles that are in place, and [the names of] the present occupants of CESO positions who are not CESOs....Lucille [chief of staff of the executive secretary] calls me almost on a daily basis. Yesterday she called me about appointments pertaining to the Department of Environment; last week we were talking about the DPWH; and the other week she was talking to me about the Bureau of Customs. And she said "Hey, there is just one CESO in customs." I said "Yes, that's [X] one of the deputy commissioners, and the rest are not CESOs." "So what do we do with them?" So I said "Well you can appoint them in an acting capacity and then require them to finish their courses." The same is the case for their collectors who, at some level, are part of the career executive service. So that's the kind of vetting that we get now. It's quite informal, given the fact they have not constituted a [search] committee at their end.'* [196]

If, as she believed, presidential management staffs were involved in these make-do arrangements, then participation was limited to their head - Julia Abad, a political appointee. She was Aquino's former chief-of-staff in the senate and the daughter of the Department of Budget and Management's secretary. As already noted, the secretariat had little or no part in appointments, and its staffs were put-out by this. '*Right now, he [the president] hasn't signed the order activating the Search Committee, so it still pending. So we're stuck.... All appointments are being processed over there by the executive secretary... Appointments issued since July 1...have been processed under the office of the executive secretary. For our part, of course, we are always here to provide assistance, and we give them information if they need information because we have the database. And we are ready with the terms of reference: what are the rules? who could be changed? who cannot be changed? We have all of these things in PMS. We provide information to the OES [Office of the Executive Secretary], but the real processing is not being done here right now. We are actually volunteering our services all over the place, and we have gone as far as offering help to department secretaries because they are the ones who need these people - they will be their staff. "Okay, we will prepare meetings for you of all the applicants, of all the people endorsed, for a particular position." So we gave it to them and it's up to them how they will screen, because the screening should have been done by the search committee... which hasn't been constituted...Although Abad and executive secretary Ochoa are more or less the same level, still the executive secretary is considered the higher official. So we try to work together, so when they need any information we give it to them... But we are just hoping that the search committee will be constituted because at our end we are blindsided, we don't know what's going on there.*'[197]

In the absence of clarity, rumors circulating in the press gained traction. Aquino's sisters and cousins were having their say on appointments. And, it was said, two competing but poorly defined cliques were pursuing their own interests. Both had supported Aquino's campaign, and each had preferred different candidates for the vice presidency. The *balay* cheered on Roxas (who stepped aside in favor of Aquino) while the *samar* stood behind Binay. These stories were not without foundation. '*I know some of the people there [on the search committee]. I know that two of those were the sisters of the president – they went through the lists...And [X] was the person that the president sent...to speak with me. I knew him because... he's related to the family - a cousin... I was working with [him] during that whole movement for change [against] the last administration...We were advocating the same thing, we organised a lot of public protests and actions.*' There was recognition that '*improvements are really very important [for] the search and vetting process, and that's what they are trying to do now: [to] remove as much as possible - how do I say? – the influence coming from relatives and friends and that sort of thing. However, I wouldn't say that the appointments of Aquino are characterised by classmates and friends getting appointed in high positions.*'[198] The latitude given to cabinet secretaries to determine appointments in their departments left many feeling that Aquino did not have a grip on government. '*With the GMA administration.... she [Arroyo] was going through the appointments all the way [down] to director III. With Aquino, it's really the secretary, and sometimes the under-secretary....Most of the time they leave it to you [the secretary]. For example, for me now, I am recommending one undersecretary and one assistant secretary ...... and as far as I am concerned, and as far as they are concerned, they [their appointments] are ...going ahead.*' She had also advised Luistro in the selection of his 'God-given' appointments. Soliman had known Rivera for some ten years. He had worked for NGOs and a consulting firm and was then active in the anti-Marcos and anti-Arroyo campaigns. He took up an academic post at Ateneo and helped organize local groups supporting Aquino. His understanding from discussions with Soliman during the election was that he would work with her at the Department of Social Welfare and Development. But he now found himself in Education after determined lobbying by Brother Amin Luistro. Amorphous and loose, the search committee seemed to comprise no more than conversations amongst a few actors: the president, the executive secretary and his chief of staff, and Julia Abad, who would consult the executive secretary of Career Executive Service Board, Constantino-David, and few others as much or as little as they thought necessary.

There is no doubt that the dimensionality of relationships, and the tension this generates, bring uncertainty to the Search Committee at the start of administrations. This is also evident during presidencies and especially at times of stress when the committee is needed most. The farsighted will have begun to think about appointments long before the election results come in. But events usually move faster than expected, and there is a danger of being overwhelmed by the number of appointments. In this case, it is not long before the president and his confidants will begin to rely upon recommendations further and further removed from the original source. All this allows bad apples to get through, no matter how well-intentioned the administration. As time goes on, mistakes build. The next election closes in, and within the cabinet ambitions strengthen. Soon the equanimity with which the president left appointments to the search committee is replaced by a desire to make decisions for oneself.

Nevertheless, the committee appears repeatedly and frequently takes on a formal quality. Its secretariat is staffed by permanent civil servants with their Weberian ideals, databases, and processes for checks, investigations, shortlists, and signatures. The committee modifies its decisions in recognition of agencies (such as the Career Executive Service Board) with the authority to determine who is qualified for posts and their criteria for assessment. It has its own clusters and procedures, and there is some accumulation of experience beyond the political life of any given actor in that the committee has its own conventions. These conventions shape its activation, its leadership, the relative status of the executive secretary and head of the Presidential Management Staff, its size, its probable membership, the levels of appointment scrutinized, and the manner of scrutiny. These conventions are settled enough for some to take exception to attempts by others to block or circumvent them:

'I had a run-in with another member [of the search committee]. He is a cabinet member without a portfolio. His work was to liaise with a particularly important religious group. But he didn't want to attend meetings. We [the committee] chose, and we submitted, a number of candidates for a particular position. So he went to the president and said "You know, this particular religious group, which is very influential, prefers person X rather than person Y which they [the search committee] nominated." And the president goes with person X. So I said to the [the minister without portfolio] "If you're going to do that to me, why don't you sit here and run this office yourself, be-cause as far as I'm concerned you're a deceitful..." He had a row with me and we didn't speak to each other for quite a while. Later, he 'phoned me and said "Why did I get upset? It's just one position." I said "Yes, but you forced it, and it wasn't the best candidate who got the job......"' [199] The constant re-creation and periodic formalization of the committee are highly significant. They suggest that there is in circulation a representation of the committee and how it works – an idea shaped as much by immediate circumstances as earlier practice. That is, the committee meets a perennial need for some kind of forum where strands of relationships can be drawn together and managed, compromises made, and different interests at least partially satisfied.

Chapter 17

Understanding Informality: enabling growth

Informality is a way of describing affective relationships and so effective organizations. It also cultivates flexibility more generally and ensures that redistributive and commercial channels are established and kept open. Resisting the West's fetishistic treatment of rules and processes helps insulate the Third World from confusion and disorder.

Being informal is not a peculiarly Asian or African or Latin American, or Third World characteristic. It is how societies pattern themselves naturally and progress materially. Knots of relationships are sources of capital. They are the means through which new outlets and inlets create new wants and markets and encourage subsistence producers to turn out new goods and buy new wares.[200] They allow economies of scale to operate. They protect against the misinformed decisions of organizations at home and overseas. They act as switches or turntables, steering resources. They are society's redistributive channels.

Many businesses start with scatterings of small loans scraped together from the owner's family. Sometimes the money is lent directly; sometimes, it is routed through parents who borrowed money from family and friends on their child's behalf. Some loans bear an interest; most often, they do not. Running the businesses also involves all kinds of subsidies. Sometimes relatives are hired because they are felt to be more reliable. Sometimes they are excluded because they are relatives. Sometimes they are hired despite the fact they are more awkward to handle and costly. Mr. Cui, the owner of a restaurant in Pingshan, Shenzhen, puts this well. '*Relatives, on the whole, work hard... they will do their best.... for the restaurant, like washing dishes or vegetables... the plates and the food will be cleaner if they do it. Relatives who are paid a wage regularly are even more likely to do a good job as they feel embarrassed if they don't get things done.*' But his responsibilities to relatives did not end with the wage. '*You know my cousin is here working in this restaurant. In addition to paying him a normal salary, I will buy some clothes or whatever for him – to help improve our relationship.*' Like Cui, his cousin was young and had dropped out of school early because he didn't enjoy it and his parents had no money. He had come to Cui to pick up a trade and learn about 'life.' When differences or refusals did arise, Cui felt he couldn't push it too far because he was family. '*I can't say too much. So I will have to do the work myself.*' Workers he hired 'off the street' might want to finish a task as quickly as possible, but at least he didn't need to worry about family.[201]

Subsidies reach well beyond the extended family. It's a notorious problem for small stores: their owners find themselves doling out credit to friends and neighbors- a pack of cigarettes here, and a beer or phone card there – until they cannot re-stock and the business goes under. Most do not survive for long. But some enterprises grow from subsistence outfits into small manufacturers and retailers or even large-scale firms with a national and international presence. Redistribution, if carefully managed, is critical to survival. It is how one builds a loyal clientele. Customers from all walks of life become family friends, and friendships are handed from one generation to the next. If they are reasonably prosperous, owners and families give as businesses and individuals. They serve as a spring for their community. Money is lent to those in need without interest or fixed dates for repayment. Children and adolescents are taken into the household to work and run errands in return for board and lodging and school fees. They live with their doors open to a constant stream of people who drop by for help and advice, to explain, or just to talk. They feed the hungry, find lawyers happy to work pro bono or repay a favor and have a doctor come by and offer advice and medicines without charge. They help find a job with a steady if modest income from business or bureaucracy for a man with a wife and young children. Young men train as cooks in their kitchen, and young women in the art of keeping house. They let out small farms with little or no rent while the tenants raise their families or pay medical bills. They fund scholarships for local children.

Businesses are also involved in redistribution indirectly through clumps of social networks that fuse with landowners, professionals, bureaucrats, and politicians. They are drawn together either through work or because they live near each other or their children are friends. Or because they have run into each other before during their social rounds. They join charitable organizations, such as the Masons and Lions and Rotary, or churches or credit unions. Sometimes there is an ethnic dimension to this behavior. For example, Chinese merchants throughout southeast Asia and beyond created associations from schools to temples to help each other, feed and house, make loans, educate and care, put out fires, and bury the dead, mimicking arrangements made by countrymen migrating amongst towns in China. But none of this is uniquely Chinese.

Why do these people work to charm, plead, persuade, and exchange all kinds of favors on behalf of the community, hoping to secure a share of national funding, whether as roads, drains, water, electricity, lighting, schools, hospitals, or basketball courts or some other improvement? Votes and kickbacks are part of it. But personal courtesies, indulgences, and kindnesses matter far more. The results, on the ground, are less uncertain. In Davao City in the Philippines in the 1980s, it was often hard to tell where a squatter settlement began or ended. The comment is true of settlements all over the Third World. There were plenty of good-quality wooden and concrete houses and commercial buildings alongside flimsy, makeshift ones. Many of the squatters were young, educated professionals — including doctors, dentists, engineers, lawyers, civil servants, middle-level managers, and administrators — and a host of small entrepreneurs, from storekeepers and drug pushers to taxi drivers and petty criminals. With time, metaled roads replaced muddy tracks; ditches gave way to concrete water courses and underground sewerage tanks. Water pipes were laid, schools built, and clinics and hospitals appeared. What was once a space for a periodic market became a collection of permanent shops. It is also through these alliances that broader national programs are rolled out.

Being informal also protects and insulates society from those mechanical levers, the implacable certainties, which governments in the West and its agencies think they have their hands on, such as money supply and treasury bills, interest, and bank rates. During the early 1980s, the West's newly installed liberals brought down spending and pushed up interest rates to control inflation. The impacts domestically were disastrous. Internationally, commodity prices fell and servicing debt became more expensive. Matters were made worse by the IMF's and World Bank's determination to force the West's medicine on the more than sixty countries in the Third World. Conditions and expectations fastened to aid, loans, and policy advice - reducing spending, cutting wages and subsidies, privatizing the economy, and building rigid, formal organizations and processes – often aggravated locally generated crises. In the Philippines, rises in the price of oil mixed with political turmoil following the assassination of Aquino sparked inflation, a moratorium on the repayment of foreign debt, and a run on the pesos. The IMF demanded a sharp tightening of monetary policy, triggering a collapse in GDP to -7% for two consecutive years in 1984 and 1985. These actions would have caused even more damage if not for many 'criminal' businesses that carried on as usual and cushioned the archipelago. It was subsistence producers who dampened the effect of the West's measures in sub-Saharan Africa.[202]

A protective effect is also to be had from the allocation of land through everyday relationships or what is sometimes called 'customary arrangements.' For instance, land may be held in trust by a central authority, such as a king, whose duty is to ensure that everyone can eke out a living. The ordinary subject, even the poorest, is lent a plot and has the right to consume the crops he grows on it. But he does not own it, nor can he exclude others from grazing cattle on its pastures. These arrangements forestall hoarding and speculation and marked imbalances and inequalities, though entering land into a market is not ruled out if this is thought to benefit the wider society.

An uncontroversial opinion back in the 1950s, and one that few in the West would take issue with today,[203] was that customary arrangements frustrate the rational use of land as it cannot be freely bought and sold. Yet the link between property rights and development is not well understood,[204] and there is a weighty body of generalized studies questioning it. Customary arrangements work, while formal property rights' effect on investment, household welfare, access to water, and economic growth is mixed, uncertain, and unclear.[205] The total land area under customary arrangements varies from under 1% in India to just under half in China, nearly two-thirds in Turkmenistan, three-quarters in Tanzania, and 97% in Papua New Guinea.[206] Whether we are talking about the rise of Europe or the Third World, the term *property rights* is little more than a popular shibboleth.

A signal advantage of customary arrangements is flexibility. Land inequality is not inherently bad or good. Like any other resource, it must be concentrated and redistributed if society is to progress. Its heavy and permanent concentration only seems inevitable because land is bound to end up in just a few hands in the West's rules-based market. Around 77 million corporations and individuals own about 60% of America's land area.[207] Most of these individuals hold their meager share as part and parcel of home ownership, which accounts for only a few percent of America's total land area. By land *value*, 10% of households own 85% of the land, and just 1% of the population owns 40%. It's a similar story in England, where 1% of the population owns some 50% of the country, and in Europe, where one-fifth of holdings own three-quarters of farmland while the number of small farms has fallen by around 40% over the last twenty years.[208]

Another measure of land inequality – the Gini coefficient – does suggest that land inequality has also been growing in Asia as well as in North America and Europe. But the moderate rise in Asia may reflect government intervention (especially in China and Vietnam). The same measure also indicates marginal declines in Africa (where inequalities are lowest) and Latin America (where land inequality is the sharpest).[209] The nature of the land, its use (monoculture, ranching, and mining), and competition from Western or Western-style enterprises might help to explain concentrations in Latin America. Another suggestion is that since indigenous populations have always relied on collaborative practices and never owned the land, they don't care who does as long as they can make a living.

When income is not enough to live on, people will react differently. In the public sector, low salaries and wages are often augmented by illicit payments to levels that are still modest but now enough for officials to send their children to decent schools. These infusions stabilize bureaucracy and help establish a settled middle class. A bureaucracy whose ranks are swollen (whether through nepotism or the perceived opportunities for illicit money-making that membership offers) keeps large numbers of young, comparatively well-educated, and ambitious people off the streets, giving them a stake in 'the system.' And by accommodating the widespread expectation that officials should meet their obligations to their extended families, the number of people interested in holding on to that system is multiplied many times. Moreover, offering a way to supplement poor wages encourages those who might otherwise enter the professions or business to go into public service. It is also entirely conceivable that groups successful at penetrating the civil service through nepotism have, for this very reason, the qualities necessary to implement policies effectively.[210]

Bribery has advantages from the viewpoint of reformers and activists, too. It is a tangible and personal means of influencing the polity at many levels, from its legislature and highest-ranking executives to the everyday gritty bureaucratic routine on the ground. Even the economist demanding efficiency above all else may approve. The speed money merchants pay to public officials shortens the time they wait and the overall length of the queue. Companies that can afford to pay hefty bribes are already efficient enough to bid for tenders at the lowest cost. A more general political advantage is that payments form a common point of interest, bridging divisions along caste, tribe, ethnicity, language, kinship, ideology, and religion and working as a 'solvent' for matters over which no compromise is otherwise possible.

Integrating business with bureaucracy is vital at the other, wealthier end of society.[211] Sometimes these channels are exceptionally well organized. Power concentrated in the hands of central politicians and bureaucrats in South Korea left society uncluttered by an intermediate (or non-capitalist) class. In return for substantial payments, bureaucrats and politicians allocated rights to capitalists to maximize long-run growth. In Malaysia, though an intermediate class of Malays dominated politics and bureaucracy, payments by the Chinese minority, who held sway over the economy, were arranged such that there was little interference with the economically rational decisions of Chinese entrepreneurs. In Thailand meantime, the capitalists, who included many Chinese entrepreneurs, populated the political elite, controlled local political networks and circumvented the country's intermediate class. This allowed the elite to reallocate rights among its factions in response to the changing requirements of economic growth. All this contrasts with countries such as India, where landowners persuaded bureaucrats and politicians to make decisions that were illiterate from the national perspective but in their favor.

My examples are 'Asian,' but do not reflect peculiarly Asian qualities. If centralized and effectively monitored, bribes can produce more effective and less costly (to the briber) systems than those in which different ministries, agencies, and local governments set their levies independently. Still more efficient is a system where a firm must pay only a single, large bribe. It might be a capital payment that, if invested productively rather than salted away into bank accounts overseas,[212] can help stimulate the economy. Or it might contribute to a party's campaign slush fund and help strengthen parties. Without that funding, parties might be overcome by foreign interests, indiscipline, factionalism, and disunity, taking the entire country with them. Similar points are made in Africa about patronage. It is compatible with strong economic performance if it is centralized and oriented to the long term.[213] In other words, patronage allows rulers to exert influence and direction informally over companies and investments for society's benefit.

Creating chaos through order

The evolution of these redistributive patterns is spontaneous. Relationships - society's capillaries, its redistributive networks - keep the community oxygenated, fed, and alive. It is necessary for economic growth, and capitalism would not survive without it. The real puzzle is not why the organization in the Third World is social but why the West is fetishistic in its treatment of rules, organizations, and ideas. The simplest and the most complex organizations with the most advanced technologies are built from the same substance - every day relationships and their psychological management. To erase the *social* organization and view this as progress makes no sense. Take, for instance, those organizations described as 'highly reliable' - the aircraft carrier, submarine, nuclear power station, or commercial airline. Despite their inherent dangers, they operate, for the most part, remarkably safely day in and day out, year after year, decade after decade. What makes these organizations reliable is not merely their rules, procedures, and processes but how these frameworks are treated. The 'system' is continually questioned. What is wrong? How do one's actions or decisions here and now fit into the whole? If nothing is failing or poorly coordinated now, then there is no question that something somewhere will go wrong. Where is that problem or failure likely to occur? Where is a failure most unexpected? If this involves technology, then redundancies are built in. If it is a procedure, then people must be prepared and trained to respond, however unlikely that eventuality might seem. Nor is that the end of the matter. Is it possible that too many redundancies might themselves cause problems? Nor is there much doubt that people will make mistakes. This leaves trust - an old human virtue that also characterizes the informal organization - as the lynchpin.

The importance of doubt is most evident once the organization begins to drift into a puritanical state and the body and its processes are treated as absolute, fixed, and certain. NASA provided a very public and disastrous illustration of this. By the 1980s, puritanism had gripped the Agency, egged on by budget cuts and pressured to deliver quick turnarounds in missions. Bureaucracy trumped thoroughness and reason.[214] Staff at all levels were more concerned with deferring to layers of cumbersome regulations than with the development of the program, critical thought, and safety. As long as the bureaucratic process worked, it was felt that everything would be well with the shuttle. Previous successes only reinforced this certainty. The possibility that procedures were faulty - or had built into them an acceptance of technical issues which, though considered problems initially, had been normalized over time - was not contemplated. Instead, a deal of effort went into ensuring hierarchies were maintained and defended and information flows kept efficient, even if that meant paring away critical information. Far less attention was paid to the nature of the information and the questions and doubts it raised, especially if these were minority views.

What is true of a single organization is true of collections of them. The apparent chaos of some Third World countries is created not by informality but by the West's insistence on the rule as absolute. The Philippines, like other colonial fabrications, was to obey the regulations bequeathed to them by the Americans. Many of the Philippines' western-educated elite in the universities and press and among its business leaders, politicians, and civil servants listened and agreed. Under no circumstances should the Philippines treat the market as another form of redistribution. The lives and prospects of the majority depended upon the market and the country's political system. Rectitude and adherence to these truths defined the elite and made them worthy of their position. The more practically minded, however, understood that, to the contrary, a re-distributional state was essential. They also understood that such behavior would be regarded by the righteous as irrational, damaging, and criminal and so had to be nourished surreptitiously. Then there were those, perhaps most people, who looked at the emerging confusion, saw it did not work and concluded they would have to look after themselves and their families one way or another.

Japan and South Korea illustrate how difficult it has been for Third World countries to buck the West's expectations successfully. Both felt compelled to knuckle under and move away from redistribution and towards the market. And both have regretted doing so. By the mid-1980s, trade deficits made it evident that the United States had trouble competing with Japan and other exporters along the West Pacific Rim. Nakasone, Japan's prime minister, agreed to let the yen appreciate, making Japanese exports more expensive and less competitive. Over the next eighteen months, the yen rose by more than 40%, well above the original target of around 10%. Japan's exports were severely hit, and during the first half of 1986, GDP came to a halt.[215] The government responded by lowering interest rates and introducing other measures to stimulate the economy. But matters only got worse. Land and asset prices inflated into a bubble that continued to expand until 1991, when it burst. Tightly wound packages of credit unraveled, and banks suffered until a currency crisis struck in 1997. By the end of the century, the economy was stagnant, and prices were falling. Then, the global financial crisis hit just as deflation seemed to run out of steam in 2007. Japan was less exposed to sub-prime debts than America, so the Yen became a haven despite its flat performance. Huge quantities were bought, pushing up the Yen's value, making Japan's export expensive[216] and dampening prices at home. By 2020 there was clear evidence that the economy had even begun to deindustrialize.[217]

The reason for the debacle was plain. The government had released its grip on Japan's credit-based system (in which the state-controlled banks and other financial institutions directed subventions at will). It then shepherded it toward the West's preferred market-based system in which capital is raised by companies competitively on the market. By 2015 fewer people were buying into earlier explanations for Japan's lost decades: an ageing population; over-dependency on central government subventions; poorly judged monetary policy; ineffective, less productive, and uncreative Japanese businesses; and inefficient and corrupt banks. These seemed more like rationalizations of problems wrought by deregulation.[218] By giving up control, Japan had stepped off its redistributive path. With this has grown resistance to America's attempt to assert financial hegemony.[219]

Korea, too, came under heavy pressure to change paths. Many Koreans felt that economic and political liberalization were inextricably linked. And since political reform was well underway, greater economic freedom should be forthcoming. Korea's influential chaebols firmly adhered to this view. Externally, America demanded that Korea quicken the pace of trade and financial liberalization, improve transparency, and stop manipulating the won. In 1990, Korea's economic indicators put it into a different category of GATT and required it to loosen up its trading regime. In 1995, the WTO replaced GATT. The following year Korea became a member of the OECD. In 1997 Korea was granted an IMF bailout after the Asian currency crisis shook the country.

As externally imposed rules and demands to stick to them grew, so did the country's problems. Income distribution worsened, wages flattened, and the productivity gap improved in favor of the country's competitors. The line taken was a familiar one. Korea's development model was old and worn out. Bureaucrats were unable to make sensible decisions on the allocation of resources. Big companies were inefficient and in bed with politicians. So the market had to be allowed to take over. Private companies should work their magic in social welfare, health care, and other services. The financial sector and tourism should be permitted to blossom too. And while the corporate sector and the Korean people (and their small businesses) did all this, the public sector needed to come up with a clear vision, build 'capacity,' and develop an incentive system.[220] Yet, like Japan, Korea was not wholly convinced, and suspicion and mock compliance[221] soon grew into resistance.

Chapter 18

Authentic Democracy I

An emphasis on transfers and informality, and an acceptance of population growth, go hand in hand with patronage. Patronage delivers goods and tangible benefits in return for support. Redistribution in exchange for submission is a serviceable arrangement and a more authentic form of democracy.

Western democracy, having ceded control over distribution to the market, has little choice but to concern itself with the symbolism of the vote. Patronal rule is conditional upon the delivery of tangible improvements. It is not by chance that rapid progress widely spread has appeared outside the West. Living standards are being raised on a scale never seen before, and countless lives have been saved. Why upend a way of life that works for one that does not? When society cannot establish a symbiosis between patronage and western-style democracy, resisting the latter is necessary for economic growth.

Malaysia

Neither historical precedence nor geographical ubiquity explains patronage, but each does help to illustrate its organic and democratic nature. One example is the states that had emerged by the early sixteenth century when the Portuguese took control of the Kingdom of Melaka on the west coast of the Malaysian peninsula. The general settlement pattern comprised villages, each with its headman, grouped under a chief whose territory (a district) was often defined by one or more river valleys. Both headmen and chiefs usually arose from lineages that customarily provided those officeholders.[222] But to attain and hold power, each needed followers and the means to support his following. This required an increase in the productive population. This meant new mouths to feed, more loans to make, more favors to dispense, and more bodies to clothe and protect. Wealth channeled to the chief then had to be recycled.

These nested groupings formed the basic building blocks of states, topped off by a Sultan. Between the Sultan and the district chiefs were various other officials, the most important of which were the commander of the police and troops and the treasurer. Real power, however, lay with the district chiefs who kept the peace and collected revenue. Just as the district chiefs relied on their followers, the Sultan depended upon his district chiefs' cooperation.

This basic arrangement, which evolved in Melaka first, served as a model for others on the peninsula and in Sabah and Sarawak. But it was not copied precisely. In Kedah, for instance, the Sultan appointed his relatives as district chiefs (over whom his authority was unambiguous[223]) and dispensed with many of the grades of officials between them and himself. Nevertheless, the basic pattern of political organization was an expression of, and rested upon, patronage – the conditional upward flow of support in return for the downward flow of things and services. Political authority was ultimately dependent on a willingness to be ruled.[224]

Trade was part of this story. Trade generated the wherewithal needed to provide for and help cement those building blocks. The Chinese, in particular, had to be treated with care. They were merchants and miners and wealthy and mobile. The peace had to be kept, and they could not be over-taxed, or they would go elsewhere. Trade could also mean contact with older complex societies through which experience of statecraft could be channeled and put into practice. An ambitious man from such a background and with royal credentials could set himself up anywhere he could bind together enough villages, headmen, and chiefs who understood the value of those credentials. It was just such a roving, kingdomless prince who established Melaka. Paramesvara, a refugee from Palembang in Indonesia, claimed descent from Alexander the Great. He had tried first Singapore, then Muar, then Bertam, before trying his luck in Melaka around 1400.[225] He spent the last decade or so of his life turning the settlement into a major trading center upon which the new Ming Emperor bestowed his inscription. It was not the only trading center recognized by China, but it was the most favored. The refugee's exalted lineage and the status conferred by the Chinese court helped the immigrant win the support of local people or, at the very least, to accede to being ruled by him. Paramesvara also brought enthusiasm for Islam – a functional social kernel that Indian and Arab merchants appreciated. It put the ruler at the head of a religious hierarchy that extended to the village.

Paramesvara also brought sensible and fair judgment, or so accounts of his reign maintain. No subject should be disloyal or treacherous, but no ruler might shame even one of his subjects unless prepared to lose his Kingdom through God's actions. More practically, a King had to consult with those in authority under him, including the chiefs. Collective decision-making guaranteed that resolutions would be effective. It also prevented arbitrary rule. As important was that his lineage, recognition by China, and links with merchants, delivered tangible benefits to his followers. It isn't easy to know how far the new wealth flowed down the strands of patronage. If it meant that those higher up did not make excessive demands on those lower down, most of whom made their living from fishing and agriculture, then that was something. Better still was that they lent their clients a hand when times were hard and indulged them with opportunities and feasts when times were good.

Paramesvara's scions would, in their turn, seed other kingdoms. The son of Melaka's third-to-last ruler was placed over Pahang as its Sultan. One son of Melaka's last ruler became Johore's first ruler, while others established Perak, turning it, by virtue of their lineage, into a respectable kingdom.

It was a similar story elsewhere. It was probably a Sumatran prince who was the first ruler of Negeri Sembilan in the south. Kelantan, Pattani, and Pahang acknowledged the Thai Kingdom of Ayudhya's overlordship in the north, just as Melaka had looked to China. Ayudhya had expanded after 1351, demanding closer and more formal relationships with its Malay vassals. Its influence strengthened after the fall of Melaka to the Portuguese in 1511.

Melaka was not the first state on the peninsula. Keda and possibly Kelantan, Langkasukah, and others emerged over the six centuries or so before the arrival of the Portuguese. It is also likely that centers developed inland either independently or in connexion with trading communities on the coast. Whether these older political entities were controlled by states beyond the Malay peninsula or, like Melaka, created by itinerant princes are questions wrapped in contemporary politics.[226] Yet it is clear that communities along the coast traded with Indonesia, the Philippines, Burma, Thailand, the Middle East, China, the Ryuku Islands, and the lower Mekong. Some of their partners (like China and Funan and Champa) were well-established states; some, like Srivijaya, were thalassocracies and consisted of loosely connected trading posts, some probably no more than chiefdoms.

Yet Melaka is regarded as the first distinctively Malay polity that still exerts an influence through its statecraft. Today, the Sultans are merely advisors to the executive. But they retain their sway as leaders of the religious hierarchy and the shariah courts and mosques. The Sultans also rotate amongst themselves the ceremonial role of King. The headmen and chiefs remain part of governance arrangements, though instead of focusing on the Sultan, they look to the prime minister. In Kedah, the BN alliance continued the Sultan's predilection in pre-colonial days to appoint headmen who, in 2008, often led the party branch as well.[227] Meanwhile, in other states, they sought and received patronage even if not party appointees. For although headmen have become civil servants who report to the state secretary, their salary is poor. If they are to succeed, they must deliver to their village as well as secure their own material and social status in, say, the form of a house that is noticeably bigger than all the rest.[228] Even the river valley, which found some expression in the electoral districts of the late 1950s, still forms the basic territorial unit of the village and the boundaries of the headman's responsibilities in Sarawak.[229]

These and other techniques survived Portuguese and then Dutch rule and then a further two centuries, during which the British gradually asserted control over what was to become Malaysia. Penang was acquired in 1796, Singapore in 1819, and Melaka in 1824. These three territories, which formed the Straits Settlements, were administered first by India, then Singapore. They would not be managed directly from the Colonial Office in London and given the status of Crown colonies until 1867. It would take almost thirty years more before the Sultans of the 'Protected States' – Perak, Selangor, Sungei Ujong, and Pahang were persuaded to come together as a federation centered in Kuala Lumpur. In 1909, Siam agreed to relinquish its influence over the Keda, Kelantan, Terengganu, and Perlis and leave these to the British. These arrangements were made behind the Sultans' backs, though, in recognition of their sensitivities, the grouping (also joined by Johore), known as Unfederated states, retained some autonomy. North Borneo (Sabah) and Sarawak, British protectorates since 1888, were made crown colonies in 1946, just eleven years before Malaysia was granted independence. Neither they nor Singapore would join the Federation until 1963. Singapore had agreed in 1961 to a union subject to provisions allowing it a degree of autonomy over education and economic matters. It nevertheless found this too onerous and, in 1965, pulled away from the Federation to become a republic.

Why did Malay statecraft survive these expanses of times? The answer is the logic of relationships, loyalty, support, and power. This, far more so than the British policy of indirect rule or the workings of 'culture,' determined the continuing relevance of patronage and the details of its use in state affairs. Moreover, patronage took on even greater significance in a society rived by ethnicity. Chinese and Indian merchants had established a presence long before the British arrived, dominated the larger towns and cities, and grew in number without help. British rule oversaw more Chinese and Indian immigrants, brought in to work in the tin mines after the abolition of slavery in 1833 and, later that century, on the rubber plantations. By the 1920s, of a total population of 2.9 million, 54% were Malay, 29% Chinese, and 15% Indian. Underlying the import of labor was a belief amongst the British that the Malays were 'inert' and fit neither for hard work nor leadership. Or was it a reluctance to cooperate or do so fully and effectively, a brooding and silent resentment that stripped standing and authority from a leader who sealed his own fate should he then respond with force? The Malays certainly proved to be anything but apathetic when the British proposed a Malayan Union.[230] The Malay leadership saw what those who suggested union did not. A Malay majority in a country where economic power lay disproportionately in the hands of two minority groups – the Chinese and the Indians – would have created dangerous tensions. Concentrating in Malay hands the authority to dispense resources and opportunities to favor Malays was necessary for economic growth and political stability. It kept the Malays in the same tent. And it fostered a secure psychological base on which they could redistribute to Chinese and Indians or, at the very least, not discriminate against them too harshly. The flexibility to keep the varied interests amongst Malays, let alone the Indians and Chinese, would be extraordinarily tough and probably impossible if conducted in an open, legitimate, and planned manner. In practice, it was as likely that patronage would have to be effected through grey and often illegitimate forms. Gerrymandering and fraud; brokering promotions, court rulings, and land titles; awarding favored Malay businesses licenses, contracts, and development funds to build roads, mosques, drainage systems, dams, and palaces: these were just some of those techniques.[231] During the run-up to elections, government largesse might also include salary increases or one-off payments to bureaucrats, administrators, and teachers in universities and schools or discounts to mortgages or loans to Malays.

If there was any doubt about the danger of trying to implement exclusively programmatic (non-partisan) policies, one only had to look at the 1969 riots. Three days after the May 10th elections, violence erupted on the streets of Kuala Lumpur. The UMNO-dominated alliance ('The Alliance') retained a majority, but only after losing a quarter of its seats and seeing its share of the popular fall below 50%. The beneficiary was a collection of smaller parties favoring equality and fairness among the 'races,' each of which fought to ensure the group they represented got an equal slice.

The shift in seats and votes had come when the Alliance government was moving inexorably toward policies that favored Malays. Singapore had seceded from the Malaysian Federation. And unemployment had risen as tin and rubber prices dropped. The smaller parties, representing mainly Chinese and Indians, were confident enough to hold tongue-in-cheek 'victory' demonstrations. Malay onlookers, suffering under a hail of taunts and invectives, were shaken enough to let their insecurities get the better of them. Peevishness seemed all the more acute and productive given the Alliance had won all prior elections since 1957, and the favored position of Islam, the Sultan, the Malays, and their language would be ensconced in an amended constitution in 1971. In fact, the Alliance would go on to win all subsequent ones up to 2018.

By then, however, the Alliance's sixty-one-year tenure had bred complacency. Party and government forgot that success depended not only on keeping Malays happy and secure but on meeting some of the demands of the Chinese and Indians and keeping them on board. Patronage did not have to be dispensed equally, but it did have to be dispensed wisely and judiciously. Discontent and dissatisfaction became focussed on corruption scandals, real and concocted, involving the Prime Minister and his family. The Alliance's loss of support among Malays and non-Malays gathered pace in 2008 and 2013[232] before its fall in 2018. The winner, the Alliance of Hope, was led by a former UMNO grandee Matahir Mohammad. He had decided to recant his past beliefs and chase programmatic policies. But once installed, the party dropped him, back peddled, past the center ground long held by UMNO to a more conservative pro-Malay and pro-Islam camp. Against this new background, various factions in Parliament maneuvered to establish more favorable positions in unstable ruling coalitions. By early 2022, they had temporarily settled into a bloc, including UMNO, Bersatu (indigenous Malay), and the Pan-Malaysian Islamic Party - temporarily because UMNO was already planning to re-establish its old Alliance with *Barison Nasional*.

Despite all the political shenanigans and scandals, Malaysia has done extraordinarily well. Average rates of economic growth reached 11% in the 1970s, 9.5% in the first half of the 1990s, and 4.88% over the last two decades. It has one of the world's lowest poverty rates (0.4% in 2016); its HDI was 61 in 2019. Malaysia is also one of the 'cleaner' countries in southeast Asia. A good deal is said about why Malaysia is well-governed: well-paid civil servants, a large and educated middle class, a bureaucracy inherited from the British, a comparatively free press and a judiciary that is more or less independent, and a loud if, until 2018, an electorally unsuccessful opposition, are amongst the reason often proposed. But a more likely explanation is that the Malays are favored and know it. There is less incentive to act outside the bounds of what is acceptable (even if grey or illicit) behavior and make hay out of suspicions and allegations when those boundaries are crossed. Another way of putting this is that a certain degree of corruption keeps corruption from becoming too extensive and damaging.

Brazil

Brazil secured its independence in 1822, even before a good many territories outside the West had been colonized. Its Parliament – a council of deputies and a senate – dates from the late 1820s. Its members were chosen indirectly through an electoral college. Real power lay with a monarchy transferred from Lisbon to Brazil in 1808, shortly before Napoleon marched into the capital. The Royal House eventually returned to Portugal in 1821, leaving behind hereditary rulers of a fully independent Kingdom. The monarchy lasted barely sixty years, edged out as interest groups multiplied and jockeyed for wealth and influence. The Royal House had sat above a hierarchy whose apex comprised landowners - a non-hereditary aristocracy in its own right. Slaves suffered at the bottom of the hierarchy. They formed both the workforce and a status symbol owned by everyone who was anyone in a society that despised manual labor. Between landowners and slaves lay plantation owners (sugar, tobacco, coffee, and rubber), mine owners, cattle ranchers, bureaucrats, and professionals. Because of their wealth, merchants engaged in foreign trade were accorded a place at the high table with the landowners. But their poorer domestic cousins sat with the artisans and workers.

None of these groups was entirely homogeneous. The military was thought to be full strivers who languished some way down the hierarchy. The navy was a cut above the army. Army officers tended to come from the provincial backwaters, the sons of families who, at one time wealthy, could no longer afford to educate their children. The military, in turn, looked down on the politicians - the *legista* who spent their time drawing up unnecessary laws and regulations, which they then offered to circumvent for a price.

During the nineteenth century, tensions amongst these groups intensified. New classes emerged, and allegiances changed. International pressure (especially from Britain) for the abolition of slavery put the owners of land, plantations, and mines in a tight spot. The sugar market declined while the introduction of coffee encouraged a new kind of commercially driven plantation owner who was, in the eyes of Brazil's landed aristocracy, very nouveau riche. Industries grew, further increasing the demand for workers. Immigration partly compensated for the shortfalls in labor. Many new immigrants were from Italy - rural workers and one-time small landholders with ambitions.

The groups began to line up on either side of a divide. The wealthy landowners, the merchants involved in overseas trade, and the bureaucrats tended to be pro-slavery and pro-monarchy. The commercializing plantations, the military, domestic merchants, artisans, budding industrialists, and workers saw things differently. And two of the most frustrated and aggrieved - the coffee growers and the military – finally did for the monarchy. The military organized a Clube Militar to represent their interests in 1887, one year before the abolition of slavery and just two years before the removal of the monarchy in a bloodless coup and the establishment of the Republic.[233]

By 1890, Brazil's population was around 14.3 million, some three times what it had been seventy years earlier. Most people were illiterate and most worked in agriculture. But some ambitious rural workers and former small-holders who had arrived in the country before the Republic were now substantial landowners, property owners, or industrialists. Another 3 million immigrants from Portugal, Spain, and Italy were added to the working population before World War II. Governments oriented policy toward industry, urban workers, and the armed forces. Traditional oligarchs found themselves replaced by the people they had looked down on – the military, the merchants, the artisans, and the industrialists.

Something of the old still hung about. Support for the new was offered in return for minimal change in their neck of the woods. Individual serving officers often ran for political office, but the military as a group stood back and operated more like a pressure group. Junior officers felt stifled: the best jobs were cornered by their superiors and politicians. A similar feeling was growing within Brazilian society more generally. Change had slowed to a crawl. The open and competitive society brimming with opportunities many had hoped for was not evolving fast enough.

By the end of the 1920s, patience ran out. The military still had allies amongst the coffee growers who were suffering as the depression gripped the international markets. And many of the grower's sons had gone into politics. Together, they deposed the president, set up a provisional junta, and a few days later rallied behind a single figure – a *provinciana* named Vargas. They promoted industrialization and modernization through authoritarianism. Basic industries, chemicals, and pharmaceuticals prospered. Attendance at school and university in a population that had risen to 41 million improved markedly. The pace of development, though not galvanic, laid the groundwork for the post-war era.

Following a war against dictatorship that Brazil, under American pressure, had joined in 1942, an authoritarian government was hardly a realistic option. After 1945, the military stepped back and, for the next decade, watched events from the barracks, occasionally champing at the bit. Governments shifted money from agricultural exports to industry, often behind trade barriers. They created public monopolies, established public banks (including a development bank), and spent on infrastructure. They created state-owned steel firms, oil firms, and the car industry. The workers who not so long ago had been a small and insignificant group were now both numerous and their unions powerful. Communist sympathies were also on the rise. At the height of the cold war, the military stepped in. A purge of union leaders rolled into a general cleansing of the judiciary, congress, the civil service, state governors, and even the military. Democracy, said the new regime, had to be limited if Brazil was not to self-destruct. Reforming capitalism meant tightening control over urban and rural workers, outlawing strikes, restricting the number of political parties, and brutally treating those who took up armed struggle against modernization.

In the heat of the moment, the rebels either misjudged the times, the state's reach, or the government's nature. Resistance was not widely supported. The military had not concentrated power on one man. Instead, it rotated the titular head of government amongst its own: Branco in 1964, Coste de Silva in 1967, Media in 1969, Geisel in 1974, and Figuerido in 1978. Moreover, each relied mainly on civilian politicians and technocrats to devise policies and run the economy, which they did with some success. The years under the generals between 1964 and 1985 saw import substitution policies and inflationary financing of fiscal deficits. On average, Brazil witnessed growth rates of around 7% from the 1950s to the 1970s. True, social programs were abandoned, and inequality sharpened. But from 1969-73, growth was high, inflation was low, and from 1974, a transition back to civil rule began. In the minds of the soldiers, the coup was not just about defeating communism or promoting the economy but also about democratic tutelage and rebalancing interest groups. In 1985, a civilian president oversaw the final transition. This involved formulating a new constitution and direct presidential and congressional elections. The new document unveiled in 1988 marked the start of universal suffrage in that even illiterates were now entitled to vote. Universal access to the Single Health System was also introduced.[234] Political parties were legalized. Direct elections were held the following year, and a new president took office in 1990. Parties multiplied, and thousands of unions sprang up, along with all kinds of organizations formed by students, state enterprise employees, federal employees, religious bands, professional groups, and social movements.

In 1995 state monopolies in telecommunications, oil, gas, electricity, and mining were opened up to private capital in the form of concessions, though Petrobras remained in state hands. Brazil joined the WTO and a customs union with Argentina, Uruguay, and Paraguay. China became Brazil's largest trade partner in 2010. Steel producers (such as Gerdau, CSN, and Usiminus) were thrown up along with aircraft manufacturers (Embraer), car manufacturers, telecommunication companies (Oi and Telemar), oil producers, and ethanol production.[235] Foreign capital increased from 400 million in 1985 to over 400 billion in 2019. There has been heavy and sustained spending on education. Brazil's tropical agriculture is one of the most competitive in the world.[236] Cash transfers to various groups helped reduce the poverty rate from 40% in 1990 to 20% in 2010 and lifted more than thirty million from low to middle income. The middle class now forms about 50% of the electorate. The government also purchased land and redistributed it to poorer families, increased spending on students from poorer backgrounds, introduced minimum wages, created new state companies, and restored defunct ones. Growth in GDP has been volatile, swinging from 9% to -4.5% over the last forty years but averaging at around 2.4%.

Perhaps the sheer scale of Brazilian society (now at 200 million) and the complexity of development persuaded the military to remain in the wings, influencing government rather than being of it. Events over the previous century - the slow extension of the franchise, military interventions in 1930 and 1964, and the proliferation of parties following the new constitution – reflected tensions present even before the founding of the Republic amongst landowners, plantation owners, miners, merchants, artisans, industrialists, professionals, intellectuals, workers, military and others. As the population and the economy grew, and as these groups specialized and fragmented and new ones appeared, their relationships became more complex. Policies favoring one or other helped reinforce identities amongst the beneficiaries, who would then lobby for their privileges to remain. The technical complexity of shunting around resources, materials, funds, and people, favoring one sector and then another, and asking for sacrifices from here to deliver benefits there, and thus lift all boats, was overwhelming. It could not be managed by the military or by any single party. Temporary coalitions built mostly from patronage rather than formal processes were the only arrangements flexible enough. And these involve all kinds of undisclosed and off-budget transactions: transfers and tax incentives;[237] subsidized loans and cross-subsidies through the credit markets; price controls; transfers from one firm's payroll to other organizations with social functions; transfers of a portion of a firm's wages to government investments and subsequently returned as pensions; kickbacks to fund election expenses; kickbacks to buy votes and support policies that favor one or other sectors; and payments to bind and divide. These practices are a necessary part of economic and political management but politically risky in that they are easily tarred as corruption and lie at the heart of many a scandal. The most recent and most salacious has involved the state-owned Petrobras and state officials (elected and non-elected) who accepted kickbacks from contractors following the award of contracts. The corruption was said to have spread throughout the economy and helped push it into a recession. The atmosphere of blame and suspicion enabled opponents of the former leftist president de Silva to chase him and undermine his protégé - the sitting president Rouseff. She was subsequently impeached not for any matter related to Petrobras but for using funds from state banks to hide a budget deficit.[238] It also set the scene for the election of the populist and right-wing Bolsonaro in 2019.

Chapter 19

Authentic Democracy II

Patronage does not limit the size of society. But effective redistribution and political stability require a sensitive appreciation of and response to different groups' requirements.

Botswana

Botswana was one of the poorest countries in 1966 (when its GDP per capita was just US$80) and faced an uncertain future. Its population was tiny, but its land area is about double that of the UK and Eire combined. It is landlocked. It was administratively weak, had poor infrastructure, little industry to speak of, and 90% of the population lived in rural areas. Its largest town was less than 10,000 people. It and the rest of the country largely depended upon financial support from the UK, development aid, and a negotiated customs union with South Africa.

By the early 1970s, UK financing ended, and revenues from newly discovered minerals began to flow in. The government started to spend on improving water supplies, primary schools, health, roads, and a cattle industry that could sell meat in the EU. In the 1980s, income from mining was redirected from cattle to manufacturing and services and arable farming. Public enterprises in housing, railways, civil aviation, electricity, water, and telecommunications were set up and expanded; and, through the Botswana Development Corporation, the government held shares in manufacturing firms. Because spending geographically was roughly in line with population and, as a whole, less than revenues, the country accumulated a substantial reserve and kept both external and domestic debt low. Over the next thirty years, mining's share of GDP fell from over 50% to 20% in 2017. Manufacturing expanded in absolute terms though its share of GDP remained at around 5-6%. Agriculture fell to 2.2% in 2017 from its peak of 3.4% in the 1990s. Services increased their share of GDP the most, from 45% in 1986 to 89% in 2017. Consumption by the bottom 40% of the population grew a little more than that of the top 60%. Cash income amongst the poorest remains stubbornly low. But improvements in health, safe water, subsidized housing, and education (spending on which amounts to about 8% of GDP, one of the highest in the world) have meant a dramatic cut in the poverty rate, from over 50% in 1966 to 19% in 2014, and 16% in 2019.[239]

The lives of the poorest were not bettered as quickly as the discovery of copper, nickel, and diamonds made possible. As in Malaysia, networks of patronage and nepotism, and the interests of politicians and their families, and those of state and private firms overlapped. Nevertheless, the country has broadly succeeded in being redistributive.

One party has won the election every five years since 1965, with the last held and won in 2019. From the start, the Botswana Democratic Party made good use of its natural advantages. One of these is that the majority of the country's small population (just under 3 million) are Tswana-speaking, as are the party's founders and successors. From the start, the party was careful to bring in the various Tswana-speaking tribes and leaders (the chiefs) upon whose territories the country's administrative districts are based and to campaign and attract the remaining twenty percent of the population. Once in power, and ever since, it has also been careful to distribute goods and services fairly, regardless of linguistic and tribal differences in a society that has become increasingly mixed geographically and amongst whom there is a good deal of intermarriage.[240]

The other advantage is its pre-colonial governmental arrangements, preserved in legislation and grafted onto modern forms such as parliament, councils, village development committees, and land boards. The chieftaincies (the heads of tribes) and the *ktloga* are particularly important.

The chiefs (hereditary positions) are brought together in the House of Chiefs to advise the national assembly and the executive. They also administer justice according to customary law and dispense it in more immediate, direct, and understandable ways than any provided by judges and magistrates.

The *ktloga* are communities into which the tribal territories are divided. These were based on kinship - true and fictive. At assemblies in these communities, anyone could have their say about important decisions made by the headman and chief. The practice continued after independence in 1966. Today these meetings are also attended by government ministers.

Political stability, then, is achieved by distributing goods, services, and positions to different groups, maintaining direct contact with leaders, and cutting the ground from under opponents. The result is a polity that is one of the most clearly patrimonial[241] and in which tribal, linguistic, and ideological divisions are not especially significant. Opposition groups, even amongst Tsawan-speakers, have found it difficult to become more than small regional or local parties. Of these, there are about 30. Support for BDP has slowly eroded since 1965, and in 2014 the opposition coordinated better than before. The Umbrella for Democratic Change and Congress came close to victory. But by 2019, the BDP took a majority of the popular vote and 38 out of the 57 seats comprising parliament.

China

Patronage is also central to the most populous society – China. Already weakened by warlords and foreign concessions during the nineteenth century, China was finally torn apart in the early twentieth century by different visions of what the country should be. It was a tough lesson in the importance of unity and discipline, one taken to heart. Throughout the decades after reunification in 1949, competition amongst groups, though no less energetic and impassioned, has been shrouded by allegiance to a single party. It serves as a parliament where leaders fight it out and decide who will govern for the time being and how. The public forums, such as the NPC and the State Council, are idealized reflections of those gritty discussions and debates. Disputes and clashes about who should get what rarely break cover and, if they do, emerge sanitized as changes in policy or as incidents of incompetence, illness, or corruption. Less often, it signals the replacement of one group with another and a major shift in policy and practice.

Leadership is, as noted earlier, essentially collective. Myriad interests are competing behind the scenes, which must be considered, persuaded, bought off, soothed, and rewarded. Leaders who are insensitive and unresponsive to what is needed, what is wanted, and what is felt will not last long. But throughout all these maneuverings, it is not 'done' to disturb the public face of unity and calm because to do so is dangerous and may encourage those splits to be quickly replicated throughout society.

Academics often referred to ideal types to characterize factional disputes during the last half of the twentieth century. The radicals viewed the world through the lens of class conflict; the marketeers were determined to free up the economy and improve productivity; and the bureaucrat was concerned above all with state control. The bureaucrat, a moderating influence, would put China back onto an even keel following the wild excursions on which radicals and marketeers took it. The marketeers had the upper hand between 1953 and 1955, only to give way to bureaucrats and radicals between the late 1950s and mid-1960s when China pulled away from the edge after the Great Leap Forward. Ascendant radicals then launched China into the long decade of the Cultural Revolution until the bureaucrats turned the country around and the marketeers lurched to the right.

These descriptions are gross over-simplification. What was being discussed was who got what and how, and this ran the whole spectrum of possibilities. The strategy - to gather up and redistribute in such a way that allowed the entire material platform of Chinese society to be raised – was sensible and entirely necessary. But a determination to disavow any role for non-state commerce and price, to substitute bureaucratic management for the art of logistics, and to present market and state as opposites, made that strategy difficult, if not impossible, to realize in practice. Vast shifts in materials and people from one sector to another were insensitive to the dangerous tilts in the country's economic platform. The consequence was that policy and practice zig-zagged from one sector to another as government and party tried to bring the platform level before embarking on another effort to raise it once more.

Private businesses flourished after 1949, even as the nationalization of industry gathered pace. By 1953, most, if not all, businesses were brought under state control either as vast state-run companies run directly from central ministries or as collectives - industries owned by the state but managed by local government units, provinces, or municipalities. At first, steel plants, power stations, heavy machinery factories, and oil refineries were favored in what amounted to a grand bureaucratic exercise in which money and prices followed materials and goods. The kind and amount of raw materials supplied were planned, as were timings and prices. The state also planned and fixed what was produced, how much of it, when, and at what prices. And state determined how much of what was then bought and when and where it was delivered.

Heavy industry was concentrated in existing large cities in eastern China, but the construction and expansion of new cities in the interior were also encouraged. These inland cities, allocated about half of all investment, increased their industrial production from about one-quarter to a third of the national total in 1958.

All cities, in the east and inland, were to serve as growth poles. Development impulses from these regional growth poles were to filter down the settlement hierarchy so that even the smallest towns in the countryside would benefit. One consequence of this strategy was rapid growth in the urban population – by 14 million in the first four years after 1949. The government tried to constrain the distention of larger cities by moving people into satellite towns and industrial dispersal. It also lowered rural-urban migration by controlling the birth rate and sending educated youths and technicians into rural areas. Even so, by 1957-8, the urban population nearly doubled from 57.6 million to just under 100 million.

In the countryside, meanwhile, land expropriated by the new government from the landlords and richer peasants was redistributed. In theory, this created the basis of an equal society and provided everyone with the means to produce enough food to feed themselves. In practice, it resulted in holdings too small for successful farming. The solution to this problem was thought to lie in the introduction and development of cooperatives and collectives. Initially, it was envisaged that agricultural producer's cooperatives (in which land, labor, and assets were pooled) would be developed and expanded over 15 years. Higher-stage cooperatives would follow. But events moved far more quickly than planned. By 1956 the private ownership of land had just about ended, and over 90% of the Chinese peasants found themselves in 680,000 Higher Stage cooperatives. Agriculture, too, had been made an extension of the bureaucracy.

It became apparent in 1957 that agriculture was failing to supply the raw materials and food for non-agricultural workers. The emphasis now switched from industry to agriculture and rural development, and the country took a 'Great Leap Forward' the following year. The sending-down policy was intensified, and industrial activities were diffused into rural areas. From then on, until 1976, urbanization in China showed only a marginal increase of just 1.1%.

At the heart of this new movement was the commune. The typical commune contained around 50,000 people spread over several villages. Each commune was organized into brigades. Each brigade comprised about 8-12 teams, with 15-20 households in each team. It was intended as the basic unit of administration and production in rural areas and was soon applied to the cities. Every commune and every urban settlement was, as far as possible, to be self-sufficient in industry and agriculture as well as producing for the state whatever the state asked of it. There was little or no free commercial exchange. The whole country fragmented into cells. Workers in the town tried to plant crops, while people in the countryside poured resources into technically inferior backyard furnaces producing steel and iron so brittle it was useless. Each cell made whatever it could in an uncoordinated manner.

Disconnecting what was produced from what was needed ended with disaster. By 1960-61, starvation and disease had spread to many parts of the country. The leadership knew things were going seriously wrong even as early as 1959. But it was not for another two or three years that the restoration of central planning and limited private markets, a reduction in the size of communes, and the abandonment of experiments with urban communes in urban areas began to show their effects. These same measures, however, were attacked even as the economy was being returned to a reasonably even keel. Excessive centralization meant taking power away from the people. Material incentives, private plots, and the resumption of trade were capitalist tendencies. The Party and China, said Mao, had fallen into the hands of a capitalist bourgeoisie in alliance with the Soviets. A cultural revolution starting in 1966 was necessary to set China on the right path. The people's thinking had to change once and for all. Old ideas, old habits, old cultures old customs were attacked, as were bureaucrats and people in authority. Again, the country slid into anarchy until Mao called on the army, who restored order. The economy was not quite as radicalized as it had been during the GLF. But the communes kept everyone in their place. Rural development and, as far as possible, self-sufficiency came first and foremost.

Mao's death in 1976 and his gang's collapse brought opportunities. Over the next forty years, there emerged all kinds of factions. The 'taizi' or princelings or elite - the children of former or current political leaders. The bureaucratic bourgeoisie and the 'tuanpai' - those who cut their teeth in the China Youth League. The new leftists and the Maoists or populists. The rightists, who desire political liberalization, and the Deng Xiaoping faction. And Shanghai, Guangzhou, and Chongqing factions. Factions are also to be found in local (provincial and sub-provincial) politics, sometimes mirroring, sometimes adding to, an already complex national picture. The boundaries separating them are uncertain, shifting, blurred, overlapping, drawn in different ways, and open to different interpretations. But the essential split is between those who support China's middle class and big business; and those who sympathize with, and draw support from, the vast number of people who have been left behind in rural and urban areas and who have lost their share of China's wealth. As many commentators note, politicians on both sides of this split need to work together; both sides need each other. Those not yet absorbed by a self-conscious and often self-regarding middle class must be brought along and provided for.

Power was dispersed in many ways. Most apparent was the distribution of posts amongst competing groups. Another was the slow but constant reform of the legal system since the early 1980s. The stated aim - to regulate government behavior by making all people equal before the law - was entirely understandable in the wake of the Cultural Revolution. The jolts from Tiananmen Square and the fall of the Soviet

Union probably brought still more pressure to bear. By 1997, 'governing the country according to the law' had become the guiding principle of government. There was also growing attention paid to international law, especially to those aspects of it which have a bearing on commerce and China's concerns overseas. The courts remain under the Party's thumb. For instance, politically connected firms are more likely to resort to legal action in commercial disputes precisely because they can exert influence over the courts.[242] But while the Party is shielded, Party members involved in corruption are not, and this is especially true if their political opponents have sufficient clout.

Power was also dispersed through fiscal decentralization and localism. One obvious instance is the percolation of commerce throughout society and the rise of small businesses. Another is the financial independence of provinces. They have their own revenue and are responsible for most of the country's public expenditure. Provincial leaders have the same bureaucratic rank as central government ministers. Some of them sit on the Party's Politbureau. Beijing is, therefore, keen to reserve the right to confirm appointments of provincial leaders and key subordinate posts and move appointees around. Books are audited in Beijing. Allegations of corruption are investigated in Beijing. Beijing also ensures that military districts fall across provincial boundaries.

Whatever the assessment of China's economic performance from the establishment of the Republic until the late 1970s, the Party and government learned - through bitter experience and occasional success - much about the art of shifting goods, materials, and people. Now they learned to do so in ways that would raise the economic platform for all. This required it to put to one side the distinction between market and state and the notion of a mixed economy. Once ideological tags were removed from notions such as 'market,' 'trade,' 'profit,' and 'state ownership and control,' they were just standard, interchangeable techniques. State-, collective-, and privately-owned units were extensions of society, whether entrepreneurs understood this or not. Precisely what the practical arrangement would look like was unclear and remains so because development and progress are a matter of gradually feeling one's way ahead.

China's success over the last thirty years or so has drawn mixed responses from the West. The West's policy in the late twentieth century towards China was 'constructive engagement.' If the West conducted business with China, drew it into global and regional institutions and gave it a stake in the international community, then China would be socialized and become more like the West. There was a debate to be had over how quickly this would happen, but it would happen eventually. That was the firm belief amongst academics, policymakers, politicians, and journalists.

When it became clear China was taking longer than expected to become 'one of us,' academics concluded that China was nevertheless evolving some remarkably modern elements - precursors to democracy - that keep it stable. These include institutions so valued and respected in Chinese society it is more rule-bound than many other authoritarian regimes.[243] Furthermore, relationships within and amongst China's organizations are more impersonal than in many countries dominated by neo-patrimonialism. *Guanxi* (connections or reciprocity) and corruption are breaking down. 'Factionalism' in China is maturing. A quarter of a century ago, informality was dominant. Formal politics often provided no more than a façade. Individuals established formal bases more as fall-backs in the event their informal bases (and their patrons) should weaken or be removed. And while the formal members of the elite were supposed to be equal, there was amongst them an informal hierarchy of patron-client relationships. Yet, '*the historical trend is to formalization.*'[244] This is especially true since the death of Mao, for the '*overall thrust of development since the advent of political reform....has been towards increasing formalization, as measured by the frequency, length and regularity of meeting sessions, and the number of people or procedural stages involved in drafting legislation.*'[245] The secularisation of Mao Zedong's thought and Deng's pragmatic focus on growth, and '*attendant dismissal of the specter of an elite "struggle between two lines" and "people in the party taking the capitalist road," have reduced the ideological barriers to the operation of factions.*[246] The ebbing of ideology, combined with an easing of disciplinary measures against officials and attempts to legalize their tenure, and restore popular respect for officialdom, have allowed factional behavior to become somewhat less clandestine. Elite factions have now begun to pursue and represent the interests of their constituencies. Indeed, in the wake of reform, elite coalitions have even begun to move away from 'factions' towards 'policy groups,' the next stage being the formal structures and formal alliances which make up a 'bureaucratic' polity. Of course, few things are certain: informal politics in China tends to '*reinforce traditional hierarchical relationships (including the "cult" of leadership inherited from the empire), and culturally embedded relationships more generally (for instance, time-honored primordial "connections") at the expense of rational-legal and meritocratic arrangements.*'[247] Nevertheless, bureaucratic systems were being formalized at all but the highest levels. The reliance on explicit rules and procedures was strengthening. Informal groups, now oriented more towards policies designed to enhance bureaucratic interests, were being transformed into professional, vocational, business, and pressure groups – and even, as in the case of the reformists and conservatives, into quasi-parties. Moreover, as a political form, '*informal politics...tends to be progressive in terms of policy, as its flexibility facilitates more rapid change by offering shortcuts to standard bureaucratic procedures. This has helped make China an extraordinarily well-led country compared to others in the Third World (albeit not always wisely governed).*'[248]

However, when it appeared that China would not become like the West, it was decided that China could not succeed and must be facing imminent collapse. Marked inequalities of wealth between east and west and urban and rural China, together with questions about levels of debt and toxic assets, suggested comparisons with the west's economic conditions shortly before its financial crisis in 2008.

And when the crisis did not come, the West lost patience and decided that China was a threat. Thus, was the intellectualized, other-worldly China of the 1990s begging for Westernization, replaced by a cartoonish villain.

The specific catalyst or initiator for this change in sentiment was the rise of Huawei and its threat to the dominance of American IT firms – especially Apple. The embodiment of the West's frustration is Xi Jinping and his regime. China is said to be regressing. Xi is a reincarnation of Mao. He has concentrated power in his hands, stuffed the upper echelons of the party and government with yes-men, and is putting personal loyalty and the party's security before economic growth. So twitchy is this cabal that it would probably take the opportunity presented by Russia's invasion of Ukraine to attack Taiwan. Meanwhile, the gaps between rich and poor are too wide to be remedied. An emphasis on the market and money is too powerful to be tempered. And wealthy, sophisticated, and educated urbanites encrusted with impenetrable snobbery are becoming caste-like.

The truth is that the West does not want to see China for what it is. China is readier to make transfers to its people and nimbler at this. Debts are written off, subsidies are made, and prices are controlled. Giant state-owned behemoths are used as conduits, disguising transfers as inefficiencies and losses. State enterprises and collectives and their descendants retain a role more critical than mere numbers of organizations suggest. Some of these are natural monopolies. Many others have formed oligopolies into which private enterprises are bound. Nor has China's government lost sight of just how vital its relationships with its people are and of those relationships' patronal and pragmatic quality. The generation that knew the make-do spontaneity of guerrilla war is almost gone, and those who learned its application during the thirty years after liberation are ageing. But a willingness and ability to take risks and experiment remain. Finally, the polity is extraordinarily stable. Despite the formidable might that can be brought into play - a police force [1.5 million] under the Ministry of Public Security, an army of 2.5 million, and the courts and the prisons - small beer given China's huge population. A leadership that relied on sticks of this kind would already have been handed its hat. Instead, it provides security, jobs, and rising living standards and, believe it or not, listens to its people.

Chapter 20

Authentic Democracy III

Patronage is one facet of transfers, 'informal' behavior, population growth, and government, and so is part and parcel of economic growth. For this reason, the case made to foist Western-style democracy on the Third World is unconvincing, resented, and resisted.

The West assigns patronage to a specific category of relationship described as unequal, vertically aligned, manipulative, and personalistic. It is said to convey a sense of dependency and control. It concentrates power in the hands of a single leader or small clique who uses it to dispense favors, backed up with the threat or use of violence, in return for support. As primordial, traditional, and artful behavior, patronage differs from sincere and purely social relationships and from interactions that pervade formal organizations and democratic politics. The essential features of these polities - free and fair elections, the separation of powers, the rule of law, and limits of authority on rulers - can be found in no other form of state, whether chiefdom, oligarchy, absolute monarchy, limited monarchy, military dictatorship, communist, or socialist. When democracy is equated with a republic and excludes constitutional monarchies such as those found in the UK and Europe, we can draw an even sharper boundary.

The problems and difficulties created by patronage are widely discussed. Leaders who use patronage to compensate their followers - and cultivate amongst them fear that other venal and ineffective rulers favoring other groups - will rive states into pieces.[249] The harsh truth is that patronage vests arbitrary power in the hands of unaccountable appointees who emerge from, and disappear back into, a secret world where corruption is practiced with impunity.[250] It encourages different factions within organizations to pursue their own interests, generating distrust and poor organizational commitment.[251] In these and other ways, patronage undermines attempts to reform organizations and governments and improve the lives of the poor and disadvantaged.[252] It disrupts formal politics nationally and locally.[253] It breaks up horizontal or community relationships and disorganizes and perpetuates inequality and dependency.[254] And it interferes with the impartial management of the economy.

These problems are found throughout the Third World (including former communist and socialist states). In Africa, south of the Sahara, post-colonial rulers often bought loyalty by redistributing resources and assets as patronage. Initially, this was effective in building power bases but meant less was available for the rest of the population. It also weakened supply organizations. This gradually compelled the ruler to parcel out economic opportunities and markets to loyal supporters locally while marginalizing others. As a result, local networks strengthened, political networks replaced formal organizations, and national channels fell apart until, eventually, the power and influence of the ruler collapsed.[255] Corruption, poor infrastructure and communications, dysfunctional economies, weak organizations, civil unrest, political instability, authoritarianism, armed conflict, and state failure are all laid at its door.

Even those countries successfully establishing stable democracies are not free of the problem. Patronage is a danger that requires constant vigilance. It rears its ugly head wherever a political system fails to adapt to changing circumstances. It is persistent because indulging family and friends is a natural and basic human propensity and will constantly reassert itself without countervailing incentives. It is especially likely to reappear when long periods of stability give way to financial or military crises.[256] Hundreds of thousands of South Koreans demonstrating in the autumn of 2016 to demand the resignation of President Park Geun-Hye, who they believed was corrupt, did not so much indicate the strength of the country's democracy as a lack of trust in its formal channels.[257] The president was the daughter of Park Chung-Hee, a military general who had ruled South Korea from 1963 until his assassination in 1979, some eight years before the country finally dispensed with autocracy in 1987. Like her authoritarian father, who isolated himself, she didn't hesitate to use whatever elements of autocratic rule left open to her, such as the National Security Act, the concentration of power in the Blue House, and its informal alliances with the National Intelligence Service and chaebols. She disbanded a minor opposition party. She conducted a wrongful election. She failed to investigate a ferry disaster that killed more than 300 people. She doled out money to family and confidants. And she left the chaebol to dominate an economy where most young adults had to work long hours in low-paid and insecure jobs.

Unconvincing?

It's true that patronage does not always benefit society or facilitate growth. Societies are messy. Coordinating actions so that they promote economic growth is not always the best or most sensible or most human thing to do. People create ineffably complex and varied contexts. They often find themselves in situations where the same action has different, contradictory, and sometimes harmful meanings and effects. Few of us are strangers to venality, selfishness, and destructiveness.

Yet, as we have seen in earlier chapters, assumptions underlying darker characterizations of patronage are questionable. For example, do inequality and dependency inevitably taint relationships with immorality and damage them? Surely the answer to that is no. Think of the relationship between parent and newborn infant. Aren't patron-client relationships just a way of arranging unequal power generated by complex circumstances?[258]

A more telling criticism of patronage is it leaves open the possibility that those who think they can offer more effective leadership are entitled to seize power. Indeed, those who feel this way might say it would be immoral to avoid that responsibility. The result is political instability and worse. Thus, we are brought back to the need for a process that allows the governed to remove and appoint leaders: Western-style democracy.

This argument has some purchase but fails to distinguish political power from mere control. Control is fragile. In a Western-style democracy, electoral rules provide 'the people' with only fleeting, momentary control. The people have no power because the elected politician only needs to obey the system's rules. Under those rules, politicians 'owe' their supporters nothing, and, in any case, they have nothing to offer because they have ceded decisions over distribution to the market. By contrast, reciprocity lies at the core of an authentic democracy. If it were the case that a group felt it could improve a society's lot and it seized power successfully, it would immediately find itself on notice. Forever in society's debt, it would have to live out its days knowing that if its ambitions exceeded its abilities, the people would eventually raze it from history.

The case favoring Western democracy also rests upon a series of claims that do not match experience. One claim is that politicians held to account (through elections, the rule of law, the separation of powers, and limits on a government's authority) are unlikely to rush into wars with other states, and the norms of peace and non-violence will soon reshape relationships among countries. Violent domestic conflict is also less likely. Western democracies are, therefore, inherently peaceful.

But is this true? A defining element of the state is often said to be a monopoly over violence and the legitimate right to use it. Like it or not, violence is necessary for the democratic process.[259] And when it is used, it mustn't be allowed to escape democratic control. Moreover, it isn't clear that levels of political violence in repressive states are necessarily much higher than those states categorized as non-repressive.[260]

There are other uncertainties. For instance, what is a democracy, and precisely when does a state become one? What is meant by war or violence or coming to blows? At what point does armed conflict turn into a war? Are there different categories of 'war'? If so, how is one distinguished from another? Is the use of battlefield casualties sufficient? Or should one rely on the total number of deaths caused by fighting and the breakdown of agriculture, food distribution, water supplies, and healthcare? Or is the proportion of deaths as a percentage of the population a better measure? And what kinds of numbers separate one type of conflict from another? These questions might seem pernickety, but they are not superfluous. On occasions, democratic states *do* have a go at each other. Examples are not hard to find: India and Pakistan have fought each other three times. Nor are Western democracies (and their predecessors) less likely to start wars and become embroiled in conflicts with non-democratic states. On the contrary, Western states have been a party in more recorded conflicts than any other part of the world for the last two hundred years. Since the early nineteenth century, two-thirds of the 95 or so wars between states have involved North American or European powers or Israel and Russia. About one-half of these took place after 1945.[261]

A second unsubstantiated claim is that democracy is more conducive to economic growth and development.[262] Democracy, it is said, makes it easier to remove ineffective and dishonest leaders and do so peacefully and regularly and do away with unrestrained squabbles, turmoil, violence, and anarchy. Even the threat of removal mitigates the effect of incompetence, disinterest, and corruption on economic growth.[263] At the very least, politicians are unlikely to participate in corrupt practices that affect the economy. Undergirding the politicians' willingness to leave and avoid corruption is the rule of law. Everyone must account for their actions, and everyone has an equal right to redress for harm, whether caused by another person or the state. To this extent, everyone is equal and equally free to live their own lives. It also means that we are free to own property and that agreements concerning livelihoods should be honored and protected. These assurances bring stability, give everyone a stake in the community, and encourage some people to set up businesses, take risks, invest, and make money. The rule of law also helps ensure that power is less centralized, less personal, and less uncertain and that the state's bureaucracy is more effective. And because politicians have a more effective bureaucracy to rely on, democracy is also better at distributing wealth and opportunity and improving health and education.

A society whose population is becoming wealthier, healthier, and better educated is also a society with a larger market and better labor force. With better-educated people come more ideas and a more intense exchange of ideas, information, and funds. And with more people coming up with ideas comes greater scrutiny and better policy, better organizations, and better practice. These traits also make for a more competitive society. Even if labor costs and taxes are higher than elsewhere, a competitive society remains attractive because it has skilled labor and the dense and creative exchanges of information and ideas that companies need.[264]

So closely entangled are growth and democracy that each creates the conditions necessary for the other. The strong parliament that arose at the crown's expense after the English civil war was monopolized by a landed gentry who also filled the cabinet. Parliament settled disputes peacefully amongst the gentry's competing factions and drew traders and manufacturers into its arena. And both groups – landed gentry and new business – were willing to alleviate mass distress and, during the 19th century, make popular concessions in return for mass support.[265] Europe's history might also be thought of as one in which claims and counterclaims were made by competing groups and settled through an 'unstable blend of law and violence.'[266] Today, the European Union (neither state nor collection of autonomous states) is simply an expression of competing interests focussed on national parliaments who together now exercise their claims and counterclaims within an international forum.

Nevertheless, it is non-democratic countries that more often experience marked economic growth. Indeed, this seems to be the norm. Examples include Brazil, South Korea, Taiwan, Indonesia, Thailand, Vietnam, Hong Kong, China, and Singapore. Nor were Western countries democratic when they underwent industrialization and rapid development. Free and fair elections, a genuine choice of candidates and parties, and true universal suffrage in Britain and the United States are no older than the Chinese communist party. Britain was no democracy in 1914, four years before all men over 21 and women over 30 could vote, and 14 years before the franchise was extended to all women over 21. Nor could America in 1941 be called a democracy, 23 years before segregation was banned in schools and public places and 24 years before the Voting Rights Act prohibited states from using one pretext after another to disenfranchise African Americans. The fact is that many democratic countries do poorly as far as economic growth is concerned.

Why is it hard to establish a positive connexion between democracy and economic growth? One popular answer is that political and economic development are separate phenomena with their own logic. If one outruns the other, they both suffer. Another – and its one formulated more than two thousand years ago - is that it gives the whip hand to those who want to see governments spend[267] and dispossess the rich. A third is that under democratic rule, groups of all kinds flourish, lobbying for their interests, clamoring for support, and complaining that they and the people they represent are being left out or left behind because they are a minority. Society is prone to social, ethnic, and sectoral struggles. Government is loaded down with contradictory policies. Resources can't be mobilized quickly or managed sensibly enough. Lee Kwan Yew, who led Singapore into, through, and beyond secession from the Malaysian Federation, was fond of saying that his tiny island, crammed with Malays, Chinese, Indians, and workers from around the world, could not have flourished without restrictions on civil and political rights.

Democracy is said to be self-destructive in other ways. It tends towards political decentralization, making it difficult to avoid the minority's domination of the majority. Having traveled around America shortly after 1776, Tocqueville concluded that he knew no country where people were less open-minded. An associated quality cultivated by democracy is elitism. Party leaders might be selected because of their accomplishments within and outside parliament. But to gain mass electoral support, they must become mass demagogues. Democracy, Weber argued, is a way to select would-be Caesars.

Yet another objection to Western-style democracy is that its imposition creates the very problem – corruption - blamed on patronage. Democracy removes the personal and emotional quality from transactions by emphasizing process and transparency. It thus restricts the conduits through which goods and services can make their way to the general population. Only official and transparent channels are possible. And only during official and properly conducted elections can an unspoken *quid pro quo* be offered in the form of votes. Anything else will be treated as grey or elicit. Consequently, many opportunities and possibilities for exchange are blocked off. Even if democracy operates properly, the vast number of people trying to petition a tiny number of politicians guarantees that the political class will ever hear only the most powerful, well-organized, and well-funded groups. Everyone else will have to rely on a single vote amongst tens or hundreds of millions of others, cast every few years. Frustration and corruption erupt as people try to re-establish the deals and opportunities they are used to.

Democracy also cultivates self-centeredness. By treating the vote as a symbol of the individual's pre-eminence over the state, democracy encourages citizens to place themselves at the center of the state, its interests, and its political processes. If voters feel reasonably content with their lives, they will likely withdraw from society into their private world of family and friends and leave society to itself. But if and when the state fails to deliver, and people find they are without influence, they slip into a downward spiral of frustration, alienation, and self-interest.

A third claim often made on behalf of democracy is its inevitability. Many countries in the West are democratic now but first became rich under very different political regimes. This is because economic growth produces an educated middle class whose members want more say over their own lives. It also leads to greater urbanization, improvements in technology, better communications, and faster movement of more people, things, and money at home and overseas. Sophisticated, coordinated, and effective political opposition groups are more likely to evolve in these circumstances. For all these reasons, authoritarian rule necessarily gives way to democracy.

Some writers, notably Fukuyama, went so far as to argue that with the collapse of communism in eastern Europe and Russia, and with the metamorphosis of communism in China (and we might add states such as Vietnam and Laos), we have reached the end of an era of ideology. Variations on a liberal democratic theme will become the global norm, occasionally modified by local managerial practice.

Fukuyama wrote his book towards the end of a century over which democratic progress had been slow and hardly spontaneous. It had taken more than a hundred years for democracies to grow from ten to 119[268] (or about two-thirds of independent states).[269] Many appeared during the last quarter of the twentieth century when seeding democracies across the Third World had become a point of principle for the West's universities, non-governmental organizations, development agencies, journalists, and politicians. Nevertheless, the 'rush' to democracy struck the West as significant. The correlation between democracy and economic development is among the most well-established relationships in political science, proclaimed one writer after another.[270] Even in Africa, nearly every peaceful state (with the exceptions of Eritrea and Swaziland) had by 2005 committed itself to hold competitive elections.[271]

Yet resistance brought this surge to a halt and forced it into a retreat as the new century progressed. In 2016, sixty-seven countries suffered a deterioration in political and civil liberties – more than double the number of countries registering progress. That was the eleventh successive year in which declines had outnumbered improvements. Human rights and democratic norms were rolled back in countries from Poland, the Czech Republic, and Hungary to Turkey, Azerbaijan, Cambodia, Thailand, the Philippines, and China. African democracy was in reverse, even though 45 leaders had by 2016 gone through some form of multiparty election to secure their position; by 2019, only eleven percent of the continent was politically free. Globally, the combined GDP of autocracies now equaled or exceeded that of liberal democracies. With some justification, it was enough for Putin to declare that modern liberalism was now obsolete.[272]

Part III

The Decline of the West

Chapter 21

Affective and Puritan Revolutions

Decline is better understood as part of a long series of pulses that raise, shape, and undo society.

Lifted slowly by possibility and worn down gradually by a yearning for certainty, society is always on the rise and in decline. Rome was no different. Its collapse meant disassembling flows of agricultural and manufactured goods, materiel and coinage, people and ideas, amongst two thousand cities from which even the lowliest farmer found himself cut loose. Turbulence and plague followed in the late fifth and early sixth centuries, leaving populations on the Apennine Peninsula with little choice but to seek refuge in the countryside. But it had not come apart all at once. Five centuries earlier, Rome had been fretting about its collapse. Pliny blamed the large estates, and Seneca warned against the acquisition of yet more land. Livy and Horace lamented the all-pervading moral corruption wrought by property and wealth. Others worried about the barbarians scratching away at the Empire's borders. When Rome decided it could not, or would not, conquer still more territory, it struck agreements with the invaders. Not only that, it absorbed them: they were admitted into the armies and even the praetorians; they were awarded Roman titles and honors; they were settled in the provinces. The policy was Augustus's but adopted by most of his successors. The new blood became part of what Rome had already become: a society in which self-aggrandizement had taken hold. Politicians and soldiers, barbarian and Roman, all vied for posts and land and influence and wealth. Some believed they deserved more than they had been given; others simply demanded it or took advantage of circumstance when it presented itself. Misrule by one emperor and then another, too venal, too weak, or too naïve, or merely disinterested, added to the distractions the ambitious who hovered within the Empire and just outside it were quick to exploit. Only occasionally did an Emperor provide the leadership to restore a sense of direction or restore the territories ceded for peace or temporary alliance to play one group of barbarians off against the others.

Into all this, Christianity also insinuated itself and was taken up by Constantine and the aristocracy nearly three centuries after Augustus. It had traveled far since its revolutionary days and became as effective as the imperial bureaucracy at squeezing the peasants. The old divinities of Athens and Rome were outlawed. If this was not enough, Constantine transferred the capital to Byzantium, stretching the distance between the center of power and the troubled northern borders by a thousand miles. The pagans received a brief respite under Julian (d. AD 363), who disliked the vehement zeal of the Christians until the pious Theodosius (d. AD 395) sanctioned it. By the sixth century, so closely associated was Christianity with affluence and the state that the senatorial aristocracy and the moneyed blocked off opportunities for the bureaucrat or soldier, barbarian or Roman, to rise through society. Thus was 'the fate of the Empire sealed by Christian prejudice.' [273] No later than a year of Theodosius's death (and the Empire split into east and west between his sons) were the Goths up in arms and at the gates of Rome itself. They were bought off that first time and a second, but on the third occasion, they took the city aided by its slaves. The Goths stayed there for six days before moving on, though it remained under their control for nearly another year. It would take another century, and almost a dozen more emperors, before the western Empire was finally extinguished. Each ruled only with the support or disinterest of the barbarians who were busy carving the empire amongst themselves, each finding a spot in the sun. When, at last, the Empire gave out, its death was hardly noticed.

Affective revolution 450-700

As the cities drifted away from each other, remnants of the imperial bureaucracy and secular municipal schools with their curricula of grammar, rhetoric, logic, arithmetic, geometry, and music sloughed off gradually.[274] Before the end came, literacy was widely disseminated among the urban population.[275] Parents handed on what they had learned or hired private tutors if they could afford it. The new rulers who carved up the Empire amongst themselves were happy to let the Church step in to administer and organize. Monastic communities sprang up all over Europe as far north and west as Iona in Ireland, and were joined by episcopal schools. Together they provided men and women for cloisters and scholars and scribes for administration, teaching, or the priesthood. The Church could not expect to spread the word of God unless the laity, too, could read. With that in mind, song schools taught Latin and music to the children who would sing at church services.

The best of the Church's congregation discarded wealth, rank, privilege, and such insulation as it afforded at a time of great uncertainty. At seventeen, Benedict (480-555) cut himself off from his family of wealthy country landowners. He planted a dozen or so monasteries in what is today Italy's southern Lazio region. More than 25 years as their superior preceded his Rule – his set of instructions for how monks should live their lives. It treated the house as a family and the abbot as a father who, in the exercise of authority, understood human weakness and frailty, and imperfection. It eschewed Celtic and Egyptian monks' treatment of corporal punishment and physical penitence as an instrument of perfection. Yet it retained something of their asceticism, carefully tempered, in its demand on the individual to renounce his will and adhere to strict routines.

The bureaucracies of the new barbarian kingdoms included within their ranks men determined to keep alive the classics and establish programs to educate the public. At about the time Benedict set down his Rule, Boethius (480 -524) wrote his *Consolation of Philosophy* – his imaginary discussion with Lady Philosophy, who led him to recognize just how worthless riches, office, fame, status, pleasure, and glory are. Happiness is to be found in obedience to God's commands. This was a choice made freely and made easier because God ensures that humans are inclined to pursue goodness and happiness. Free of bitterness and full of contentment, this was an extraordinary piece from a man in prison awaiting execution. A man born into aristocracy, primed for imperial office, appointed ceremonial counsel and then elevated to Master of Offices as Theodoric's (454-526) court only to be caught up in its intrigue and rivalry.

In the years between Boethius's execution and Benedict's death, Gregory (d.604) was raised by a wealthy and devout family. He was educated in preparation for a career in the imperial bureaucracy and rose to high office as Prefect of Rome, only to turn his back on that life. Instead, he sold his patrimony and used that money to establish six monasteries in Sicily and turn the home where he grew up opposite the empty palaces on the Palatine Hill into a seventh – St Andrew's. The remainder of his fortune he distributed amongst the poor. He entered St Andrews and lived under Benedict's Rule as an ordinary monk. Over the next twelve years, he served as one of the seven archdeacons of Rome and then as nuncio to the imperial court in Constantinople before returning to St Andrew's as its Abbot. In 590, he was elected pope. He adopted Benedict's Rule for the Church and, in his own writings, made plain the moment of humility and compassion. It was under him that the Church took over many functions of the imperial bureaucracy, including responsibility for feeding Rome's population. Using the papal patrimony, he saw to it that the infirm and sick in the suburbs and coastal towns, as well as in Rome itself, were fed and sheltered. And he interposed to protect laborers from the corruption and oppression of bureaucracy and the Church. Such was the esteem felt for Gergory the Sees continued to multiply a century after his death.

Precisely how much wealth the Church committed to helping the poor, the sick, the old, the widows, and the orphans are unknown. That Bishops were expected to set aside at least a quarter of their income to the poor might give some indication of what the Church itself was prepared to redistribute. The willingness of many landowners to donate large portions of their holdings to the Church greatly expanded its authority. The Church also worked assiduously to influence marriage patterns, the legitimacy of children, strategies of heirship, and so the distribution of property between generations.[276] About one-third of the Frankish Kingdom was transferred to the Church by the early eighth century.[277] Keeping tags on its far-flung properties and paying for new buildings, ceremonies, lighting, manuscript production, and feeding and housing all those who worked for it directly also involved the Church in the gamut of economic activities from beekeeping to minting coin.

So it was that affective pools gathered and slowly amalgamated into a tide that washed over Europe. Even the mood in Ireland began to thaw by the seventh century. Windswept and bare and hanging off the edge of Europe, Ireland initially attracted a strongly ascetic version of Christianity - one forged in the Egyptian desert. The spartan existence demanded in life was promised in death. The good and the bad would be raised into heaven or cast into hell. Middling souls, aided by an entourage of angels, were offered no guarantees. They should expect to battle with demons immediately after death and before God decides their fate. For Irish Christians, there were no luxuries, not even a long wait for Judgement Day. Stringency in education was required, too. Yet by the time literacy was well established in religious centers throughout the island in 600AD, monkish communities were softening into lay communities or civitas led by a priest.[278] Some took in visitors: the sons of kings and nobles who came to learn to read and write Latin or Ogham; and artisans who came to teach or to learn how to work gold, copper, iron, glass, and leather or make bells.

Puritanism Returns (700-1250)

Far to the southwest, however, on the Arabian Peninsula, events were underway that would encourage a new Puritan surge in Europe. From the Hejaz came tribal raiding parties; then, an entire army pushed north and east to harass Byzantium. It also drove west. By the middle of the seventh century, it occupied northeast Africa; by its end, Carthage had fallen. It moved on to Tangiers and Spain and across the Pyrenees into southern France, reaching Poitiers by 732.

Although nominally separate from barbarian royalties (many of whom had long since converted to Christianity), the Church depended upon their goodwill in times of peace and their soldiers in times of war. The strongest of them, Charles Martel (688-741), the leader of the Franks, repelled the Arab invaders and established himself as the political chief of Christendom. He used the Church as his treasury, rewarding his supporters, who rewarded theirs with offices in the Sees. It was also under him that the Church began to return land to those families who had donated it.

After Martel's death, the Church, which still looked on Gregory's stewardship as a golden age, began painstaking reform, only to find it faced another threat, this time from Martel's erstwhile allies, the Lombards. They ruled nearly all of Italy save a sliver of land that ran across the peninsula from Rome on the west coast to Ravenna on the east and included Perugia in the middle and Bologna in the north. It split their Kingdom in two. To the Lombards, it was a thorn in their side for obvious reasons. Rome called again on the Franks, led this time by Martel's son, Pepin (714-768). He had received a monastic education and, he claimed, for the love of St. Peter, threw out the Lombards. He then pronounced the Church independent from any temporal rule.

His statement, intended as a gift, turned the Church into what neither he nor the Church hierarchy had supposed it to be – a worldly kingdom. Nor did it alter the Lombard's strategic calculations. In 771, they again marched on Rome. This time it was left to Pepin's son, Charlemagne (742-814), to defend the Church. This he did with decisive action. He ended not only the Lombard's incursion but their entire kingdom and absorbed it into his own growing empire, which at its height united the Frankish dominions, parts of Spain, the old Saxon kingdom, and the Slavs. Having dealt with the Lombards, he also began to exert personal influence over the papacy. To forestall any further interference, Pope Leo crowned Charlemagne Emperor of the Romans. In doing so, he wedded the Church to its protector, leaving Charlemagne secure in the knowledge that Rome was his and that he was free to concentrate his energies and imperial ambitions elsewhere. By 814, when Charlemagne died, nearly all Christians in Europe lived under his rule.

As the eighth century rolled on, puritanism strengthened. This was as much a reaction to the threat posed by Islam, and a remedy to internal politicking, as it was a consequence of affective drift. Martel put paid to Ulmahad's ambitions in Western

Europe. His son Pepin, who had put a stop to the Lombards and finished off his father's work by chasing the Islamic armies back over the Pyrenees and down the other side, also had time to develop a strong interest in Theology. In addition to bringing his grandfather's and father's achievements to a head, Charlemagne also desired nothing less than to establish God's Kingdom on earth. This demanded, amongst other things, raising the educational standards of the clergy. Scholars were shipped from Ireland, England, and Italy to bolster existing schools and establish new ones. In the monastic foundations, cathedral schools, and Royal Palace School of the Frankish Kings, they were set to work preserving and imitating the works of Rome and Greece.[279] Louis the Pious, Charlemagne's son, who was just as determined to establish God's kingdom on earth, pursued canonical reforms, making a physically ascetic version of Benedict's Rule obligatory for all monasteries. Louis intended to model the real world in a monastic community where everyone knew their place and performed their duties correctly. Bishops became equivalent, if not superior, to kings who were expected to obey moral laws fixed by the Church. In setting the Church and worldly kingdoms against each other, Louis's desire for perfection only hastened the collapse of his father's empire. So did Louis's decision to divide its territories amongst his sons. He died, leaving his inheritance riven with bitter feuds, civil war, and vulnerable to invasion.

In England, monastic, episcopal, and song schools appeared during the sixth century, a little time after they had in Europe and Ireland. By the eighth century, schools in Northumbria (where links to Ireland were strong) also taught a much broader curriculum from grammar to astronomy, geography, music, and scripture. It was supposed that all clerics were competent in Latin. In practice, many could not read it; only some were fluent, and even fewer could produce sophisticated prose and verse.[280] This state of affairs Alfred (850-899) was determined to change, or if not everyone could manage Latin, then the vernacular would have to do. In fact, usage of the vernacular in legislation, documentation, and poetry was already established; and literate noble laymen could be found.[281] But Alfred gave education a shot in the arm. And within a century, the vernacular was firmly entrenched in religious and secular life, and it was taken for granted that the better-off layman could read.[282]

In common with Charlemagne, Louis the Pious, and Ireland's first priests, Alfred was driven by a severe form of Christianity allied, in his case,[283] with an intensely neurotic disposition. The teenage Alfred had prayed to God to substitute the hemorrhoids from which he suffered with a lighter illness to control his sexual desires.[284] He was rewarded, it seemed to him, with a worse condition. It struck on his wedding night and stayed with him for the next twenty years, during which he remained preoccupied with chastity and penitence. The new affliction remained centered on his anogenital region though its exact nature remains a mystery. 'Fics' – or pustular eruptions – and a lot of pain were involved. Beczeks disease (an inflammation of the blood vessels) is possible as it links together several of his complaints - hemorrhoids, genital abscesses, folliculitis, and, as suggested by his fear of blindness, problems with his eyes. Whatever the truth, health anxieties, extreme religiosity, and an obsession with ritual were re-presented as suffering and piety, responsibility and wisdom, and learning and morality. The model of correct behavior so formed, he projected through practice at court and as bookish learning.

Religious devotion throughout Europe lost none of its fervency over the next two hundred years, driven as before by internal concerns and external threats. Charlemagne's empire barely outlived the death of his grandson Louis II (806-876). It would take another sixty years before a different house assembled something like Charlemagne's Empire under Otto (912-973). It did not match Charlemagne's creation. But Otto descended on Rome, where he was named Holy Roman Emperor in 962. He drew the northern half of Italy into a thick wedge of territory, which extended from Hamburg in the North to Rome in the South and from Lyons in the West to Moravia in the east. And he, too, was driven by the vision of God's Kingdom on Earth. To this end, training the clergy to interpret the scriptures and administer church properties was necessary.

The return to monastic asceticism set in motion by Louis the Pious strengthened through the tenth century. It centered on Cluny, founded in 910. Benedictine in name, it took on a regimen made popular by Louis and, with the encouragement and support of the papacy, led a general reform of monastic life. House after house, abbot after abbot, was made dependent upon Cluny, jettisoning another principle of Benedict's - that each monastery should be independent rather than an extension of worldly ambition.[285]

External threats, meanwhile, were issued not from the Caliphate in the West but Turks in the East against Byzantium. The papacy whipped up hostility and promised immediate remission of sins to all those who died in battle against the pagans. One war after another was launched, each no more than fifty years apart. The first campaigns in 1095, 1147, 1187, and 1201 intended to capture and hold Jerusalem. The next in 1229, 1249, and 1291 saw the crusaders cling to their gains before they were expelled. The third continued sporadically over the next 300 years until 1571 when they had become a sorry anachronism and little more than an excuse for looting. The early crusades, however, strengthened the Church's standing in the eyes of its congregation. This fed enthusiasm for conflict and encouraged the Church to become more assertive over temporal matters. Was it not already accepted that Bishops were at least the equivalent of kings? Is not every human creature subject to the papacy if there is to be salvation? Is it not apparent that temporal powers are instituted by, and subject to, the spiritual?

Religious fervency had yet another effect. The crusades (to say nothing of domestic conflicts) were costly and weighed heavily on the royal houses. Feudalism had outlived the Empire in which Charlemagne had enshrined it, and the burden it now carried was too great. Restrictions on commerce were lifted, and merchants were left to operate freely. Where this was done, towns and cities sprouted up in small pockets of land in an otherwise feudal landscape. Stirred partly by the Clunaic drive for ecclesiastical autonomy[286] and sensing the weakening of central political authority, urban settlements grasped the opportunity to manage themselves. Towns along the north coast from London to Novgorod in the east organized themselves into the Hanseatic league. Trade routes stitching together settlements by road, river, and sea also ran south and east to Genoa, Venice, and Constantinople – a network on which German cities grew extremely wealthy by the mid-sixteenth century. In England, by the fourteenth century, a commercial web threaded by merchants amongst competing towns had helped to shape a sense of national identity. By the fifteenth century, the expansion of foreign trade through the Company of the Staple and the Company of Merchant Adventurers had transcended the urban guilds. By the late sixteenth century, the regulated companies - organizations designed to regulate the trade of their constituent merchants – were being replaced by joint-stock companies.

Commercial development meant that there was more wealth to give. The moral obligation to do so and the enthusiasm with which it was done intensified with Clunaic reform. Giving also became more focused and better organized. And what better way to demonstrate one's prosperity than by saving souls and investing in salvation, including one's own? Nobles and guilds, like the monasteries, furnished the beggary with food from their tables and feasts. The manor courts made arrangements for the elderly, infirm, and orphans raised by substitutes until they were old enough to work their parents' holdings. By the eleventh century, welfare provision was extensive in many parts of Europe. With a population of some 2-3 million, and more than 1,000 monasteries (each with infirmaries), England could boast one monastery for every 2,000-3,000 people.[287] There were, in addition, some five hundred hospitals - places where the old and the sick prepared for the end rather than sought a cure. This number had risen to 885 before the end of the twelfth century. Hospital numbers on the European mainland are less precise. Still, figures for particular towns at the beginning of the fourteen or fifteenth centuries are striking: Burgos had 30, Astorga and Valladolid 20, Leon 17, Salamanca 28, Arezzo 26, Pia 27, Rome 25, Paris 60, and Florence 30.[288] Hospitals of one sort or another shaded into all manner of places offering clothing, food, shelter, and care.

There seemed to be a place or community, religious or lay, to help whichever category one fell into - old or young, adult or child, man or woman, single mother, prostitute, clergy, traveler, pilgrim, sick, disabled, or poor and destitute. The number of people working for the Church who had to be supported also grew. England's secular and religious clergy multiplied three- or four-fold between the late twelfth and late fourteenth century to around 33,500 men or some 3% of the male population.[289] How much did the Church and charities redistribute? This is unknown, but around a sixth to a fifth of taxable incomes is a standard estimate for the fifteenth century.[290]

Schools - monastic, episcopal, song, and others – also flourished. In France, in the eleventh century, traces of elementary schools dating back to Charlemagne could be found in most provinces.[291] In England, grammar schools, business schools, and higher schools appeared in the twelfth and thirteenth centuries. Loose groups of teachers and students followed the lead of urban artisans and merchants and established their own *universitas* or guilds. The practice began informally, even spontaneously,[292] amongst the medieval guilds. Networks of students clustered around itinerant teachers; the clusters became faculties, and faculties became the university. It was no coincidence they appeared when towns and cities were multiplying. Professionals of all kinds were needed in these dense and complex societies. The Church desired to reconcile Christianity with Plato, Aristotle, Euclid, Archimedes, Porphyrus, and others whose original texts were being discovered or re-discovered. The uncertainty of individuality, the perishability of the soul, the eternal nature of the world, the bare and impersonal perfection of God, and Man's existence for the polity, were views not easy to square with Christian beliefs. The pope or local royalty gradually assumed authority to establish a university, issuing a license as a papal bull or a charter. They remained, in essence, nurseries for church and bureaucracy. A degree was needed for those entering the church but not for practicing law or accountancy. By 1300 there were 20 universities; by 1500, seventy were strewn across Europe.

Chapter 22

A Second Affective Revolution, 1250-1550

An affective mood, having permeated the arts, charity, and learning, dissipated and dried out during the sixteenth century. Magic, mysticism, religion, mathematics, geometry, astrology, and numerology, melded during that long affective spell, were now infused with certainty. Thus a new approach to the natural world crystallized - science.

Puritanism was fading by the end of the twelfth century, if not earlier. After more than two hundred years of commerce and urban living, a powerful affective mood suffused Europe by the mid-thirteenth century. It vented itself through sculpture, music, art, literature, and philosophy - activities concentrated in the relative wealth of the urban islands. It blew first where Puritanism and alienation were most intense. Cluny was such a place. The liveliness, fluency, and self-delight wrought into human figures by the masons there seemed like a gibe at the po-faced and marked the beginning of a movement that would take Europe by storm. The 'Clunaic' style later shone through Brunaschelli's humanistic architecture (1379-1446); through Giotto (1266-1337), who translated life naturally and unforced onto flat canvas; and through Donatello (1383-1466) and Pisano (1250-1330) as it made its way to Chartres and on to Pisa and Pistoia and Florence.

It was at Cluny - under its Abbot, Peter the Venerable – that Abelard (1079-1142) ended up shortly before his death. He argued that a doctrine is not to be believed because God had said it but because we are convinced by reason that it is so. A century later, Aquinas (1225-1274) managed to suture humanism to the supernatural throughout vast tracts of Christian thought. Understanding and acknowledging God is neither a given nor dependent upon faith but realized through reason and argument. And while we can experience true virtue only through divine intervention, we must consent to be infused with those virtues. Even without such intervention, we can still be virtuous as humans.

By the mid-fifteenth century, the Church had joined the humanistic movement. Pope Nicholas V (1447-55) appointed Lorenzo Valla (1406-1457) as apostolic scribe and, later, as papal secretary. A scholar, priest, and humanist, he declaimed monastic life, sympathized with the indulgence of natural appetites, and accused St. Augustine of heresy. The next pope but one[293] *was* a humanist, though during his tenure Pious II curbed the license he had shown earlier in his life.

As the affective mood strengthened, the charitable revolution of the eleventh and twelfth centuries matured. Charity became less about giving and more about devoting one's life to service, just as it was for those who had witnessed and survived Rome's collapse. When the Black Death swept through Europe in the mid-fourteenth century, and for a decade or more after it had passed, fear, hope, and relief turned giving back into a transaction once again. Then came simple disobedience as peasants refused to pay rents and dues and an unwillingness and inability on the part of the landowners to do much about it.[294] Vocational charity returned in the fifteenth century. Charitable organizations – from hospitals and bedehouses and Maison Dieu to beguines - grew in number. Redistributive channels proliferated: clergy and Church gave to parish fraternities; manors gave cash and grain and helped with building expenses; food was left at monastery gates and with beggars' guilds; the crown ensured that bread and ale were sold at fair prices and that grain was not exported during times of shortage.[295]

Education was vivified, though more so outside the educational organization than within it. The universities had not taken long to become conformist and staid and attracted criticism for being overly technical and rigid in thought and style. They were also expensive. Parents, sponsors, or patrons hired private tutors. Nobles placed their sons in court or a bishop's household for their upbringing. Those further down the social hierarchy hired the local priest, his assistant, or the parish clerk.[296] In Italy, boys were commonly sent to work with an artisan. Da Vinci trained at a workshop in Florence. Michelangelo was tutored in Florence until the age of thirteen. But otherwise, he learned his craft informally, except for a year or so at a workshop and then two or three years in a discussion group (described as an academy) in the de Medici's household. Indeed, it is fair to say that the most important intellectual developments before the twentieth century took place *outside* the universities. Renaissance humanism grew up in Italy from the thirteenth century amongst professionals and officials and did not enter the universities' curricula until the fifteenth century.[297] More than two hundred years later, another dramatic shift in thought (the Enlightenment) swirled around them.[298] Not until the late eighteenth and nineteenth centuries did universities become more secular. Even then, many discoveries that helped drive the industrial revolution were not theirs or were made only in loose association with them.

A Resurgence of Puritanism (1550-1750)

'Germany' comprised more than three hundred principalities, making up a large part of the Holy Roman Empire. Each principality was independent, and each town and city within it had a deal of autonomy. The settlements were planned and organized well, and life within them became evermore routine from the end of the fifteenth century and through the sixteenth century. The townspeople became wealthy on trade. They were patrons of the arts and standard-bearers of the Renaissance. Architecture and material culture followed tastes, styles, and fashions made popular by the elites. The burgers (the citizens) patterned their domestic lives around the family. Their lives outside the family were organized according to profession and guild or reflected their status as patricians. Manners became more standardized and complex and covered everything from behavior at the dining table, bathing, and toiletry to the colors and style of clothes – a matter with which sumptuary laws were also concerned. By the mid-sixteenth century, mechanical clocks were commonplace. City officials made official time as precise as possible, divided it into thinner and thinner slices, and scheduled the day accordingly. Living became predictable, ordered, and constant. The stage was set for a drift into Puritanism.

Luther (1483-1546) did not object to certainty. He railed against wealth, high culture, and intellectuals; against Michelangelo and Raphael; against the Church and its indulgences; and against the complacency that certainty bred. He branded the Church materialistic and hypocritical and demanded that true Christians withdraw from the world, renounce wealth, and commune with God. Luther's ideas struck a chord with the peasants at first. Only when he turned on them and sided with the nobility did they discover that he was a political operator and a social conservative at heart. He demanded unquestioning acceptance of the princes' divine right to rule. It was a shrewd move. The princes objected to political interference from the Church and emperor and distrusted the merchants' enthusiasm for amassing wealth. Thus Luther carved sure footholds in northern and eastern Germany, Denmark, and Scandinavia. Southern Germany, Austria, and the Rhineland stayed Catholic, though urban communes inspired by him there and in Switzerland refused to tolerate Rome.

Calvin (1509-1564), who was Luther's junior by more than twenty years, found life in France easygoing at first, if only because it was a much larger territory than any of the fragmented German principalities. But society was tightening up quickly and noticeably. By 1515 a kingdom whose ruler was expected to rely on income from his own land was becoming more like a monarchical state with authority to extract revenue from everyone and everything. Francis I made Paris his Chief Residence and firmed up his control over tax and the more important towns and cities. Other settlements he viewed primarily as a source of income and was content to leave them with substantial autonomy as long as they coughed up. A council - a corporation of magistrates and administrators who controlled prices, supervised the market, organized defense, and maintained the city walls – was given power over high justice. Lawyers replaced the artisans who once dominated the urban government. Throughout France and much of Europe, the legal profession flourished. Law courts grew in number and influence. So did university law schools, high-court magistrates, and lowly rural practitioners and their office staff. The profession helped order and legitimize the monarch's control over income and was itself a source of income.

But Calvin, who had his own *idées fixes,* saw nothing wrong in profit and wealth, provided it was earned fairly and honestly through hard work (rather than off the back of the poor) and not displayed ostentatiously. Nor was there anything respectable in poverty if down to idleness. The real world, he believed, is where the true Christian must live and, through living, do God's work. His natural ally was the merchant.

One did not have far to travel from these assertions to disdain for sacred images and grand religious buildings. Nor was the threat to the Catholic Church and the social order posed by these ideas lost on monarch, priest, and lawyer. So Calvin retreated to Geneva, a prosperous market in the grip of merchants whose government was ready to turn the city into a version of Calvin's model Christian community. The Netherlands, the Rhineland, northwest Switzerland, and south and southwest France also favored Calvinism. His ideas found support in Scotland and England, where the monarchy created the Anglican – a blend of Protestant and Catholic.

In response to northern Puritanism, Rome rediscovered the will to reform, to harmonize education and even the dress of its priests, and, through the confessional box, to wheedle its way into the most intimate thoughts of its congregation. Nevertheless, the growing religious divide created insoluble problems for the Holy Roman Emperor, Charles V. His domains included Germany, Switzerland, most of Italy, parts of France, and slices of the Netherlands, Austria, and Eastern Europe. Charles had also inherited Spain together with additional possessions elsewhere in Europe. 'Germany,' the Empire's heart, possessed a rallying point of sorts in linguistic commonalities and the idea of a Reich. But in practice, it was little more than a bundle of territories whose members alternately fought each other and banded together as allies. The whole body comprised feudatories stretching from the Atlantic to Hungary in the east. Unable to square the circle and drained by the futility of trying to do so, Charles abdicated, handing title and possessions to Ferdinand, his brother, and Philip, his son. Neither man fared any better. Philip quickly took up the sword, and his campaigns in the Netherlands and against England succeeded only in pushing all sides further apart.

In the first decade of the seventeenth century, Protestants and Catholics organized themselves into a Union and League respectively to defend their interests. Any religious unity that the Holy Roman Empire professed broke down. The war, which came eventually in 1618 and lasted for thirty years, was part religious and part imperial conquest of the German princes in whose defense both France and Sweden became embroiled. The war decimated settlement after settlement and delivered the coup de grace to an economy suffering even before conflict broke out. And as routes to the East via the Cape opened to avoid mainland Europe's fractious states, trade shifted to the Atlantic coast.

The princes, though, had their liberty guaranteed by the Treaty of Westphalia in 1648. Over them, the Hapsburg emperor now had no more than titular status. But he did not go unrewarded: Hapsburg's rule over Austria, Bohemia, and Hungary was recognized. The Church was left with the least. In a rage, the pope, in his bull '*Zelo Domus Dei,*' proclaimed the treaty null and void. Promptly ignored, his declarations merely confirmed just how impotent the Church had become.

In England, meanwhile, civil war ripped apart the Kingdom and left it under Puritan rule for nearly twenty years. Ordinary lay courts were charged with quashing sin. Adultery was rendered punishable by death. Soldiers entered private houses to ensure the Sabbath was being observed (and being observed correctly). Sunday sports in villages were prohibited. And Maypoles were cut down. The counter-reaction was, as on the European mainland, decisive. Anti-clerical feelings were primarily responsible for the Restoration of 1660 and the anti-Romanist or Glorious Revolution of 1688 after James II tried to foist Catholicism on a people already tired of religion.[299]

Welfare and colonialism

The dissolution of the monasteries in England in the 1530s hit the poor badly. In response, a direct chain of administration from the monarch's privy council to local grandees (county magistrates and local property owners) was established.[300] It marked the start of a taxation system to finance discretionary assistance to the elderly, the ill, unemployed, and others hurt by high food prices. The poor laws introduced in 1597 and 1601 subsequently extended and codified existing practice, compelling each parish to provide basic food, shelter, and clothing for the needy, financed by local taxation on the well-to-do.

Putting figures on transfers such as these before the late nineteenth century is little more than guesswork. Most acts of giving – official, unofficial, secular, religious, individual, and collective - went unrecorded or, if recorded, are too patchy to make any overview reliable. Estimates vary from 0.05% of Finland's GDP in 1880 to 2.5% in England and Wales in the early nineteenth century[301] and 11% (of GNP) in 1850.[302] However, an indication of their significance can be derived from the timing of economic growth and surges in poor relief.

Take, for instance, the increase in per capita GDP after the Black Death. This marked a step-change in economic growth. The new income level was sustained over the remainder of the fourteenth century, through the entire fifteenth century, and into the sixteenth century. Two gentle pulses were experienced during this period. One occurred after the dissolution of the monasteries and the reorganization of welfare by the monarch. The second pulse coincided with the poor laws introduced at the turn of the century. It is also worth noting that the shift to commerce from a dependency on land continued in the background.

A second step change in income occurred in the second part of the seventeenth century but then stalled in the first half of the eighteenth century. The market wound down as the inequalities it created deepened. Attitudes towards the poor became more hostile. 'Rogue' came to be used more commonly than 'poor.' Workhouses sprouted up. Colonialism flourished, driven quite explicitly by the need to expand English markets. Two English companies, Virginia and Massachusetts Bay, spent large sums (equivalent to an economic cost of about £10 billion today) financing 20,000 colonists in New England between 1630 and 1643. Twice that number of colonists were sent out to Virginia and other colonies. More than a century later, shortly before the American Revolution, the colonial population had risen to 2.5 million. About half of the colonies' exports were destined for Great Britain and Ireland. The colonies were also the motherland's most important customers, just as it was the colonies' most important supplier. Many of the colonies' exports were more expensive for Britain than they would have been if the colonies had been independent.[303]

Throughout the eighteenth century, the trade of the English East India Company also prospered, largely at the expense of the French and Dutch, and other Europeans. By the start of the nineteenth century, Britain was the source of at least half of the value of India's imports and the destination for the bulk of India's exports either for use in Britain or for re-export to Europe. Whatever costs the British government shouldered, English companies and merchants had made hundreds of millions of pounds by 1813.[304]

Education

Schools in England grew from around three dozen or so in the fifteenth century to about five hundred during the second half of the seventeenth century. These included: petty schools, which catered to the bulk of the population and taught basic reading and writing; the lower grammar and free schools, which taught advanced English, mathematics, and accounting; and grammar schools where classical language, grammar, and religious instruction were taught in preparation for entry into Oxford and Cambridge and the Inns of Court. The number of university entrants also increased, peaking between the late sixteenth and early seventeenth centuries at around 2.5% of seventeen-year-olds - a figure that was not matched again until after World War I and not exceeded until after World War II.

This educational pulse reflected various concerns. One was a desire to avoid the sins of ignorance, purposelessness, and idleness. Favoring a university with a donation and creating opportunities for the less well-off was also a way of demonstrating success without committing yet another sin – bragging. The rigid curricula, severe instruction, and spartan life appealed to the students' parents and sponsors, too. An ability to hold one's own around the dinner table counted just as much. It was not, therefore, primarily in schools or universities that intellectual development took place. There were one or two bright spots – Newton had pursued gravity and alchemy with equal vigor at Cambridge. But, as during the Renaissance, it was outside the universities that new thinking flourished. They suffered further by association and fell into decline when the Puritan state collapsed, the monarchy was restored, and religion slipped into disrepute. The Enlightenment and the industrial revolution washed around their impermeable walls and lapped at their gates. Slow to take on humanist ideas, universities and schools were now reluctant to consider science.

Science

The affective surge had petered out by the seventeenth century leaving a concoction of religion, mysticism, magic, animism, legalism, humanism, music, mathematics, geometry, medicine, and numerology around which boundaries were uncertain. Possibility, allegory, and analogy were allowed free play. It was extraordinarily fertile ground.

Copernicus (1473-1543), a contemporary of Luther, found amongst Greek philosophers those who believed the earth moved. Philolaus and Hicetas thought it a sphere that, together with the sun, revolves around a central fire that regulates the universe. Aristarchus thought the earth and other planets moved around the sun. This idea Copernicus revived because it made for a mathematical account of planetary movements that was simpler and more effective and therefore closer to God's mind. In doing so, he broke with Ptolemy's conception of a stationary earth around which the sun and other bodies revolved and explained why the stars appeared fixed - an idea that also suited the Christian because it put man and earth at the center of God's creation and interests. Copernicus's theory was attractive to other astrologers and astronomers, not least because it could interpret many existing observations of planetary movements. But he provided no proof to set aside Ptolemy and settle the matter. So his theory remained just that during his lifetime and for some time after his death in 1543.

The following year Gilbert (1544-1603) was born. He came to favor the Copernican view. First, though, he spent a good deal of time and money experimenting with iron and loadstones to test their properties and significance. In doing so, he confirmed some and rejected many of the supposed medical and other properties often attributed to magnets. He distinguished between the attractive properties of electrics (which would attract most other objects) and magnetism which existed only amongst magnets and between magnets and iron. The earth, he concluded, was a giant loadstone. He believed this explained the movements of the heavenly bodies and kept one side of the moon facing the earth, whose ability to move testified to its animate nature.

Galileo (1564-1642) also favored Copernican theory. And, like Copernicus and Gilbert, he explained the forces which ordered the universe as a natural desire or appetite established by divine providence. God chose not to interfere in these desires because to do so would nullify the abilities he had given to man to understand them. That ability was gifted as mathematics - a nexus between the thought of men and the mind of God. Aside from mathematics, only empirical observation was needed to understand the world. These trumped 'authorities' (the referencing that we rely on today) who were merely assumed to give clear witness to the truth. Descartes (1596-1650) went further, arguing that the only way to reach truth was to begin by doubting everything, including Aristotle, Christianity, and tradition. But in his Delphic pronouncement that the pineal gland anchored the soul, he kept good company with Galen and many others over the previous fourteen centuries.

Galileo had much in common with Gilbert. In Gilbert's case, though, observation and experimentation were traditions in which the practices of elite artisans and manual workers in mining, smithing, compass making, navigation, and sailing were rooted. The techniques of magicians (especially as set out in Pierre de Maricort's epistle on the magnet) also owed a great deal to experimentation and observation. Nor was astronomy easily separated from astrology, in which Kepler (1571-1630), Galileo, and Copernicus were each accomplished. For Kepler, it was a way to understand the influence of the planets and stars on weather, geology, state affairs, and other aspects of human behavior and the human body. He also drew on Pythagorean mysticism and numerology. He suggested that Euclid's five regular solids determined the distances between the six known planets. He saw a relationship between these shapes and the lengths of strings whose vibrations produced music consonances (an interest of the Pythagoreans). Beyond all this, and operating on these phenomena most directly through geometry, is God. In dealing with how the planets, the moon, and the sun exerted the influence they did upon the earth (and with how the earth reacted to those influences), Kepler invoked: light (from the planets and the moon); heat from the sun (warming the air around the earth and so altering its weather); and 'forces,' which he referred to variously as power or laws (in the legal sense). He also invoked the Trinity: the sun was the father, the fixed stars were the son, and the ethereal medium through which the sun worked to move the planets, was the holy spirit. This was probably more than allegory.

From around 1560, attitudes began to harden noticeably. For Luther and Calvin, an understanding of the planets' movements enriched the adoration of God so long as the interpretation of their significance remained the business of scripture alone. But now, one man was dead, and the other dying, and neither had control over how their ideas would be shaped and plied. The Bible was treated as an encyclopedia of facts and knowledge. Further strands of thought that Gilbert, Copernicus, Galileo, Kepler, and others had worked with likewise ossified.

Only in the aftermath of conflict, once religion thoroughly discredited itself and an affective mood gathered, were ideas about the natural world and methods of understanding disentangled from the spiritualism and mysticism from which so much was borrowed. Defense of literal scripture also quickly fell away in the second half of the seventeenth century, and theologians, taking a leaf from Aquinas, began to stress once again the need for evidence to explain. It was in this atmosphere that Newton published his *Principia* in 1687. In it, gravity supplants motive intelligence, souls, animism, and magnetism as explanations for the movement of the planets and sun. It was a measurable force, and its effects were predictable and understandable. It did not invoke Greek philosophy, the occult, or a hidden purpose. Yet, like Boyle, Newton retained his Christianity. Newton also spent at least as much time and energy on alchemy. In his psyche, natural laws operated separately and objectively in one sphere, while religion and mysticism were confined to another. Yet the two mixed and had some influence on one another. The supernatural was not allowed to dictate to the natural, but, somewhat immodestly, he looked to God (who, Newton believed, was constantly perfecting and tinkering) to explain the differences between the predictions he made and the exact movements of the planets.

The arts

Puritanism benefitted science in some measure, but cast a chill over the arts. Painting in northern Europe remained medieval in its rigidity despite Italian influences and the Eyck brothers' innovations. Only portraiture survived in England, where the Puritans questioned the legitimacy of religious paintings.

The written word broadcasts meaning with greater ambiguity and is better suited to intolerance. Friendship, heterosexual and homosexual passion, and every other aspect of human relationships and emotion were expressed and, at least in Shakespeare's (1564-1616) writing, without dogma. Yet by 1640, as Puritanism neared its zenith and reached every corner of life, his sonnets were either changed or excised as new editions sought to cut out the ungodly, unwholesome, and impure. In the face of this silliness, writers and their characters turned to pretense, to ludic selves that were not quite one thing or another. Milton (1608-74) wrote plainly if he wished but preferred the allegorical and uncertain. He laid a path through obstinate devotion – for he was Puritan and supporter of Cromwell and regicide - to an affective world in which ideas are merely hinted at. Wren (1632-1723) also found his way there through ambiguity. Astronomer and architect, neither entirely classical nor baroque in style, his sense of beauty was neither customary nor natural. The

Dutch genre, too, let simplicity speak. Painters caught people at unremarkable moments in their everyday lives. Yet the plainness and ordinariness of the best of these artists, notably Vermeer (1632-75) and Hooch (1629-78), puzzles. Silent but pregnant with meaning; precise but fuzzy and ambiguous; intensely atmospheric and evocative, but evocative of what is hard to say. To look at the *Lady Standing at the Virginal* is to be brought into a somehow familiar room and thrown a glance by someone in whom your presence stirs a fleeting memory before her mind returns elsewhere. Like Titian in his later work, Caravaggio brings an extraordinary 'thereness' to religious and mythological scenes and their allegories. Emotional immediacy is realized through exactness and obscuration, the brightly lit and almost black, leaving the mind to establish 'the truth' for itself.

The philosopher has a harder time of it. Locke gets there on occasions, intentionally or otherwise, not through precise statements but fitful rawness and doubt. People have natural rights independent of the mores and laws of any given society - a view that rendered illicit any claim by a monarch to rule by divine right. But he left so much that is contradictory and seemingly incomplete. Where do laws come from? What are their first principles, and how does one get to those laws? What do rights mean for the duties that exist if society is to work? Many writers have tried to provide answers. Though perhaps it is those gaps that keep the writing fresh and powerful and immediate.

Chapter 23

A Third Affective Revolution, 1700-1830

The irruptions and intolerance of the seventeenth century created conditions from which an affective surge and an industrial revolution emerged.

If the application of the steam engine is its defining quality, then we can push back the start of the industrial revolution in England to the late seventeenth century. The engine was at work in mines up and down the country from that time on (see Figure 23.1[305]). The reasons for its spread are not complex. It was applied first to the manufacture of textiles. Cotton could not be grown in England, and its import, especially from India, was expensive. Mechanization made it possible to bring in raw materials and make and sell the cloth in England or even India for less than Indian-made cloth. Once it was shown to work for textiles, why shouldn't mechanization work for other materials and goods too? The principle was simple: the production of more and more goods brought down the price for more and more people. In the eighteenth century, the number of engines used in manufacturing in settlements could be counted on one hand. A hundred years on, the substitution of wood and stone with iron had begun in earnest. After another fifty years, it was at full tilt.

The industrial revolution presupposed competition, population growth, and commerce. Each element quickens the other and is further enlivened by the higher densities they foster together, creating a virtuous circle. The switch from agriculture to commerce supplies the wherewithal for population growth. Higher densities facilitate the flow and movement of people and ideas. It also encourages population growth by presenting more opportunities for sexual liaisons and marriage outside kinship groups. Higher densities also excite technological and organizational change and constitute a ready market and labor force.

Density also helped cultivate emotional change, which eased the path to more effective organizations, creating yet another virtuous circle. Love had had little to do with marriage in the mid-fifteenth century. Discipline within the family was harsh, and children were still 'counters in a game of family aggrandizement, useful to buy money and estates or to secure the support of powerful patrons.'[306] A century later, matrimonial freedom and the 'love marriage' were viewed more sympathetically, at least on the stage. In practice, child marriage was still common. Another century later and the great crisis of the seventeenth century generated the conditions for affective individualism[307] or what some have called an affective revolution.[308] By the eighteenth century, an interest in relationships and people in themselves was permeating one society after another. Love was more likely than not to be accepted as the basis of marriage, and children treated were no longer pawns in games of power. [309] Explored and experimented with, [310] emotions were concentrated in the arts, literature, and music. The intellectual constraints imposed by Bach (1685 - 1750) on his music gave it remarkable intensity and directness. Mozart (1756-91), whose life was confined to the last half of the eighteenth century, poured out music so unencumbered it seemed to have written itself.

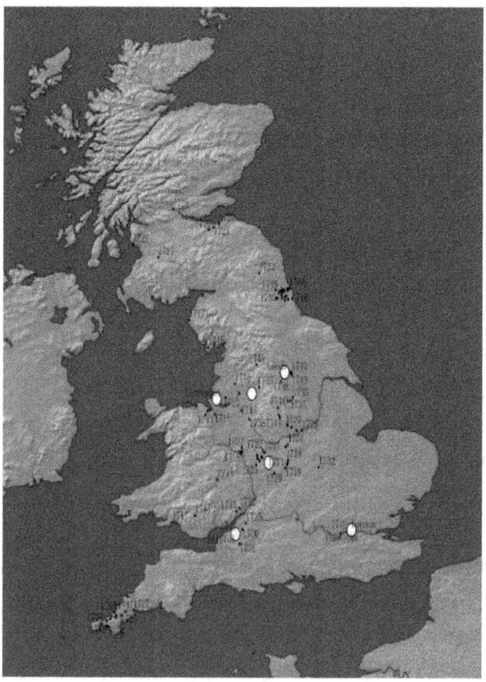

(Left) Figure 23.1 Location of Steam Engines in England, Wales and Scotland upto 1750

It might be asked how densities rose and remained high before the industrial revolution, given the problem of disease? Cities, it is often said, were so unhealthy they had to be fed by streams of young migrants who died in large numbers. Life expectancy in England in 1700 was 36. By 1811 it had risen to 41, and there it stayed until 1871. The average height of adults, which increased until the later eighteenth century, fell during the first half of the nineteenth century.

Improvements in health came eventually, but not until the last quarter of that century. So why, for 120 years, did young adults throw themselves into these death traps? Better wages cannot be ruled out, but that is not convincing. It is more likely that cities then were not as dangerous as we think today. There are several reasons for this.

First, we cannot be sure of the available figures. Before the start of the nineteenth century, there were only estimates of the population. These are arrived at and take on a certain firmness through consensus and the habit of citation. Moreover, the first census in 1801, the first attempt since Doomsday at a systematic and empirical description of the population, might have found people that no one had bothered looking for, armchair scholars had not envisaged, and records had overlooked. Parish records, for instance, noted baptisms, burials, and marriages, not births, deaths, and sexual relationships. There may have been more people than records show: population levels might have been higher for longer before industrialization took hold. Various events may have pushed up and sustained these levels. These include the practice of inoculation against smallpox in the latter part of the eighteenth century. Another was an improvement in domestic hygiene when brick floors in houses were laid, doing away with earthen ones. And a series of good harvests in the 1730s.

This first problem may have accentuated a second. High infant mortality from infectious diseases (especially gastrointestinal) creates short life expectancies statistically. But if children survived their early years and made it to the age of twenty, they had a good chance of living to 60 or longer.

Third, life in the countryside could be riskier than in the cities. Links between a person, vectors, pathogens, and environmental conditions vary greatly. Smallpox, for example, preferred dense populations, young hosts, and relatively dry conditions. It could spread rapidly, killing mainly the young, leaving nine out of ten alive, and conferring a degree of immunity. Primary pneumonic plague spread at a slower pace through close and sustained contact - usually with whoever was caring for the sick. It circulated more quickly in rural areas because people were more likely to spend more time in each other's homes than urban dwellers.

It's also possible that centuries of relatively dense living conditioned people to survive the crowded conditions brought later by industrialization. This also helps explain why atherosclerosis and cancers are so common in the West today: such diseases might originate in unrelenting attacks on the body, its constant state of defense and inflammation, and so are associated with aging. Medical advances are just beginning to mitigate the downside of immunity generated by high population densities over long periods.

The fact is that commercial settlements were, in most cases, already densely populated. They had become so over the previous centuries of development. A large population comprising both market and a workforce right on its doorstep made those first engines, which were expensive, viable. Londoners were packed together, more than 700 to each hectare in 1720, falling to 500 by the middle of that century. In Leeds, the figure was somewhere between 400 and 500 by the 1720s. Liverpool was close to 200, Birmingham was nearer 400 and Manchester 450. The fact that the engine could be run twenty-four hours and demanded shifts of workers sucked still more people into the mill. The construction of houses around the factories to shelter their workers further swelled the population. The physical expansion of the built-up areas and populations then saw densities fall over the next 180 years despite occasional spikes. London's density nearly hit 700 again by 1790 before falling to 480 by 1832. Densities in Leeds rose again by the turn of the nineteenth century before dropping sharply in the 1850s. Liverpool, Birmingham, and Manchester experienced similar fluctuations.

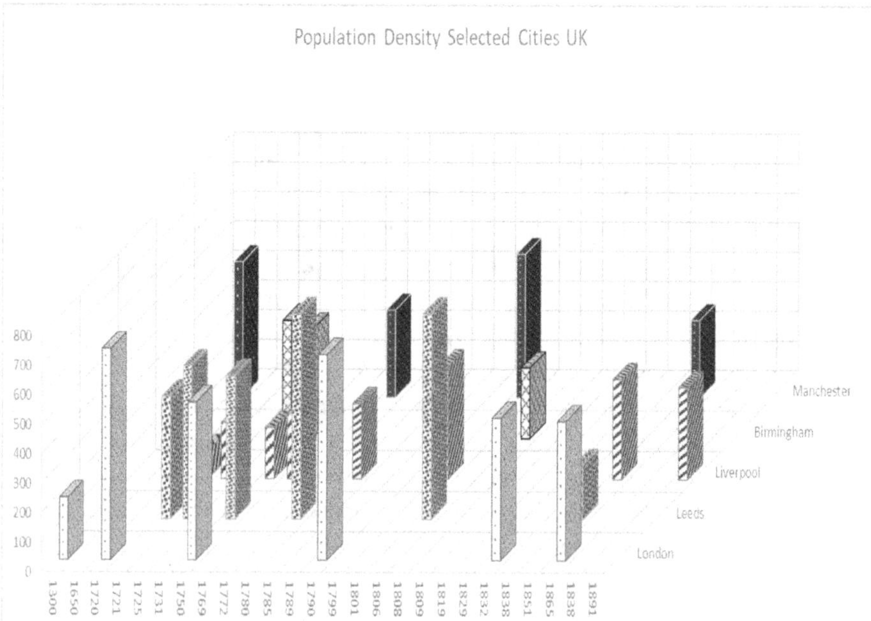

Figure 23.2 Population density, selected English cities

That settlements were not too distant from each other magnified density's influence on economic growth via markets and labor. A figure that keeps repeating itself is 300 kilometers: the distance within which preindustrial settlements that subsequently industrialize clump together. The distance is manageable in about a week by wagon or three or four days on horseback or coach when the weather is good. This is enough to keep an eye on commercial interests and feed manufacturing with everyday items.

High-density clumps, set within striking distance of each other, made the comparatively fast exchange of information and ideas possible. The evolution of science and technology in Europe owed a tremendous debt to commercial and other contacts with the Middle East, India, and China over many centuries. But as important as this was, the generation and transmission of knowledge built up through trial and error by those who often had more practical experience than formal or theoretical education. Even without a systematic understanding of the principles of nature, great things were possible, as Europe's cathedrals showed.

Germany

Germany's population densities equaled or surpassed those found in English towns and cities before the introduction of steam engines. It is also notable that a version of the steam engine had powered a fountain in Germany in the seventeenth century before it was used in Altenweddingen's mines in the 1770s. It took another hundred years before the application of steam to manufacturing was widespread and rapid industrialization was underway.

One reason for the comparatively slow build-up was that 'Germany' comprised congeries of independent states. It had taken more than two hundred years for these to be united through the efforts of one - Brandenburg. It had swollen into Prussia as it expanded west, east, and south. It also benefitted from Napoleon's decision to organize the German states outside Prussia and Austria into a confederation and bestow a constitution and a French code of law or something close to it. They retained complete sovereignty after his defeat, though, in practice, they relied on Prussia and Austria for physical protection. In 1818 the Zollverein – a unified tariff system, or common market, centered on and extended from Prussia - made trade between the confederation and the rest easier. Thus, by degrees, the impotence of the states and the necessity for German unification became evident.

Another reason was that towns and cities were slow to recognize the advantage of unity. They had long enjoyed a good deal of independence, and their guilds did their utmost to resist outsiders. Migrants drained the communities, disturbed their social balance and hierarchies, and were often seen as little more than vagabonds, shit-hens, shiftless, and poor.[311] The new machines and engines from England were blamed for creating migrants, attracting them, employing them, and thus threatening the livelihood of the towns.

Nevertheless, people were on the move, and they had to go somewhere. Population growth and crop failures in 1845-6 highlighted the point. The states recognized this and did what they could to persuade their towns to yield. And not all the towns resisted. Saxony, already a center for textiles, was the smallest and most densely populated kingdom with well-established long-distance routes dating back to the fifteenth and sixteenth centuries and peppered with inns and paved sections. It saw a ready labor force and market in the growing population and migrants. And, in new technology and practices, it saw a way to improve production, reduce costs, secure larger markets, and generate more wealth. The kingdom's first water-powered spinning machine was built in 1782 in Chemnitz, whose population density had already returned to about 156-200 people to each square hectare, figures last seen before the Thirty Years' War. To the east of this town lay Dresden (469 in 1790) and, still further east, Breslau (443 in 1757). To the south was Munich, where, early in the nineteenth century, densities had climbed back to levels (over 400 per hectare) last experienced in 1300. To the west lay Frankfurt-am-main (300 in 1700). Leipzig (555 by the middle of the eighteenth century) to the northwest was already the most important trading center in eastern Europe. And 150km to the north was Berlin (with well over 300 per hectare in 1700). Each settlement drew on the other. A carding machine followed in Chemnitz in 1792. By 1800 a fully mechanized cotton mill was operating. By 1817 Chemnitz was known as Saxony's first factory town and given the name Manchester of Saxony. By 1864 there were 64 machine factories and 57 steam engines at work employing over 6,000 people.[312]

Another clump of densely populated centers developed further to the west on the Rhine – an area that would quickly match and surpass Saxony's economic significance. Like Saxony, densities before industrialization were already comparatively high. By the eighteenth century, towns with populations in the tens of thousands hugged both sides of the river. There were also generous deposits of ore and coal to be found.

Two years after a textile factory appeared in Chemnitz, another was put up at Ratinger just a few kilometers from Dusseldorf (148 per square hectare in 1800). But the industry that would soon come to dominate was iron and steel. A steam engine, brought into Bochum in 1799 to raise water from the mines, was followed by iron and steel at Essen in 1812, by a rolling mill at Stervede in 1830, and coke smelting at Mulheim.

Powerful though the resistance to factories and migrants was, greater still was political drive and competition, population growth, and the demonstration effect of Chemnitz and other towns. Steam engines popped up all over Germany. Town walls came down. The momentum for unification gathered pace.

The new German Empire was established in 1871. Prussian functionaries took to heart the ancient goals of economic growth and population growth. If kingdoms were to survive, they needed people; if the crown were to meet its responsibilities to the people, commerce would have to be encouraged. It was the only way kingdoms and populace could compete with the evident power amassing in England, Belgium, and elsewhere as the industrial revolution spread. Austria was formally excluded from the new Empire. Five years earlier, in 1866, Prussia had launched a short war, defeated the Austrians, and compelled them to accept its ambitions. Remnants of the Hapsburgs and memories of the Holy Roman Empire lingered and made it too cumbersome to digest. Yet it was too valuable an ally against radical liberals in Germany, and the sheer number of soldiers it could muster was vital to Germany's strategic interests. In return for people – men to support the English against Napoleon – an infusion of gold temporarily stimulated the Austrian economy in the 1820s and 1830s.

America

The colonization of the United States began with a ring of small settlements along the Eastern seaboard, the southern coast, and the west coast in the seventeenth century. The settlers moved inland slowly. They followed the rivers where they could, and where they could not, they forged land trails. They circumvented the Appalachians to the north and breached them to the south. As they went, they established way stations – landmarks, defensive positions, victualling points, trading stations, or places to exchange goods with native Americans or other Europeans.

The general movement inland halted in the 1840s, after which land purchases opened up the remaining territories. Migration then resumed: north along the Missouri River before striking west over the Rockies and down the other side, meeting up with those who had settled along the west coast after arriving there on boats.

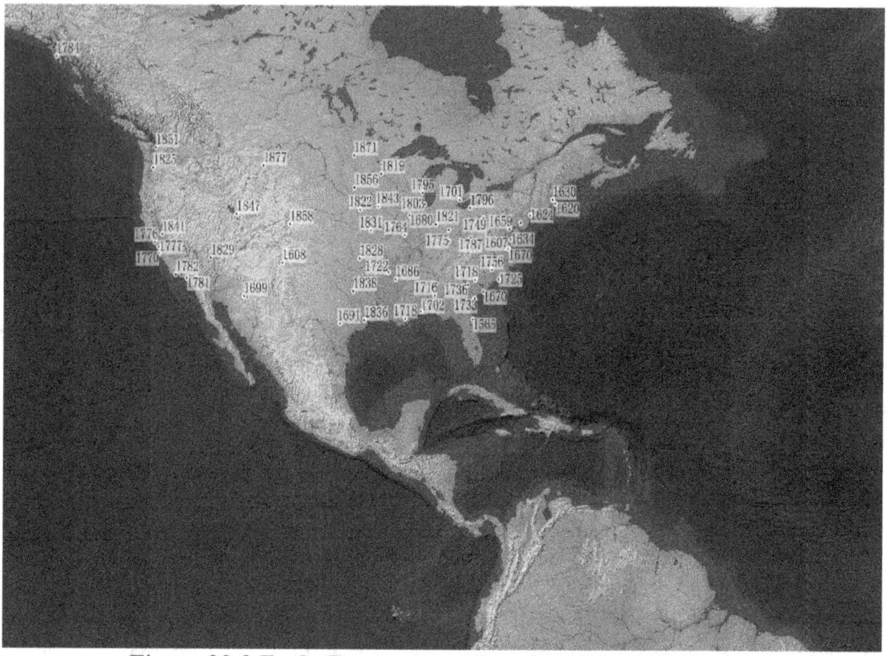

Figure 23.3 Early European settlement of North America

Meanwhile, the first towns on the east coast grew denser even before introducing the steam engine. These settlements were often sited on small tracts of land, circumscribed, and easy to defend. Boston (287 before 1830) perched on a land-tied island; New York (281) on an island proper; Philadelphia (227) on a stretch picked out by the Indians; and Baltimore (140) nestled between two points of land at the head of a river. The people who settled there brought crafts and knowledge of urban life. In Boston, as early as 1647, there were six woodworking trades and seven metalworkers as well as leather manufacturers, weavers, ropemakers, feltmakers, brickmakers, and other industries.[313] In Philadelphia, there was anything and everything from blacksmiths and wheelwrights to hatters, brewers, cabinet-makers, and lime burners. As in Europe, they relied on muscle, the wind, and waterpower. Manufactories were set up in and around the new settlements. Ironworks were ubiquitous because they used a good deal of water and other heavy raw materials. Twenty forges lay within a twelve-mile radius, from Jamestown in 1621 to Lyn, Bridgewater, Easton, and Middleton.

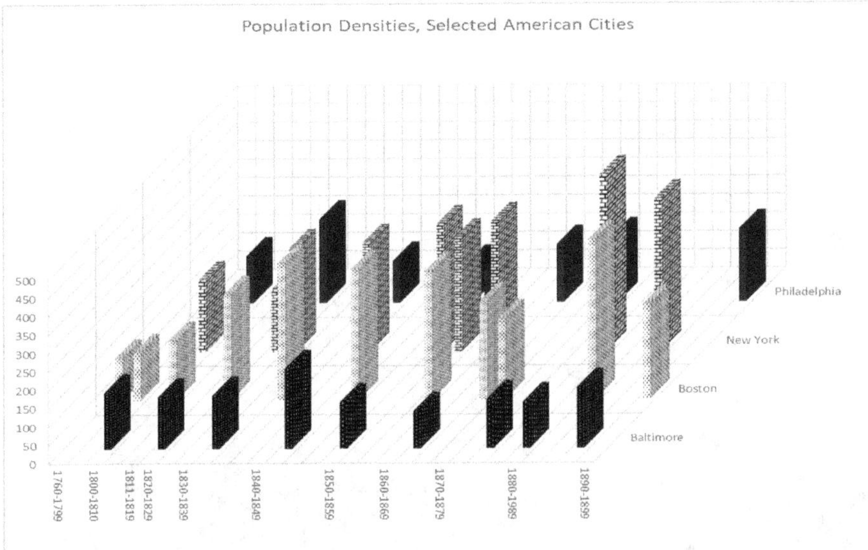

Figure 23.4 Population densities in selected American cities.

The first steam engines appeared in the last three decades of the eighteenth century. At first, their use to propel boats on water and carriages on land attracted more interest. Their application to manufacturing emerged only in the last decade of the eighteenth century. Over the next thirty years, they spread along the eastern and southern coasts as far north as Main and as far east as Pittsburgh (see Figure 23.5[314]).

Although widely spread, they were thin on the ground. The main concentrations were in and around Boston, Philadelphia, Baltimore, and New York. They were the largest and most densely packed settlements, constituting a ready market and labor force. They were also within striking distance of one another. New York lay 300 km as the crow flies south of Boston. From New York to Philadelphia, it was another 300kms; and from Philadelphia to Baltimore (where many Boston residents had their summer homes), it was another 300km. Moreover, these cities were linked to Europe and had established connections west of the Appalachians. Thus, the distribution of the engine reflected the pull of eastern cities on places to the west that could provide raw materials and goods - from sawn wood and grist to animal pelts - and funnel still further west goods manufactured far to the east.

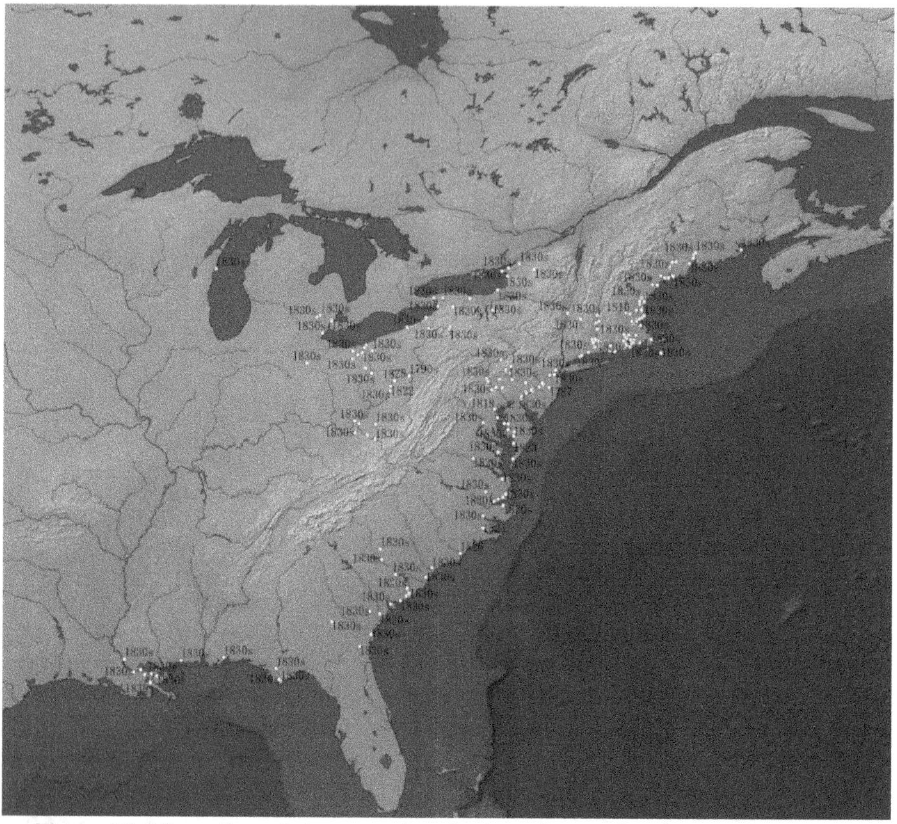

Figure 23.5 Location of steam engines in America, early nineteenth century.

Chicago supplied grain to help feed the eastern settlements. At first, loaders shoveled grain by hand into boats. Then came the horse-drawn elevator. Steam replaced horses in 1848, so it took just an hour to load what had once taken a day. The faster the loading, the quicker grain could flow from the farm to the docks. The dirt tracks that ran through Chicago were upgraded with wooden boarding to speed up the journey. Then came railway cars rattling their way directly from the farms. At the same time, a factory was built to produce mechanical reapers to expedite grain harvests. Thus, by increments, Chicago became its own market. And just as Chicago had been an outlier for cities to the east, newer settlements to the west became outliers for Chicago.

Kansas City, for example, had been little more than a collection of outfitters, general stores, and warehouses at the junction of two rivers – a convenient place to switch goods between boats and wagons. It was still little more than this well into the 1830s and 1840s when it reached a population of around 4,000. Ammunition, mining implements, and other goods were sold to homesteaders and prospectors heading north and west, and animal skins were bought and stored before being shipped east and south. It was also a way station for drovers heading to Chicago. If Kansas was ever to become more than this, it needed people. The Gold Rush of 1849 swelled the city with prospectors and land speculators, but the civil war ended that. Only after the war did people make their way to Kansas in large numbers, either on their way to somewhere else or settling in the town or farming around it. There they fattened cattle and pigs. People in the east wanted to eat meat as well as grain. Rather than lose weight by driving or shipping livestock east, why not slaughter them in Kansas City? And why not mill the grain before sending it east? Slaughterhouses, meatpackers, and flour mills were thrown up. So were factories producing agricultural machinery. By 1870 the population had increased seven-fold to 35,000. It would increase another sevenfold over the next thirty years.

Now that the city was becoming a substantial market in its own right, it made sense to use the engine, its high initial costs thus mitigated. It was first used as a fire engine to protect warehouses. Then the meatpackers and millers got hold of it. Then it was used to produce agricultural tools such as hay presses and scales. Then it was producing still more steam engines and rolling mills. By 1870 there were steam engines in just about every state and territory. Pennsylvania had three times as many as the whole of the country had had in 1830.

Chapter 24

The Return of Puritanism After 1830

Industrialization and the regimens and certainties it imposed stimulated a new and powerful Puritan surge that culminated once again in fragmentation, intolerance, and war.

Even as a long affective wave propagated through the eighteenth and early nineteenth centuries, memories of Puritanism continued to worry and bother well into the latter part of the eighteenth century. Some wondered about its origins. Did these lie with disputes in the established Church over clothing, ceremony, worship, godliness, and truth? Was it the consequence of non-conformity or doctrine? Or did it reflect a particular worldview within the Church of England?[315] For Hume, enthusiasm marked out the Puritans. They were fanatical in celibacy, fasting, penance, and mortification and eager to proscribe human wit and learning. They encouraged cant, hypocrisy, intolerance, and '*harangued and launched invective with noise and vehemence.*'[316] Might Puritanism show its face once more? The fear was justified. But it discarded its religious form for the most part and declared itself loudly and triumphantly as reason even before the eighteenth century was out.

At a gathering of Versailles, around six hundred delegates of the Third Estate (the French commoners) made clear their desire and demand for representative government, economic freedom, and an end to ascription. The monarch would have to share power with elected representatives. The king agreed reluctantly and then turned up at the newly created National Assembly with mercenary troops to re-establish absolute rule. It was a foolish move. The king was executed, and the Catholic Church separated from its head - the Papacy. The clergy was forced to choose between an oath of loyalty to the Church or the new Republic. Tens of thousands chose the Church and were driven out. Even this was not enough. In 1793 an attempt was made to erase Christianity from France altogether. It was now the turn of the remaining constitutional priests to abandon their parishes. 'Reason' was elevated in status and idolized, first as a young goddess, then as a supreme being (represented by Wisdom), and then as a kind of philanthropic deism. Having empowered Robespierre to crush dissent and now concerned that he might turn on them, the National Assembly executed their fixer.

As a semblance of common sense returned, a decree was issued in 1795 granting freedom to exercise any religion. Nevertheless, the Directory, the Council of Elders, and the Council of Five Hundred proved unable to govern effectively, leaving an opportunity for an ambitious young general, Napoleon, to seize power in 1799. He oversaw the completion of educational and legal reforms that started just after the revolution. High schools were established in every major town. Military and technical schools were formed under state control and supervised by a national university. The Napoleonic Code toughened property rights and authorized new methods for drafting contracts, leases, and stock companies. And a diluted Church of Rome was reunited with the state. The Church could discipline bishops and lower ranks, and it received, as did Protestant Churches, an income from the state. In return, it had to relinquish any claims on landholdings throughout France. The idolization of reason thus gave way to enlightened despotism.

Puritanism also manifested itself through the idealization of emotion or, in other words, romanticism. Venerated and made routine, emotions are easily divined, categorized, and symbolized by a repertoire of techniques that become worn and obvious over time. Disentangling faux emotions from the real thing becomes impossible. Playwrights and their literary characters struggled with this in the seventeenth century. Christianity - which focused on collective worship and community and a power far greater than oneself - allayed self-centered and self-obsessed concerns. Emotional enthusiasm turned outwards. But now that Christianity had been diluted or set aside entirely, the affective risked unrelenting introspection and a downward spiral into nihilism.

It was possible to avoid this danger if you were prepared to admit God, thought Kierkegaard.[317] To him, society and its dominant organizations – most especially the Church, which, in his view, ought to be destroyed – do not allow people to work out their own unique identities and be themselves. Each person is expected to be like everyone else. Excessive adherence to rationalism was to blame. One was, or pretended to be, whatever society, the crowd, had decided was rational and logical. Moving beyond this state and being honest with oneself demanded self-reflection, inwardness, and an emphasis on emotional life and subjectivity. But there's the rub. Contemplation of one's own emotions, thoughts, and physical sensations leads to self-absorption, alienation, and nihilism. So Kierkegaard chose to allow Christianity to rescue him. The truth, not an approximation of it, is brought from the outside by God, who takes on human form. He takes on human form because, otherwise, the truth would be little more than instruction. The realization of truth is nothing less than a miracle.

It was all a question of choice. In the moment before one acts is a realization that it is your choice and your choice alone, your desire, and your responsibility to take that action. It has always been so. Hence, the struggle to take that first breath at birth. The panic experienced before the newborn understands it can choose to breathe through its mouth rather than through the caked mucus in its nose. Or, later in life, the allure of the cliff edge and the rocks below and the choice they present.

Nietzsche (1844-1900) gave himself no way out. Precisely what he believed and argued is often subject to a good deal of interpretation. He did not feel bound by what he took to be foolish consistencies, nor was he afraid to be enigmatic, contentious, obtuse, brutal, and lucid in equal measure. He was a romantic and rationalist; he defended Jews and attacked them; he was contemptuous of Christianity and aware of its artistic achievements. But there are matters over which there is no doubt. He was highly critical of European morality. Notions of good and evil, right and wrong, were to his mind historical relics. They were accepted and mouthed out of habit and had little to do with modern society and living. This did not mean that specific actions regarded as moral or immoral should be encouraged or avoided. But what was done should be encouraged or avoided for reasons other than mere routine. He was critical of European morality because, at its core, lay a desire to live a pious existence while judging others, apportioning blame, and determining responsibility. The entire pattern of European morality and religion, and the envy, humiliation, and powerlessness it engendered, would have to be uprooted and rebuilt. Otherwise, western society would crumble into insignificance as its values became unintelligible, leaving its people shallow and insincere.

Nietzsche had created a playground for adolescent iconoclasts, an emotional Cockaigne where they could always triumph. Each of them could say: If society does not recognize why and how it should mold itself to *my* worldview, then I will take society by the scruff of the neck and reshape it!

Nietzsche's ideas became increasingly popular after 1870 and the creation of Germany and even more so after his death in 1900. His ideas appealed not only to young adults (especially young men) but to a nation that felt other European powers were holding it back while building enormous navies, dominating shipping routes and trade, and gathering up colonies for themselves. The individual struggling against the herd was a narrative that could lead to only one place – a sink of introspection. It allowed no one, no collective, no community to rescue Nietzsche or, years later, Germany.

He probably realized these dangers and found just such a community earlier in his life on at least two occasions. Once with Wagner, who considered himself the personification of a uniquely German cultural revival. (Many others looked at him in the same light). And then with a woman he thought his equal intellectually and who appeared to be just as critical of petty values and just as willing to abandon them. When he discovered Wagner had turned to Christianity and she to another man, Nietzsche was compelled to search elsewhere unsuccessfully.

Had he remained lucid and lived into his nineties, might he have found community again? Maybe temporarily. He would have seen his books stuffed into backpacks of young men sent off to the front. He would have exerted some measure of influence over the Nazi party. More importantly, from his perspective (for musical composition had been his first calling), he would have seen his ideas influence the course of German music. Richard Strauss - who, like Wagner and Dietszb and Sibelius, was commended by the Nazis - entitled his first tone poem *Also Sprach Zarathustra* after Nietzsche's eponymous book. Strauss saw in it an account of man's evolution from his origins to *ubermensch* (superman or overman) – the man who had overcome frippery, unleashed the true potential of human beings, and had thus shown the will to engage in that struggle. This, at least, was one of Strauss's stated intentions. In practice, it was a musical exploration of emotions that Nietzsche's message evoked in him. *Ein Heldenleben* adheres more closely to Nietzsche's basic narrative. A man (represented by the French horns, an instrument his father played) at first shrugs off his critics (described by the woodwind, amongst whom the whining and nasal oboes are especially grating) before he finds himself in a pitched battle with them. Only then, having emerged victorious, can he enjoy the peace he has always longed for.

But the community would still have eluded Nietzsche in the end, for none who held to his ideas could survive for long. He would have been part of a collection of like-minded souls teetering on the edge of a chasm, each convinced that if they jumped together, each would be saved from his own self-imposed darkness and isolation.

As for Strauss, he was rescued from Germany's descent into the abyss by his wife, son, and daughter-in-law (a Jewess). And unlike Wagner, who never really escaped his penchant for long and dreary grandiosity, Strauss found a sincerity and serenity that otherwise eluded him until his *Four Last Songs* composed in 1947.

Emotional and intellectual solipsism was not peculiar to either man. Composers from Beethoven to Mahler were often a mere breath away from bombast, pomposity, mawkishness, self-conscious dourness, or unabashed self-indulgent misery. Rachmaninov barely avoids maudlin and cloying sentimentality through sheer pace and technical brilliance, while Ravel does so through precise orchestration and tonal ambiguities.

Puritanism's influence on painting was just as powerful. The two dominant movements - the neo-classical and romantic and their close variants (such as the Nazarene, Pre-Raphaelite, and Orientalism) - began falling apart by the second half of the nineteenth century. The academies established in 1648 (in France) and 1768 (in England) had once determined good art and who could make a living from it. After 1850 a desire to escape the conservatism they cast over neoclassical and romantic movements became overwhelming. Forewarnings of that counter-reaction are found in Turner and Goya. Both were breaking away from the rigidities setting in all around them. Turner used color and uncertain forms to suggest a oneness with the sea and the storm, an atmosphere that could not otherwise be conveyed on canvas. The best impressionists, too, by departing from objective details, transformed an observer's first look, that casual glance through the corner of the eye, into an extraordinary moment of reality imbued with movement and atmosphere. More than any other artists, they were isolated from society and, in their best years, '*were treated as madmen or completely ignored.*'[318]

It was as though the bindle holding the impressionists' techniques – and those of the realist, post-impressionist, expressionist, primitive, experimental, cubist, surrealist, art nouveau, art deco, nihilist, symbolist, and modernist – had been torn open and its contents scattered about. Each movement became increasingly self-conscious, determined to be different from what went before and from each other, and wedded to their defining principles and philosophies. By the 1920s, painting became something so pure, so absolute, and so free of insincerity that it had to be about itself rather than everyday objects and life. And in being so pure and abstract, it risked becoming little more than an instrument. How art organized itself reflected this trend. What had been looser arrangements to select, exhibit, buy, and sell art became concentrated, commercialized, and just as effective as the academies at limiting style and taste.

Music, too, abandoned form, melody, and tonality, along with the discipline that made it possible to convey emotion. It became so abstract, intellectual, and self-conscious that it was transformed into material for analysis in bureaucratized academies and badges for the Highbrow. The best composers - those whose music will probably last the longest – such as Elgar and Walton - were outsiders with virtually no formal training. Vaughan Williams kept his own counsel regardless of fashion and reputation.[319]

English literature, complained Orwell, [320] became self-conscious and intellectual and thickened with orthodoxies: pessimism, social resignation, weariness with industrialized life, and the evaporation of religion and moral certainties was 'the line' taken through the 1920s. It was commentary without purpose, reports of the ordinary, observations supplied with the detachment of a cat. That sense of '*I don't care*' was replaced in the 1930s with communism's steely sense of purpose. Both these lines were possible, thought Orwell, only because English writers were too comfortable. Bustling economies produced plenty of cash, and social taboos fell away during the 1920s. No one wanted to look at or think about Europe's political irruptions. Writers were protected by wilful ignorance and cossetted by their safe and routine English lives. They had no dealings with murder, street violence, persecution, massacres, prisons, and torture. It was easy for them to indulge in ideology with such enthusiasm.

Education also felt the chill. Thought petrified while the number of educational organizations and the volume of people they processed grew. The temperature dropped slowly during the nineteenth century. In France, Napoleon imposed on schools and universities an almost military discipline. In Germany, knowledge became a valuable instrument for lower-middle-class men determined to build themselves a new profession. Learning meant selfless dedication to years of study - the only sure way to master philology, philosophy, history, or natural science. And it required gatherings of like-minded souls and collections of journals through which they spoke to each other, appraised each other's work, and assigned each other posts based on what they took to be merit. Their new profession claimed to stand alongside law and medicine. Perhaps it was even a cut above those traditional, somewhat technical, and narrow trades. It offered trained generalists for administration and government and marked out as truly educated those who could afford so much time and money on its pursuit. Americans looked at Germany with admiration. Ambitious would-be economists made the trip over, determined to build their own professions back in the States once they had learned what they needed there.[321]

Attitudes in England also became severely functional. Worried about the country's standing in Europe, Parliament compelled factories to provide some basic reading, writing, and arithmetic in 1802. It prohibited the employment of children under nine and, in 1833, legislated compulsory attendance at school for all children aged nine to thirteen for two hours a day. It set up a state training college for teachers in 1835. In 1870, all children between five and twelve were brought into a national public system. By 1891 attendance had become both compulsory and free. By 1900, the number of public elementary schools reached 34,300. A secondary education, though, would take longer to realize. Some elementary schools in 1907 offered a secondary education up to fourteen, and scholarships and free places were available. Yet even by the 1930s, only 10% of public elementary school children went on to secondary education. In 1944 secondary and elementary education separated from each other and further education, and made free of charge. By 1951 there were 27,700 primary schools and 5,900 public secondary schools housing some 7 million children.

In the same year (1870) that a national system for children was created, Oxford and Cambridge were compelled by an act of Parliament to open their doors to non-Anglicans and women and expand their curricula to include natural sciences, history, and foreign languages. Pressure on both places to loosen their monopoly on university education had already been underway for some years. The first non-Anglican college in London (University College London) was built in 1828. In response, Anglicans founded King's College in 1831. The University of London, established in 1836, subsequently grew by merging UCL, King's, and other existing specialist organizations – the medical schools, the Royal College of Mines, the Royal College of Science, and the Central Technical College, and, in 1898, the London School of Economics. Universities also appeared in Southampton, Leicester, Birmingham, and elsewhere.

To frame and flesh out the professions evolving in these new organizations, intellectual creeds, old and new, were taken up. Ideas once passed around the dinner tables, chewed on over coffee and tea, and aired in growing numbers of periodicals, were transformed into implacable certainties. Adam Smith's *Wealth of Nations,* for instance, was, from the start, treated respectfully as a thoughtful, subtle, and, just as importantly, well-written and engaging piece full of valuable and interesting examples. It quickly became one of those books on which any educated and well-read person should spend time. It drew the attention of all sorts of readers, from those interested in the evolution of language to those intrigued by Smith's comments on the fecundity of Highland women. It also contributed to political economy, a wide area of thought catered to by wide-ranging, quality journals such as the *London Review*, the *Edinburg Review*, the *London Magazine*, the Monthly Review, and *Critical Review*. (*The Economist* was not up and running until 1843; and there were no specialist academic journals in the field until the end of the century.) The book also received a tremendous fillip from Pitt the Younger, who saw in it a case for undoing the corn laws and undermining smugglers. Two years after the book's publication, Smith was appointed Commissioner for Customs and financially set for the rest of his life.[322] But though he was respected, known, and rewarded in life, Smith's death in 1790 did not interest the English greatly.[323] Obituaries were skimpy. The man, his ideas, and the book were subsumed by political debates on the relative influence of landed classes and merchants, the revolution in France, and war. Not until events moved in favor of merchants did that change. When the corn laws were repealed and Britain's trade expanded, Smith was raised from litterateur of repute to prophet. His ideas became statements of how the world is. The prices business sets are not what the owner thinks society will tolerate or which circumstances wrought by chance or design allow him to demand. It is a phenomenon that naturally and logically resolves itself into labor, rent, and profit. Profit is not whatever the business can get away with. It naturally presents itself as the surplus left over from the risks and trouble of employing stock. The increase in stock determines wages, and this behooves the business community to employ free men rather than slaves and pay liberal wages sufficient to keep the worker and allow him to keep his family. Free men are cheaper than slaves because the owner must bear the cost of his property's wear and tear, whereas free men will bear that cost themselves. And liberal wages, from the perspective of society, lower child mortality and keep the supply of workers coming. Moreover, the rise in labor costs is more than offset by new machinery and labor-saving devices. The government's role is not to favor one business, manufacturer, or trade but to stand back.

These kinds of absolutes stopped politicians from taking even basic and remedial action. Sympathy for the poor was not entirely absent. Limits on the working hours of children had been imposed in 1833. Further restrictions on working hours were introduced in the following decade, and women and children were forbidden to work in mines. The public health act of 1848 followed the Municipal Reform Act of 1835, though it would be some twenty years or more before either act was properly enforced and municipalities were made responsible in practice for lighting, housing, public health, and education. Working men in towns were given the parliamentary franchise in 1867. And between 1871 and 1875, trade unions received their charter of rights. But the general mood was hard. Government should have no place in planning, sanitation, housing, or control of slum landlords and jerry builders. Under the poor laws of 1834, outdoor relief was abolished, and the workhouse test was imposed on those applying for welfare. Employment was made attractive by making conditions in the workhouse as miserable as possible for its inmates. The poor relief's share of the economy stagnated between 1820 and 1880, and the area covered by industrial slums grew.

Marshall's *Principle of Economics* was an attempt to introduce a more affective feel to economics so that it was more about men and less about mathematics. Yet by the end of the century, the university men had made sure that any hint of genteel amateurism still left was erased. Free enterprise, the survival of the fittest, self-reliance, utilitarianism, Malthus's population thesis, Ricardo's economic laws, and Smith's principles were fixed like stars in the firmament. A new type of economics - separate from political economy, philosophy, morality, and thoughts about the nature of human beings - claimed to know the world as it is.

On the other side of the Atlantic, the United States was industrializing rapidly. The word 'system' entered the vocabulary as life was standardized, and what had been an agrarian society of small towns erupted into dense metropolitan centers. 'Captains of industry' or 'robber barons' grew rich through the monopolies they created in the steel, petroleum, and transportation industries. The best-known were John D. Rockefeller, Andrew Carnegie, Cornelius Vanderbilt, Leland Stanford, and J.P. Morgan. They instigated state-organized violence and murder, dispersed native Indian societies in the West and, in the Mid-West and East, pitted workers and federal troops against each other in the railroad strikes of 1877 and 1894.[324]

While economists were carving out their discipline, another set of university men – the Geographers - were staking out another. The Royal Geographical Society (RGS) was established in 1830. University College opened four years earlier, and a new London University was being readied. It would include a Chair in Geography. Captain Maconochie, founding secretary of the RGS, was appointed in 1833. In 1835 Geography attracted only 5 of the university's 136 students. The following year Maconochie resigned to take up an appointment as Lt Governor in Tasmania.[325] The chair was readvertised but left empty, as were classes, and soon post and classrooms were forgotten.

Not until 1903 did London appoint a professor - in economic geography. The chair was preceded by a handful of lectureships at Cambridge starting in 1888 and a readership the year before at Oxford, held by H.J. Mackinder. The purpose of Geography, declared the Faculty of Arts, was '*to explore the portion of space allotted to man; to portray his habitations therein, diversified as they are in geological structure, in clime, in vegetation, in animal life; to show their connection with his form, his habits, the temper of his mind, his language, his laws, his institutions; and to deduce general principles by which, under similar circumstances, similar results may be inferred.*'[326] Mackinder's interest was what came to be called geopolitics. The strategic position of states and alliances had long played into the calculations of politicians and military commanders. But Mackinder transformed this into something akin to natural law. In 1904[327] he published a paper in which he argued that control of the pivot area – a wedge of territory stretching from Afghanistan, Iran, and Pakistan in the south to Russia's northern coast from the Barents to the East Siberian Seas – meant control over vast continental resources sufficient to build a massive fleet. It also meant control over a place to launch that fleet and dominate the world. This might happen if Germany were to ally itself with Russia or if the Chinese, organized by the Japanese, were to overthrow the Russian Empire. This was powerful stuff from Germany's perspective. It fitted with its ambitions for expansion in the East (preceded by a knock-out blow in the West). It also chimed with its imputed romantic soul: Germany would have to struggle to fulfill its destiny. Many on the General Staff already thought war inevitable. The build-up of the German fleet alone would ensure the future hostility of England. Winning that war required decisiveness and speed. Even as Mackinder was preparing his paper, Schlieffen, the Chief of the General Staff, was arguing for a short campaign against France that same year. In 1906 he was replaced by Moltke, who did not resist the decision to prioritize the navy financially. Not until 1911 did he and his staff push for a substantial and rapid expansion of the army.

The pools of affect collecting in the aftermath of the first world war had no time to amalgamate. Europe had broken up into four blocs: liberalism, conservativism, communism, and fascism. It was, wrote Hobsbawm, an age of extremes. When Spengler looked across Germany to an exhausted Europe, he saw in its buildings, literature, arts, and technologies the end of a Culture. He saw the West frozen and intellectualized. Its cities were obvious expressions of a culture at its height but, committed to stone, were dead and dying. This last stage in a Culture's evolution is obligatory. It is a process insusceptible to modification and limited to a few centuries. Classical civilization's transition can be dated to the fourth century, and the West's to the 19th century. Equally relentless is the path leading up to that final stage.

Different forms characterize it. These include the apollonian, which describes an interest only in the contours of the world as they appear to be. And the Faustian – a concern with the soul and a world defined by shades of light and dark. But whatever its morphology, once petrified, it is finished.

Spengler's galumphing, grandiose, and melancholy images appealed to the Nazi party. His style captured what he hated: a heavy, concrete, enormous, machine-run, rationalistic, money-centered world. And what he loved: flesh, blood, and soil mixed with emotional, spontaneous, and intuitive action, shaped by Caesars and political dynasties touched by destiny and commanding loyalty. If he were right, the world he loved would rise again. But in the romantics' collective mind, the working through of geopolitical certainties left unfinished at the end of the First World War demanded a reckoning. And that, General Foche predicted, came just 20 years later. By then, romanticism had dissolved into the entirely selfish cult of Nazism, whose leader's introspection and concern purely with himself gave us the most eloquent definition of evil.

Chapter 25

A Brief Affective Respite, 1945-1980

An intense affective surge in the second half of the twentieth century found expression through a dramatic expansion of the public world and welfare. Organizations and formal rules came to dominate everyday life. By the 1980s, Puritanism reasserted itself, sparking rancor, ressentiment, obduracy, and despair. This behavioral cascade generates incoordination and may eventually lead to society's effacement.

The brutality and uncertainty of two wars and economic depression left survivors with simple gratitude for life and an untrammeled ruth for others. The new affective surge, which probably equaled in intensity those experienced during the Enlightenment, the Renaissance, or the collapse of Rome, took the form of the welfare state. Governments, which had learned through the industrial wars to involve themselves in the lives of citizens intimately, now placed center stage the family, children, education, health, relief from cruelty and economic hardship, the importance of emotions (especially love and compassion), and freedom of expression. Hospitals were placed under central government's control, and health was made free to all. Dramatic improvements in public health and falls in infant mortality followed. Slums that had survived the bombing were cleared away with all the damaged buildings. Whole new towns, replete with schools and shops, were constructed. Universities were expanded, and the state paid for those who gained entry. American money poured in to help repair Europe and Britain. By the mid-1950s, economies were humming; unemployment was low, as was inflation, and wages rose. Women's employment, which had been growing since the start of the twentieth century, continued to accelerate. Those who, before the war, would have had little choice but to go into domestic service were now taking up clerical, sales, managerial, professional, operative, and craft work.

Economic stimulus and the return of men from the war led to a long-term rise in population, which further excited the economies. Fridges, washing machines, vacuum cleaners, and all sorts of new devices became widespread. New channels and broadcasting stations filled the air. Televisions were brought into homes, and families organized the furniture, their meals, their routines, and their lives around it. Life outside the home was ruled by the car as it became more affordable and miles upon miles of motorways were built. Internationally, the jet airliner and long-distance phones began to knit countries together. Security was provided by a voluntary alliance –NATO - in which the greater power allowed smaller ones much authority, while the number of democracies worldwide more than doubled even before the collapse of the Soviet Union.[328] Throughout the West, societies became increasingly relaxed. Hierarchies became looser or broke up along with deference to them. People and their relationships and how they felt about and treated each other mattered rather than ascriptive rights or social position. Speech and the written language became less formal. Hats, gloves, ties, and formal attire were abandoned, and first names were used to address one another. Demeanour and practice became less mannered and more spontaneous.

This profoundly affective mood complemented what was already a commonplace feature of life - the organization. In England, the share of labor working in organizations (public and private) rose from about 40% in 1861 to 60% by the turn of the twentieth century and to 97% by 1945. After that, it stabilized at around 94% for the next thirty-five years before dropping in 1980 and steadying at about 80%. Over the same period, the share of the workforce employed in large organizations grew from just under 7% in the 1850s to a little under 40% by the second decade of the twenty-first century.

A similar description can be made of America. Here, public and private employees accounted for 75% of the labor force by 1948, stabilizing at around 90% by the early 1970s. The proportion of workers in large organizations (public and private) had reached one-third by the second half of the 1940s, rising to more than half by 1989. Thirty years later, nearly 60% of the labor force works in large organizations.

The upshot is that about half the labor force spends their working lives in large organizations, which also help order everyone else's lives outside them. In its turn, the organization cultivated the affective, initially at least. But as the organizational routines became entrenched, so did the mundanity of life. Anesthetized and alienated, the population drifted into a puritanical state.

Festering international tensions aided the shift. Even before the end of World War II, the lines for international rivalry, and the fate of eastern Europe, had been decided. The Soviet Union kept Poland, occupied east Germany, and ensured that countries it bordered would be 'friendly.' In practice, all Poles, Czechs, Romanians, and Bulgarians were brought into the communist fold. Yugoslavia and Albania declared themselves communist republics, though neither shared a border with the Soviet Union. In the East, China proclaimed itself a republic in 1949. North Korea and North Vietnam had done so four years earlier. Then came the North Koreans' invasion of the south. These ructions, and the successful detonation by the Soviet Union of its own nuclear bomb in 1949, together with revelations that the Soviets had been spying on the Manhattan Project, handed McCarthy, a young senator from Wisconsin, opportunity enough to whip up anti-communist hysteria in the United States. The worst of the frenzy was over by 1954. But military insurgency, already in its sixth year in Malaysia and eighth year in Vietnam, seemed to demand military responses from Britain and France. In 1959, Cuba transformed itself into a communist republic less than a hundred miles from the American mainland. By then, like some helpless neurotic unable to stop picking at a sore, America had become fixated on Vietnam.

Détente in 1969 was accompanied by a rash of communist revolutions in the Congo, Yemen, Somalia, Mozambique, Benin, Ethiopia, Kampuchea, and Afghanistan. Many other countries, from Tanzania to India, were already strongly socialist. They brimmed the West with sympathizers, provoking loyalists to raise their totems: market, freedom, democracy, individual, and the rule of law. The most dangerous part of the cold war ensued in the early 1980s. But when the gamble paid off and the Soviet Union fell, the West was left in the thrall of its own idols.

Perhaps its least contentious impresa is the claim that Western societies are rule-based. Rules form a complex within which both people and their organizations are meshed and anchored. This system is crafted such that no one person is favored and rules are enforced equally. And when rules are broken, redress is certain and proportionate. In this way, everyone is protected, disputes are solved peacefully, justice and fairness are guaranteed, and order and predictability reign. Without its system of rules, society cannot function properly, advance materially, and none of its members is genuinely free. There is a debate to be had – and it is a long and distinguished one – on what is meant by 'law,' 'the rule of law,' 'justice,' and 'freedom' and many other related matters. How is the rule of law realized? Who enforces it? What is justice? How does a society come to be just? Is justice a property of the distribution of goods? Is it the deserts of one's actions? Is it synonymous with the avoidance of breaching rights? Is it to preserve equality or to allow inequalities to emerge? Societies rarely have answers with which everyone agrees. Still, there is no question that they must establish rules based on answers that people can live with if the community is to survive long enough to have those debates let alone come up with definitive solutions.

These arguments are not unimportant. But they do reek of justification. They do not explain why legislation and official regulations have ballooned at other moments in history. One such pulse gathered during the sixteenth and early seventeenth centuries. It was marked both in its volume and in its nature. It comprised ordinances drawn up and issued by a council of 15-20 men, headed by Cromwell, who had the final say on the content of items and whether they passed or not. A second legislative pulse built up during the latter half of the eighteenth and early nineteenth centuries. The third and current pulse is the most spectacular. The last forty years account for about 60 percent of all legislation generated by English parliaments since the thirteenth century. Most of this takes the form of statutory instruments. These are rules, orders, and regulations that ministers issue under the authority established in a parent act. These regulations have legal force and can only be challenged in court if doubt exists over whether the parent act confers such powers. Specific instruments are scrutinized by parliament, but many are not. The sheer number and length of statutory instruments in practice mean they receive a very light touch. Scrutiny committees are scheduled late in the day or delegated to a sub-committee. Most are passed unless an objection is raised in parliament within forty days of being laid before parliament and is described tellingly as 'a prayer.'

Earlier legislative pulses also occurred in the United States. One long wave crested during the civil war. A second peaked early in the twentieth century, shortly before the first world war. The momentum for a third gathered during the immediate post-war decades accelerated after 1980 and may not have yet reached its apogee. It took the form of official regulations measured in thousands of pages and millions of words.

Back in England, the authority delegated by parliament through acts to ministers is frequently delegated again through ministerial orders to organizations that go by many names: quangos, arms-length bodies, non-departmental public bodies, executive bodies, quasi-judicial bodies, and regulatory agencies. In the late 1970s, around 490 and 1561 organizations were characterized as executive and advisory, respectively, alongside nearly 70 tribunals.[329] There were under 1000 in 2008 and less than 500 in 2021. Such numbers, however, are unreliable. Organizations are often reclassified. Some are merged with others. And some are left unclassified and uncounted and do not publish data.

Quangos sometimes include organizations that were once private but have taken on government functions. One example is the National Trust, which owns around 2550km2 of what is widely thought to be Britain's most beautiful land, with properties and gardens. Entry fees are expensive, and so are annual memberships. Consequently, the Trust has become a middle-class preserve.

Varicose regulations and quasi-government regulators alter how societies are run. Commands and plans issued through congeries of ministries and publicly owned corporations are being replaced by minimalist governments whose primary function, as they see it, is to guide the market and society through the lightest of touches and only when necessary. The government makes these adjustments through 'hard' legislation and legal actions.[330] But it prefers to persuade and nudge through proxies (the regulators) who network with each other, the government, and the people they regulate. These arrangements have attracted all kinds of criticism. Governments are abdicating responsibility for political decisions and have become more interested in regulation than provision.[331] There is confusion over who is responsible for what. Regulators lack the money and teeth to do their job properly. They are influenced too easily by the organizations they regulate. The arrangement is vague, allows evasion, appears stacked in favor of the private sector, and seems undemocratic.[332]

The source of the West's love of rules, I suggest, is not primarily a sense of justice. Affective states of mind and the creation and operation of organizations are part of it. But so are other immediate practical considerations. All sorts of matters, from the construction of railways, airports, and roads to disease control and food processing, may require legislative responses. It is, however, the drift into puritanism and a desire to perfect society that makes recourse to rules irresistible and entirely logical.

In this connexion, it is worth drawing attention to debates on whether the nature and origin of law are natural or man-made. Natural law, rather like laws of nature, just are. They go beyond the authority of any person or organization (whether legislator, judge, court, or monarch) to confer or take away from anyone else the protections or rights laws offer. They have this quality because they are God-given. Or because all rational beings have the right to be treated as such. Or it is because laws (especially common law) emerge from judges whose reasoning, like all human reasoning, is a mystery. In its more recent iterations, natural law is represented by morality.

The alternative view is that a legislature or king posits laws, and there's an end to it. Laws are positivistic. Legal positivism emerged during the seventeenth century. It strengthened in the wake of the Enlightenment. Its anti-religious sentiment was formulated most clearly during another pulse in the latter part of the eighteenth century and early nineteenth century. It became orthodoxy between the world wars of the twentieth century and has remained so despite a brief challenge during the second half of the twentieth century. Legal positivists are generally dismissive of natural law but see the relevance of morality, which they treat as an add-on, a matter of interest, once rules on any given issue have run out. Morality there is, but it is a matter entirely separate from law.

Arguably, any claim to have identified the source of law appeals to absolutes of some kind. And any appeal to absolutes transforms law into an instrument. If everyone believes without a doubt that the source of law is the legislature or monarch or God or morality or that morality has no bearing, then there is little to be done. Society must be shaped by those originators' visions or interpretations of them. The law can only be an instrument of policy. The separation of judiciary, executive, and legislature from one another offers not protection but delay and obfuscation.

The most effective protection lies in uncertainty about the nature and origin of law: that it remains a mystery; that it is treated *as if* absolute only for immediate practical reasons and is therefore always subject to doubt. Tear off that mask, and the law reveals grim certainty and flinty intolerance.

Puritanism's effects on the West

Thought hardened into rules entails a deal of intolerance and easily splinters. It sets in motion behavioral cascades with the potential to scour and efface society. First come rancor, ressentiment, and Machiavellianism – emotions and behavior that suit the market just as the market suits them. A sense of accomplishment and pride swells with physical wealth and the ranks of the poor and worthless. For when Puritanism has not yet passed its nadir, affirmation and pleasure are found in the immiseration of others, and relief for mounting alienation is sought not in relationships but in further isolation.

Next, the market severely limits the politicians' choices about redistribution, leaving them powerless and ineffective. Instead, it redirects concern and interest to the vote and selection of leaders. And as the ineffectiveness of elected officials becomes apparent, disillusionment and despair set in.

At the same time, sclerotic and fractionated thought encourages an emphasis on process and routine. Coherence and flexibility, it is hoped, can be re-established by rearranging fragments into an optimal pattern. Systems are idolized, demanding obsessive attention to procedures and a degree of obduracy. These qualities are antithetical to instinctive thought and its development. The more sophisticated the function intended, such as education and repair and maintenance of biological life, the more ineffective and clumsier the organization to deliver these becomes.

Chapter 26

Rancor: creating divisions

Thought's petrification sharpens existing divisions and heightens intolerance. However well-meaning, a desire to perfect society by including people who are excluded or feel so produces new splits.

Left and right, conservative and liberal, religious and secular, mystical and scientific, artistic and mechanical are a few categories drawn from a list that grows as thought indurates and fragments. Common ground disappears, intransigence grows, and thinkers ignore one another or gird themselves. Debate is no longer about substance. There is no need to find out what is in the person's mind and look under the hood. You do not have to imagine the other person's feelings, as that might taint you. It is better to assume that whatever festers there is beyond the pale and act accordingly. A word or phrase is enough to symbolize reams of thought and sentiment.

One manifestation of this behavior is known popularly as political correctness - a reference to campaigns by the communist party in the early days of the Soviet Union to ensure compliance with political and policy lines. Today, conservatives in the West view it as an expression of the left's dogmatism. Many on the left see it as a trite label or myth[333] attached by conservatives to arguments they dislike while demanding airtime and a license to speak with impunity. The ploy, complains the left, is remarkably successful. It has never been easier to speak out and repress those who are least able to defend themselves.[334] Nor has the banal, absurd, crazy, ridiculous, offensive, xenophobic, insincere, and untrue been more commonplace. To those who see themselves as a-political, down-to-earth pragmatists, the dispute is, at best, little more than a storm in a teacup: silly, parochial, limiting, limited, and insignificant.

Yet, the quarrel is consequential. Language is about matters other than accurate communication. It is about being part of a group and being excluded from one. Vocabulary, accents, humor, likes and dislikes, food, manners, drink, judgments about what is proper and improper, and worldviews (however stale and predictable, whacky and distorted they may be) are all a part of belonging or not belonging. Legislation and rules applied to language bring a blunt axe down on society, cleaving it in two.

During a live broadcast of the Brexit shenanigans in 2019, Anna Soubry took great offense when men in luminous jackets shouted ‘Nazi,’ ‘scum,’ and ‘traitor’ at her while police looked on.[335] She was jostled by jeering crowds as she made her way through the streets around Parliament. Other MPs were treated similarly and received all kinds of insults by email. Soubry later called for a police investigation and a change in the law to preclude such behavior in the future.

I do not think it harsh to say that however unpleasant Soubry found her experience, her response suggests a sheltered life for an MP and criminal barrister, at least in comparison to earlier generations of public figures. The open-air political meetings that characterized politics in the nineteenth and the first half of the twentieth centuries brought politicians and voters face-to-face. It was an opportunity for the men and women on the street to say and show what they felt about the people affecting their lives. The vital, genuine, and raw grilling that ensued demanded resilience from the politician who was heckled, shouted at, sworn at, pushed, manhandled, and worse. And if he, like Soubry, were spotted walking along the road, he could expect stones, mud, and dead animals to be flung at him.

More genteel modes of criticism were available for the genteel. Caricatures were rich with meaning amongst the swathes of people who could not read. Coffee houses were places where you could be yourself, and conversations were treated as private. The ruling orders feared the cartoon more than the printed word and censored it in most European countries[336] except England. Charles II tried to shut the coffee houses in 1675, some twenty years after they first appeared in the 1650s. It was not for another century, with the French revolution in the air,[337] that one had to be more careful about what was said and overheard.

But invective was the mainstay of gritty politics. Invective and - if people had *really* had enough of what was troubling them - rioting. Rioting cut near to the bone. People died, property was destroyed, and the status quo was directly challenged. When the Gordon Riots erupted in London in 1780, it felt as though civil war had broken out again.[338] Downing Street and the House of Lords were attacked. So were many of the prisons. Newgate was razed. [339] Thirty years later, workers in Nottingham, Yorkshire, Lancaster, Leicestershire, and Derbyshire, led by the fictional Ned Ludd, took matters into their own hands. Having lost jobs to machines and seeing wages cut and standards in their trades decline, they broke into factories, destroyed machinery, and sent threatening letters. The government ignored their requests for minimum wages, controls over child labor, and restrictions on certain types of machinery. Instead, it made breaking machinery a capital offense in 1812 and, the following year, executed seventeen men. It had been even more ruthless in its response to the Gordon Riots. These were fuelled by a concoction of grievances, from hunger and poverty to fear of the press gangs roving the streets, oxygenated by American and French revolutionary sentiments and explicitly anti-Catholic. Troops shot dead four or five hundred people. A further sixty or more were sentenced to death, and a third of these were hanged.

Yet, for all that, rioting had a ritual quality. It was frequent, occurring at least every other year in one or other part of the country during the eighteenth and nineteenth centuries. It was treated with less tolerance from around the start of the nineteenth century, but the Old Bailey resorted to the death sentence permitted under the Riot Act of 1714 less frequently than it had in the eighteenth century. The right of 'patriotic Englishmen' to protest was a long-held convention amongst ordinary folk. Rioters focused on legitimizing notions, norms, or obligations, which justified their actions. Events were punctuated with banners, horns, bells, trumpets, and drums. And while they did not often achieve their specific ends, they shared goals and, collectively, helped bring to bear pressure that encouraged reform. Even when rioters went away empty-handed, they had defused tensions, avoiding more violent explosions. Frequent rioting, irreverent cartoons, coffee houses, and plain rudeness probably helped spare England the revolutions that swept through Europe before WWI.

Radio and television became a reason and excuse to end all that. Journalists and legislators controlled the radio and TV forums where citizens questioned politicians and spoke their minds. Only the language, manners, and deference of the middle-class dinner table were acceptable. And if you couldn't or wouldn't adopt that style or some version of it, you were given short shrift. The politicians found these manicured events comfortable and helpful enough. So did the journalists, even as they became fashionably less obsequious. Their careers as influential mediators between the people and the political class turned them into personalities and commanded generous incomes. So did the millions populating the closes and cul-de-sacs, villages and shires, determined to be middle-class or at least 'ever so' respectable. Any hint of rowdy behavior, unruly dress, or balky demeanor was enough to have the channel switched or the current turned off. When email came along, and politicians again found themselves uncomfortably close to the people, they complained. When they received thousands of offensive words on their mobile phones, that avenue, too, was narrowed and monitored or shut down. The demonstration became superfluous, even a drawback, and raucousness, let alone riot, put any cause beyond the pale. During the twentieth century, the frequency of riots dropped to one every three years, and restrictions on demonstrations were progressively imposed.

Exasperation with politicians who enforced on everyone else manners with which they are comfortable was bound to grow. Soubry's reaction was just a small instance of a broad determination to instantiate her version of polite society. It declares to large chunks of the populace that they and their kind are unacceptable. It polarizes and alienates on a grand scale. It shuts down the tiny release valves, without which tensions and resentments build and sour.

It also breeds a resolve to feel aggrieved at pressure to self-censure or moderate one's language or views. In 2006 *Charlie Hebdo*, a left-wing satirical magazine published in France, reprinted a cartoon of the Prophet Mohammed, which had first appeared in a Danish paper. The cartoon ridiculed fundamentalists, not Islam – a distinction and motive accepted by French courts after a suit brought by the Union of French Islamic Organizations citing antiracist legislation. In 2001, *Charlie Hebdo's* offices were fire-bombed. In 2015 two men armed with automatic guns broke into the office and shot dead eleven staff. Two more were killed later that day by the gunmen. Several others were killed during attacks in the following years, in which hatred against the magazine was an ingredient. In 2020, the magazine received threats from *Al Qaeda*. *Hebdo* claims to be indiscriminate in selecting the people it writes about and does not set out deliberately to rile them. That might be true, but it takes a good deal of pride in its criticisms and plain-speaking regardless of what anyone might think or do, for it sees itself as upholding what it takes to be the most important principle in life – free speech. And it enjoys doing so:

> '*The pleasure of saying "fuck off" to these new gurus of formatted thinking. In the past we said "fuck off" to God, the army, the church, the state. Today, we have to learn to say "fuck off" to tyrannical associations, navel-gazing minorities, bloggers who slap our wrists like little schoolmasters when, at the back of the class, we no longer listen to them but come out with rude words: "wuss, prick, queer, cow, tart, bitch, arsehole, dickhead, cumsack." Write these words in your Twitter account and 10,000 little Torquemadas will tie you to the stake. Does that mean you should let yourself be intimated*

by this pack of jaws waiting to tear you apart? On the contrary, let's have fun making the wolves howl. Because you only have to pull their tails to make them whine: Charlie Hebdo still has a rosy future.'[340]

The magazine went on:

'I think I can say that at Charlie everyone is relieved that the trial has finally taken place, and that it has established responsibilities.... The message the specially constituted criminal court has sent to society is thus very clear: radical Islamism is illegal and contributing in any way whatsoever to the preparation of a criminal act in its name leads to a double-figure sentence..... As Riss reminded us, the fact that they were all found guilty means that Charlie Hebdo is innocent. Apparently, what seems obvious to us is not obvious to society, which includes people who continue to say: "they asked for it, it's their fault." Nor is it obvious to the media who, more slyly – because they have a fantasy of Islam defending the proletariat – stigmatise cartoonists and journalists who mock fanatical Imams and who must, in their eyes, be racists. In the 1950s, Sartre said that we should not dishearten. Billancourt in 2020: we must not offend the mosques. The truth is... Islamists have chosen to complain about the cartoons in order to justify their death drive. So there we are: French society... considers that Islamic fundamentalist terror merits the severest sentences, and that it is unacceptable to compromise with evil.'[341]

This attachment to absolute freedom of speech is extraordinarily selfish. Not all those who have, or may yet, die or suffer in one way or another share the magazine's uncompromising stance. *Hebdo* neither asks nor demands: it expects everyone to sacrifice themselves for the principle. Despite the phrase '*war on terror*' neither France nor the West is at war. And it is unlikely that those who cry '*Je suis Charlie*' the loudest are those most at risk. This pure attachment to absolute principle is still more distasteful because its writers make hay out of the tragedy by blowing their own trumpet.

Equally objectionable is that those who favor speech restrictions feel increasingly vindicated as other people's frustration with those restrictions grows. And grow they do, once in place. Initial legislation tends not to refer to specific words or phrases. But particular terms must be offered in evidence if there is to be a conviction. In this way, lexicons are built up. An arthritic man riding his mobility scooter on his way home from a pub made one contribution. Finding himself unable to pass three young women in the street, he chased them into a shop, calling them '*bloody foreigners*' and telling them '*go back to your own country.*'[342] In another case, a young, pregnant woman on a bus with her small daughter was berated: '*I don't fucking like you people because you're fucking rude. You come to England and you have no fucking manners... Go back to your fucking country where they're bombing every day. Don't come to this country where we're free... You're lucky I don't kick you in the uterus and you'll never have a baby again.*'[343]

The problem is tricky for the police, who must not be heard using offensive language. Among the lists of their proscribed words are '*son*' or '*wee girl*' along with '*kids,*' '*children,*' '*love,*' '*dear,*' '*pet,*' '*policeman,*' and '*fireman,*' and phrases such as '*are you married?*' and '*what does your husband do for a living?*'[344]

Over time, the solons (those who believe legislation is essential) and the principled (those determined to oppose restrictions and stick absolutely to their principles) entrench their positions. Nuanced arguments that might have prevailed in a more tolerant atmosphere are forgotten.

The principled loses sight of the protections that limits on speech bring and how they change. Blasphemy laws and lese majeste failed to attract much attention during the eighteenth century and gradually fell into disuse. Laws restricting obscene language such as 'cunt' and 'fuck' and descriptions of sexual desire and practices between adults eventually melted away. Other concerns have emerged: prejudice towards race, nationality, ethnicity, religion, or gender. Thus, whereas nigger is largely unprintable, fuck appears quite regularly. Society changes with assessments of limits on some aspects of freedom to protect liberty for all.

The principled also turns a blind eye to the fact that words *do* hurt. Think of the politicians who encourage people to turn on their neighbors. Think of books that instruct readers on how to make bombs. Think of sexually themed magazines and websites[345] and the dependency they breed. Think of how hostile behavior toward women becomes more likely as derogatory language about them becomes second nature. Words *are* used to incite, denigrate, dehumanize, and set the stage for violence: descriptions of Jews as rats, the Tutsi as cockroaches, and Muslims as Black Crows are all infamous examples.[346]

Meanwhile, believers in the necessity of legislation, the solons, release themselves from doubt over deterministic links between words and actions. They are less inclined to recognize that words provoke and aggravate and incite only as part of a complex of stimuli. Among young males (who are most likely to be violent), biology and upbringing are the most consistent influences. These include low heart rate (around 65 beats a minute), impulsiveness, and levels of chemicals such as serotonin, testosterone, or lead.[347] Of these and many others, the most reliable predictor appears to be a low heartbeat. Upbringing refers to circumstances such as disinterested or neglectful or violent or young parents, broken families, deprived neighborhoods, and delinquent friends.[348] But the proximate cause is the situation that people find themselves in – one that creates fear and panic and snarls them up in each other's emotions.[349] Those who, for whatever reason, then learn to profit from violent behavior will probably remain violent for the remainder of their lives. It is also worth remembering that it is easier to point to instances where it appears words led to violence than it is to cite cases where language helped avoid conflict for the simple reason that there is no violent incident to investigate.

The solons also seem to forget that the same word may carry many different senses, making it easy to get around restrictions. When Nigel Farage said he would take a knife to the civil service and was then accused of using inflammatory language, he said he meant an axe, as this would have been the usual metaphor. Intentionally or not, he drew more attention from the press and got his message across twice over.

None of this is any consolation to the frightened mother and child on a bus, even when prosecutions are successful. The focus on language is unlikely to stop those people intent on intimidating others from doing so. Energies are likely to be directed at cultivating 'undertones' that are just as nasty. For this reason, the number of racist incidents at schools might be even greater than thought and may grow, demanding still more legislation.

The tendency of rules to beget more rules is evident in other areas of social practice. New legislation that dissolves or supplants customs that once helped regulate behavior may require further legislation. Holding doors open for someone else, rising when a woman enters the room, offering a seat to a woman, shaking her hand only if she extends hers first, and so on. These were, at one time, everyday courtesies that were just 'the done thing.' Reasons were not usually given, but if the question was asked, the answer probably was that preference given to the strong would make for an unpleasant and self-destructive society. Today, such considerations have been forgotten or are seen as condescending, old-fashioned, and unnecessary as an emphasis on gender equality grows.

One consequence, however, is the return of the ungentle men. There is no shortage of anecdotal instances. A woman, heavily pregnant and walking slowly in the London rush hour, is muttered at and pushed aside. She doesn't expect to be offered a seat on a bus or train except perhaps by another woman. Doors are allowed to shut on her. "*Do you have to travel at rush hour and waste so much space?*" a man in his forties says under his breath, but loud enough for all to hear, as a guard helps an old, disabled woman sitting in an electric wheelchair onto a train. And now that the ungentle man is back, more rules are needed: 'Stop the Spread' plead New York's posters, while Spain's phones circulate *#MadridSinmanspreading*, hoping to free up seats on metro lines and buses.

The populace must now rely on explicit rules, without which they are dehumanized or left treading on eggshells. A man in the office reaches for a file behind a woman sitting at a desk. Was that an unwanted sexual advance? Is it unwelcome attention to comment on how lovely a woman is looking? Did the boyfriend force himself upon his girlfriend? Did the husband rape his wife? Did one partner abuse the other, if not physically then emotionally or psychologically? And who owns what, who inherits what, and what responsibilities do they have to each other and any children? Relationships become hedged with formality spelled out in statutes and judgments. One alternative, influential, and strongly held view is that marriage and domestic partnerships should be treated like any other contract. People should decide on the details of their relationship and set these out in a contract. No law of marriage is needed. Either way, relationships are converted into a web of formal rules, incentives, and punishments. One consequence is a withering of intimacy and trust, deepening alienation and instrumentalism. Another is a tendency for sex to be displaced outside these 'agreements' and sought as an anonymized performance, free of contractual and legal complications.

Smacking children

Legislation on this sensitive matter is bound to look and feel like one set of people is imposing their preferences on others. A ban was implemented first in Sweden in 1979, followed in 1983 by Finland and 1987 by Norway. Since then, Australia, New Zealand, and most European countries have applied bans or are committed to doing so,[350] and momentum for one is gathering in England, the USA, and Canada. Under pressure from the West, the UN, and numerous NGOs, a few other non-western countries have complied, but they remain in the minority.

The argument for a ban is straightforward. Corporal punishment does not make children conform or encourage them to accept or act on moral principles. Nor does physical discipline make children less aggressive or antisocial. On the contrary, corporal punishment leads to mental disorders, worse academic results, and troubled relationships between children and parents. It encourages more violent behavior in the child and more abusive behavior in the adult. Bans instill changes in attitude and practice and promote non-violent methods of childrearing. One common assertion underlying these statements is that smacking *is* violence and creates ‘toxic stress’: the body’s response to fear and tension is overworked, changing the brain’s structure and functions.[351] Up to three-quarters of substantiated physical abuse cases begin as attempts to ensure compliance. The connection is so routine that it can be quantified monetarily. Poor academic performance, lower earnings, and greater demands on mental health services due to smacking amount to 7 billion dollars every year in India.

Yet, doubts are raised. One is the ease with which smacking is equated with violence. This implies a continuum of acts that include murder, war, and genocide at one end. We must believe parents smack their children with the intent of inflicting harm. One can even conclude that the intention to damage and destroy lurks behind every physical action directed at another person. If so, why not restrict all physical activity in which children are involved? And why regulate only physical actions? If parents intend to harm their children by smacking them, a ban is unlikely to remove that intent. It will, at best, merely deflect the intention to harm into more subtle and damaging behavior. In this case, more legislation and monitoring are required. Society must either develop methods of surveillance that reach into every dark corner of the home or establish a specialized class of surrogate child-rearers. Perhaps this is what schools and social services will eventually become.

A second doubt is that smacking is singled out and isolated from parents’ more complex strategies. Parents do not *just* smack their children. Indeed, smacking makes other forms of punishment more effective[352] and is most likely between the ages of 3 and 5[353] when parents are at the end of their tether, frustrated, or fearful. The circumstances are familiar to every parent. One child has just pushed another into a road. A toddler trying to touch the wheels of a bus drawing out from the curb is pulled back out of danger. A small arm is grabbed as it reaches up to a pan of boiling water.

A third doubt surrounds the effects of bans. More than forty years after Sweden’s prohibition, the point rate of mental illness is about 18%. In other words, about 18% of the general population suffers from mental illness at any given moment. In Finland, seven years after the ban, the figure was around 17% for men and 19.5% for women. Some thirty years after its ban, the figure stood at 19% - the highest in Europe.[354] In Austria, the point rate for adolescents is around 24%,[355] and the lifetime rate (the proportion of adolescents who will at some time in their life have a mental disorder of one kind or another) was around 36%.[356] Of the children aged 0-10 years at the time of the ban (2000) in Germany, 21.9% were, by 2007, suffering from mental disorders. Between 2009 and 2017, rates amongst 15-19-year-olds (the eldest of whom would have been ten at the time of the ban) nearly doubled. In Denmark, of the children born between 1995 and 2016, 15% were diagnosed with a disorder before the age of 18.[357] The Danish Health Authority put the proportion of children who fulfilled clinical criteria for a diagnosis of anxiety or depression at 20%. In New Zealand in 2019, rates of depression in adolescents (aged between 1 and 7 at the time of the ban in 2007) were around 23%. That's about twice the rate for 13-19-year-olds in 2012. In the 3-4 years immediately before the ban, when 29% of youths (16-24-year-olds) had experienced disorders of some kind in any one year, the average point rate amongst 13-17-year-olds for depressive disorders was 10.4%.[358]

It is difficult to demonstrate a general decline in mental health, whatever its cause. But rates among children and adolescents have not improved or have worsened. The same can be said about rates amongst the general population. Many commentators back in 2000 thought that a ban would do little for the simple reason that a smack is, for the most part, a trivial incident in most people's lives. And where smacking did give expression to abuse, a ban would only misdirect public attention from other forms of maltreatment and cruelty. So far, rates of abuse have not declined. Nor is it clear if the ban has obviated brutality and heartlessness among children.[359]

Questions and disputes over speech and childrearing will not bring the West down. But they help fatigue society which might, on a sudden, tear apart.

Chapter 27

Rancor: fear of criminalization

Where smacking is banned, the courts are not dragging in large numbers of parents. Nor has speech legislation set off a rash of new prosecutions. But amongst populations obsessed with adherence to rules, these measures aggravate deep-seated fears already stirred up as governments across the West collar and imprison large numbers of fellow citizens.

Since 1945 there has been a marked rise in court activity and incarceration across the West. The figures are striking. Some 2.3 million people in America are confined. Numbers began to climb in the 1970s and grew in earnest before plateauing in 2000. For nearly two decades, the United States had the largest prison population and the highest imprisonment rate at 700 for every 100,000 people. Surrounding the inmate population are another 840,000 people on parole and 3.6 million on probation. By 2018, around 28% of all Americans had a criminal record.[360]

What are the reasons for these astonishing figures? One explanation is that more rules make it more difficult to avoid infringements. The result is a growth in court activity, both civil and criminal. The connexion between legislation and court caseloads is evident in the UK. In the United States, the split between federal and state (local) systems of justice and the uncertainty of local statistics (which describe the bulk of court business nationally) make it difficult to get a handle on trends, though the growth in civil cases and federal regulations in the US seems to be especially close.

A second reason is a determination by government to pre-empt crime. The number of prison inmates, which fell slightly during World War II from already low figures before the war, remained low until the later 1950s. It began to rise during the civil rights movements and anti-war campaigns from about 1967 onwards. These provided foci for a generational shift against social and political conservatism – a rebellion baited with attempts to normalize drugs, defined by a youth culture of music, dress, and lifestyles from surfing to back-packing, and cemented by radio and television. The conservative counter-reaction morphed into what was and still is a pre-emptive strategy to deal with any form of behavior that might lead to more serious criminal acts. A slew of new laws aided this: some 40% of all criminal legislation enacted since the American civil war emerged over the last forty years. The hope was to remove petty criminals and the doggedly antisocial from the street before they turned into hardened criminals.

A large segment of America's prison population is interned for less than one year for misdemeanors, minor offenses, or bad behavior. The jailed include those mentally ill but for whom care is unavailable, those involved in property crimes, and those caught with drugs. This last category embraces a complex of offenses and penalties. In Texas, for example, Xanax (used widely to treat panic attacks) is a schedule four drug, and many cough mixtures bought without a prescription are schedule five. Possession of Xanax without a prescription or in amounts greater than specified by a doctor is illegal and carries all kinds of penalties, including life. Possession of schedule five medications may bring up to four years on a second offense.

Also included among short-term prisoners are those who claimed admission of a lesser crime they may or may not have committed in lieu of a more serious one. A further proportion of inmates – comprising around 25% of the prison population – are neither convicted nor sentenced: they are merely awaiting trial.

Whatever the justifications offered, the effects of incarceration and the processes of justice on behavior and mental states can be hugely damaging. Most people imprisoned are poor, and poverty often shades into mental illness and vice versa. The commission of a crime, almost by definition, reflects disenchantment with society and its legal norms. Having a criminal record makes it difficult, in many cases impossible, to escape poverty and claim a stake in society. Imprisonment also disrupts relationships, further alienating the criminal. As a consequence, re-offending rates are high.

Ethnicity supplies a further dimension to this vicious circle. A disproportionate share of prisoners is black. In America, this helps fuel the sense that society is endemically racist. And it reinforces widespread cynicism: the justice system generates cheap, unskilled labor (a practice that emerged in the south after the abolition of slavery) and drums up business for the private commercial interests in the correctional system.

As the weight of legislation grows, the fear of being criminalized or branded a civil delinquent becomes more oppressive. Little is said about this except to the extent that punishment is or is not a deterrence. Arguably, such fear is both expected and precisely what is needed. Law is, by definition, coercive. Its rituals and its punishments are designed to intimidate and instill fear. If innocent citizens exhibit irrational responses, this is of little interest to the profession. The law is rational, and there is no reason to lay other people's frailties at its door. Whatever social scientists, social psychologists, and neuroscientists bring to the legal profession is neither here nor there.

Mental disorders are usually explained as disruptions in the brain's structure and functions. Faults, dislocations, or disturbances of neural connexions and chemical balances produce aberrant thought and behavior. Some illnesses such as intellectual development disorders, language disorders, autism spectrum disorders, attention deficit, and hyperactivity disorders probably look to genetic and physiological influences right from the start. Others are the product of a mental context formed over many years from the accretion of problems, specific events, and situations, often repressed or ignored. The behavior that surfaces years later may seem crazy to everyone else but reasoned, logical, and explicable, given that person's mental context. Untwisting the two and explaining why, in similar circumstances, some people survive and some do not is beyond our ken.

Even the most basic questions seem to defy clear answers. What is meant by mental disorders? How is their extent measured over time? Two hundred years ago, most disorders were classified as either melancholia or hysteria. By the end of the twentieth century, most delusional ideas were categorized as paranoia. In Germany in 1874, somewhere between a half and four-fifths of patients admitted into hospitals and asylums suffering from delusions (as symptoms of functional [or non-organic] psychoses) were said to be paranoic.[361] Criticism of paranoia as a broad class and the emphasis on nosology grew, but to little avail until after 1945. By then, America had become the center for the discipline internationally. Boundaries amongst different conditions blurred to the extent that schizophrenia became the catch-all for mental illness, and paranoia was just one of its subtypes. By the end of the 1980s, the emphasis shifted again toward establishing diagnostic criteria, sharp classifications, and clear labels. Again, the number of conditions billowed, such that paranoia was just one of a long list of delusional disorders. The meaning and usefulness of these boundaries were further complicated by the discovery of new drugs, especially SSRIs. Developed for one disorder, they were often effective across many others. All this only went to show that categories of mental illness are ungainly, though they have a bureaucratic value for legal and statistical purposes and the management of treatment programs.

Despite these points, and a general unwillingness to broach connexions between mental illness and society's regulations, it isn't difficult to appreciate how the burden of rules might drive the population along different paths. For most people, these paths are survivable. But for about one-fifth of the population, thought and behavior adapts poorly and exhibits what are today regarded as pathological features which may descend into psychosis - a catastrophic response in which the mind withdraws from the world and focuses solely upon the self.

The first path is compliance, passivity, and wanhope - turning oneself into a rule follower or an obedient rule enforcer. It is the path of least resistance. Collectively it amounts to apathy for the problems and even the misery and desperation others face. This is especially true if those in difficulty are thought to have brought their problems on themselves by not playing by the rules or falling foul of them by inattention, naivety, or bad luck. Passing judgment in this way, and comparing one's avoidance of wrongdoing with the failure of others to do so, brings a sense of achievement and relief. Along the first path are found obsessive-compulsive disorders, depression, anxieties, panic disorders and phobias, gender dysphoria, hypersomnolence, and conversion and feeding disorders. Trauma and stressor disorders are also more likely.

The second path is for those who flail against the rules. Some travelers seek punishment and atonement to elicit recognition that they have faced overwhelming odds created by circumstances outside their control. Some are resentful and angry and imagine the people and systems behind it all bearing the guilt and responsibility. Those who travel the second path are most likely to experience disruptive, impulse control and conduct disorders, elimination disorders, personality disorders, and paraphilic behavior.

Travelers along the third path seek out a new society or forge one in which they lead and other people follow. They live above rules, survey them, dispose of them, or make them. In some instances, they literally are rule makers: legislators or heads of large corporations or illicit organizations. In other cases, they are fantasists who assign themselves a mythical influence. Rule-makers are prone to more assertive personality disorders – narcissism, bipolar, or cyclothymia.

What evidence is there for these paths? It's difficult to answer when we can't even be sure that the incidence of mental illnesses today differs from the past - recent or distant. As a state that goes beyond momentary fear, breathlessness, concern, or restlessness and pervades the mind, gripping it, darkening it, wringing it dry, and leaving it exhausted, anxiety was known to the ancient Greeks and their physicians, such as Aretraneus, Galen, and Rufus. It was known in the mid-eighteenth century to writers such as Beard, Levy-Valensi, Kraepelin, and Kierkegaard. Auden sealed its status as a modern disease in his book *The Age of Anxiety,* which Bernstein gave musical form the following year. But there are no reliable figures. Today's numbers for Generalised Anxiety are around 5% (lifetime prevalence) in the West, with highs of about 8% in the USA, New Zealand, and Australia, compared to lows of under 1% in Nigeria and Shenzhen (China).[362] In England, increases are marked for young women and men, rising from around 10 to 20 or 30 per thousand between 1998 and 2018.[363] The incidence of OCD, too, remains consistent at around 1-2% (lifetime prevalence) in northern Europe, the UK, and North America. Figures for OCD are more variable in other parts of the world. For instance, Catholicism's emphasis on ritual purity, the prohibition of sin and shame (especially in sexual matters), warding off blasphemous thoughts, and repeated prayers seem to aid and abet the disorder.[364]

But perhaps description, not statistics, is a better way of looking at the question. Rules bring pressure to bear mostly indirectly by creating finer and finer cells – boxes of circumstances in which each person's mental states evolve and where so much is hidden, left unseen, misunderstood, misdiagnosed, and assumes such different expressions. Only by examining particular cells can we understand what is happening. The rules of the market, the bank balance, and accounting practices, for instance, mean a rise in the number of people living alone and determine a single-minded pursuit of wealth. The rules of the mobile phone, its modes of communication, and its features can reduce lives to staged images and aphorisms and perfectly curated beings. Alienation and anxiety follow soon after. Or perhaps the truth is we love rules because we think they will protect and insulate us from feelings of anxiety. Yet, in binding ourselves so tightly to our rules, we cut ourselves off from the freedom and possibility in which anxiety is rooted. And *that* concerns us still more. Strange as it may seem, we are anxious about not being anxious.

Look more carefully at the rules and processes that frame these grids, and we see detailed routines validated and normalized. Doctors, lawyers, psychiatrists, social workers, schools, and teachers, have taken over many aspects of the child's upbringing from parents. Routes are prepared to protect and nurture the child's sense of self and to provide for every need. Technology and industry cater to every want. The child emerges into a ready-made world. Rights are established and canonized in law. Education, healthcare, university, and income are just 'there.' If they are not, then we feel they ought to be. Objects of every description - from telephones and computers to buses, trains, the internet, airlines, and roads - make life more convenient, interesting, and safer. From the child's perspective, the conclusion is quite logical: the world is shaped around *me*.

It is a worldview confirmed by advertising, films, television, electronic games, literature, and music. At its center is the hero or anti-hero. Heroes are young, athletic, physically appealing, and outstanding at what they do. Heroes do what they do effortlessly; their talents are just 'there.' But they must struggle against people who are older, envious, jealous and trying to prevent them from securing what is naturally theirs.

The hero is reminiscent of Nietzsche's *ubermensch* and his influence less than a century earlier. Another more recent and, for many, more powerful statement of the hero's fantasy world is conjured up by Ayn Rand's *Fountainhead* and *Atlas Shrugged,* published in 1947 and 1958, respectively. Both novels owe much to the period between the wars. It is a kind of art deco literature that invokes a world of steel, smooth iron, glass, stone, and concrete. It is solid, monumental, spacious, clipped and neat, and sparsely decorated with rounded, geometric simplifications of nature. Its characters are laconic and clear-headed. They are detached because their actions are bound to clear values at odds with a society populated by looters and *Ein Heldenleben's* mean, thin, reedy, chattering critics who, driven by spite or envy or unthinking habit, are determined to subordinate the hero to the mass.

The books appeal to young adults - and young men especially – and were bestsellers when first published. They sharply distinguished the Soviet Union from an America that had not yet given up on Keynesianism. But the central message - the remarkable man or woman succeeding against a grasping herd - would later come into its own. Sales of both novels and Ayn Rand's other books found a steady market in the 1960s and 1970s. From the 1980s, sales picked up markedly: around 74,000 copies a year during the 1980s, 95,000 a year through the 1990s, 1.67 million the following decade, and over 3 million annually from 2015. Her books also claimed an influential readership: from Alan Greenspan (who was a member of Rand's intellectual clique), President Trump, and Sanji Javid (former Chancellor of the Exchequer and then Secretary of Health in the UK) to a rash of actors in the USA including Sandra Bullock, Brad Pitt, and Angelina Jolie.

The hero against the herd was a theme in popular music, too. In the 1950s and the 1960s, the coquettish fun and passing sentimentality of songs like *Be My Baby* (the Ronettes) lived alongside self-conscious protest songs, narratives, and ballads on love and loss from writers such as Joni Mitchel, Simon and Garfunkel, and Fleetwood Mac. Old and young enjoyed Abba's playful kitsch during the 1970s. But confirmation of your love *for me* in the teeth of the world's opposition took pride of place. *We're living in a world of fools, breaking us down, when they should all should let us be, we belong to you and me, how deep is your love*? That is the question. If you *really* love me, prove it and join me in my world. It's an obsessive romance in which how 'I' feel is all that matters. I can take you or leave you. If you want to be with me, '*it ain't complicated*' - be as I want you to be, declares Avril Lavigne. Self-love was now the '*greatest love of all.*' Traveling this road alone sings Carey, makes it a long journey, but that's the way of the Hero.

By the 2000s, the message had become even less subtle. I'm going to sing about what I've done in spite of the rest of the world, including friends and family who wanted me to fail and who quickly changed their tune and said congratulations when I succeeded: that's Post Malone's revenge. The world is mine for the taking, and other people, especially women, are disposable objects, boast Eminem, Kanye West, and Lil Peep. Yet I can live quite happily in my own self-indulgent misery. Billie Eilish's dirges, sulky rather than sultry, sodden rather than smoldering, offer up a world where I feel everything while nobody else cares or notices or is trying to take from me. I am here, feeling, but the world's gone blind. Occasionally there is a *you* who causes me to feel and offers relief from my self-imposed isolation, but *you* are little more than ghosts or shadows of the self. Music rooted in the slave spirituals and work songs, in deeply shared emotions born of base hardships, was reduced to a thin, weak pastiche.

Chapter 28

Ressentiment and Machiavellianism

Twisted around rancor are ressentiment and Machiavellianism. Ressentiment vents through aggressive depressives who do their best to destroy society if it does not grant them the recognition they feel they deserve. The Machiavellians leave in their wake a cardboardy, bromidic, insipid, and fragile version of what once had purpose and meaning.

Although not classed as a mental disorder, ressentiment feeds on the depressives' sense of inferiority, fragile self-worth, shame, unattractiveness, and social ineptitude. Its sufferers travel the third path. They seek attention and admiration for their inflated or imagined success and put themselves forward to champion a populace that, unlike them, has not managed to shake off society's restraints. Between the wars, the strongmen - Mussolini, Stalin, and Hitler - and their followers undermined the courts and judiciary because they saw them as an extension of the ruling elite's interests. They set out to break up current political arrangements because they thought them unfair and obstructive. They attacked the press because they said it was biased and conservative. They assaulted what they saw as the combined means with which the unworthy protected their wealth and privilege. Out of envy and spite, having once felt excluded, they denied others and took from them. Ressentiment found its simplest collective expression as Germany's frustration with its place in the world.

Ressentiment is again at work through populists today in America, the UK, France and Germany, Italy and Greece, and elsewhere in Europe. Each side - elite and underdog – is vengeful and resentful. Each attempts to disparage the other. In America, Bannon, the architect of Trump's electoral success in 2016, was open in his stated aim to bring the establishment crashing down and destroy the state. In England, Johnson's 'advisor,' Dominic Cummings, engineered a successful Brexit referendum and election, handing Johnson his own mandate. Cummings was equally plain in his determination to upend the establishment, wipe away the civil service, marginalize the press, and create a new revolutionary state. Like the populists between the wars, today's levelers feel they were never taken seriously. Having been ridiculed, disparaged, and left in the cold, it is their turn to exclude and demean by tapping into a reserve of similar resentments simmering in people like them from all walks of life.

Journalists are not immune from these feelings. They are not shy to describe themselves as seekers of fact and truth and raise their profession to stand alongside the judiciary and legislature as guardians of democracy. And in this, they regularly call upon the past. For Scharma, a contributing editor of the Financial Times, Milton's *Areopagitica* is a majestic articulation of the principle of press freedom.[365] But is that what Milton had in mind?

Writing some 20 years before the first newspaper appeared, Milton's *Areopagitica,* for the liberty of unlicensed printing,[366] is more of a gentle argument for common sense and tolerance. England had had enough of schism and sectarianism. Was it not time to show each other a little charity? Licensing did no good and could do great harm. To suppress books was to suppress reason itself. It was an affront to learning. It left men suspicious of each other and fearful of every book, pamphlet, and conventicle. Who would decide what should be printed? Anyone learnéd, capable, and experienced enough would find the job impossibly tedious and soul-destroying. Anyone who wanted to do it would be ignorant, imperious, base, pecuniary, and in every other way unsuited. And what would be the point? The dissolute, ignorant, heretical, evil-mannered, and foolish do not read books and do not need them to spread vice and immorality.

Today's modern 'press' is a world away from Milton's plea for a bit of goodwill. It is a complex beast because it, like democracy, has been turned into an absolute. As such, it has been fashioned into a tool for attack and defense, pushing this policy or party or politician and damning that one, setting agendas, changing attitudes, fighting campaigns, stoking tensions, suffocating one point of view, and oxygenating another. It works day and night to catch the eye, entice, evoke, provoke, tickle fancies, wheedle, stimulate and simulate outrage, fan the flames, misdirect, and build up heroes and demons it then tears down or forgets.

Unlike ressentiment, Machiavellianism is a recognized aspect of various personality disorders. It, too, has been normalized. Ideas and practices turned into absolutes (so that faith, belief, and argument are no longer required) need only be applied and used. Instrumentalism is no longer a problem but an attribute. All walks of life are tainted. In administration and organizations, the self-centered operator, the callow fantasist, and the narrow careerist are rewarded. The arts are driven by galleries, curators, collectors, and firms. They advise on what to buy and who to sponsor. In their words, they help identify 'investment-quality stores of value' and provide well-informed advice on financially sound transactions. Precisely which artist and which pieces are valuable is determined through a consensus arrived at by these players. Each listens to what others say about an artist or artwork, who is exhibiting what, and who is buying. Neither the work nor the artist is of much significance. What matters is their bankability. Released from any need to mean something, a piece of art can mean anything or nothing.

English literature also became decidedly highbrow between the wars and continued to be so after 1945. It became about its techniques and philosophies just as art became about art and music about music. To criticize a writer whose vocabulary and fine-grained description get in the way of whatever the writing is supposed to be about is to miss the point. Technique comes before all else. Rather like the chromium-plated Liberace or sparkling Lang Lang, the display is everything. The writer, who is bizarre for its own sake, is putting on a show of imagination. Writers specializing in soul-destroying banality or the iconoclastic are vaunting perspicuity and dissent. The trend is encouraged by publishers, agents, awards, and juries with at least one eye on the bottom line. The pensions or patronage some writers were lucky enough to receive up until the end of the nineteenth century were replaced by prizes. A work, like its authors, has to be categorized and marketed, identified and sold, placed within a literary school, and assigned an influence. Even when the master self-deprecatingly reveals the fakery of the whole shebang, that mockery is itself a claim to originality.

As philosophy became more gaunt, severe, and proscriptive, it became more instrumental. The notion that language signaled concepts and reflected the mind gave way to the certainty that thought and language were the same. Sapir and Wharf made this explicit when they concluded it was difficult, perhaps impossible, for two people who, from birth, did not share the same language to think in the same way. Each was forever barred from truly understanding the other. The exclusive nature of language and mind implied was later turned against the world in general. What was said only had meaning if it was either true or false. All concerns which had no meaning were of no interest to Philosophers. There is little point in debating issues that could not be verified - such as religion, metaphysics, or ethics. Frege devised a language of logic that subsequently overturned Aristotle's. It led him to design a similar system for mathematics and language that would influence Russell and

Wittgenstein. Russell supposed that once the correct logic is established, the philosopher can work out what is *really* meant and do away with ordinary language altogether. Because so many problems were created by trying to say what could not be said in plain words, Wittgenstein supposed that he had answered all philosophy's major questions through logical calculus.

What had been a medium through which ideas were formulated and presented now became the subject of analysis. The philosophers' task was to expunge the unverifiable and devise a communication system through which the verifiable could be discussed without ambiguities or mistakes.[367] Natural or everyday language was ill-suited for this. A system of logic was needed - symbols that could replace the uncertainties and ambiguities of words. Philosophy *was* the study of language - a belief that soon infected all its branches.

By the early 1950s, the mood had begun to warm a little. From his substantial contributions, Wittgenstein walked away. He had, he said, been too dogmatic. He was now interested in how human language, despite its fallibilities, nevertheless managed to communicate. There was no fundamental, underlying logic operating, no ultimate standard of correctness to uncover and work to. There was only public practice. This alone governed language. Strawson saw little purpose in reducing common-sense ideas to what were supposed to be bare, error-free theories of logic and science. Nor could one understand one's own experience without admitting that other people have those experiences. Even the just society that Rawls' imagined for America seemed far more down to earth than many of Frege's, Wittgenstein's, and Russel's imaginings. In post-war Europe, too, the mood changed. Gadamer rejected the notion of objective, universally valid principles of logic and rationality. Too many equated truth, knowledge, and reason with instruments of power. When Russell, Frege, and Wittgenstein described routes to the truth, they claimed not only '*to know*' but that '*you do not understand what you are talking about.*' Habermas agreed with Gadamer that truth has to be arrived at through consensus and conversation; otherwise, it is impossible to organize and arrange. Husserls' desire to establish philosophy as a rigorous science (focused on the essential structure of consciousness) was supplanted by Heidegger's concern with relationships among people. Reason and science, argued Foucault, defined themselves in terms of the people they excluded. Culture, Levi-Strauss believed, was a systematic reflection of human mental structures.

Yet these arguments, too, once they hardened, once doubt was removed, became as intolerant and exclusive as logical positivism. By the late 1970s, ideas that were self-consciously radical, or a snub at the status quo, had become instruments of identity, power, and influence. Philosophy, like other areas of inquiry, also became fragmented. Attempts at large-scale works by individual philosophers – the systems of thought which touched on many aspects of human interest – were replaced by shorter discussions on matters of 'relevance' as utilitarianism invaded the universities. Philosophy, like all subjects, had to show materiality and function. Philosophers had to professionalize. That meant specializing and demonstrating influence through the application of philosophical 'approaches.'

Logical positivism of a kind returned just a few years into the twenty-first century. Not only were ideas fetishized, but evidence was transformed into an absolute. It followed that actions couldn't be taken without facts, whose generation depended upon those actions. If there is no evidence that masks prevent the spread of covid-19, then masks should not be worn. If there is no evidence that the virus spreads among children, the schools should stay open. Turning evidence into an absolute also demanded bold verbal redundancies. An organization can no longer be called an institute for healthcare, a center for medicine, or just an institute. It becomes an Institute for *Evidence-Based* Healthcare, a Centre for *Evidence-Based* Medicine, or an *Evidence-based* Practice Institute. If the phrase conveys any additional meaning, it is a desire to establish the truth *and* root out, categorize, and catalog everyone else's faults and prejudice.

Of all the West's organizations, families probably suffer the most from ressentiment and Machiavellianism. Whatever its legal status or makeup, the family's idealization has turned it into a political constituency to be chastised or rewarded, but always entered into the books as a cost and made to remember that. It is a rigid bastion of social conservatism and champion of trite cant. It is a kit and caboodle of chaotic lives, ill-discipline, and state-appointed wastrels and scroungers to be ridiculed, rejected, and kicked into the long grass and forgotten. Where pro-lifers get their way, it comprises young women corralled to satiate society's moral appetites. It is the shiny, young, and above all, 'hardworking' couple lost and subservient in an empty desert of identical homes. It is the screaming child with an embarrassed mother in a train hedged in by self-important singletons tut-tutting silently at all the subsidies they must pay for. It is the parents and children obediently crowded into the family coach. Saying the West's fertility rate has been under two since 1980 and does not seem likely to get above that is to say that it's dying.

Chapter 29

Market over Society

The market is a necessary and pragmatic response to a growth in population and density. It trains resources on the manufacture of goods in demand. From the perspective of society, however, these concentrations are potentially damaging. They suck resources away from other activities which, though necessary, do not attract sufficient interest or on which claims are seemingly inexhaustible. Resources accumulate in preferred sectors while others lose out. Puritanism transforms the market into an absolute and - by dint of rancor, ressentiment, and Machiavellianism - favors it beyond all practical advantage. Society thus renders itself temporarily incapable of balancing out the material flows vital to economic growth.

In response to depression and war, Keynes handed governments an intellectual rationalization for redistribution. He was ambivalent about the market as he was about most things in life. He was not anti-capitalist, or at least not enough to unnerve the Treasury or Churchill. On the contrary, he appeared to think that capitalism was, for the time being, essential to generate wealth but had to be controlled and managed. It's a view familiar to all those who favor a mixed economy. The market leads, and society follows. The market creates wealth, and society redistributes it. And for some thirty years after Keynes's death in 1946, the West experienced remarkable improvements in educational opportunities, living standards, and health.

However, the mixed economy couldn't be sustained for long. Few people accepted that redistribution is the key to economic growth. Nor was the market thought of or treated as a mode of distribution. Consequently, it couldn't be integrated organically into society. Instead, society was bullied into believing it depends on the market, and the market resented society for holding it back. Keynesians fixated on employment numbers, and marketeers on tax cuts and keeping the upper hand over labor. Socialists, who once had demanded state ownership, tempered themselves and accepted the market as a wealth creator just as long as they could be its conscience. Conservative 'wets' stomached transfers as a reluctant concession either to their sense of charity or to real politick and what they felt to be the politics of envy. There could be no coherent arrangement to move funds, people, and materials around so that populations, sectors, and organizations could support each other and grow a stable economy. If there is any sense of direction, it is overwhelmingly to protect business and minimize the drag as it moves through society. And all the while, the market undermined itself and the communities it fed on.

Policy and politics degenerated into chants of 'you said this,' 'I said that,' 'your fault, their fault,' which translated into stop-start, one-step-forward, one-step-back, economic jolts. When the economy stumbled badly during the 1973 oil crisis, the market began to reassert itself. The marketeers scoffed at Keynes' belief that inflation and unemployment exclude one another. A little inflation and rising employment should go together, he had said. Growing demand pushes up prices; this encourages firms to expand and hire more staff; these new staff, in turn, push up demand. So why were both unemployment and inflation now picking away at western economies? The Keynesians stuck to their guns. The oil shock had driven up the price of everything all at once. There was no cash to expand businesses, causing employment to stagnate and fall. Wage and price controls were needed to limit increases in the cost of labor and materials. This would enable companies to expand the supply of goods. The marketeers threw cold water over that analysis. Rising inflation and unemployment revealed a basic flaw in Keynesianism. Government had spent too much and left too much cash sloshing around. This pushed up prices so quickly that the value of savings and investments tumbled. The only solution was to tighten the money supply. Higher interest rates and tax increases would suck cash out of everyone's pockets until prices stabilized. Tax cuts, not government spending, would see businesses expand and their products bought.

Thatcher's election victory in 1979, and Reagan's in 1981, sealed the market's dominance. Keynes was just plain wrong; in any case, the cold war required clarity between America and Communism, which Keynesianism did not provide in many people's minds. One had to have the correct theory, declared Friedman,[368] and that, he asserted, the central banks had not had before the 1980s. The notion the market is organic to a complex of transfers was either dismissed as a brand of oriental serfdom or simply did not register. When Friedman looked at the economies in East

Asia, he saw only the free market. Keynesian and welfare socialists had had their day, and it was time to redress the wrongs.

Transfers or subsidies in their different guises in the West became the target of lacerating and often moralizing criticism. Subsidies encourage companies (and whole sectors) to improve alliances with politicians rather than innovate. Companies producing inferior or more expensive goods put more creative, efficient, and effective competitors who make better, cheaper goods out of business. Subsidies also encourage people and businesses to consume more than they need, generating more waste and pollution. Goods manufactured in one jurisdiction are bought up and then sold elsewhere. Subsidies are paid for with higher taxes, a bigger deficit, and heavier debt, which means less spending on education, health, and other public services and goods. Poorer households will benefit the least from subventions because the rich buy up a much larger share of subsidized goods such as electricity or fuel. What is true of subsidies is also true of other kinds of transfers, whether as welfare or unrealistically high wages. They reward failure and destroy incentives to work, innovate, and invest. They undermine productivity,[369] distort the market, and cultivate dependency. This is not what rational economics is all about. Indeed, subsidizing a few selected 'winners,' a common practice in North and South in the 1970s, is still widely regarded as an example of disastrous industrial policy.[370]

And at first sight, subsidies were used sparingly. Amongst OECD members, industrial subsidies were no more than 0.2% of GDP for most countries. Only in Hungary did they exceed 1% in 2002. Attitudes to farming subsidies were a little more relaxed. Agriculture is now only a small appendage to the West's economies and employs few people. Governments are also sensitive to food safety and security, dietary preferences, the preservation of the landscape (which depends upon the farmers who husband it), and political constituencies. In absolute terms, agricultural subsidies in the US were amongst the highest in the West – an average of 66.2 billion dollars (though this was still less than 1% of America's GDP). EU subsidies were estimated at 97.1 billion euros. These figures were higher than Japan's 41.8, Korea 7.5, Brazil 3.5 and Thailand 1.9 billion (the averages for each year from 1995-2001). For WTO members, agricultural subsidies fell from 272.9 billion to 193.8 billion (2001) and, for OECD members, rose to 279.5 billion (in 2004).

As a percentage of GDP, general subsidies in the EU remained modest (if one excludes aid to railways, agriculture, and the financial sector), rising from 0.49% in 2010 to 0.76% in 2018. About two-thirds of these took the form of direct grants, and the rest were made as exemptions, reductions, or deferrals in tax. In America, subsidies paid to private businesses and government enterprises have risen steadily since the mid-1970s. Not until 2020 did subsidies jump (by about 1300%) to US$1.3 trillion.

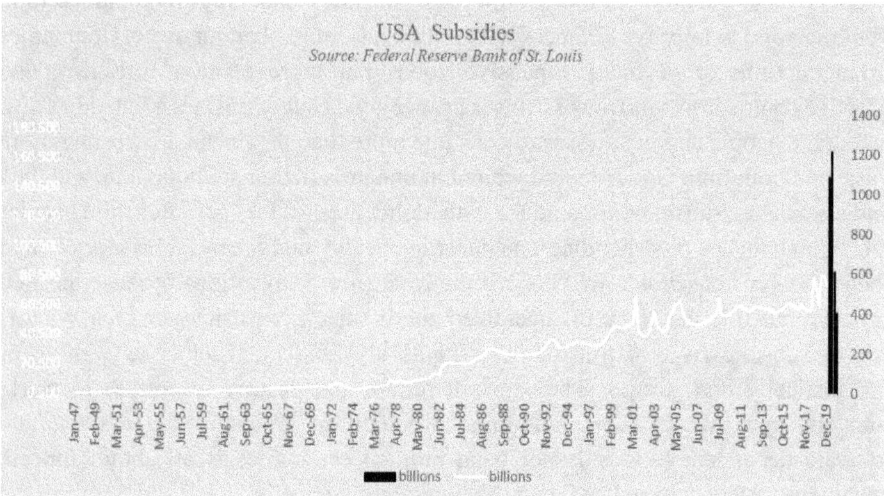

Figure 29.1

Nevertheless, putting the market first demanded a shift in resources from the general population to business, though in guises other than those plainly labeled industrial or agricultural subsidies. Wages were held down, and taxation moved even more decisively in favor of companies. Utilities and transport were privatized, and fuel taxes grew. The population had to shoulder the full price of energy. The cost of getting around became prohibitive. Welfare payments and social housing were pared down still further while the price of a university education soared.

The results were predictable. In the early years of the marketeers' victory, the determination to expunge inflation dovetailed perfectly with the main agenda: less government spending and less regulation. Increases in interest rates served the banks well. Large profits accumulated in the UK, where banks had already established an oligopoly. The general population suffered as incomes stagnated. Manufacturing sectors were either erased or lopped off, packaged up, shipped out, and sold to various parts of the Third World.

It was the same elsewhere, provided banks were not themselves heavy borrowers. In the 1980s, when again oil prices jumped, and inflation crackled, the rise in interest rates precipitated a crisis in Sweden. Real estate and stock markets flared up in the wake of deregulation and the abolition of restrictions on the volume of bank lending. When interest rates soared, the markets collapsed, and bad debts gathered, the banks faced insolvency. In 1991-2, the state had to step in and rescue the entire financial system. A slower but similar crisis was already underway in America. Banks and savings and loans associations (responsible for about half of all mortgages in 1980) went under. They had lent too much following the removal of restrictions on their activities.

Governments across the West ignored these warnings. If the market dictated the expansion of finance and services, then that is what would happen. The drive for less government, less regulation, and less public spending was not just about eradicating inflation. They were about putting the market first. All sorts of 'traditional' enterprises became involved in finance and were soon just as active in financial markets as they were generating ready cash on the high street.

There was nothing new about financial instruments and their inveterate use. That's clear just from their definition as documents (paper and, more recently, electronic) identifying ownership of companies, rights to assets, and responsibility for liabilities, and traded privately or on a central exchange. However, they have multiplied enormously in variety and volume, and nonfinancial companies have also become involved.[371] Financial instruments are, it is frequently said, a way to manage risks created by movements in exchange rates, interest rates, and commodity prices, ensuring the flow of cash to cover operational expenses. And the somewhat prim and proper declaration that such instruments are never used for speculative purposes is routinely included in companies' financial statements.

Some writers say that, empirically, nonfinancial companies derive little or no income from such instruments. Some claim otherwise - and do so with a deal of supporting evidence. The fact is that estimating a firm's income from financial markets is made difficult by different classifications of revenue streams and assets and by networks of company ownership. In America, nonfinancial companies' financial assets[372] began to exceed revenues from sales and goods and services in 1986 and have since pulled away.

As the trade in financial markets grew, so the company was further distracted from what used to be its main production activities, such as manufacturing cars or selling clothes or prepared foods. Instead, these came to be seen mainly as a way of bringing in a steady flow of cash through the shop's front door – proof to the world that the company has the hard cash to back its plays (and finance its debts) on the markets. It doesn't matter too much how or why the money flows in so long as it does. Only when revenue slows does the company think about why that might be and how to remedy the situation. Yet by then, the people who manage the company no longer live and breathe the business, especially if it has become part of a bigger group. They no longer have the experience, enthusiasm, understanding, or freedom to do what is needed, and the company begins to founder.

As wealth gathers in financial and nonfinancial companies (and in the hands of their owners, managers, and investors), demand amongst the general population thins and weakens. What production does take place tends to favor luxury items. This has been a noticeable feature of the last forty years. Precisely what comprises 'luxury' goods and services is widely discussed, and classifications of all kinds have been devised: from high-end and low-end to old luxury and new luxury, real and faux. These gradations reflect efforts to lift sales by stretching desirability and 'aspiration' as far down the income hierarchy as possible. Estimating its value is not especially helpful. The true luxury market is, by definition, limited, exclusive, inaccessible, and indicative of weak demand rather than a substitute for it.

The simple truth is that financial services flourished initially because everyone else suffered. Demand was needed, and that could be puffed up with loans. This strategy was inherently dangerous, as Sweden and the US had shown many years earlier. Yet loans were allowed to collect like pick-up sticks. The pile finally collapsed in 2007-8. First came bailouts on an unprecedented scale. In Europe, the numbers jumped to nearly €1 trillion in 2009 (around 10% of GDP), falling steadily to €150 billion (or just under 2%) in 2017. Estimates of subsidies paid out across the West to patch over the financial crisis vary greatly, but around US$551-993 billion annually from 2008-2013 is a fair guess. [373] It includes subsidies paid to organizations deemed systemically important or 'too big to fail,' making it easier for them to attract equity, reducing the amount of debt they had to take on, and their operating costs. It also covers subsidies to offshore financial centers (worth around 21-32 trillion), sovereign wealth funds, equity funds, and organizations such as money market mutual funds, hedge funds, special purpose vehicles, the repo market, and private equity funds. Together, these make up the shadow banking system. The 'system' is centered in the US and Europe, and its transactions amount to $71 trillion annually.

Chapter 30

Madness in the Method

The Great Crisis persuaded marketeers to double down on the market. Resources continued to be driven away from the population through taxation, lower wages, and higher prices for necessities such as water, energy, and housing.

The Great Crisis was an expression of decay, not a cause, and the West's response has only made matters worse. Governments restated their determination to adhere to the market with still greater vigor. Money spent on the financial sector would have to be repaid. The shift in resources away from the general population, which had helped bring the crisis about in the first place, would continue. Austerity was the solution. The Puritan's enthusiasm was plain in the UK. If the budget deficit – the difference between expenditure and revenue – was not brought under control and reduced, the government's creditors at home and abroad would lose confidence in the British economy, borrowing rates would shoot up, and this would ruin the country for decades to come. Blinded by their assumptions about how economies work, the government ensured that resources continued to migrate from society to the market. In this topsy-turvy, back-to-front understanding of wealth creation, politicians and economists thrashed about trying to put together fugitive transfers and mitigate this or that problem. How resources were moved before, during, and after the crisis are described below. As such, it describes how 'the economy' grinds down society leaving it thin and ragged.

Real wages – the value of wages after it is gnawed at by inflation - have not done much for the last forty years. In America, real wages in 2018 had about the same purchasing power as fifty years earlier.[374] In England, the incomes of the bottom 10% of earners in 1991 were no higher than in 1967.[375] Between 1997 and 2002, the median wage grew 2.2%, slowing down to 1% until the financial crisis, before falling by around 1.5-1.8% over the next eight years.[376] It was similar in

Australia, with real wage growth of about 1%[377] from 2003, dropping to 0.4% in 2013. In 2018, median real earnings were still 3% below their level in 2008.

That more people were working helps illustrate just how soft wages had become. Minimum wages backed with legislation are standard throughout the West. Though these were supposed to keep wages from sliding any further, they gave plenty of employers reason to bring wages down to the lowest common denominator. Government after government also introduced scheme after scheme to encourage businesses to take on and train workers. These may have affected the availability of labor, enlivening wages locally, if not internationally, but they aim primarily to reduce unemployment for political effect.

What governments have conspicuously failed to do is compel businesses to improve wages. On the contrary, governments weakened the power of unions, making it clear that businesses had the whip hand. Losing the 'old' manufacturing industries at the start of the West's 'restructuring' made that job easier. Unions had been at their strongest when activities such as shipbuilding, steel, and cars focused the energies of large numbers of workers. As manufacturing dissipated and services took up the slack, more part-time work and less pay were offered and taken.

Taxes were also skewed in favor of business.[378] This redirection is a modern invention of the marketeers, determined to get society to pay for its own foibles and unyoke business from it. For most of the West's history, commerce had carried that weight. Having been allowed to establish commercial islands in a feudal sea and link them together at home and overseas, merchants financed the crown's whims and wars. During the fourteenth and fifteenth centuries, taxes on goods and services became the primary revenue source. If merchants at home wouldn't or couldn't finance the crown, then the crown could always go to merchants and moneylenders in Europe. It was not very becoming for Royalty to run around looking for subventions, but needs must. These sensibilities, and the continued expansion of commerce, led to a change in financing. With sufficient command over commerce and consumption taxes, the crown could promise future earnings to those willing to lend to it, thus establishing a market in government debt.

At the end of the eighteenth century, emergency measures - an income tax and a tax on all kinds of luxuries - were introduced to cover the cost of war with France. The government targeted wealthier members of society who, in practice, ended up supplying about 60% of the revenue. Nobody liked it, and in 1816, it was abandoned. It was reintroduced at 7d in the pound on annual income above 150 pounds in 1843, again hitting the affluent. This was better than a tax on goods which, the merchants argued to some effect, ought to be allowed to move freely: duties on 700 items were removed. Nevertheless, consumption taxes remained the state's main source of revenue.

The first world war saw an increase in all taxes so that the general populace now found themselves paying for a war in which they also fought. But profit-makers also took a hit and would do so again in the second world war. Income and consumption taxes and national insurance contributions took on more strain throughout the fifties and sixties. But the big shift came in the 1970s with the introduction of value-added tax and a substantial increase in contributions from income tax and national insurance. The pattern was entrenched during the following decades. In 2018, corporate tax collectively paid around 60 billion – equal to about 30% of the profits of one company - BP. Meanwhile, 'ordinary' people had stumped up more than half a trillion pounds.

The privatization of utilities - energy and water – also shifted costs onto the general population. In 1948, myriad gas distribution companies were nationalized and integrated into a single unit called British Gas. Prices were set by negotiation between the company and producers. Its monopoly and the fact that it was also an important producer meant that prices could be controlled easily. In 1965, gas was discovered in the North Sea. When the market took over the gas industry in the mid-1980s, prices rose consistently and sharply. Changes in the cost of production (from extraction and refining and its delivery to the point at which it enters the national distribution system) explain these rises only in part.

Between the time gas reaches the earth's surface and the moment it is burnt on the kitchen stove or in the house boiler for hot water and heating, its price increases by more than 1000% (figures for 2016/17). How is this extraordinary rise explained? One reason is that gas must be transported through a lattice of pipes, refineries, storage tanks, and compressor stations under constant pressure, requiring the amount of gas entering the system to match the amount leaving it. This is managed by the national grid, which also maintains and upgrades the distribution infrastructure. The gas then enters one of eight regional distribution networks – the webs of fine pipework from which homes and smaller businesses draw their gas. Finally, suppliers arrange the metering and billing of gas flowing into houses and collect payments.

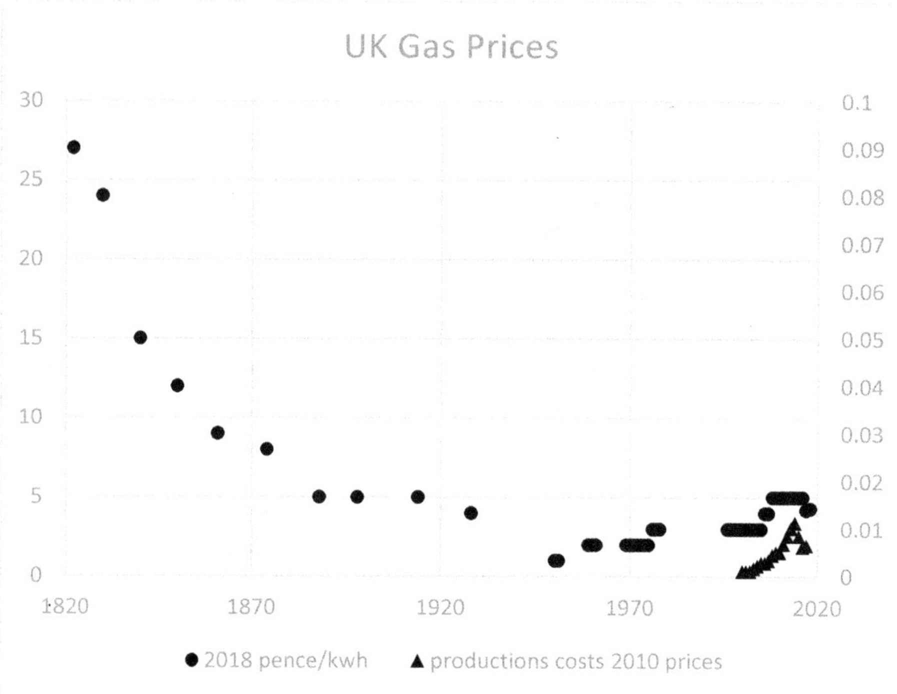

Figure 30.1

The costs of producing and distributing gas into the home are comparatively modest. Production in the North Sea (the site of the world's most expensive fields) was around 1.067pence per kilowatt-hour in 2016. This figure excludes capital costs. The National Grid adds another 0.02229 pence to each kilowatt-hour. The largest of the distributional networks, Cadence, manages four of the eight regions. Its costs amount to 0.26 pence for the same unit, while the suppliers' costs add another 0.42 pence. Put these costs together, and each kilowatt reaches a little under 2 pence per kilowatt-hour. The National Grid, distribution networks, and suppliers also demand profits, and Ofgem regulates these, effectively doubling costs.

But that still leaves quite a gap between the actual price of gas and the amount paid by the general population. One other link in the chain accounts for this – the gas shippers. The shippers make up 'the market,' which is now international in that they trade in gas across national boundaries through pipes and in liquid form on ships.

The lion's share of the price consumers pay is neither for the gas itself nor its distribution, but for what shippers are prepared to pay amongst themselves. Once the gas is in the distribution system under pressure, it must move through the system no matter what. In effect, traders do not more than buy and sell rights to quantities of that gas. They intend to buy low and sell high. Traders can be anyone with money. They include all the players in the distribution system: the producers (such as Exxon, Shell, BP, Elf, and Gazprom), the distributors (such as Cadence), and the suppliers (such as Southern Electric, Scottish Power, and Powergen). They also include banks (such as Deutsche), hedge funds, and specialized traders. The distributors are not allowed to buy and sell gas directly, but they can do so through other companies in the groups they belong to.

It is not difficult to see why prices in the market, and the final price carried by the general population, grow. Even traders with no vested interest in production or distribution profit from buying low and selling high. Meanwhile, companies involved in producing, shipping, and distributing – and especially those related to distributors whose profits are capped - will want to make as much as possible by ensuring that the price of gas flowing through the pipes is as high as possible. When legal techniques are not enough, then they will manipulate the markets. The extent to which this happens is unknown, but it would be naïve to think it is merely occasional.

The financialization of the supply companies also influences the costs homes must bear. Companies find it relatively easy to attract loans and investments with a guaranteed and predictable income, which can be recycled through the financial markets or other economic activities. This improves returns for managers and shareholders, but the consumer is on the hook for a bailout should the company over-reach itself.

The price at which gas is delivered to homes today is not wildly different from that at the end of the nineteenth century and early twentieth century. But the context has changed dramatically. The quantity of gas used has increased enormously. Once, it was a luxury that only those with money could choose to adopt. Now it is ubiquitous and built into houses and workplaces. It is essential to sustaining domestic and working lives and biological existence. One can no longer *choose* to have gas and electricity. Yet the state treats energy as an option and hands it over to the market, which remorselessly loads costs onto every person and family. These arrangements enable rapid expansions in resources drained away from the general populace under the guise of what is presented as a universal law - 'supply and demand.' Today it is a cut in supplies from Russia. Tomorrow it will be excessively cold or hot weather.

The price of water is even more iniquitous. Its supply is an obvious necessity for any large community. It was usually treated as a civic duty fulfilled by providing a tank or pump from which citizens could draw. Once pipes were laid and water delivered to houses, 'the cost of this, not the liquid itself' justified payments. By 1908 its price ranged from about two and a half old pennies/m3 (about half of today's price) to around 5% of the rateable value (which is not so different from 2021). Again, however, the context has changed in two respects.

First, the amount of water used has increased enormously. Piped water used to be a luxury or convenience that one could choose to have or not. And while essential for drinking, one could decide not to wash bodies or clothes or dispose of sewage. Running water is now ubiquitous. It is built into life and is essential to public health and used for certain things more frequently than in the past: washing hands, brushing teeth, washing more clothes, and flushing away small quantities of sewage. The result is standards of bodily hygiene about which the room for discretion is limited. Nor are there many choices over mechanization - from washing machines and dishwashers to toilets and showers – which multiply the amount of water used. For instance, a proper wash of a family's clothes by hand would occupy a good day's work about twice a week or more, equivalent to around £230 or so in lost wages.

Secondly, while its retail price has remained reasonably stable, the cost of harnessing water, purifying it, and recycling it has fallen despite becoming more complex. But instead of allowing prices to fall, the gap has been filled by 'the market.' Financialization compounds the problem.

The use of cars has long since outstripped any other mode of transport. But since the 1990s, the distances traveled have fallen, and the number of trips has increased: people are moving locally more frequently. This trend is stronger amongst those with the lowest income. They are also four times less likely to be at the wheel of a car than people with high incomes. This means that people on low incomes are moving about eleven miles a day – the distance one expects in preindustrial societies of people making their way to market or fetch water.

Cost is part of the explanation and reflects a willingness to treat mobility as something a person can do without. Indeed, it is treated more like a privilege to be paid for. Tax on petrol was lower when cars were the preserve of the rich, while taxes on car ownership have also remained high. Estimates of mobility's demands on income today average at about 13-14%. Those figures are probably too low. It is easier to cut back on travel than heat, food, or housing, and people who earn less walk more. But as the car took over, trains and buses were degraded and became more expensive. A century ago, 2.186 billion trips were made on trains annually by a population of 45 million people. That's about 55 trips by each person a year. The length of the track was some 32,000 kilometers. A century later, those numbers had fallen to 1.76 billion or 26 trips for each person on track half as long. Commuters from the wealthier end of society make these trips. Only about 9% of the population travel once a week or more, and only 10% of those on the lowest incomes ever travel by train. Two-fifths travel once a year or never. Bus services, too, have deteriorated. In 2018 buses traveled 2 billion miles, just over half of which took place within London. Eighty years earlier, buses carried passengers some 19 billion miles. Much of the decline occurred before privatization and has hovered at around 2 billion ever since. A national service accounts for an increasing share of this, while local services outside London wither away.

Since the 1960s, road deaths have fallen dramatically. Improvements in engineering and planning are the reasons usually given for this. But people have also been doing their best to keep off the roads precisely because they are, in many respects, more dangerous. Parents drive their children to school whenever they can and rarely let them into the streets or parks by themselves. Inside hermetically sealed, sound-proofed, air-conditioned cocoons, quiet and comfortable, decorated with safety devices and screens and buttons and lights, a sense of control and serene detachment quickly takes over. Outside, narrow paths for walkers scarcely separate flesh and blood from the road. Green men flash resentfully and impatiently. Planners are reluctant to add new crossings or lengthen timings. They might think about it: if traffic flows are high (6,000) a day; if the fragile pedestrian has a hard time 'asserting precedence' (as one report advises) over hunks of metal driven at speed and often with remarkable callousness; and if prior accidents have shown the dangers. But don't hold your breath. Consequently, the elderly and the cyclists, especially those 'asserting their precedence,' are most likely to end up dead on the road today.

It does not take much imagination to appreciate what happens when people are pushed from the car onto trains, buses, or streets. Every aspect of life, from medical care to shopping, becomes difficult. Isolation and alienation quickly build. Alcoholism, drugs, suicide, risky behavior, and other pathologies are common, whether in sparsely populated, rural communities or in cities where people are divided by poorly organized, fragmented, over-crowded, and expensive transport.

If providing enough food to the population is a primary criterion of legitimate government, then the West has been extraordinarily successful at first sight. It was not always so. In Britain, hunger and malnutrition were still widespread at the beginning of the twentieth century, though famines had been left behind. Earnings largely determined whether a family ate and whether they ate adequately or not. But with many living so close to the edge, all kinds of other considerations might decide whether you and your family clung on or fell: an understanding of food and how to prepare it and cook it; seasonality and weather; the age of children in the household; whether or not a child could bring in additional income; an effort to get to the market on time, to organize meals, and to clear up afterward. During the first world war, a good proportion of men presenting themselves at recruitment offices were turned away because they were too sickly. And many who were accepted visibly flourished once they were given the ingredients they saw little of in civilian life - regular meals, exercise, and sunlight.

With that lesson in mind (and experience organizing supplies nationally), England could say with reasonable confidence that by the 1920s, its people had enough food. And for the next thirty years, the kind and quantity of food consumed altered little. By the 1950s, the population was not only better fed, but spending on food as a proportion of gross income had fallen into single figures where it remained for the next half-century or so.

The market, though, threw up new problems. Businesses involved in producing and delivering food must deal with the fact that a person can only eat so much. A growth in population, technological improvements, and higher production volumes allow prices to fall, but only up to a point, as there are still limits on how much one person can eat. Corralling supplies through a smaller number of larger and well-integrated businesses also helps tap demand. But then what? Greater variety, better packaging, better advertising and marketing, and a yet more sensitive and responsive distribution system can help. Yet the fact remains that any one person can only eat so much. The obvious solution is to make food in its natural state - food that has not been manicured, processed, or packed - the most desirable and expensive. Food now supplied in a condition taken for granted sixty years ago is around 2-3 times the cost of its processed counterpart.

The effect of 'adding value' in these ways is to keep the cost of food higher than it needs to be. Food as a proportion of income is said to be low. But raw life knows nothing of the statistician's version of it. Include another adult or teenager in the household who does not earn or throw in the changing demands of growing children, and economies of scale that might exist quickly evaporate. Add in and deduct all manner of personal allowances, national insurance contributions, council taxes, and benefits that the bureaucracy is increasingly unwilling to grant or pays late, and food as a percentage of income regularly hits 16%. If eating out and alcoholic drinks are included, that figure rises to 43%. This means that the cost of food as a proportion of income is about that last experienced in the 1920s.

While costs to the general population have risen, the quality of diet has deteriorated. Fresh food has become more expensive while consumption of other modes (frozen and processed) has increased enormously. The consumption of cereals, bread, and fresh green vegetables has declined. And while the consumption of meat has remained fairly steady, processed meats as a proportion of this have grown dramatically. Most people are eating cheaper, highly processed foods. The market has managed to pull off the unique trick of making food more expensive and less healthy, leaving between 4% and 5% of the population malnourished and nearly 30% of adults obese.

From a mathematical point of view, a housing shortage ought not to exist. The number of people for every dwelling slipped to less than 2.4 by the end of the twentieth century, from nearly 5 at its start. Today, if every discrete group or person living on their own were allocated a house, there would be a surplus of some two million units. Yet there is a shortage. The number of homeless – adults and children living in temporary accommodation or sleeping rough or put up in hostels - is around 320,000. If those who need supported accommodation, but are without it, are included, then the number of homeless rises to 350,000.

Part of the explanation is that people move and houses (on the whole) do not. The result is a mismatch between what is available and demand in any given area. Although the problem is both obvious and predictable, little has been done to deal with it over the last fifty years. The reasons are three-fold.

One is that the planning system is slow and ineffective, and governments are not prepared to remedy the matter. The slower the release of land for building, the more prices are likely to rise and the higher the building companies' profits. Existing residents are also unlikely to want more buildings thrown up near their homes.

A second reason is the financialization of the housing market. Debt makes up for the shortfall in the general population's income. Housing provides collateral. As collateral rises in value, so does the level of debt. A rise in value usually reflects a shortage. Why end that when extending loans is good business for banks and other financial organizations? The subsequent hawking of mortgages and loans further stokes the market. It also drives up rents, encouraging people to take on mortgages. Rent paid is frequently seen as money lost, whereas mortgage payments are treated as investments.

A third reason is the sale of social housing, reducing its stock to about 2 million units, while the number of households in poverty has grown to nearly seven million. People are funneled into temporary accommodation or bed and breakfasts, the cost of which predictably escalates. The number of families now 'homeless' is approaching 90,000. This includes 123,000 children. Without social housing to compete with, builders and landlords have had incentives to lower prices removed.

The problem is just the tip of an enormous iceberg. The roofs over the heads of the old and young are often in poor shape. Shortages and high prices and their use as collateral keeps decrepit housing in service and encourage shoddy conversions or the construction of small and fragile new buildings. Somewhere between 8 million and 15 million people live in such places. The rise in illnesses that poor housing creates is one way of viewing the problem. It is not a peculiarly British problem. Across Europe, the deaths attributed to shabby housing number 100,000 a year.

As well as shifting costs onto the general population, expenditure on welfare has been limited. The amount spent on various kinds of benefits from the late 1940s up to today has risen from around 4.5% of GDP to 8.5% today, peaking briefly in the early 1990s at 10.5%. These figures, though, are not quite as they seem.

First, state pensions account for the largest share of spending. The national insurance scheme funds this. Each worker pays a proportion of their income into the scheme, together with a contribution from their employers. In theory, this should be sufficient to look after each member after retirement if properly managed. The state pension (which excludes all other benefits available to older people) is greater than the sum paid to adults of working age and children. If pensions are excluded, benefits dropped from 3.5% of GDP in the early 1970s to under 3% today, peaking at just over 5% in the early 1990s.

Secondly, an increasing proportion of benefits is paid as tax credits. This grew from 0.03% of GDP (in the mid-1980s) to somewhere between 1.5 and 2% in the last decade or so. Tax credits are deceptive in that the state is not required to make any new subventions. They merely allow employees to keep a larger proportion of their earnings rather than make it over in tax. Yet it is entered into government books as an expenditure. If tax credits are deducted, the welfare bill falls to about 4% or less of the GDP. The share of GDP spent on children and working-age adults also declined, even though they comprise more than a quarter of the population compared to a fifth in the mid-1980s.

Chapter 31

Corruption

Resources are also transferred away from the general population through behavior that, although recognized as corrupt, is being standardized.

In part II, I argued that corruption emerges in the Third World as society rationally and logically feels its way against practices and priorities imposed, demanded, and expected by the West and moves resources to patrons and their clients in bureaucracy, politics, and the general population. In the West, resources often move in the other direction towards business and away from government and the general population. Moreover, these movements are justified and protected by an armature of legal and semi-legal measures and accepted conventions. In the UK, this is not generally understood as corruption. Sleazy and gray, perhaps, but not corrupt. Such movements do not break the rules or do so only unintentionally: there is said to have been some misunderstanding, or the rules are not clear enough or not adequately enforced. This flexibility is inevitable. When the mood turns puritanical, and rules are idolized, alienation builds, and instrumentalism sets in.

One measure used to systematize corruption is the notion of a *legal person* or *limited liability*. It describes the distinction between the company (the organization) and the people who comprise the company. It is legal parlance for what we have termed 'psychological distancing' and is in no sense a peculiarly European invention, nor a nineteenth-century one. A legal person is an important idea, but not because it enables the accumulation of capital and risk-taking that would not otherwise be possible if shareholders and officers were asked to put up their own personal fortunes. Nor does it explain the industrial revolution. But it does make prosecutions difficult. In the UK, for instance, 'piercing the corporate veil' is improbable unless wrongdoers are demonstrably at one with the company's core leaders and decision-makers (essentially at board level) and there is intent to do wrong (such as commit fraud). Shareholders and officers know this. Consequently, trails of evidence rarely lead any further than middle management.

Another set of legal protections allows tax avoidance so that companies and individuals keep more of their income than the 'advertised' rate allows. This enables businesses to split off from society, whose ability to redistribute is weakened. Justifications for avoidance are various. It is said that life for businesses is unfair and impractical unless, for instance, depreciation is factored in and the tax burden is reduced correspondingly. Society will lose income and employment as businesses move elsewhere if other jurisdictions provide more favorable tax rates. Thus, while the revenue gleaned from a single company in a single instance might fall, the overall amount harvested from many successful companies is greater than it otherwise would have been. Growing numbers of thriving companies paying less tax generate more revenue than a few struggling ones paying more tax.

These arguments are widely accepted but spurious. On the one hand, profits are not regarded as transfers. Instead, they are plucked out of thin air and claimed as a reward for the risks of making outlays on, say, new machinery and its adoption. On the other hand, society is expected to make transfers through depreciation, tax reductions, and low pay. In other words, businesses are treated as part of society except when profits are earned, at which point they become entirely separate entities.

As for the argument that tax rates must be competitive, one must ask, why are tax havens retained if that is the case? They undermine competition and make it unlikely that, as often asserted, they keep other governments honest about tax and collecting revenues. At the time of writing, there are around eighty, usually small territories, often islands, with relatively small populations and little else to offer. (The exact number of havens worldwide depends on changing definitions and policies.) Many are found in Europe. They include Switzerland, Ireland, Luxembourg, the Channel Isles, Guernsey, the Isle of Man, and Andorra. Others are located in the Caribbean, the Pacific Islands, Singapore, and Hong Kong and are often associated with former colonial powers. In recent years, those judged less cooperative about sharing information have been blacklisted. Yet, despite objections and much hand-ringing, they survive and prosper.

A third convention protecting corruption is known popularly as the revolving door: the movement of people back and forth between the government and the private sector.[379] This is justified on the grounds that it allows former government officials to make a living while businesses come to understand better how bureaucracy and government work and vice versa. Close relationships between business and government are also a feature of many Third World states – both those economically successful and those unsuccessful. But whereas these relationships are, in more successful parts of the Third World, integrated into state-run development efforts in which business is a subordinate and organic part of society, the West tends to treat companies as quite another thing. Politicians in the UK are mesmerized by businesses they merely assume are beneficial and see themselves as facilitators rather than as planners and administrators. This attitude is evident in two arrangements intended to restrain corrupt behavior.

One is the Committee on Standards in Public Life. The committee has four independent and three political members. Johnson gave one of the four 'independent' seats to Ewen Fergusson, a solicitor and old friend of his. The committee is chaired by Evans, former director-general of the MI5 and a non-executive director of the Hong and Shanghai Banking Corporation, who also sits on the accountancy firm KPMG's UK Public Interest Committee. Evans also retains interests in several other companies, including Darktrace, a cyber security company. The company, which provided free services to the NHS at the start of the covid pandemic, was floated in 2021 at £1.7 billion and reached £7 billion within five months. Shirley Pearce (a former Vice-Chancellor of Loughborough University) is another independent member of the Committee. Her husband was chief executive officer of Mowlem (a company bought up by Carillion in 2006) before joining Cleshar Contract Services to maintain the East London Line under a contract held by Carillion before its liquidation in 2018.

The second arrangement is the Advisory Committee on Business Appointments, established in 1975, which regulates the movement of people from government and civil service into the private sector. The committee has few powers, is run by political appointees who are members of the ruling conservative party, and seems to have little effect. The inadequacies of both committees are easily demonstrated.

In 2010, shortly after his election, prime minister David Cameron established a Business Advisory Group. Its membership numbered around twenty or so people at any one time but altered frequently. Over the years, it included business leaders from Rolls Royce to Lloyd's of London, British Petroleum, and the ASDA supermarket chain. It also included Sam Laidlaw, who was, until 2014, Chief Executive of Centrica, a large energy firm, whose public affairs manager and lobbyist Tara Singh became a personal advisor to Cameron on energy and climate in 2013. Laidlaw also served as a non-executive director to the Department of Transport which commissioned him to write a Laidlaw report exonerating ministers over allegations of bias in franchising rail services to private companies.

Two years after resigning as prime minister in 2016, Cameron himself became a lobbyist and a paid advisor to Greensill. Lex Greensill had worked at Morgan Stanley and then at Citibank as head of supply chain finance before being appointed government advisor on supply chain finance, initially for three months from January to March 2012. Two months earlier, in November 2011, he had declared no conflicting interests, citing only his family's agricultural businesses in Australia. In April 2012, a month after his initial contract ended, he set up Greensill Capital Management and Greensill Capital Ltd. Before his subsequent appointment for three years as Crown Representative (for supply chain finance), beginning in 2013, he stated in his declaration of interests that he was a director, not owner, of those two companies. He said both were owned by the parent company Greensill Capital PTY in Australia, for which they provided services. None, he said, was active in the UK. However, both companies started operations in 2013 and were involved in paying pharmaceutical companies on behalf of the NHS. They gave NHS workers, especially the low-paid, advances in their salaries. Greensill was also in discussion with other parts of government, including the Ministry of Defence, to provide supply chain finance for major procurement items, including submarines.

By 2020, Cameron was finally earning his pay from Greensill by telephoning the Chancellor, the Economic Secretary, and the Financial Secretary persistently and trying to persuade them to give the company access to the Covid Corporate Financing Facility. The application was rejected on technical grounds, though, after a good deal of to-ing and fro-ing, it secured a line with the Coronavirus Business Interruption Loan Scheme through the British Business Bank. In 2021 Greensill collapsed.

Despite these facts, a report into the matter absolved Cameron and the rest of the government. Johnson, who had ordered the report, selected Nigel Boardman as its author. Boardman was a former Tory candidate for a parliamentary seat and had previously worked as non-executive director for the Department of Businesses, Energy, and Industrial Strategy.

The affair revealed several other curious intersections of people and events. Cameron's acquittal had relied a good deal on a statement by Charles Roxburgh, the second permanent secretary. Roxburgh said he felt no pressure from the Chancellor or Economic or Finance Secretaries to supply finance and had rejected the application. Yet he had joined the government in 2013, working previously with

McKinsey, a management consultancy firm. In this capacity, he had advised the government in 2012 to support the kind of financing offered by Greensill. McKinsey had also provided advice to the government on defense procurement when Kevin Tebbit had been the MOD's permanent undersecretary. Tebbit left the government in 2005 to become chairman of the Italian defense contractor Finmeccanica from which the MOD subsequently bought 62 helicopters. It also bought voice and flight recorders from Smith Industries, whose board Tebbit joined in 2007.

Boardman himself provided another intriguing twist. In 2016, Greensill had agreed with Carillion to provide supply chain finance a little over a year before it folded in January 2018. This was the same Carillion with which Gains - the husband of Pearce who sits on the Committee on Standards in Public Life - was involved. Bankruptcy came only a few months after KPMG (on whose Public Interest Committee the Chair of the Committee on Standards in Public Life also sits) had signed off on its accounts and four months after a series of profit warnings. Also involved in the collapse was the firm Slaughter and May, one of whose senior partners was Nigel Boardman. The firm provided Carillion with legal advice and presented it with a bill on the day it failed. That same day, £6.4 million went missing from the company.

When appointed to undertake the review of Greensill, Boardman was also a non-executive director of Arbuthnot. Another was Angela Knight. After a stint in parliament as MP for Erewash and as Economic Secretary to the Treasury, she became chief executive of the British Banker's Association, tirelessly and vigorously defending the sector and its practices throughout and beyond the financial crisis. She then became the Energy sector's champion as chief executive of Energy UK. She later apologized for the banks' behavior as quid pro quo for her appointment as Chair of the Office of Tax Simplification. Throughout this time, she held non-executive directorships in a range of finance and energy companies.

The close connexions between politicians and businesses make it easier and provide an incentive to protect cartels and cartel-like behavior. The fact that KPMG was able to sign off on Carillion accounts reflects the dominance of four accounting firms in the UK - Deloitte, EY, KPMG, and PwC. They audit all but nine of Britain's 350 largest listed companies. Their market share has only grown despite an investigation by the UK Competition Commission — the predecessor body to the CMA. It is not just their market dominance that raises concerns. The same firms also advise companies on securing better profits and avoiding tax, for which they also receive hefty fees. There are calls to separate auditing from advice and impose heavier fines on accounting firms for 'serious' misconduct. Ten million pounds or more are mentioned - about twice the record £5.1m meted out in 2017 to PwC over one of its audits. But the big four can easily afford these, and there appears to be no criminal penalty for those involved in what amounts to corruption and fraud.

Cartels also exist in the energy sector. Natural gas price assessment is left to reporting agencies who use underpaid reporters to glean information from talking to highly paid and partisan gas traders. It is difficult for price reporters to check the deals the traders give them, and they are often lent on to "correct" their numbers. For instance, traders on Dominion's natural gas trading desks knowingly reported false, misleading, and inaccurate figures for natural gas trades, including price and volume information. A $4.25m fine was imposed. This is just the tip of an enormous iceberg. According to the French oil firm Total, prices are deformed at every point in the chain. And plenty of academic studies indicate market power abuse, such as capacity hoarding practices, high transaction costs, information asymmetry, and insufficient disclosure. Yet their reports are used as reference points for prices and taxation calculations across Europe. One influential player is ICIS, part of FTSE 100-listed Reed Elsevier publishing house. This same company also publishes getting on for twenty percent of the world's academic research papers through its journals.

That such cartels operate with impunity also casts the CMA (and its predecessors) in a poor light. So does the revolving door between the CMA and private business. Its board and panel are all appointed by the Business Secretary. Its present chief enforcer was formerly a partner at Norton Rose Fulbright – a global law firm with special interests in antitrust and competition work. This same firm has also acted as legal advisor to Cinven – a company fined nearly £52 million by the CMA for overcharging the NHS. The matter for which Norton Rose was hired was not related to Cinven's fight with the CMA, but the potential for informal advice and information to flow amongst the various parties is obvious. This is not the only dispute between Cinven and the CMA, and all, one of which dates back to 2016, are still open. In 2021-2022, £13.6 million[380] was collected by CMA - about 12% of its annual budget.

There is no question that what we see here is corruption and a determination to entangle countermeasures in bureaucratic, legal, and social niceties. These practices would be declared as turpitude and dereliction loudly and confidently were they to occur in Nigeria or the Philippines. Greensill obviously had it in mind to use government as a platform to develop his business interests. And government officials and former officials benefitted or would have benefitted financially. These are old-fashioned kickbacks. Johnson appointed[381] a solicitor with 'form' who not so much whitewashed the whole affair but tried to explain away what happened, throwing up more red herrings and opening up more dead ends than the best 'whodunnits.' Angela Knight made a career out of describing black as white and apologized for doing so only to obtain another sinecure. The chair of the Committee for Standards in Public Life also works as a non-executive director for a bank that has been involved in drug laundering and does his best to heighten concerns about electronic terrorism and fraud while getting paid for cultivating young firms that make money by countering those threats.

It would be naïve to think such behavior is out of the ordinary or the product of carefully organized conspiracies. On the contrary, it is entirely routine. More often than not, people find themselves in situations that, to their surprise, are of broader interest and a matter of controversy and criticism. This is precisely why such behavior is so damaging and corrosive. Corruption is how Britain's government and business works, not because secret plots and intrigues are afoot or because of some profound moral decadence affecting the Great and the Good, but because such behavior seems normal, even ethical, and is so often protected.

Why does this happen? First, society, including government and bureaucracy, sees itself as dependent on, and in debt to, the market and business and is enthralled by commerce. The government needs services, and companies provide them. Businesses supply the government with a large chunk of its revenue, if not directly, then indirectly through the salaries and wages it pays its workers. And since business is said to create wealth, it is to business that resources and opportunities must flow.

Secondly, Puritanism abhors complexity, doubt, uncertainty, and possibility. Where such imperfections exist, they must be shaved away. Puritanism transforms the market into an objective, rational, law-induced ideal. As such, the market stirs up and satiates rancor, ressentiment, and Machiavellianism. The stronger the Puritan's faith in the market, the more determined the believer is to rationalize bending its rules when it does not work as expected. As alienation sets in, they seek comfort with the like-minded until the ends justify the means.

Chapter 32

Poverty and Rancor

As resources are directed away from the bulk of the population, poverty and rancor grow.

There is some merit in the argument that poverty in the West is not comparable to poverty in the Third World or the destitution experienced historically in Victorian Britain or rural France during the eighteenth century. There have been marked improvements in living standards in the West over the last 300 years. People are undeniably better off. A boy classed as poor in the UK is not as poor as his contemporaries in the Philippines or Nigeria. Even if he is completely deprived of all possessions, he still has a vast health service, schools, and other services at his disposal. Poverty in the West today is about inequality at a time when overall living standards are higher than ever before.

So where and how should we draw the 'poverty line?' Does it, or should it, reflect a level below which conditions are unacceptable to the observer or society? Does it mark a point below which people cannot afford the kind of lives that most other people enjoy? Should it be drawn at 60% or 50% of the mean income, and why there? Or should we concede that all poverty is relative and, so long as a degree of inequality and difference in society is accepted, there will always be poverty?

These arguments and questions are not unimportant, but they do somewhat miss the point: that there are a good many people whose material circumstances threaten their very existence and egregiously restrict their quality of life. Whether they are as badly off as the Victorian pauper or a Filipino street child hardly matters. They face real difficulties and represent a huge loss in the potential for society.

It is for these reasons that most people know poverty when they see it. (Whether they admit it is another thing, as Andrew Ure[382] and Timothy Worstall,[383] both Adam Smith enthusiasts, illustrate). Consequently, estimates of poverty at different times and places end up being pretty reliable, despite the variation in criteria and techniques used. In Britain, the rate was around 30%[384] (a figure for London) at the end of the nineteenth century. It fell to a low of about 8% in the mid-1970s. (These estimates are based on the number of households with incomes below 50% of the median income). By the start of the twenty-first century, the figure was back up to 20% or more. (This is based on the number of households below 60% of the median income). It has since remained there. Figures around 20% pop up again and again in estimates for specific parishes, counties, and settlements reaching back to the third quarter of the eighteenth century.[385] The picture is similar across the West. In 2015, almost 119 million people, or 23.7 % of the EU population, were poor or excluded. The West, it seems, has had great difficulty over the last 300 years in keeping poverty rates below 20-25% or about 1 in 4 or 5 of the population. During that time, something of poverty's sharp edge has been dulled by technology and state services, but the West is still willing to accept the dreadful waste and risks it entails.

Mention also needs to be made of labor's falling share of income in the West. That share remains high or at least within normal historical limits of variation, or so a good number of conservative and orthodox economists claim. They also claim that too many commentators rely on unreliable statistics and techniques and don't understand what is, after all, a complex topic. Business incomes are lower than they appear to be (and so labor's share of the pie is higher) and are used to cover the rising depreciation costs. Computers and advanced electronics date quickly and must be upgraded and replaced frequently. The growth of value-added is another reason labor's share of income remains high at 60%, despite labor-saving technology and the migration of companies to countries where wages are cheaper.

There are answers to these claims. Depreciation is merely an accounting technique with a chequered past, as noted in part 1. As for value-added, this describes many different activities, none of which guarantee improvements in wages. Pharmaceuticals manufactured cheaply from inexpensive raw materials can be sold at extremely high prices. The wider the gap between production costs and the price, the greater the value-added is said to be. It is justified by the time (often years) and expertise it takes to uncover the combinations of materials, forms of delivery, and doses required before an effective and safe drug for specific conditions or diseases is manufactured. Value-added also describes fancy packaging, slick presentation, more attentive service, faster delivery, or the addition of a brand or logo, to rationalize a generous markup for otherwise plain goods. Take, for example, a box of loose carrots at a greengrocer. Wash the carrots, trim them, sort them, and put them in a bag. The convenience this offers allows the carrots to be priced above production and preparation costs. This is the value-added. But this does not mean the people who picked, prepared, and packaged the carrots are paid more. Even if they are, they must also pay more for the carrots. Any increase they receive is unlikely to be as large proportionately as the gain made by the business.

The unreliability of data is a double-edged sword but tends to favor the case that labor's share of income in the West is worse than it seems and probably better in the Third World. This is because it is impossible to quantify with any precision the relative share of total income labeled as wages and salaries (compensation) and profits (operating surplus) across many different countries. One immediate difficulty is the size of the informal sector. Another is that businesses classified as formal are often small and make no distinction between wages and profit. Large and wealthy corporations don't make a distinction either, at least as far as their owners and directors are concerned. In all likelihood, they retain far more income than official figures suggest.

Wages have not been growing fast or by much, and people are worse off. Moreover, any improvements are spoken for, even if incomes rise on paper. The basics - heat, light and water, and a roof over one's head – continue to take the lion's share of income. Personal mobility is being restricted by the cost of travel and by cities built around motorized transport. Food, the best of it, is all too often beyond reach and competes with other basics. Take welfare services away, make them unobtainable, or watch them fail, and children, the weak, the old, and the sick, have nothing to fall back on. The poor in the West can be just as badly off as in Africa or the Philippines, sometimes even more so, as informal relationships that support and buffer are so often absent.

People and families with little or no income, except the state, are especially vulnerable. They have become accounting units with little discretion, shuffling funds on behalf of a state bureaucracy that has become unresponsive, punitive, and determined to instill fear.[386] They must behave perfectly in line with the accountants' demands. If the accountants get their calculations wrong, there is no alternative source of relief. And any additional earnings are either treated as illegal or taxed at 63%. It is partly for these reasons that food banks have grown to around 2,500, and the number of people using them has swollen to over two million.[387]

One must also remember that irrespective of vociferous denials, absolute poverty exists in the West. In 2013, 3.2 million lived in absolute poverty in the United States, and another 3.3 million in high-income countries on less than $1.90 a day. If you try to buy goods bought for $1.90 in the Third World, then you need a sum closer to $4 in the United States.[388] And if you take $4 a day or less as the cut-off point, then there are 5.3 million Americans who are absolutely poor. This is a small number compared to India's 175 million, for example. But it is more than in Sierra Leone (3.2 million) or Nepal (2.5 million), about the same as in Senegal (5.3 million), and one-third less than in Angola (7.4 million).

Move away from the statistics and whether someone's income is $4.20 or $3.80 within this or that accounting period and look at people searching for shelter and food, and the scene is nightmarish. The toll on health is dreadful. There are places like the Mississippi Delta and much of Appalachia, where life expectancy is lower than in Bangladesh and Vietnam. Even when national estimates dilute these figures, life expectancy in the US is lower than its national income suggests it should be. Many Americans are in trouble, especially those with only a high school education. Mortality rates from drugs, alcohol, and suicide are rising. The long historical decline in death from heart disease has stopped. There are millions of Americans whose suffering, through material poverty and poor health, is as bad as the poor in Africa or Asia.

One obvious indication of transfers made to businesses and away from the general population is income growth only among the top 10% earners - the owners, managers, executives, professionals, and technical specialists. [389] Most other people's incomes have stagnated or fallen. One explanation offered is improvements in education and the quality of the workforce: competition is tough amongst a well-educated and well-trained workforce. But this is quite the wrong way around. People do not spend on education and training to better their chances. Rather, people are paying the vast sums now required for education *because* they are wealthy. It is one way they can pinch themselves off from the rest of society. The popular shorthand for this emerging caste is 'the elites.'

The destructive nature of market forces compels governments in the West to instigate counter-transfers back to the general population. Because of these expenditures, governments have taken on large domestic and external debts. The UK's domestic debt (public and private) is around 90% of the GDP. Its external debt is also high. If everything that the UK owes and owns overseas is deducted from everything foreigners own and owe in the UK, then Britain has a shortfall of 318 billion dollars. It is a debtor nation. The UK's external debt, calculated as a percentage of exports, is running at about 120% compared, for instance, to Thailand's 8.3%.

But marketeers turnabout cause and consequence, like parents unable to reconcile the adult reprobate standing in front of them with the memory of the child they lovingly favored. Loudly they complain that the market is being smothered by bureaucracy and bled white by transfers and requires more freedom. The market is being weighed down by people who live beyond their means and expect and demand too much. Public spending, they say, must be reduced.

Yet, the more society is compelled to subsidize businesses through low wages, high personal tax, higher interest rates, and larger debt repayments, the more anemic demand becomes. And the more anemic demand becomes, the more businesses either suffer or turn to the luxury sector or various financial techniques to inflate their assets.[390] A vicious, downward spiral is set in motion, increasing the calls on welfare. This, it is asserted, must be paid for by the people who benefit, further weakening demand and business. Standards of nutrition, housing, and health decline, and education becomes a mere gesture. Poverty becomes normal, acceptable, and even deserved. And as the means and the will to redistribute are eroded, the notion that the state has obligations to provide for its people becomes facile, immature, incredible, and naïve. The result is an economy that staggers and jolts from unplanned and irregular infusions while the general population suffers.

The provision of health care, education, housing, water, and energy is the simplest and most basic indication of a government's willingness to nurture society. These services keep the population active, push up demand, and keep the economy humming. On the other hand, if a government has the wherewithal, technical proficiency, and organizational ability to provide for its people, but chooses not to, then its trustworthiness and legitimacy in the eyes of the governed will soon evaporate along with their willingness to comply. Arrangements that stack the odds against most of its citizens are bound to suffer instability at some point.

Redistribution is wealth creation, and trade is another form of transfer; price movements are ways to transmit and track currents of demand and supply, not iron laws for allocating resources: statements and practices such as these are essentially anathemas in the West. There, the market comes before society. It is widely believed that this must be so because otherwise, there will be no wealth to redistribute, and redistribution is a choice, not a necessity. Ideally, the market conforms to economic laws, not the whims of government. A clear line is drawn between, on the one hand, the market's purely economic transactions and, on the other, transfers. The former is rational and competitive economic behavior; the latter is quite the opposite, though it can make political sense. The West is foundering because governments have forgotten how to get the basics of statecraft right.

Chapter 33

Obduracy: health

As the organization and its procedures and rules harden, its members feel that to run it properly they must identify detailed chains of causality and devise stringent operational processes. True mechanisms crystallize in their minds demanding additional responses. But acting as a cog in an imagined machine feeds alienation and other pathologies. Behavior becomes more calculating and artful. Discrediting and disposing of other people demonstrates the ruthlessness necessary to advance. Helping others, self-sacrifice, and decency equate with naivety, dullness, softness, and sentimentality. One practical response to growing instrumentalism and ruthlessness is more red tape imposed with more enthusiasm, followed by greater efforts to evade and play the system. Private and public organizations become uncoordinated and then disintegrate.

Since the last war, providing free or heavily subsidized health services has become a symbol of the West's economic rise and its states' commitment to its people. One of the most well-known arrangements is Britain's National Health Service. The amount spent on the NHS since its establishment in 1948 has risen from around 3% of GDP to more than 8%. Yet the organization has become increasingly shaky.

Take, for instance, the procurement of drugs and labor. The cost of drugs is only slightly more than the amount it pays to the private sector to deliver various services, or about 13% or 14% of the entire NHS budget. Branded and generic drugs are dispensed by hospitals and GPs (or general practitioners, who are the first port of call for someone who feels ill or suspects a problem). The cost is often calculated from the list price (set by the manufacturer). But the amount paid is usually discounted under schemes agreed upon by the NHS and pharmaceutical companies. Precisely how much lower is varied and often subject to confidentiality. For example, according to the government, the average price increase for 2015-16 was 8%, but the ABPI cited 2.4%. The leeway given to pharmaceutical companies to raise list prices artificially cushions the effect of any discounts agreed on, makes it easier to raise the cost of generic compounds, and leaves the whole process looking even more byzantine.

Warnings about the rising cost of medicine and calls to limit purchases have been made regularly since the NHS was created. No health service, it is said, can afford to pay for everything. Hard choices must be made. The state must ensure 'value for money.' These and other catechisms are chanted again and again with missionary zeal. The National Institute of Clinical Excellence was established in 1999 to give rationing a more objective and independent air. Its slogans were no different. In the real world, budgets are finite. The NHS and the country can only afford so much. Prices rose by 19.4% between 2010 and 2014 and 8% annually between 2014 and 2016, well above funding levels and inflation.

The lion's share of NHS expenditure, though, is on its staff which has grown to just under 1.1 million. Of these, only 10% are doctors, and 30% are nurses. If doctors are excluded from these calculations, then most staffs (a fraction over 50%) in the NHS are on bands 5, 6, and 7 of the NHS pay scale. This means they earn somewhere between £24,000 to £44,000 depending on how long they have been working and their success in jumping through various assessment hoops. Another forty-two percent of staff earn less – anything between around £17,000 to £23,000.

These are not generous salaries. For those on bands 1-4 (about 40% of staff), salaries lie around the London living wage (£20,500), the UK living wage (£17,500), and the minimum wage (£16,000) and are said to furnish an 'acceptable' standard of living, whatever that means. In truth, life is a struggle, especially if workers are the sole breadwinner or have children. Life is even more difficult if they live in London or one of the more expensive cities, just about anywhere south of a line running through Peterborough and Birmingham, or in northern cities such as Leeds and York. After housing, utilities, tax (national and local, and VAT), and food, it would be surprising if much is left for transport, telephone, internet, or TV (which is taxed at £150 a year), let alone childcare or any luxuries (such as nights out or holidays). The NHS also charges its staff for car parking. Even for those towards the higher end of these bands (after several years' service and who are more likely to have started families), life outside work is, at best, likely to be frugal and reduced to basic routines.

Restrictions on medical treatment and staff pay mainly affect the sickest or those who are sick for the longest. This is an obvious but important point. Only a small proportion of the population (about 5% or so in the West) requires the most care and resources (about 50-65% of total expenditure). Type of work (or its absence), bad housing and diet, and forms of enjoyment and relaxation injurious to health make sure that this segment of the population is also the poorest. Economic ups and downs appear to make little difference to them, judging by evidence from between the wars. In England in the 1920s, inequalities in mortality amongst occupied and retired men declined. The United States also saw a decline in mortality and improvements in life expectancy during economic downturns and quite the opposite during upturns. The effects of deprivation lag the experience of it, so when the economic wheels grind faster and harder during a recovery, the poorest are most likely to be worn through in the scramble to make a living. Establishing a health service in the UK mitigated the effects on the poor. But it is the educated and wealthier people who benefit the most. They are most able to get what they want out of the NHS and feel the physical and psychological effects of material deprivation and economic upturns the least.

Health inequalities thus prove extraordinarily resilient. Since the end of the seventeenth century, there have been improvements in the proportion of people living in old age. Much of this has been due to falls in death rates amongst the very young (under five years old) during the eighteenth and nineteenth centuries and then, after 1867, amongst older children and adults up to the age of fifty or so. This was accompanied by widening gaps in the quality of general health and life expectancy between those on low and high incomes. In 1688, the life expectancy of peers (members of the House of Lords) and commoners was about the same. By 1867 a difference of 15 years had opened up. It narrowed between the wars only to widen again despite the establishment of the NHS. By the 1970s, the gap was as pronounced as it had been earlier in the century.[391] By the end of the twentieth century, those living in poorer areas of Britain were nearly twice as likely to die in any one year as those in wealthier parts. By 2020, and before COVID hit, the poorer were dying ten years sooner than the rich. The poor also spent one-third of their lives in ill health compared to the longer-lived wealthy, who spend about one-fifth of their lives with some form of disability.[392]

A society wedded to the market slams the poor twice over. First, when it refuses to make the transfers necessary to lift them out of poverty. And second, when its accountants and treasurers look to claw every penny back as bodies start to fail.

As well as having to bear growing niggardliness, the health service has suffered increasingly frequent bouts of reform. Its first iteration in 1948 lasted 26 years before upheaval in 1974. The second version lasted 17 years before it was replaced by the third version in 1991. This was superseded by the fourth version in 2001 and the fifth in 2012. In all likelihood, it will see reform again in the 2020s.

The first configuration was clear, simple, and hierarchical. The Ministry of Health ran hospitals through regional hospital boards and management committees and directed family practitioners (the first port of call for most people except in an emergency) through Local Health authorities. It delivered materials and funds to doctors and nurses as necessary. Increasingly, however, the government saw medical staff as the tail wagging the dog and sought to strengthen management. The result was a strange, cumbersome machine with additional layers between the clinicians and central government. The Ministry of Health was merged with social services to become the DHSS. Its Secretary worked through regional health authorities, each of which operated through area health authorities and district management teams before contact was made with the hospital. Family doctors, too, were separated from area health committees by family practitioner committees.

The third iteration was driven by an economic crisis in 1987 and a belief that costs had to be contained. Contented with centralized management until that moment, the conservative government now upended the service. In 1988, health was distanced from social services and, over several years, an 'internal market' engineered. This purported, somewhat confusingly, to separate those who provided healthcare (the hospitals) from those who purchased or commissioned it (family doctors). The split was observed in new organizational arrangements at the level of Regional Offices. Under these were placed both hospitals (now designated as Trusts) and health authorities (responsible for GPs). The Regional Offices answered to the NHS executive, who answered to the Secretary of State.

The fourth version emerged at the start of the new millennium. It flattened the hierarchy a little further. The Secretary of State worked directly through Strategic Health Authorities, where the division between Trusts and GPs (organized into primary care trusts) was maintained and services commissioned. In 2012 the Strategic Health Authorities were replaced by NHS England, beneath which clinical commissioning groups contracted hospital services from the Trusts.

The willingness to shift more authority and money into the hands of those making clinical decisions and let the tail wag the dog again might have seemed like a reversal of strategy, taking the service back to its early days. But gaggles of smallish agencies strengthened regulation and monitoring. Various forms of evaluation and surveillance constrained and second-guessed health services more than ever, despite claims that clinicians had greater freedom and that the flow of money and materials was tailored to meet clinical needs. Five new agencies were established in the four years after 1997 to regulate the NHS. The National Institute for Clinical Excellence, the Commission for Health Improvement, the Modernization Agency, the National Patient Safety Agency, and the National Clinical Assessment Authority. These new agencies have themselves undergone reform. For example, the National Patient Safety Agency was folded into NHS Improvement; and the Healthcare Commission replaced the CHI. The Modernization Agency was replaced by the National Institute for Innovation and Improvement, which gave way to NHS Improving Quality, which the Sustainable Improvement Quality Team then took over.

None of this makes for better care. Accurate estimates of the number of inquiries into the service are hard to come by as definitions are somewhat nebulous. In addition to statutory inquiries, there are non-statutory ones which include Royal Commissions, Committees of Privy Councillors, and Departmental Inquiries, as well as those conducted by Parliamentary Select Committees and Independent Reviews by segments of the NHS (such as the Trusts). Not all of these report on specific events: they also cover more general questions, such as the social care system for older people or, as in the case of the select committees, high-level appointments. On the other hand, reports by agencies supposed to monitor the NHS are not included in these estimates.

With those comments in mind, around 126 inquiries were completed over the first 60 years of the NHS, the majority of which were produced in the 1980s and 1990s and during the first five years of the 21st century. Another dozen or so were completed over the next fifteen years. To these, just under 100 investigations by select committees can be added and, between 2013 and 2020, around 172 independent reviews. These were conducted against a background of medication errors, about 237 million each year. These are responsible for around 700 deaths and contribute to another 2,500. Other medical errors (such as misdiagnosis and other aspects of daily practice) number somewhere between 800,000 and 1 million. This is not too different from the proportion of similar events in daily practice in the US (4%) or Norway (17%).[393]

Why does an emphasis on systems, monitoring, productivity, and targets not help or even aggravate existing problems? For starters, it creates additional work. In 2013, managers and administrators spent up to two days a week dealing with requests from various agencies (excluding NHS England). Clinical staffs were spending up to one day a week.[394] GPs currently spend about a quarter of their time on administration instead of reading the medical literature, catching up on new developments, and reviewing decisions. Nurses spend about one-third or more of their time gathering information and completing the paperwork required by monitoring and evaluation agencies to inform their decisions.

Secondly, a focus on process distracts staff from thinking about the consequences of their behavior. They are presented with a body and treat one limited aspect of it in a process they are not otherwise part of. They may not know what happened to that body before it arrived or what will happen to it after it leaves their room. But they are safe in the knowledge that their compliance with rules protects them and that others in the organization, including those higher up, are interested only to the extent that the system works.

Thirdly, by following the rules and only following them, the sense grows that all they need to do is *appear* to follow them. Cynicism and purposelessness set in. Managers do not want to know or ask questions[395] that need asking. Since staff and their overseers' only purpose is to keep the organization running correctly (according to its processes), anything that might disturb this is unnecessary. Staffs become manipulative. Criticism becomes extremely difficult. Groups formed around their part in the organization's processes become entrenched, focusing only on their role and interests, reinforced by a kind of 'club' loyalty or tribalism.[396] New rules and systems and people might help at first, but new cliques soon rear their heads. Wrapped in their procedural cocoons, they are free to have their opinions and draw their own conclusions. Why shouldn't we be annoyed and frustrated at the chronically sick, the old, and the mentally ill? They are the ones we deal with most frequently, making timely and correct processing more difficult. Why should we bother? It's clear from our frozen salaries, thinning ranks, and tightly rationed medicines and equipment that society doesn't care. Politicians and newspapers constantly ask if we should blithely accept the financial burden caused by someone else's unhealthy living.

Fourthly, attempting to impose certainty when there is inherent uncertainty only creates a false sense of security. For example, removing discretion from treatment programs can *potentially* improve results. Studies might show that procedure X is the most effective and safest for 91% of patients with condition Y. This can be statistically accurate *and* misleading. It shows that a procedure is best for most people, but it does not mean *your* risk is about one in ten. It may be that you will always respond adversely or will never do so. Medical knowledge is not sufficiently advanced to say for sure one way or the other. Another set of studies might show that if people drink more than five cups of coffee a day for twenty years, they are at risk of Y. Those studies might also show that the risk is reduced if less is drunk.

Again, this might be statistically accurate *and* misleading. It does not mean *you* are at less risk if you drink less coffee. It may be that however much coffee you drink, you will suffer Y or never suffer Y. Nobody knows.

One striking feature of the Mid Staffordshire National Health Service (NHS) Foundation Trust debacle was the emphasis on targets and cost reduction to the exclusion of other considerations. Procedures that enabled staff to hit targets at the lowest cost - and on which they felt their jobs and prospects depended - were all that mattered. Other procedures governing complaints, staff appraisal, and communications between management and staff were, at best, secondary concerns. The sick were more often than not ignored. Even when enough staff was on duty, patients were time and again roughly handled, deserted in states of undress in full view of passers-by, abandoned without food or water, and left in their faeces and urine.[397]

But the solution to all this was thought to be more or the same: more rules and processes, new official bodies, and the removal or revision of existing ones. Francis demanded more integrated systems, closer monitoring, genuine honesty and compassion, and a service that prioritized the patients' interests. Rules and processes were the means to that end and mattered above all else. And treating compassion, respect, and patient-centeredness as absolutes turned these qualities into material for gaming.

That rules still trumped people were evident in the first spontaneous responses to the Francis report. The Dudley and Walsall Trust set out absolute criteria which had to be met and, above all, had to show they had been met on paper.[398] At the start of the Board's '*Winterbourne, Francis, Cavendish, Keogh and Berwick Report Overview Report*,' a chart (with the equally ungainly title *Patients First and Foremost-System Response Timeline*) is presented. It notes the publication date of each report and the consequential measures taken by the Trust. 'Overarching themes' are then named and 'mapped' to those reports. A table of initiatives follows, linking each theme backward to a report and forward to action taken by the Trust. For example, 'increased staff engagement' (a theme mapped to the Francis report) is partly met by 'service line quality groups,' 'team meetings,' and a 'trust escalation framework.' Thus another set of absolutes ('care' as defined by documentable criteria) is added to the first set (an organization capable of high turnover at least cost).

Universities responsible for training nurses reacted similarly - by establishing new sets of absolute criteria and documenting processes to meet those criteria. In the case of the University of Plymouth – renowned for its teaching and learning excellence – compassion is turned into an itemized and measurable 'skill.' This is achieved in two ways.

First, students must write 150-200 words on an aspect of the 6Cs (care, compassion, courage, communication, competency, and commitment) identified by Britain's Chief Nurse in the wake of the Francis report. An example of a possible question is: 'Why do you think compassion is important in nursing?'[399] A pass (without which candidates are rejected) is fixed at 40%.

The second is establishing clear sets of program aims and Intended Learning Outcomes (ILOs), which are 'mapped' to the criteria defined by the NMC. There are nine program aims. ILOs number close to forty and are divided into five groups: knowledge and understanding; cognition and intellectual skills; key and transferable skills; practical skills; and eleven employment-related skills, one of which is to 'engage and interact with patients and clients of all ages in a sensitive, kind, and compassionate manner.'[400]

Signs that process trumped people were also evident in the flood of reports on homicides committed by mental health patients 'cared' for in the community. 'Tragically' and 'sadly' are used so routinely to describe victims' deaths that these reports - poorly written, in desperate need of editing, and often left unpublished - come across as obligatory and shallow displays of compassion. Their commissioning instructions were ludicrous: to establish whether the murder would have taken place had employees of the NHS acted differently. They are not serious attempts at establishing culpability. They are sloppy, half-hearted gestures - self-indulgent exercises in semantics and epistemological and metaphysical debate.

The signs were also evident in the way 'care' is depersonalized. Care was treated as a product or 'outcome' of the correct and impersonal 'systems.' '*Shrewsbury and Telford Hospital NHS Trust*,' wrote its CEO[401] following a meeting with the CQC, '*needs the strong support of the surrounding system and also needs a further and strengthened package of support including more senior on-site support, additional measures which you have indicated you would be supportive of. ..... We have agreed to hold a Board-to-System meeting where Baroness Dido Harding and I will meet system leaders from Shropshire, Telford, and Wrekin Sustainability and Transformation Partnership……to review the wrap-around support that is being put in place.* A list of bureaucratic measures then follows. These include 'embedding professional accountability,' appointments of an on-site senior improvement director, and support from an integrated care expert on 'Making Data Count' so that better charts, narratives, and performance reports are produced. It also includes '*pump-*

priming for a dedicated head of training and development to build a quality assured leadership development programme and refresh staff training to ensure it is aligned with strategic requirements and embeds trust values.' Bureaucracy is the focus; care and compassion are hoped-for side effects.

The signs are evident in an ambulance service that, in the name of the greater good (a more efficient and less costly organization), is working to reduce the number of people it takes to hospital. The initial response to the growing burden of calls and patients was to demand greater 'productivity.' More patients had to be 'conveyed' further per unit of expenditure until paramedics were left exhausted and paying for equipment out of their own pockets. Not conveying patients became official policy, accompanied by a mass campaign for self-triage. People who are frightened and confused and have no medical knowledge are instructed to ask themselves and others if they really need to go to A and E? Then comes triage over the phone. Is the patient breathing? The third stage is triage by the paramedics: does the patient *really* need to go to A&E?

Some doctors and administrators think this is sensible. Mike Berwick, an experienced doctor, GP, medical administrator, and management consultant (who set up a consultancy firm confidently named *IQ4U*), is clear on this.[402] In his independent investigation into raised mortality rates at one hospital's A&E, he points out that 49% of the patients brought to A&E by ambulance would have died anyway. So rather than waste time 'humanely processing' these deaths in the hospital, why not do it in the community?

Some studies estimate the effect of this policy on deaths will be negligible. Others predict a rise of between 3.5% and 10%. In raw lives, that's another 2,500 people a year at the lower end of estimates, or double the number who arrive dead at A&E each year. This excludes those who died before they reached hospital either because the ambulance failed to arrive within set targets or did not have the equipment to keep patients breathing. Nor does it include the 17,500 who died in A&E after arrival (regardless of whether an ambulance brought them). Perhaps someone somewhere has calculated that redirecting ambulances to those more likely to live and away from those more likely to die will reduce deaths overall. That is Mike Berwick's point. But then one must ask, what is the purpose of a health service that puts the eldest, the sickest, and the oldest, to one side, whether by prior agreement or by force of circumstance and does so during peacetime? There are also practical difficulties. Unless an agreement has been reached with people very near the end of their lives, it is a supremely confident doctor or paramedic who, at someone's home or on the street or at a roadside, would claim to know in every case who will and won't live. It is also brave unless they are sure the hospital trust will always back their decision: after all, no one gets fired for taking someone to hospital.

The despair and desperation these questions evoke are all the more potent given that the ambulance service (including air ambulance) brings to A&E less than a quarter (and slightly more than a fifth) of the 22 million or so patients who attend A&E each year. The busiest hours are between 9 am and 5 pm. Most of the 22 million attending A&E are between 20 and 54. Only 17% are aged 70 or older. More than a third of those who visit need only guidance and advice and receive no treatment, and a further 10% walk out without seeing a nurse or doctor.[403] In other words, pressures on A and E reflect broader problems in the NHS: insufficient GPs and poor social care. There are too few doctors, nurses, social workers, and carers. Low staffing levels mean that an ambulance and A&E service that costs around £2 billion and £3 billion, respectively (or 4% of the total NHS budget), must cope with about one-third of the entire population. That is remarkably efficient. Yet A&E's budget A&E has been cut.

The penny-pinching and false choices (older and sicker people versus the retrievable) and consequent risks derive from an unwillingness to spend more on staff to keep GPs and other treatment centers open for longer. Urgent care centers are now being established. At the time of writing, there are about 100 of these. If they were to take everyone who currently goes to A&E and receives only advice and guidance, each center would have to deal with 9,000 people every day. The pressures on general practice are also racking up more deaths through delayed diagnoses and treatment.

Health care has become the NHS's secondary function. Clinicians and support staff have become, first and foremost, followers of rules. This state of mind was at its starkest when the government's first instinct in response to COVID was to ask people to sacrifice themselves and save the NHS. The emphasis on system, rule, and process will mean that untoward instances will still occur, possibly with greater frequency. Death rates at A&E and across the service and generally poorer health and shorter life expectancy in the population will become entrenched.

Chapter 34

Obduracy: education

Puritanism snuffs out education by turning school and university into penny-pinching accounting units dealing in measurable certainties.

The meaning of a decline in education is difficult to pin down because there is disagreement about what constitutes a good education. Is it about knowing things and establishing competencies? Is it about reading and being well-read? Dazzling others with information and taking on a veneer of cleverness at the dinner table can impress some. Explaining and understanding are easier with examples. Knowing the eight times table, how many centimeters there are in an inch, or why one should not iron clothes in bare feet while standing in a puddle of water can help us get through the day. But an education can't just be that. We can write things down, print, and have tablets capable of storing thousands of books in our hands. Pens and paper, the press, and computers make retaining facts in our heads less important than in the past. One does not have to remember vast stores of information. It is not especially helpful to know all the kings and queens of Britain. When a professor of history laments that a child cannot say who Elizabeth I was, when she was born, or when the Spanish Armada sailed, the child can always retort with some justification, 'who lives at Pontypandy?' The teenager might reply, 'Do you know the local drop points in Croydon?' Both cite knowledge important to them and their understanding and experience of society. Flexibility is needed. Lore does not mean that much on its own. It needs interpreting, and its context and interconnections need to be understood. Education is not just about Mr. Micawber's facts.

Is it, then, about knowing how to perform a task, serve a function, and earn a living? There is little to disagree with there. But one also needs to understand why that task is being done. How does it fit into the world more generally? Understanding that makes adjustment possible: one might then predict what changes are needed or when the job won't be needed anymore and what will take its place. 'Fitting in' matters in other ways, too. An understanding of the rules and expectations of society is essential if they are to be challenged and changed if needed. For all these reasons, questioning, criticizing, analyzing, and debating matter greatly. Above all, perhaps, education is about learning to work out all these things for oneself and work out responses to problems one hasn't come across before. It is about helping people (especially the young) become familiar with all these aspects of being and thought and to further our collective understanding. Society will not survive, thrive, and grow otherwise.

Even if we agree on what education is about (which we don't), how do we know education is declining? What is being measured, and how? Can it be measured? Does it need to be measured? The evidence usually cited includes scores on 'objective' tests such as Scholastic Aptitude Tests and College Testing Program in America. The OECD's PISA tests in reading, writing, and math, and the TIMSS and PIRLS tests in mathematics, science, and reading show a consistent picture. The Far East - represented by Shanghai, Singapore, Hong Kong, South Korea, Taipei, and Japan – tends to dominate the rankings. Lower down the list is the UK and America. For example, America ranks 24th in reading and 36th in math in recent PISA tests, while the UK fares a little better at 23rd in reading and 26th in math.

Another symptom of the decline is national grade inflation. This has been noticeable in America and England over the last thirty years or so. University professors often complain that students lack the knowledge sufficient to argue for their own opinions and beliefs and to do so cogently. Employers complain that the pool from which they can draw competent workers has shrunk or no longer exists. Children are pushed out of school gates and universities with certificates which, in many cases, add little to whatever job they find themselves in. Some will train for a year or two in this or that government scheme, but they will never be as skilled as they would have been if they had started in the workplace earlier. The lucky ones will find employers interested in them and commit to bringing them on.

Once it has set in, decline reinforces itself because the next generation of teachers is less interested in transmitting those standards they couldn't meet. These weaknesses, it is often said, can be found in teachers' letters and communications. Here are two examples of students just months away from becoming classroom teachers who find putting ideas together difficult.

Example A:

'*One of the most severe consequences of the Green Revolution is the conflict and violence that it produced in Punjab, India. Punjab was one of the most celebrated successes of the Green Revolution. However, there was a dark side to it that was often hidden. At the heart of the conflicts in Punjab lies the Green Revolution, with nature being seen as a source of economic scarcity. Scarcity has been a source of conflict over scarce resources and conflicts have turned into a source of violence. New scarcities were produced through the Green Revolution which ultimately turned into new sources of conflict: within six years 15,000 people lost their lives. The Green Revolution tried to exert control over the people and nature. Many of the Punjab residents experienced exploitation and discrimination which led to this high number of killings. Therefore the Green Revolution turned out to be conflict producing instead of conflict reducing... (sic)*'

Example B:

'*Firstly, it critical to define Corruption* [as] *lack of integrity or honesty (especially susceptibility to bribery); use of a position of trust for dishonest gain. Therefore corruption in the form of politics in the third world is larger more wealthy nations states taking advantage of lesser third world states, for gain of their own, thus causing corruption in the third world... (sic).*'

These are in no way unusual instances. One trying aspect of marking essays is the pressure on examiners to impose a coherent line of thought on the script so that the student will pass, expected grades are maintained, and the university hangs on to its fees.

It is true that perspective is needed. Contrary evidence can always be found. The West's scores in international tests are not all bad and have improved in more recent years. Charges of decline often reflect a distaste for change rather than reliable analyses of its meaning. Generation after generation before and since the second world war have commented upon a general decline in literary culture. Conversation, reading, and writing are no longer considered arts, nor are they respected as they once were. I am sure this is so. Yet life continues, and GDP has improved. Perhaps concerns of 'decline' are little more than a kind of fogeyism. The same might be said of the hostility often directed at technological devices, from television and computers to tablets and phones, that emphasize image and choice and make it easier to communicate quickly and informally. It is possible that through its technology, society is learning to transmit ideas in ways that, while different and admittedly less elegant, are just as subtle and effective.

Claims about the quality of education are often heavily influenced by broader disputes between left and right, progressives and conservatives, secular and religious concerns, believers in state or private education, government and opposition, and theoreticians and practitioners. In New Zealand, responsibility for what is perceived as a decline is placed squarely on child-centered learning.[404] This describes how children are gently nudged as they follow their noses and pursue whatever they find interesting, engaging, and relevant. Classrooms are open plan, and pupils sit in small clusters, each child facing the others across a table. They discover and create their own 'just-in-time' knowledge through their own initiative and as team players. They become critical and creative thinkers and learn how to learn – a competency they will take with them throughout their lives.

The approach is an understandable reaction to the impermeable disciplinarians of the first half of the twentieth century. It boasts a grounding in pedagogical theory from Rousseau to Dewey and Freire. A hundred and twenty years ago, schools had set out to establish a compliant workforce and, in doing so, destroyed motivation and smothered creativity. In its report on the nature of higher elementary education for 12-15-year-olds, a British parliamentary committee in 1906 wrote that these schools should be for 'brighter' children who, at the age of 16 '*would go out into the world to earn a living in the lower ranks of commerce and industry.*'[405] The education they receive, the report went on, '*should be of the kind that is likely to make them effective members of the class to which they will belong.*'[406] The easy unstated assumption that it is possible at such an early age to tell who is intelligent or bright or able and who is not was even more damaging and dangerous than the narrow and paternalistic vision of education in which it nestled.

Yet the child-centered revolutionaries are open to similar criticisms. In the London borough of Greenwich during the early 1990s, the sight of children sitting around looking at the pages of books they could not read under the guidance of teachers who believed (with a zealousness worthy of the most committed Puritan) that reading was best learned through 'exposure to whole texts,' made for a sorrowful and pathetic scene worthy of a Dickens' novel. Nor had it occurred to these revolutionaries that the sheer arrogance and complacency underlying the ease with which they labeled this or that child as 'bright' still blighted any good the school did.

We should not underestimate the damage wrought by intellectual snobbery as it insinuates itself throughout these debates and so many other aspects of our lives. And if you are prepared to live by the sword, then expect to die by it. Education departments in universities throughout the West are judged critically and found wanting. They are often thought of and treated as second-rate. They are, it is alleged, infested with bizarre theories and techniques, populated by second-rate ideologues determined to preach against the family and marriage. And, like the rest of the university, they are obsessed with research and unwilling to spend time in the classroom.

New Zealand's counterrevolutionaries are just as culpable. They want to replace one expression of fervency with another. They gaze longingly at England's curricula with its emphasis on facts and instructions, the measuring and accountability it allows, and its 'evidence-based' identification of the 'brighter' children. They laud its scientific foundations. And they claim, without any hint of irony, that the uniformity it brings dispenses with groupthink and sameness. Their emphasis is on facts because facts, they believe, are the way to establish competencies.[407]

What, then, is going on? Is education in decline? The answer to that is a clear yes. But decline cannot be boiled down to measurable standards or rates of 'employability.' Nor is it that schools and universities are unsure about what education is, or should be, although that doesn't help. When we talk about a decline in education, we mean a decline in the willingness and ability of society to do what it takes to bring up its young and shoulder the burden of doing so. That is a dreadful indictment of any community.

This reluctance manifests itself as two problems. The first is a lack of funding. Funding matters because any educational organization's most crucial task is recruiting and retaining teachers – people who want to be there and want to teach and become good at it. This does not mean schools and universities must pay the very highest salaries. There is, though, a trade-off between the conditions people work under and their pay. The worse the conditions, the less likely people are willing to stay regardless of their salaries. The gap between pay and conditions has worsened, partly because of the second problem - an obsession with process. This is discussed in the following chapter.

Since the mid-1950s, spending by government on education has risen nearly eightfold (in 2020/2021 prices). That translates into about 4-6 percent of GDP each year. That is not generous. Expenditure includes capital spending and outlays on student loans (since 2015) and help with pre-school childcare and payments by schools to cover local rates or taxes. Moreover, the costs for the general populace have increased more than twelve-fold over the same period. As we have seen, house prices are a big part of this story. These have accelerated faster than wages. Housing is now such a large proportion of teachers' salaries that any raise usually feeds back into higher prices, especially in the catchment area of schools with good reputations.

While living costs have climbed, salaries from the perspective of most teachers have improved marginally or remained where they were. In the 1960s and early

1970s, the average teacher's salary was equivalent to about £30,000 (2020/21 prices). In 2018, the average was £38,000. 'Averages,' though, are skewed upwards because school leaders are now paid many times more than teachers in the classroom. In 2018, around a fifth of the profession (state sector) earned £25,000, 12% took home £32,000, and a little over a quarter earned £37,000. That is to say, about 60% of the profession made less than the 'average.' Those who reach the pay scale's upper levels are doing much better. The head teacher who, in 1978, earned anything between £30,000 and £63,000 (2020/21 prices) can today expect to take in anything up to £120,000. The difference between salaries at the top and those at the bottom has risen from a multiple of 2.5 to 5. The result is a sharp division between the 'leadership team' and everyone else - a sense that members of the 'team' are different animals who are less involved in teaching and must take on the attributes of the manager. They must transform themselves into wannabe corporate executives with pencil skirts and power ties. The story it tells is simple: teaching doesn't pay; management does. It is just the grunts who stay on the frontline.

Funding also matters because of the condition the children are in. How are they learning if they are not eating and sleeping well, are not dressed and washed, and do not have a secure roof over their heads? Aren't these questions for welfare, health, and social services? Society's failure to deliver children to school in a fit state has forced schools to become surrogate parents and keep adults at work in low-paid jobs for long hours. This puts schools in an invidious position. They must find the money to pay staff from a budget determined by a complex formula. Since teachers are not paid directly by the government, staff must compete with the school's other demands, and it is the school that must decide whether, within certain limits, it should pay staff more or spend the money elsewhere.

As for businesses, they lost interest in educating and training their workers long ago. Education, they might argue, must be conducted in more abstract terms, separate from practice, because society has become more complex and technically advanced. It requires detailed technical training that can be completed only in specialized educational organizations – the school and the university. There may be some truth in this, but it is mostly about economies of scale and the reluctance of businesses to take on the expense of training employees in the specific roles they want. Companies prefer schools to take on the responsibility. Spending on adult education, apprenticeships, and workplace learning fell 35% over the last decade from an already small total of about £5 billion.

Universities have also suffered indirectly: the state has shifted the burden of funding onto students, turning them into second-class citizens even before starting their post-graduate lives. In America, nearly 70% of students graduated from public universities with a student debt of more than $30,000 each, rising to $37,172 in 2016. A total of 44 million Americans are currently in debt due to student loans. Thus aggregate student debt is higher than the GDP of Australia, the world's 13th-largest economy. Compare this to the sums paid out to rescue the banks and pay for the Iraq war. Meanwhile, the universities, even those with large endowments, risk becoming publishers of credentials.

Chapter 35

Obduracy: education as a process

The transformation of education into a process and failures in other public services have turned many schools into little more than day hostels.

A second manifestation of the West's reluctance to nurture its young is a determination to rely on short-cuts - packaged philosophies and ready-made techniques, all encapsulated within a process. Formulate the right approach, implement the right policy, and get the process right, and the result, it is vainly hoped, is a well-educated society.

Throughout large stretches of Europe's past, and most obviously during affective high tides, what we might call *education-the-activity* took place outside the educational organization. Children, adolescents, and young adults learned remarkably well at home or under the care of a local patron or private tutor, in the artisan's workshop or studio, local choir or gild, or just about anywhere other than a school or a university. Learning inveigled everyday life rather than excluded it. Obversely, marked expansions of educational organizations have often coincided with cooling artistic and intellectual developments. This is not to say that education-the-activity and the educational organization cannot live together on good terms. But they fare best when an affective mood prevails. Education-the-activity is extremely sensitive to the puritan state into which the organization, by its very nature, eventually slips. At that point, education-the-activity and education-the-organization part company: Puritanism cannot bear possibility, doubt, imperfection, the rough and ready, the experimental, mistakes, argument, or any departure from its prescriptions.

Opportunities had broadened slightly over the previous half-century before the Education Act of 1944. The cost of primary education was brought within the range of most parents in 1891. By 1900 more than 34,000 of these schools were scattered across England and Wales.[408] In 1918, their fees were abolished entirely. Nine years earlier, state-aided secondary schools, nearly a thousand in all, could be found together with collections of charitable schools. These opened up routes for advancement to a few lucky children from poor families whose parents were often either uneducated or had to teach themselves to read and write.

But matching a child's proclivities with a suitable teacher still relied all too often upon chance and circumstance, as it had throughout the previous centuries. Did parents recognize that ability? Did they have the money, contacts, or knowledge to help cultivate it? Was there someone around who was able and ready to do so? Did the child understand their own talents?

The new Act would change all that and bring education and opportunity to every child and adolescent. The Act divided education into three phases - primary, secondary, and further. Secondary education was, for the first time, provided free of charge. Local Education authorities were responsible for providing schools, employing teachers, and setting the curricula. Alongside the new state secondary schools, other kinds of schools (private or independent or, in other words, fee-paying schools, voluntary schools, and state-funded selective grammar schools) continued to live together in reasonable peace. Voluntary schools (most of which were religious) could attract state funding in return for ceding a degree of authority to the state. The number of state secondary schools rose quickly from about 1400 at the start of the 1940s to more than 4,500 by the end of that decade. Over the next fifteen years, schools grew in number from 5,900 (in 1951) to just under 6,500. Meanwhile, primary schools fell to 27,000 by the early 1950s while they grew in size from around 150 to 170 pupils.

In 1965 secondary schools were reorganized into comprehensives and opened to all children regardless of ability. Grammar schools were encouraged to make the switch, too. Much of the interest, energy, and work focused on undoing crude attempts during the first half of the century to select and sort children according to intelligence, type, or class. Children from different backgrounds were brought together and encouraged to follow their own preferences and interests. That meant flexibility in what was taught and how. The point was made with great clarity by a teacher in America who wrote that most children fail because

> '*they are afraid, bored, and confused. They are afraid, above all else, of failing, of disappointing or displeasing the many anxious adults around them, whose limitless hopes and expectations for them hang over their heads like a cloud. They are bored because the things they are given and told to do in school are so trivial, so dull, and make such limited and narrow demands on the wide spectrum of their intelligence, capabilities, and*

> *talents. They are confused because most of the torrent of words that pours over them in school makes little or no sense. It often flatly contradicts other things they've been told, and hardly ever has any relation to what they really know - to the rough model of reality that they carry around in their minds.'*[409]

By the late 1970s, the puritanical streak running through British society began to surface again and widen. A series of measures in 1980, 1981, 1986, and 1988 asserted more control over schools. The intention was to give parents and children more choices about which school to attend and influence the schools' governing bodies. The other side of this coin was less influence for local authorities, of whom the Conservative government had a poor opinion. The 1988 Act also increased central control by introducing the National Curriculum, which, it was said, made it possible to bring consistency to standards and comparisons. At the same time, budgets were delegated to schools, enabling them to opt-out of the Local Education Authority if they wished.

The state also brought nurseries under its wing, and in 1998 local authorities were required to provide good quality nursery places for all children aged four. This duty was expanded so that by 2006 local education authorities were expected to provide sufficient places to allow parents to work. A curriculum was also established to cover children aged three or more, and then from birth. This was known as the Early Years Foundation Stage.

Strings were attached to what appeared to be greater freedom. Surveillance, advisory, and evaluation organizations were set up and underwent reform after reform. The Teaching Regulation Agency replaced the National College for Teaching and Leadership. Central government agencies were merged and split and merged again. Between 2007 and 2010, education became the joint responsibility of the Department for Children, Schools and Family and the Department for Business, Innovation, and Skills, until the Department of Education was re-established.

Schools also had to take on a variety of functions other than education. They had to ensure children were safe from each other, their teachers and parents, and other adults outside school. Local Safeguarding Children Boards were established and replaced by multi-agency safeguarding arrangements (under the children and social work act of 2017). The government also determined that children would have to be protected from political extremism and parties and, to that end, learn about British Values.

Centralization and control are reflected in the sheer volume of legislation. All in all, education since 1980 was subject to over 190 pieces of legislation (acts and statutory instruments). This is just the start of a monumental bureaucratic project. Teachers must consume what amount to something in the region of 17 million words or 50,000 pages of legislation and statutory instruments and notices laying out everyday practice within the school in extraordinary detail. This must be read and summarised along with the duties and demands condensed through statutory guidance and other issuances. The schools and their staff must then interpret measures and devise procedures. All this is, in turn, monitored and evaluated by around 236 organizations that are constantly demanding information from schools. Staff must become observers of rules and procedures above all else to avoid falling foul of the government and its enforcers.

Centralization, control, and homogenization are also reflected in reductions in the number of schools. The tendency is justified on the grounds of efficiency or value for money. An increase in the number of secondary schools ended by the mid-1960s. Existing schools absorbed further increases in children, growing from around 500 children for each school to a little over 800 by the late 1970s. The average of about 960 reached by 2020 hid that 60% of schools had more than 1000 and, in many instances, over 1500 children.

The primary justification for all this has been efficiency and standards. Local authorities retained some powers, but OFSTED waved the big stick over schools and later nurseries. The crucial measure of success, however, is exam results. There are two sets of exams that have an inordinate influence on the lives of students and schools. The GCSE (General Certificate of Education) and the Advanced level qualification or A-levels sat every summer. The former is a ticket to spend two years studying for the latter, which is itself a ticket to read for a degree at university where 40% of England's schoolchildren will end up. Ofqual (The Office of Qualifications and Examinations Regulation) releases the results every August.

The A-levels are not just a passport to university. A school whose students' average grades fall too far will come under greater scrutiny from the government. And this can end in sanctions of one sort or another. These include changing staff's pay and conditions, removing staff and governing bodies, turning the school's budget over to an interim board closing the school, or handing it (minus its former staff) to an academy. Academies, though state-funded, have more control over management, curriculum, pay, the selection of students and staff, and the freedom to attract money from private sponsors. Of the 3,400 or so state-funded secondary schools (with 3.25 million pupils), nearly three-quarters of those schools (with about

2.3 million children) are now academies. If an academy fails, it is either absorbed by a more successful one or closed. Independent schools judged to be failing can also find themselves in trouble. For instance, they may be prohibited from taking on new pupils, fined, or closed. Proprietors who do not respond adequately to enforcement notices can end up in prison.

What began as a wish to remove the random nature of opportunities for children to develop their potential has turned into something very different. The marginalization of both teacher and student is obligatory in many state and private schools: time in the classroom is taken up with lesson plans, assessments, mapping, and 'evidencing,' which occasionally includes photographs to prove that practical lessons took place. The problem is not just that teachers are weighed down and worn out by red tape. It is that 'education'– or rather the fulfillment of 'standards' fixed by the government - has become a glorified bureaucratic procedure in which content, imagination, experimentation, and sustained and unconventional thought no longer matter. Children and teachers must do what they are told to do in the way they are told to do it. 'Best practice' holds sway over fresh thought. The student must see the world as directed. Thus, for instance, a play is a composite of meaning shaped by literary and dramatic devices. History is an unstable melange of constructions arrived at by historians through their interpersonal relationships. Economies must be studied through the application of the correct economic models. Only by breaking the mind into a kaleidoscope of skills through which patchworks of information are collected and assembled, declares the geographer, can social and natural worlds be understood. Facts, interpretations, and evidence are set out in neat bullet points to be memorized and marshaled in the correct way and in the correct place. All of this and more (such as precisely defined 'command' words like 'analyze' and 'suggest' and the marks to be awarded for each correctly placed fact or argument) is found in thick, glossy volumes of specifications, amendments, example assessments, published resources, mark schemes, specimen paper, exemplar materials, schemes of work, skills for learning, and work topic materials, produced by exam boards for each subject.

This herding towards process begins at an early age. In nurseries in the UK, children's actions and mental states are treated as interconnected but discrete blocks of phenomena to be broken apart, categorized, analyzed, and recorded. 'Learning' is underpinned by play and exploring, 'active learning,' and 'creating and thinking critically.' A child's development is divided into two blocks. One is *prime areas*. These comprise three sub-categories - personal, social, and emotional, communication and language, and physical development. The other, described as *specific skills and knowledge*, include literacy, mathematics, understanding the world, and expressive arts and design. Each of these block's sub-categories is split into a further two or three categories. Thus, playing and exploring are divided into finding out and exploring, playing with what they know, and being willing to have a go. Each of these third-level categories is fragmented into several fourth-level categories. Fourth-level categories are sets of behavior to be performed by adults. These are organized into two kinds: positive relationships and enabling environment. Thus, having their own idea is associated with respect for a child's ideas and effort (positive relationships) and planning of linked experiences (enabling environments). These fourth-level categories, and attached sets of adult behavior, are split yet again into age groups. There are, for instance, categories of practice held to be indicative of third-level mental states that a child of a certain age ought to experience. Under the *prime areas* and its second-level category (personal, social, and emotional development) and third-level category (making relationships), a child at 16-26 months should play alongside other children and play cooperatively with a 'familiar adult.'[410]

To survive this barrage of tautologies, children, students, and teachers must perform their assigned roles in a defined process and do no more than that. Take what might happen in a British nursery if a child does not manifest the categories of mental states that it should when it should. A departure from these absolutes inevitably signals a problem, setting in train another bureaucratic process that extends way beyond the nursery. A child whose interests are too focused in one area and insufficient in another, or who is unable to form balanced relationships with peers and adults, or who constantly misbehaves, or who in other respects departs from expected absolute mental states and practices, becomes a matter of concern for staff, parents, and authorities and is likely to require special intervention.

Responsibility for raising children has been shifted onto the school, which has become a surrogate family. This grim role was plain during the COVID pandemic. In 2021 government and its scientific advisors busied themselves saturating the press with its claim that if schools stay closed, children's 'life chances' will be damaged irreparably. A generation will 'fall behind.' Many of those who rely on schools to feed them will go hungry. And others, forced to stay at home, will be at greater risk of physical, sexual, and emotional abuse. The government's chutzpah was breathtaking. To indict the produce of its own policies and then use that indictment as cheap moral blackmail to support those same policies is the height of contempt. A fifth of the population is poor because of government actions and inactions over many years. These 'ordinary' people (as ministers like to call them) are most under pressure to go to work because of cuts to welfare, changes in benefit rules, and threats by the state. It was also they who suffered most from a virus left to spread. And it is their children who were most likely to bring it back home after struggling on public transport and spending hours in crowded classrooms working on pointless and soul-destroying bureaucratic techniques.

The only strand of reasoning that made some sense in this tangled web of lunacy was a ruthless one: the primary function of the education system is to keep Britain's labor force (especially its cheaper end) at work. England's A-level fiasco in 2020 offers a glimpse into an education system's seedy and cynical nature. That year there were no exams because the country locked itself down against Covid-19. Teachers supplied predicted grades. Teachers make these predictions every year, and universities offer a place with these in mind. Offers are either unconditional or made with the proviso that predicted grades are realized or bettered. More unconditional offers were made immediately before 2020, which now comprise around a third of the total. Universities do this because they depend on each student's fees: no students, no fees, no university. The pressure rises as universities expand, and each has to attract a larger share of a shrinking number of school leavers. Restrictions imposed by a hostile immigration service on international students' movements, and then in response to Covid-19, worsened matters.

That year, 2020, was also different because when the results were issued on August 13, it was evident that Ofqual had intervened. The grades awarded to many students bore little resemblance to the schools' predictions. Worried that teachers were being too generous and that this would undermine the credibility of the exams, Ofqual devised and applied a mathematical formula to moderate the results. The formula took account of the students' mock results and each school's performance in previous years, amongst other variables. Based on these calculations, Ofqual reduced 40% of grades, threw offers and plans into doubt, and annoyed students, parents, teachers, and universities.

Gavin Williamson, the education secretary, stuck firmly to his guns. By August 17, he abandoned them, and the initial results were re-instated. He claimed he had been blind-sided by Ofqual and only became aware of the full implications of the re-calculations over the weekend. Ofqual struck back, saying that Williamson had known difficulties were brewing ever since March when he ordered the regulator to adjust grades if they appeared inflated. It was then made known that the head of

Ofqual, Roger Taylor, established and ran a firm implicated in the Mid Staffs Hospital scandal. His firm – Dr. Foster - had come up with an algorithm enabling the hospital to present its mortality rates as low when they were, in fact, dangerously high. One reason for this was that the hospital was treating its patients dreadfully.

The squabble between Williamson and Taylor was wholly avoidable and unnecessary. No exams were taken, so no exams were brought into disrepute. And there had been no exams because of exceptional circumstances. Why treat the teacher's predictions as an assault on standards, especially when predictions are made every year and unconditional offers issued to a fair proportion of students as a matter of course? The answer was immediate. '*He's fucking useless,*' declared one vice-chancellor. Then came emotional outbursts from students worried their lives had been ruined, parents trying to deal with the fall-out at home, and university staff whose breaks in Italy were interrupted. All parties likely suspected that things would eventually sort themselves out, if only because vice-chancellors are desperate to fill seats. But the government and Ofqual displayed a complete absence of trust in teachers and schools. Most disgraceful was the treatment of students who had worked hard against the odds in schools assessed as poor over the last few years. An education secretary, whose only claim to the job is that he was not educated at an independent school, and did not go to Oxford or Cambridge, wilfully took away the ladder from the very people it is meant for. A more callous and spiteful decision in the name of quality is difficult to imagine.

The farrago matters for yet another reason, too. It illustrates just how superficial education has become. Lifting a corner of the veil exposed a little of the humbug swirling around the government's education 'system' and something of the cynicism with which the government treats the people it claims to represent. Just how deep this cynicism goes is revealed by a matter from which the farce distracted public attention during a week that was proving deadly.

Rather than find common cause with schools, universities have gone along with government reforms all too easily and are becoming more like brash, over-confident schools. The university has become a brand, experience, or rite, designed to extract as much cash as possible from students. Walk away with a good degree, the student is told, and our brand will confer upon you a charisma, a light, or Duende, that will set you up for life or at least give you a foot in a door so that you can show an employer what you can do. Behind the brand is a business that has the instincts of a business. In America, where enrolments have been falling for years, the university has learned to diversify with '*high-value, non-degree offerings, become customer-*

centric, and invest more so that it can generate larger volumes of higher quality products while reducing costs.'[411] 'Business speak' is also common parlance in the UK, and the 'missions' of the university are those of the corporation. The academic has become a worker at the coalface, the professor a shift supervisor. Above them stand the corporate team: the men dark-suited and gold-tied; the women in their straight-leg, bootcut, cigarette pants or pencil skirts and structured handbags. All want to nail 'the look,' walk the walk, and talk the talk. While behind all the pizzazz, the degree's content is scratched away, and the process through which the certificate is awarded becomes more bureaucratic.

The trend is pronounced in universities without a well-established pedigree. They are unsure of themselves. They are unsure of themselves because of an immovable and crushing presence in British society – intellectual snobbery. They are asked why a student should pay tens of thousands of pounds for a certificate from a university no one has heard of? Their answer is 'relevance,' and relevance means 'skills.' As the degree is hollowed out, the space is filled with an omnium-gatherum of skills: cognitive skills, intellectual skills, key skills, transferable skills, employment-related skills, practical skills, applied skills, interpersonal skills, writing skills, reading skills, thinking skills, networking skills, team-working skills, observational skills, speaking skills, speech-making skills, analytical skills, editing skills, note-taking skills, research skills, computing skills, entrepreneurial skills, lab skills, creative skills, leadership skills, work ethic skills, and ethical skills. Take a verb or adjective, put the word 'skill' after it, and it becomes teachable, assessable, and marketable. Writing an essay or thesis or sitting an exam is to engage in bureaucracy, an updated form of medieval scholasticism, and show how these skills are stitched together, tracked, and traced.

No longer about ideas, a degree today describes a repertoire of distinct skills and, more importantly, the 'evidenced' processes through which those skills are delivered. Any remaining attention students might pay to the development of ideas is diluted by bureaucratizing what few opportunities are left to forge extended debates. The student is faced with an array of distinct pieces and asked to combine these into an acceptable narrative. These parts include, for instance, 'content and structure,' 'critical evaluation and development of arguments,' 'literature,' and 'presentation and written style.' Each of these categories is subdivided into a collection of others. 'Critical evaluation and development of argument' comprises 'developed and sustained argument,' 'logical and realistic argument,' 'critically evaluated material,' and 'original thought and initiative.' 'Content and structure' includes 'logically organized material' and 'clearly defined aims and scope.' 'Good English' (a sub-category of presentation and style), 'logical and realistic argument,' 'logical organization of material,' 'critical evaluation,' 'original thought and initiative,' and 'literature' are all separate and distinct from each other. A good 'essay' lays out these items and, quite literally, allows all those boxes to be ticked. Each of these items can also be mapped, conveniently, to ILOs: a student can demonstrate an ability to work independently and organize their own learning (key transferable skills 2) or to 'develop a reasoned and sustained argument' (cognitive and intellectual skills 3).

This emphasis on process and the easy use of its anodyne language runs throughout education in the UK. A further illustration comes from Geography at Plymouth. Here, as in nursing, the emphasis on process is such that data on students appear to be more important than the students themselves; and the instruction process is more important than content. ILOs (with itemized skills arranged into the same categories) are paramount. 'Substantive knowledge and understanding of geography' are provided only in a limited number of option modules (which also reinforce the ILOs) in their second and third years and amount to no more than thirty percent of the degree.[412]

The Universities may say that they have had no choice about the matter. They are state-funded and student-funded and have had to become more utilitarian. Regulators surround them as the schools and include the Quality Assurance Agency (QAA); the Office for Students; Research England and UK Research and Innovation; the National Agency for the Recognition and Comparison of International Qualifications and Skills; and the National Audit Office. Parliament also directly interposes when it sees fit. For example, in 2009, its Innovation, Universities, Science, and Skills Committee (today known as the Science and Technology Select Committee) encouraged staff to obtain higher education teaching qualifications. It also recommended the QAA include a review of the quality of teaching. A system of fees - introduced in 1998 – provided financial rewards for universities accepting more students from modest or poorer families, but in return for more regulation. Of the various agencies s, one claims to represent their collective interest - Universities UK. Indicative of the universities' remarkable compliance, the agency boasts it works closely with government and national regulators and funding bodies to 'evidence' and communicate the benefits of universities for the economy, employment, and society and help shape national and international policy.

As these kinds of statements and aims suggest, and as Sorokin foresaw, research has been taken over by bureaucracies that now manage thought. Applications and justifications are made and given. The cart must be put resolutely before the horse. What will be done and how? What will be discovered? What will its impact be? How closely aligned is it to current themes and objectives? How relevant is it to society's needs? What will be published and when? Research is no longer about uncertainty, discovery, and risk but about fulfilling a process. And it must be measurable. Measurements enable universities to show their processes and policies are working. Research, like teaching metrics, has become a means to 'evidence' correct policy, governance, administration, relevance, and value for money. Thus the fact that 76% of research is international or world-leading, or that Britain produces 16% of the world's most cited work with just 1% of its population, shows that England is punching above its weight.

The aims of the universities have become, first and foremost, bureaucratic. Their collective purpose is to establish consistency and comparability so that the assessment of quality is effective and continued funding is justified. Process and procedure must be observed. Universities must document and demonstrate that they realize value for money at all levels of their operations.

As Puritanism strengthens, education is side-lined and treated as a quantifiable 'outcome' to hold 'providers' accountable. There is little choice but to accept what the figures show. Either educational organizations are failing, curricula and organizations must be restructured to suit the measurements, or measurements must be altered to make the results look good. Measurement techniques become weapons in political and ideological battles, and schools and universities become less effective at doing anything other than delivering targets. Calibration becomes everything. Puritanism has objectified both what is learned and how it is learned. Education involves getting as many people through a certified process in a specialized building. Outside these places, education in any meaningful sense is rare.

The decline in education is uneven and leaves in its wake stark inequalities. Where a good education is found in English schools, it is provided by teachers and parents *despite* the vast amount of nonsensical instructions (misleadingly entitled 'guidelines') issued by the government and agencies. In these oases of levelheadedness, staffs teach outside the system's narrow confines, introducing children to other ways of thinking and helping them to explore more rounded and deeper understandings of the world.

Officialism smothers all schools. But when parents are well educated and bring up their children to read, to learn, and to write and talk and think coherently, teachers have an easier time of it. The teacher's immediate job is to ensure the child is practiced in the bureaucracy and given the required information. This delivers the grades. The second, and more important job, is to lead their children out and beyond those limitations. This – a willingness to go further - prepares the child for university and more.

This is not a state-independent sector distinction. There are some excellent state schools. And there are some terrible independent schools. These come in all shapes and sizes, from desperately over-confident little clubs that are well-heeled, well-connected, and very chichi to unhappy and sullen communities tucked away in an old building in the countryside or hidden down some medieval alley. But teachers and parents in the independent sector can stop the system from enveloping their children in niggling and pointless tasks and dragging them into a mire of boredom and despondency. The state-funded schools are browbeaten. The bureaucracy does not allow them the time, freedom, money, or incentive to see beyond the government's petty worldview. Grades have come to mean everything. And because they mean everything, what they are supposed to signify has come to mean very little. The education system - and 'system' is a good description – barely manages to educate at all.

Chapter 36

Obduracy: ineffective government

The deterioration in the provision of health and education is an instance of a general atrophy in government starkly revealed during the covid-19 pandemic.

Alongside health and education, public life generally suffered under Puritanism. Loyalty to the market undermines its material fabric. Welfare organizations, more concerned with working efficiently and following processes than dispensing welfare and improving lives, become ineffective and dysfunctional. Their purpose is not to raise all boats: that would be immoral. Ask for more, and you can expect vindictiveness and parsimony. You only deserve what you put in, arrangements that favor those with middle and higher incomes. These leviathans are run by boards who formulate principles and procedures to guide their committees and structure the reports and minutes issued.[413] The boards delineate roles and responsibilities and methods of evaluation and self-evaluation. They define and communicate mechanisms for complaints and whistleblowing. They 'embed' codes of conduct and 'positive approaches' to risk. It is their fastidiousness in their treatment of rules and process that leaves the organization rigid and hollow.

The failures of one organization weigh upon others whose own joints are creaking. Schools try to pick up the pieces only to be overwhelmed by unstrung parents and bored and disinterested children who pour on the streets. Police forces up and down the country have retreated from towns and villages into fort-like buildings in cities left dour and drab by poverty and parsimony. Here faltering hospitals, clogged emergency departments, packed surgeries, and exhausted doctors turn out the old, the sick, the homeless, the addicts, and the beggars, onto the streets and into doorways and telephone boxes rancid with stale urine and food grease. This 'demand' - as wasted and broken lives are now euphemistically referred to - is 'met' by fewer police officers.[414]

And why not? From the start, the force was intended as a preserve for men without a 'gentlemen's rank, habits, or station.' Peel thought the ideal constable were retired NCOs – honest, reliable, disciplined, and obedient. Scullions of the propertied and wealthy. Men who knew how to handle themselves and when to apply violence judiciously. The force has remained conservative ever since. It has done so not because it is a cultural or historical relic handing down traditions unthinkingly from one generation to the next. It is conservative because of the nature of the job it is asked to do. Corps d'ésprit, soldiery, camaraderie, and solidarity are needed when confronting hostility and violence. Reliability and loyalty are enough to overlook many faults in these brotherhoods and sisterhoods. But they won't look kindly on bluenose martinets standing on the sidelines. Alternative ideas about how the job is done are given short shrift, especially if thought to be irrelevant, a waste of time, or get in the way of what they know works. Officers do what is necessary to get a result. What they do might not look good. They might appear insensitive or brutal, or discriminatory. They also know that many of the people they intend to put away will make any excuse, take any opportunity, and try on anything to make the police look bad. But they can't afford to worry about perceptions. They must deal with the facts; their priorities are life and limb. Damned if you do, damned if you don't.

Attempts are made to dilute this atmosphere. Men and women from varied social and educational backgrounds are recruited. Nearly a third of the force is now women. Credentials have become all the rage. Methods of evaluation and monitoring are commonplace. The intention is to produce a consumer-friendly and gleaming new police 'service.' But that is not the effect. Catalyzed by Puritanism, the old conservatism and shiny professionalism have bred in-betweeners practiced in polite and crafted thuggery. Intoxicated with their own righteousness, they offer conditional help with one hand and wield a 'compliance' stick with the other. A respectful 'please' is followed in the same breath by a crack on the thigh or forearm. The plain, understated dark blue tunic and tidy brass buttons they once wore to distinguish the constable from the soldier have been replaced by paramilitary gear and a swagger. They think of themselves as misunderstood heroes owed a debt by society. They no longer have the time or money to take on burglaries, stolen cars, or millions of financial crimes.

The rest of the justice system is no less parochial. Judges and barristers from a part of London that feels like a small provincial university dominate it. Which matters fall within the realms of the judiciary and which the politicians are unknown. Judges are expected to exercise restraint and stay out of political questions. But they are, like the police, tractable and their interpretation and practice of the law follow a path of least resistance. They weigh heavily on the most vulnerable, ill-prepared, and, all too often, the ill. They might sympathize with people who find themselves in unjust situations created by state policy but claim the remedy is political and their hands are tied. Thus, they ensure that the law offends a sense of justice and contrives to immiserate and cut lives short.

England is not unique in this regard. Across Europe, justice systems are not interested in being fair and just. Instead, they are concerned with efficiency, value for money, accessibility, and independence. How many cases does the justice system process? How long is each case? What is the clearance rate? Does the public feel the courts are insulated from politics?[415] Yet, for all the bureaucracy and the reforms, the Africans, Roma, Muslims, Jews, Travelers, migrants, and asylum seekers are more likely to end up in pre-trial detention and then prison for longer.[416] The poor, too – a large chunk of Europe's population – are more likely to be criminalized. If you are caught evading the public transport fares you can't afford in Germany, you'll end up in prison because you won't be able to pay the fine imposed.

The British government's response to Covid shows how weak and flimsy public organizations have become.[417] The government assiduously ignored the best strategies on display in China, Taiwan, and South Korea: physical distancing and restrictions on movement; and rapid identification of positive cases through mass testing and the immediate isolation and treatment of those cases. The pillars of Seoul's response, for example, were promptness, transparency, and willingness to learn from the 2015 MERS outbreak. Government, local and national, did not hesitate: it tested aggressively, launched epidemiological investigations and imposed quarantines, shared information, and began disinfection efforts. South Korea saw its first confirmed COVID-19 case on January 23rd, 2020. Within a week, hand sanitizers and disposable masks were distributed for free on[418] public transport. Seats and handles were disinfected. Within 16 days of the first case, museums and galleries, other cultural venues, taxis, subways, and buses were sterilized with increasing frequency. People who tested positive were quarantined and given specialist medical care. Within four weeks, screening stations were up and running for 24 hours. Bars and cafes were closed, and treatment was extended to citizens with suspected COVID-19 symptoms. Within five weeks, public facilities were shut down.

In the UK, within five weeks of the first confirmed case on January 29th, 2020, and on the best scientific advice that the country could muster, almost nothing had been done. The government's 'modeling group' had determined that isolation and tracking wouldn't do much other than delay the epidemic's peak. Life might as well go on as usual. Masks were not needed. More proactive measures were not advised until six weeks after the first case. On March 3rd, Johnson's government, having listened to the great and the good of Britain's scientific community, declared that it would be better if people did not shake hands. That same day, Johnson proudly boasted[419] that he had been shaking hands with everyone, including coronavirus patients. For the time being, people in England were being told to wash their hands frequently and for at least twenty seconds on each occasion. They were told to blow their noses into tissue and bin it. They were told not to touch their faces. They were told to stay at home if they felt unwell. This would slow up the inevitable spread of the virus and buy time, though for what was unclear. Schools, universities, and other places of work (including parliament) would stay open. Trains and buses stuck to their routines. Under no circumstances would cities be closed and their populations quarantined in their homes. Even as the number of cases grew, '*the vast majority of people in this country*' should go about their business as usual.[420] Supermarkets would remain open and stocked with food. The police would continue to police and the fire service fight fires, although their priorities might change. The NHS would delay non-urgent care. If teachers were sick, larger classes would be permitted. Schools might have to shut down, but only as a last resort, in which case grandparents (whose age put them most at risk) would step up. If doctors and nurses fell by the wayside, the NHS would take on retired colleagues and unqualified students. People over seventy (presumably except retired doctors, nurses, and teachers) would not attend large gatherings. Younger people who volunteered to fill the gaps left in public services would have their jobs in the private sector kept for them for a month. Small businesses would receive financial help. Research into the virus would be stepped up. Ordinariness was to be preserved, no matter what.

The population was also told that the chances of any single person catching the virus were small. It was a ridiculous statement to make. It might be so for you or me, but someone will catch it. And for as long as that happens, and each of us thinks the chances of infection remain small, cases and deaths would mount relentlessly. The government's officers said there would be 'excess' deaths, as though each was merely a death from one accounting period shifted to a marginally earlier one. They said the death rate was less than one percent, a figure based on the expectation that many more people have the virus than reported.[421] Meanwhile, the figure given by the World Health Organization (WHO) of 3.4% was holding up in China and other outbreaks worldwide. The global case fatality rate rose from 3.69% on March 14th, 2020, to over 7% by the end of April to 3% by mid-October 2020.

On March 9th, 2020, it was evident that the British government was not just failing to safeguard its people but willing to trade lives for economic stability and an air of normality.[422] In the following days, reported infections rose to 5018 and deaths to 233, and the government modified its advice. People were encouraged to work from home and avoid pubs, clubs, and crowds. By March 18th, people had already begun to take matters into their own hands, so doubtful were they about the advice issued. Teachers were calling in sick. Parents were keeping their children at home. One private school after another decided to close down. The Education Minister, Gavin Williamson, had even resorted to threatening court action against the heads of some state schools if they took it upon themselves to shut up shop. Anxious not to be seen to have lost credibility, let alone control, Johnson said tests for COVID-19 would increase from 5000 per day to 25000. Doctors and other NHS staff, who until then were not tested even if symptomatic, would now be prioritized. The prime minister also announced that schools would be closed to most pupils. The possibility of further measures was left open. On March 20th, places to eat and drink and entertain were closed. Anyone who felt ill was advised to isolate themselves for seven days. Later it was suggested they do so for two weeks.

These modifications did not amount to a complete volte-face. Neither social distancing nor isolation was compulsory. It was going to take about a month to reach the target of 25,000 tests a day so that, for the moment, the sick would not know if they had the virus unless they ended up in hospital – a delay that reduced the chances of survival and put families at risk. Schools remained open to the children of 'key' workers. This category included just about the entire public sector and anyone involved in food distribution and transport, journalists, the clergy, and morticians. Trains and buses ran in smaller numbers, leaving many of them packed.

On March 23rd, 2020, the measures had become a 'lockdown.' Having led the country into this too late, the government brought the country out of lockdown far too early. The re-opening, said to be gradual, was chaotic and encouraged people to abandon all pretense long before the final restrictions were lifted in July and August. Johnson was back where he started, declaring, as he did before March 23rd, that normality and the economy must be preserved at all costs. As before, infection rates began to rise, especially[423] in London and parts of the north. As before, facts were ignored. Under no circumstances would a second lockdown be contemplated. Responses to any future outbreaks will be localized and short-term. Schools would re-open after the summer break on September 1st. And the guidance handed to them was remarkably like that issued back in January, February, and March: wash your hands, clean surfaces, and, if possible, keep your distance from each other. (The government added "if possible" to its documents because it knew such distancing was impossible in most schools and classrooms.) As before, teachers or children who were clinically vulnerable (or shielding a relative[424]) could attend school and should do so when the new term began in early September. Parents determined to keep their child at home would be fined as before by the secretary of state for education. And, as before, there was to be no testing unless someone displayed symptoms. However, there was one innovation this time: children, parents, and staff with symptoms were asked to test themselves, trace their contacts, and report their findings to the school.

The origins of Britain's political tchotchkes' extraordinarily cavalier attitudes lie beyond mere political ideology or their laissez-faire approach to all facets of life. Their blasé disdain grows from emotional vacuity. They are not interested in engineering and operating the foundations of power, influence, and wealth. They yearn for the trappings. Constant attention today and posterity's recognition tomorrow. The exhilaration of the grand statement. The frisson of making 'difficult decisions' and 'tough choices.' The rush felt when their edicts impoverish others (for is not sacrificing some for the greater good the mark of the true statesman and woman?) These are the moments they live for. Blair's 'hand of history' resting on his shoulder is one such moment. Ian Duncan Smith, the architect of Britain's universal credit, moved himself to tears when he remembered his own empathy for a single mother who, in his mind, embodied the very people whose character he was on a mission to improve. Johnson, the British Prime Minister, who fancies himself as Churchill risen, talked of wars and battle plans and war rooms, and had himself photographed wearing something akin to a boiler suit[425] at the start of the pandemic.

Adolescent preoccupations left these men unable or unwilling to appreciate the humdrum successes witnessed in China. A former health secretary, Jeremy Hunt, voiced a slicker excuse: being a 'mature' democracy means that Britain's government does not need to act like China's.[426] Repeated warnings about the country's lack of preparedness and the emptiness of their plans fell on deaf ears. There were insufficient beds and health workers even at the best of times, and beds for the critically ill and ventilators were in even shorter supply.[427] 'Act now, pull out all the stops, and learn from China,' cried out the WHO.[428] 'Negligent' and 'ridiculous'[429] was how many GPs described the government's response.

The government's Chief Scientist, Sir Patrick Vallance, and Chief Medical Officer, Professor Christopher Whitty, were also startlingly complacent. This wasn't helped by a general reluctance to criticize the scientists forcefully, directly, and immediately. The two frontmen 'know their stuff' and few commentators want to risk being associated with the new right's instinctive loathing of experts and science. Some critics (like Anthony Costello and John Ashton) did speak out loudly and clearly - irrelevant and discourteous rants to Whitty's ears. On March 19th, at a news conference held at the Academy of

Medical Science,[430] Vallance and Whitty dug in. Tactics evolve as new data comes in. Different opinions are welcome, Whitty said, provided they are expressed with courtesy. He identified three categories of 'critiques.' The first - that the government scientists have the right strategy but wrong timing - he described as legitimate. The other two comprise criticisms of a technical nature; and the demand that they should act to locate the virus, break transmission, and end the outbreak. These last two critiques, he said, were not supported by science and did not fit the correct theoretical framework. This is a courteous way of saying that we won't listen to you unless you think like us. Rather than stop the virus in its tracks, it is best to manage its spread throughout society. Otherwise, the NHS

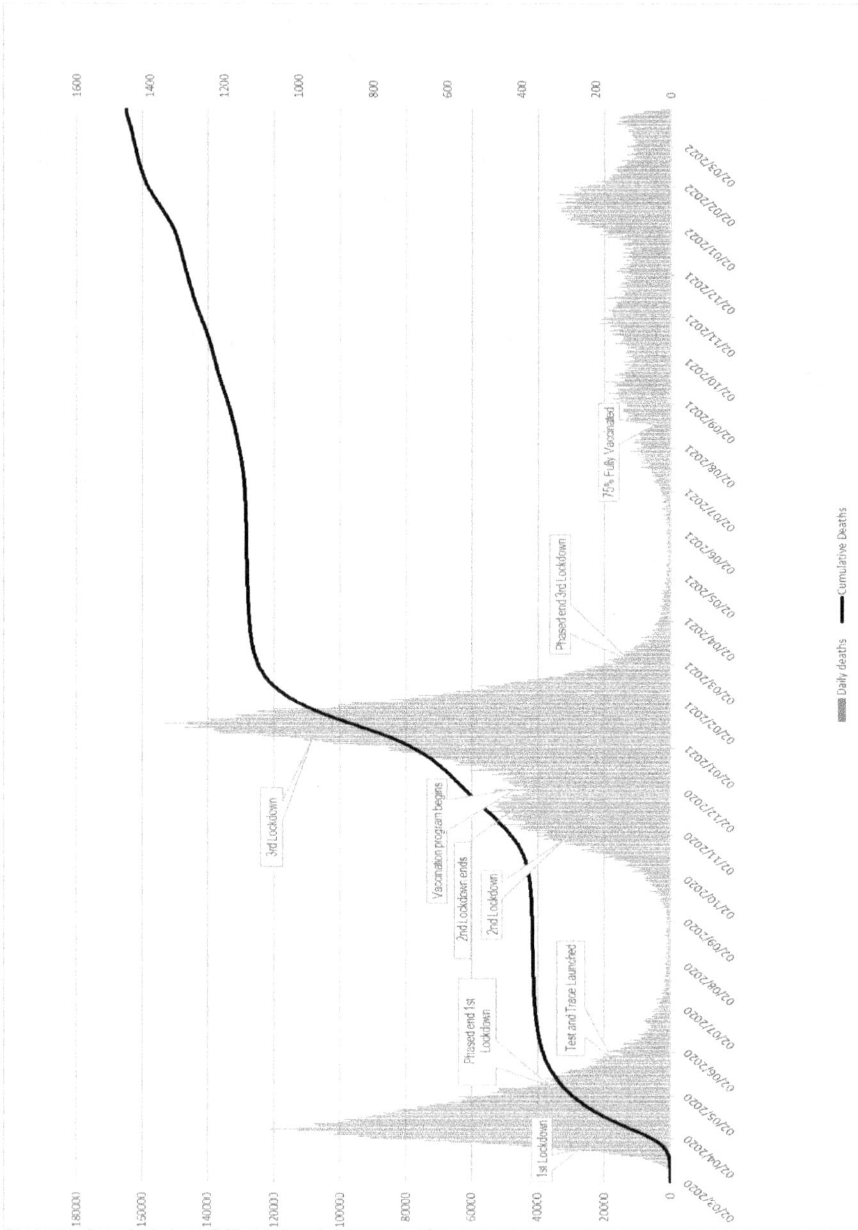

Figure 36.1 Covid-19 Timeline, UK.

will be overburdened, and herd immunity cannot be established. How else will life get back to normal, the economy rescued, and the effects of subsequent viral waves mitigated? Thus, the NHS was transformed from a complex public service that saved lives and relieved suffering into an idol for which people were expected to sacrifice themselves.

The entire debate began to sound like an academic seminar whose participants depended on each other for their reputation and station. 'I'm not sure this is the best we can do,' 'I worry that…,' 'another strategy might be..,' 'Do we have enough evidence…,' 'It is a measured approach…,' and 'We urge the government to reconsider…' Even Polly Toynbee,[431] writing for the Guardian, demurred: I can't judge who's right or wrong, she said, and, she noted, trust in Whitty is very high. Richard Horton,[432] editor-in-chief of the *Lancet*, also pulled his punches. He acknowledged that the 'best' scientists knew the bug was lethal (all the others did not?). 'Something has gone wrong,' he says, but 'I don't know why.' There has been 'a collective failure among politicians and perhaps even government experts.' But he says he knows Whitty and Vallance and 'has the utmost respect' for them and the talented researchers whose support they draw on. Vallance and Whitty no doubt nodded sagely at all this.

The governments' efforts to build up their scientists (the 'best' of whom were already brimming with confidence) also made it difficult to take a crack at them. Johnson gave his briefings flanked by the two men stony-faced and gimlet-eyed like high priests through whom the King communes with the gods. 'What we do is led by science' was the refrain uttered by every minister at every opportunity. Effusive articles[433] ('puff pieces') about Whitty were seeded in the press. When it was pointed out that the government's response was out of step with much of the rest of the world, the reply was that Britain is led by science, not by the populist and ineffective measures peddled elsewhere.[434] When more than 200 mathematicians, geneticists, and other specialists wrote an open letter expressing their doubts, the BBC[435] remarked that none of the signatories was a leading expert in the science of the spread of diseases. Matt Hancock was just as sniffy: 'What we will do is listen to all the credible scientists, and we will look at all the evidence.' When 'ordinary' people doubted, and when teachers and heads thought of closing their schools, they were patronized: You might find it counterintuitive, they were told, but it isn't necessary, and in fact, it would be counterproductive.

Treated with almost feudal deference, the two scientists were irreproachable. They were free to indulge. Why shouldn't they explore their theoretical insights?

Why shouldn't they go for herd immunity, not through vaccination, but through exposure to a disease known to be deadly? Why not blend epidemiology with behavioral science? Why not even pioneer an entirely new way of managing pandemics – one that requires minimum intervention and is highly cost-effective? No wonder they appeared so authoritative even as they nonchalantly discarded the most basic principles of disease control: stop people moving around, find out where the virus is, break the chains of transmission, and find a cure or a vaccine.

Whitty and Vallance were right, and the rest of the world was wrong. They ignored China's experience, the reports coming out of the country, and the warnings issued by the WHO. The death rate, both doctors insisted, was no more than 0.001 percent, though the rate in China and elsewhere was closer to 3.4% and much higher for older people.

The two scientists declared that schools did not spread the disease and left them open until 5 pm on March 20th. Their certainty was nothing less than bizarre. Yes, the transmission of a virus amongst children in classrooms and common areas is complex. It depends on thousands of variables: anything and everything from airflow, and types of surfaces, to respiratory rates and friendship groups. But it was evident to the rest of the world that schools are a ready-made system for transmitting the virus from hospital staff through their children back into the general population, who then turn up at hospitals to start the cycle again. Half a million teachers and four hundred thousand other staff worked in more than 30,000 schools attended by around 10 million children of all ages in England. Whitty and Vallance even made it easier for the virus by leaving hospital staff unprotected and untested, every train carriage and bus crammed with tired commuters, and every pub, club, café, restaurant, and office stuffed to the brim. Even after March 20th, schools were still being used by some children and adults, skeleton transport services were running, and people were free to move around. Local Authorities in London even had a name for this: 'clopening.'

The government's attitude did not improve in the weeks and months that followed. Grand claims that protective equipment (gowns, gloves, visors, masks) turned out to be false. Deceit was laid upon falsehood. Advice on the transmissibility and dangers of the virus and the levels of protection was tailored to match the equipment the government could supply. And when the kit arrived, it was often substandard. Not until July 2020 was the NHS getting 80% of what it needed. But only at the expense of social care, which received only 10% of what it needed, with disastrous effects. Social care is another of those awful euphemisms. It is not so much a place as a state where the old are consigned - more than 400,000 of them. They are the residual population who cannot be left alone, unlike three-quarters or more of the elderly who live alone or as couples.[436] The hospitals off-loaded them even if infected with covid to free up hospital beds. The administrators might as well have set off grenades in care homes up and down the country.

There were many other failures. It took several months to set up the infrastructure to test for the virus, trace it, and break transmission. Dido Harding, Chair of NHS Improvement, was handed the job. She had once headed a mobile 'phone company *TalkTalk* and worked as a director at Sainsbury's (a supermarket) and other companies. Friends with Matt Hancock, the Health Secretary (both are amateur jockeys), and the former Prime Minister (David Cameron), who she met as a student at Oxford, she is the daughter of a hereditary peer and granddaughter of Field Marshal Harding. And she is married to a conservative MP, John Penrose, the country's anti-corruption 'champion.' Harding's appointment came with a budget of £37 billion pounds – or around two-fifths of what is spent on education each year. The organization – *Test and Trace* - did not work. Heavily centralized and poorly coordinated, it failed to reach people who tested positive. And overall, it was unable to pass on the results of more than four-fifths of those tested within 24 hours. It did little to reduce deaths or halt the spread of the virus.[437]

Harding's appointment was part of a feeding frenzy created as the government handed out contracts left, right, and center to firms to manage the pandemic. Few had much experience for the jobs they were hired to do, and, in many cases (at least twenty percent), their only qualification was, like Harding, social connexions with politicians.

Politicians treated statistics with insouciance as well. From August 12th, 2020, as another surge got underway, a death was chalked up to covid only if the person had tested positive within the last 28 days. In the words of the 'Health Security Agency,' this would provide a 'headline figure of the immediate impact of the epidemic.' Figures derived from the previous 60-day cut-off would be kept as 'a more complete measure' of the burden of the disease. It is not easy to divine exactly what this means or what it does other than pull down the headline figure for the number of deaths by at least 12%. I say at least 12% because if one includes deaths that initially escaped any form of reporting, then around 12% can be added to a cumulative total of deaths arrived at through the 60-day limit. In other words, the 28-day limit reduces the toll by nearly a quarter. Translated into human lives, that is around 140,000 versus 186,000 as of March 2022. Most of these people were old (over 50) and amongst the poorest and most vulnerable in British society. For a government to say that these people don't count is beyond contempt.

Chapter 37

Despair: democracy idolized

Putting the market before society removes from government and populace choices about who gets what. Redistribution becomes a residual activity that, at best, expiates any lingering guilt over those society designates as the deserving poor or unfortunate. At worst, it shines a light on those society holds to be ne'er-do-wells and parasites. Democracy becomes little more than a cycle of elections for governments whose commitment is to an economy that deprives them of the power and reason to reallocate goods. Their role is to posture, tinker, and bask in the faux glory of office. Democracy is already wearing thin after barely a century of practice in the West.

To the Greeks, democracy meant provisioning the city and defending it, which depended on public-spirited rulers. It was not a form of government that thoughtful and educated men would choose. Democracy was inferior to aristocracy and oligarchy and only a notch above tyranny. Democracy threw up leaders who would dispossess the rich to satisfy the poor to everyone's detriment. The same fear echoed throughout the centuries to come. Democracy to the English in the eighteenth century meant anarchy, mediocrity, and tyranny, as the French revolution had illustrated so graphically. To Salisbury, mass democracy meant demagoguery and would tear Britain into unfriendly and distrustful fragments.[438]

During the nineteenth century, as the state became more dependent on the commoner to fight for crown and country, keep the factories running, and turn the wheels of commerce, the franchise was slowly extended, and the new voters were to be mentored. Gladstone put it more tactfully: by including more people in political life, the state would be strengthened, for it would make all men, by occupation at least, gentlemen.

A purer notion of democracy was being distilled elsewhere in Europe. Emiliano Castellar, a committed Spanish republican and nationalist, wrote in 1885 that democracy is a virtue responsible for the collective being – the nation – without which there could be no nationalities. The best democracies were to be found in Switzerland and France. And, unlike England, Spain, Portugal, and Italy with their decadent aristocracies and monarchies, and Germany with its imperial form of government, America was not weighed down by history and tradition on its journey to modern rationalism. When President Wilson set out his case for joining Europe's war, he spoke about making the world safe for democracy. When the experience of war and its fallout - not least the establishment of the Soviet Union and economic depression - severely tested such faith, democracy was re-presented as a framework that encouraged imperfect people to become better than they were. Didn't freedom, democracy, and responsibility depend upon the people's goodness and, ultimately (for those who did not insist on a secular world), upon God?

But for the most part, democracy was still a term of abuse and remained so into the twentieth century. In England before World War I, it was used more often to refer to 'the people,' much as politicians today are apt to talk condescendingly about 'ordinary' people. The idea that the democracy's ranks ought to be swollen by the forty percent or so of the adult male population (and the entire adult female population) not yet enfranchised was met with perplexity and horror, especially when it came to matters of war and peace. 'Democracy,' said Lord Charles Beresford (MP for Portsmouth and a serving admiral), '*is always on the side of peace; but, unfortunately, it is more easily inflamed than the community as a whole. That is the great danger of democracy. Let me remind Hon. Gentlemen of the Dogger Bank incident, when several poor fishermen were blown to pieces in what appeared to be a wanton way. It was not really so, as the Russians thought they were torpedo boats....and if the Russian admiral had come in and apologized, nobody would have thought any more of this incident. But democracy was angry, and I am sure that, if it had had its way at the time, it would have gone to war with Russia... and that would have been calamitous. What drove the United States and Spain to war over the Maine incident? It was democracy and the democratic press.*'[439] Nor did the idea that war should be fought over a political system figure in Ramsay MacDonald's thinking. Shortly before his resignation as leader of the Labour party, he made no mention of 'democracy' to justify support for Asquith's declaration of war on Germany. Barely four weeks later, when Sir A. Markham spoke of the war as a democratic one, he was quickly pulled up by Pirie (Aberdeen North), who said that he had 'never known a war successfully waged to be a democratic war because if a war is to be successful, it must be managed by an autocrat.'[440] Markham acknowledged his slip of the tongue, and when he mentioned democracy again well into 1915, he had no qualms about equating it with the 'halfpenny' press.[441]

As light appeared at the end of the tunnel and the debate on war aims intensified, Europe, said Colonel Lord Henry Cavendish-Bentinck, would have to rise above the old diplomatic, military, and political ambitions and the actions of Kaisers, crown princes, and, at home, the Beverbrookes and Northcliffes. The government should represent the people, not the tiny gang who owned Sunday newspapers.[442] Whether it would or not was another matter. Edward Parrot (a teacher and member of Parliament, Edinburgh) doubted the war cabinet had any particular interest in democracy. Governments, said Ponsonby, were more frightened of democracy than militarism, and '*if this war really were to end in the great ideal of the establishment of real democracy throughout Europe and the abolishment of autocracies and aristocracies and bureaucracies, I do not know that the Governments of Europe would regard that ideal with any favor at all.*'[443]

Not until the second world war did liberty and progress supplant narrow superstitions and loyalties such as God, Queen, King, and Country as the standard battle cry. The war, Greenwood argued, was not about Poland. '*We are fighting to save the whole world from the pestilence of Nazi tyranny and in defense of all that is most sacred to man. This is no war for domination or imperial aggrandizement or material gain; no war to shut any country out of its sunlight and means of progress. It is a war, viewed in its inherent quality, to establish, on impregnable rocks, the rights of the individual, and it is a war to establish and revive the stature of man.*' And to that fight, Labour had already committed itself ten days earlier. '*No democratic country will make war, but Britain, with others, will defend their own liberties and the liberties of those who are threatened by force, realizing that a threat to the liberty of one is a threat to the liberties of all.*'[444]

From then on, the freedom to choose how one lived underpinned the case for most wars. Democracy, the rule of international law, UN resolutions, and security from immediate strategic and physical threats were seen as practical measures to preserve self-determination, not as ends in themselves. Korea's government, headed by Syngman Rhee, might not be a good one, but it was a valid expression of the electorate's will, and there was no question that the north was the aggressor. The United Nations, by a majority in the security council of seven to one, agreed on military action to eject the aggressors and restore peace. The Falklands War, too, was ordered in defense of self-determination. The Falklanders sought to be British citizens. Even Lord Brockway (who stood against conscription in the Great War) could agree, though he demurred on the second justification – that this was British territory. To people throughout the Middle East and in parts of the world touched by colonialism, Thatcher could not have sounded more provocative, mocking, and cynical if she had tried when she spoke in Parliament on Iraq's invasion of Kuwait. '*There can be no conceivable justification for one country to march in and seize another simply because it covets its neighbor's wealth and resources. If Iraq's aggression were allowed to succeed, no small state could ever feel safe again. At the very time when at last we can see the prospect of a world governed by the rule of law, a world in which the United Nations and the Security Council can play the role envisaged for them when they were founded, Iraq's actions go back to the law of the jungle.*'[445] Nevertheless, while Iraq threatened western interests and the international rule of law, democracy was not invoked. Blair's intervention in Sierra Leone was also about self-determination, though, in this case, through restoring elections scheduled for 2001 before the Revolutionary United Front rebels broke their commitment to the Lomé peace agreement, attacked United Nations forces, and moved on to Freetown.

Sometimes the cry for war had to do without an appeal to self-determination. Eden did not disguise that Britain's intervention over Suez was essentially commercial and strategic from the start and had nothing to do with democracy and liberty. But he failed to reveal what the opposition leader, Gaitskell, revealed for him: a despatch from Washington that Britain and France were colluding with the Israelis from the beginning. Thus, Eden put paid to Arthur Greenwood's belief that democracies don't make war. According to one calculation, by 2011, democracies had initiated twelve out of 35 wars.[446] As with Suez, there were no credible reasons for intervention in Vietnam. There was no democracy that Americans could recognize and no prospect of it. Under Diem, the South Vietnamese government was dreadfully ineffective and autocratic and fared little better under the succession of generals who deposed him in a bloody coup. Nor was there any real commitment to the market. The idea that America's involvement would forestall wider regional or global war did not wash either. The division between North and South, intermittent conflict, and occasional unification were part and parcel of Vietnam's long history and the states that preceded it. The war - which from the start Kennedy, Johnson, and Nixon knew they had little hope of winning - was a matter of old-fashioned honor. Each felt America just had to beat the communists.

It was a different story in Eastern Europe. At the end of WWII, Churchill suggested that democracy, if established in all countries quickly enough, might put an end to war once and for all. A new generation of thinkers grew up convinced that democracy should and could be imposed. Germany and Japan demonstrated this. It didn't seem to matter that America had set about destroying their economies or what remained of them. Only when strategic realities bit did the Americans reluctantly nurture an atmosphere in which both countries could draw on political forms that existed before Japan's military and Germany's National Socialists took control. The collapse of the Soviet Union then confirmed the superiority and universality of the West's political and economic arrangements.

These new thinkers were secular, but the way they treated democracy as an absolute was faith-like. Ronald Raegan was not so bashful. He would turn the Puritan John Winthrop's 'city on a hill' into a shining city on a hill - a beacon of freedom, hope, and democracy. A few months after Raegan left the White House, students in Tiananmen raised from paper and foam the goddess of democracy, subsequently replicated in the following months and years in Hong Kong, Taiwan, and elsewhere. The West pushed eastwards through the European institutions and NATO, welcoming one country after another enthusiastically into the fold. Poland, the Czech Republic, and Hungary in 1999. Bulgaria, Estonia, Latvia, Lithuania, Romania, Slovakia, and Slovenia in 2004. Albania and Croatia in 2009. Montenegro in 2017. New Macedonia in 2020. In 2021 NATO officially recognized the' membership aspirations' of Bosnia and Herzegovina, Georgia, and Ukraine. Sweden, Finland, and Serbia were also thinking seriously about membership.

By the early twenty-first century, Bush's and Blair's idol began shaping policy and launching wars. The destruction of the Twin Towers blew away any hesitance and reticence. They elevated democracy from a preferred form of self-determination into an idol that demanded allegiance and pre-emptive action and imposed a responsibility to kill and sacrifice. It was not just proper for the West to spread democracy, but a duty. And where better to start than Afghanistan and Iraq?

Back in Europe, the warnings came thick and fast. NATO was denuding Russia by gobbling up vast tracts of eastern Europe that buffered Moscow from the West. By 2004 NATO shared a border with the Baltics. In 2014, Putin fired a warning shot across NATO's bows by invading and annexing Crimea. The West appeared to ignore Russia's concerns. Recognition of Ukraine's aspirations suggested to Putin that the West was preparing to swallow every inch of territory from the Baltics in the north to the Balkans in the south, including Russia's only warm-water ports in the Black Sea, and put NATO within half a day's drive of Moscow. Putin's response was to gather troops along the border with Ukraine. When this did not deter the West, he made for Kyiv. As he probably guessed from past form, the West left the Ukrainians to it.

Chapter 38

Despair: manipulating democracy

Populations throughout the West have lost faith in democracy. Combined with ineffective government, weakening public organizations, and self-preoccupied businesses, the West is now seen by the rest of the world to be increasingly shaky.

Not content to merely practice democracy and let that be an example, the West encourages its spread throughout the Third World, glorifies its evangelists, imposes it, and desires that it work properly. The West can't see it, but it's obvious to everyone else that it fetishizes democracy. And eventually, the fakery is revealed.[447] The West's enthusiasm for pushing democracy on others all too often ends with it pulling away its support. Having planted democracy in Afghanistan, the West abandoned the country after twenty years of occupation. Having invaded Iraq and unseated Hussein, it left the country to itself. When Yugoslavia fragmented into seven unstable republics after a referendum and descended into genocide, the West stood back, organized ineffective UN peacekeeping missions, and launched occasional air strikes. When peace eventually returned a decade later, the surviving entities were democratic in name only. The West's most recent prodigy is Ukraine. Again, the West reasons that defending the country would be too costly and bring about World War Three. That is probably right. But it should have thought about that before leading Ukraine up the garden path and turning a blind eye to the country's extreme right tendencies.

The West does not just ask Third World countries to set aside their authentic version of democracy and treat any remnants of it as underhand. It often demands this in exchange for loans, debt relief, trade deals, policy change, political support, and the like. And if they disagree, they are punished, occasionally through interference in the very democratic process that the West claims is sacrosanct.

Joseph Estrada was not the best president the Philippines had had. He admits that his presidency was a failure. But he was the president and remains furious with constant American intervention. '*They gave us so-called independence, but economically we are not independent. The colonial mentality of some of our leaders is still there. When I declared an all-out war with the MILF, President Clinton sent National Defence Secretary Cohen to me. He personally hand-carried Clinton's letter to me asking me, in the last paragraph of his letter, to desist - to desist - from continuing my all-out war against the MILF. As far as I'm concerned, he had no business telling me that. This is my country. So I told Secretary Cohen "I'm sorry I can't recall my order any more." And he answered, "But Mr. President, can I call President Clinton to talk to you?" "There's no need. Just tell him I cannot recall my order anymore." I don't like foreigners interfering with our domestic problems..... You know how important Mindanao is to the Americans? How come President Clinton personally sent his national defense secretary to personally hand carry his letter to me, when he can just call the U.S. Embassy here and send the ambassador to talk to me? Why? Why does he have to send his national defense secretary? They have a different agenda... During that time when I was senator, we kicked out the U.S. bases here in Clark and Subic. Their future enemy is China. They need the sea lanes of Mindanao for their future bases, and they cannot talk to the people here. But they can easily convince the Muslims there. They can buy them out. That is why, before President Macapagal stepped down, the peace panel created this memorandum agreement on ancestral domain giving them the Bangsamoro Republic separate from the country. It was about to be signed, and the witness will be the ambassador of the United States, Ambassador Kenney, and it will be signed in Kuala Lumpur. It so happened that, fortunately, the Supreme Court declared it as unconstitutional. As far as I'm concerned, Gloria Macapagal Arroyo has a hand in this. She should be charged with treason.*' He was, in his own words, 'a failure' but only because of the path he chose and, consequently, an establishment 'who ganged up on me.' He was now '*very frustrated. Because after I stepped down the MILF rebels were back in their camps and the insurgency has increased.*' But he had compromised neither his beliefs nor his prescription. He had, he felt, already been vindicated, and he hoped this would become even clearer in the years to come. '*When I was released from prison, through a pardon, the former president, the late President Cory Aquino....before the late president died, she apologized to me publicly.*' Vindicated, too, he felt, because of the graft and corruption that followed his removal from office. '*It's all documented. That was the worst graft and corruption that we ever had; and she was able to cheat and suppress the will of the people by cheating in the last election, in her first election, as president. It's documented. This was the worst president ever.*' Vindicated because 'even before the canvassing started, the ambassador of the United States was already in the house of Noynoy Aquino congratulating him. You see, it was designed.' He was, he thought, 'the first person to fight them – the insurgents, the Americans, and the elites – and that cost my presidency.' And he saw no likely change in his lifetime. 'I'm already 73. I've not seen any leader that has that political will as of now.' Aquino did not fit the bill and was merely an extension of American interests. The story – soft or corrupt leaders who allowed Americans to call the shots, give in to insurgents, and massage the electoral system – prepared the ground for Duterte, whose populism and anti-Americanism are now legendary.

The manipulation of democracy by the West backfired even more spectacularly in its dealings with China. By the time Mao declared the country a Republic on October 1st, 1949, it had already suffered nearly forty years of internecine conflict, having overthrown an Imperial system that had left the country prostrate before Europe, America, and Japan. At first, the West ignored the new republic. It then branded China a danger to world peace. Only when China's differences with the Soviet Union became apparent did the West see a means of outflanking the Soviets in the East. And only when its economic reforms began did the West see real economic opportunity in China. Constructive engagement became the new watchword. Once lured into the international economy, China, gently guided by the West, would be faced with no choice but to liberalize its political system and eventually allow mass representative democracy.

As these approaches to China altered, so did narratives of China and the Chinese. Whispers of Cathay had drawn traders, priests, and conquerors from Central Asia, Eurasia, India, Arabia, and the Mediterranean eastwards since the time of Herodotus and Pythagoras. Napoleon had seen China as a sleeping giant that would make the world tremble. But as the final years of the Qing ran out, the Europeans saw China as a charade, a painted edifice crumbling from within, unwilling to change, its people stifled and stultified by a rigid and ancient justification of the status quo - Confucianism. Then, as the Empire collapsed and war set in, they saw an ugly, obsequious, and obedient race. In Europe's mind's eye, this characterless mass transmuted into fanatical hordes willing to throw themselves onto the wire in Korea in the name of a vile ideology. And when communism itself appeared to wither in the late 1970s and China began to open up again, the old culture that had once enticed the West now resurfaced.

China's past and present were rewritten. Confucianism was seized on to explain China's present and past achievements. China had outdone the West long before the arrival of Marco Polo. It understood the market, banking, bureaucracy, capital, and money and evolved a range of sophisticated economic policies before Europeans grasped such matters. China was scientifically and technically more advanced than the West. And this was so because it is a moral, rational, stable, humanistic, and ancient entity with subtle democratic elements. In fact, China was responsible for the emergence of modern science in the West and its industrial revolution.

This claim is rooted in Needham's study of science and civilization in China, written in the decades after World War II. Vilified in the West because of his communist sympathies but honored in China, the significance of his ideas changed with political circumstances. As China opened up, sinologists (with Needham chief amongst them) cast themselves as cultural intermediaries: understand Chinese culture and one could nudge it, coax it, persuade it, lead it up the right path, and, with a bit of patience, get what you wanted from it. In the 21st century, China was remolded yet again by the West: the country was a bully.

Thus was China mystified, romanticized, lionized, marginalized, demonized, and then cast as a Hollywoodesque curiosity populated by people who would eventually become just like Westerners. When it was clear that this wouldn't happen,[448] China was presented as a threat: the Chinese had misled America to secure trade and other advantages.

A sideshow in this was Britain's and its actions in Hong Kong. It is easy to sympathize with anxieties over the extradition bill and worsening living standards that prompted the 2020-21 irruptions in the city. But many people were talking and behaving like it would not be fully integrated with China by 2047. This is fanciful. Who controls Hong Kong today is a question answered long before we were born.

The recent troubles are rooted in the snake oil peddled before 1997 by an English Conservative party that was then in office. Patten, the last Governor, was a parochial politician for one of the most parochial constituencies in England – Bath. He was no statesman. But he was good at presenting arguments clearly - and himself as thoughtful, self-deprecating, and wise - irrespective of the truth. He ran a successful general election for the Conservatives, though he lost his seat. And for this, he was rewarded and compensated with the governorship of Hong Kong.

Once there, his thinking didn't change. He thought that the Beijing leadership, responsible for the well-being of nearly 1.5 billion people and for lifting hundreds of millions from poverty, ought to make exceptions for an Englishman who still had his mind on home and what it would think of him after the handover. Patten created the impression that he and the British cared about Hong Kong and that Hongkongers (just like the people of Bath) would shape their destiny through local democratic mechanisms introduced by him. It was an exhibition in self-delusion and sentimentality only now matched by Boris Johnston's desire for Brexit, no ifs, no buts.

True, Patten was dealt a poor hand. Although the colonial administration could be effective when its military-style simplicity and self-imposed limitations were at their best, Hong Kong had never had a good government, let alone a democracy. Most people had always lived in cramped, mean rooms as they do today, struggling to make ends meet through work, work, and still more work. There was corruption in the administration, judiciary, business, and universities (where promotions were secured for kickbacks, and favors ran wild behind a meritocratic wall). The police were hand in glove with gangsters. Everyone from the poorest immigrant to the highest colonial officer had to pay their way somehow. Those insulated by money or passport might have found life in the territory an 'experience,' exciting, and even romantic. For the rest, it was a grubby, dog-eat-dog existence.

Patten made a bad situation worse by foisting on it the democratic pretensions of an English market town. Hong Kong had been left with no tradition of good government and no pool of committed and effective public servants. There was just a ragbag of tycoons and merchants, intellectuals and professionals, only some of whom might conceivably oversee Hong Kong's gradual integration with China. The field was narrowed still further after many of them - hooing and cooing at the world in what D.H. Lawrence called an 'Oxford voice' or, worse still, a would-be Oxford voice - wrapped themselves in Patten's democratic cloak. They were upholding democracy and defending the people's 'unique' way of life. So don't blame them if they are incompetent, if they are unable to agree on anything or do anything, if they fail the people through maladministration and petty bickering, if they have no imagination or foresight or do not care, or if they spend their time grandstanding while others scratch out a living in tiny apartments amongst the skyscrapers. Blame the outsiders instead! Blame the day-trippers who pack the shops, stuff their wheelies full of Gucci and Yves Saint Laurent, pour through the streets, clog up the trains and buses, fill the parking lots, push up prices, pick up jobs, buy up real estate, foul up the bureaucracy and public services, and are generally 'there' in too large a number.

For the last two decades, these writhing factions have preferred to engage in whatever shabby tactic is needed to get one up on their opponents. Having grown up in this morass, today's politicians and 'influencers,' professional dissenters and activists (many of whom were still only in their twenties and thirties) are just as uncompromisingly bitter, ambitious, and moralistic as their mentors. And if things were to go badly wrong in Hong Kong, that would give these careerists the profile they needed and another entry for their curriculum vitae. They might even be able to scoop up a stipend as a 'scholar' at a prestigious university overseas and write books about the crisis they saw coming.

The most critical problem confronting Hong Kong, and the source of the despair eating away at its soul, was the second-rate political leadership by Hongkongers, for Hongkongers. The solution lay just across the border. If absorbed by Shenzhen, Hongkongers would quickly see an improvement in their living standards. The high-quality government that the city so desperately needs would be forthcoming immediately, the political and physical constraints on the territory would be relieved, living spaces opened up, corruption expunged, businesses controlled, and inequalities finally tackled as subventions are pushed towards those who need it most. Beijing is sure to act positively. And then there is a simple fact that the Shenzhen government really does know what it's doing.

The solution might seem radical, even unthinkable, at present. But full integration by 2047 will take place, come what may. And Shenzhen, unlike London, has a plan. I suspect it will be necessary sooner rather than later. At the moment, Hong Kong's government probably has neither the will to make such a proposal nor the ability to win enough support for it after 22 years of misrule. The most likely scenario is that Beijing will pressure Hong Kong's tycoons to govern rather than administer Hongkongers. Hong Kong's youth will take any give and generosity as a sign of weakness and, seduced by that Oxford voice breathing gently and languishingly on the back of their necks, will cling to the hope that they can unmix Hong Kong from the Mainland. The moment for Hong Kong's big-bang integration will have arrived sooner than expected but later than needed, and in a sour and extremely unhelpful atmosphere – one, it will be said, that all along could have been avoided.

Barbarians inside the walls

The instrumental treatment of democracy within the West is no less plain. Ceding authority to the market almost guarantees it. Men and women who enter politics find themselves on a stage without lines, plots, costumes, or props. They must either make their exit or transform themselves into actors with no clear role other than to convince the audience that they are not actors and that there is no theatre. The audience is no fool and soon loses faith. Membership in political parties has steadily declined.[449] It is also widely recognized that too many politicians have forgotten how to make democracy work and why it must assert its authority over markets.[450] Apathy smothers elections.[451] Trust in the news media and journalism is also failing.[452] All kinds of other groups - so-called civil society - see an opportunity here and try to exert control and influence. Each has its own agenda. The only thing most agree on with varying degrees of enthusiasm is to preserve the market. Democracy is gradually falling apart and, if the west is not careful, will end in a whimper rather than a bang.[453]

It is not difficult to see how this lays the groundwork for populism. Across Europe, parties and politicians with communitarian and often ruthless solutions to unfairness, fissures, and material decline, have gained traction. *Alternative für Deutschland* has made it into the Bundestag as Germany's third-largest party and the largest opposition party. Hungary, Poland, and Turkey have all drifted far to the right. In France, the National Rally and *Reconquête*, and in Italy, the Italian League, The Five Star Movement, and Brothers of Italy have grown strong. Similar currents run through Norway, Denmark, and Finland. The right in Sweden has helped stir up xenophobic and right-wing parties in Britain, Germany, Italy, and elsewhere.[454] America, too, has slid to the right. This was most evident under Donald Trump, whose presidency bore all the hallmarks of demagoguery: attacks on the media and civil society, cronyism, manipulation of the courts, and scapegoating of foreigners.[455] If anything, the right's influence has strengthened in reaction to Biden's election. Groups (from the Patriot Front, Proud Boys, and Oath Keepers to the Ku Klux Klan, the American Nazi Party, and elements of the Republican Party) have ballooned and insinuated themselves into local communities across the country. The vitriol poured out by media outlets such as Fox News, Breitbart, One America, and Newsmax is breathtaking.

It should be no surprise that democracy is also retreating in Third World countries. One highly influential view is that it has become increasingly shallow wherever it survives. Democracy's technical strand (elections) is being pulled away from its liberal strand (the rule of law, the separation of powers, and the protection of speech, assembly, religion, property, and other liberties). Elections are performed to demonstrate the country's democratic credentials to the world, while in every other way, the state is authoritarian. What is worse is that many countries are becoming comfortable with this situation. The notion that the institutions and policies of the West were worthy of emulation is crumbling, and authoritarian regimes are leading the way. Among them is China, whose ability to make enormous economic strides without introducing democratic reforms has cast doubt on the notion that democracy is the only appropriate political system for wealthy countries. At the same time, China is providing African governments with non-Western markets, trade, investment, and military and development aid. It is claimed that Russia, Iran, Saudi Arabia, and Venezuela have also been learning from one another and even cooperating directly to thwart democracy's progress.

Chapter 39

The End. A view from 2120.

Over the span of the twenty-first century, development as a specialism and profession melted away. Where it remained inseparable from the vast question of how society evolves, it continued to thrive. Thought is most likely to progress when problems are approached obliquely and solutions present themselves serendipitously.

So it was countries from Africa to the South Pacific and Latin America showed that the distribution of goods, not their production, is the key to economic prosperity. They showed that effective organizations equate with nuanced and mutable, rather than formal, practice and thought. That growth demands fluid and mobile rather than fixed and cumbersome urban bodies. And that authentic democracy trumps its synthetic, purified version.

These ordinary, age-old truths were revelations to the West, not least because of their implications for two matters of pressing importance. One was the environment. The temporary concentration and rebalancing of materials needed to raise society's living standards could not be divorced from the waste generated. 'Pollution' would have to be included in the equation. The residues from burning coal and oil could not just be ignored. They were bound to influence the subsequent redistribution of goods through the lung diseases it brought on or the changes in sea levels it encouraged.

The other matter was geopolitics. The military is essentially introverted and defensive in a society arranged around procurement and distribution. It must devote itself to safeguarding the whole of society, not a part of it. In a society dominated by private commercial interests, the military is extroverted. At the start of the second half of the twentieth century, America and its Canadian, European, and Antipodean allies (who together gave the sharpest form to 'the West') proudly declared their function as the defense of the four freedoms: freedom of speech; freedom to worship

God in one's own way; freedom from want; and freedom from fear. In practice, the alliance's first and last preoccupation was the protection of commercial hubs worldwide, the trade routes linking them, and the materials that move through them. It also required training and educating the armed forces of other countries in the values and practices necessary to secure democracies and market economies. Since these commercial interests were privately owned, the military had to act on behalf of these private interests. The stance was reflected in an extensive military infrastructure - around 900 military bases globally, invasive cyber networks, the militarization of space, and frequent local conflicts.

Yet despite these realities, the West's leaders and a large portion of its populace simply could not acknowledge that what they took to be their greatest strengths were their greatest weaknesses. There was no need to admit their armies were pushy, their economies destructive, their organizations vise-like, and their cities hung as millstones around their necks. Nor could they accept that the Third World was doing anything different. China's growth, many snapped, depended on private business into which a little state capitalism was mixed - just like any other country.[456]

Scapegoats were found instead. Christianity took a good part of the blame, and not without reason. Having played no small part in the fall of Rome and promised heavenly salvation to those who submitted themselves to the Last Judgement, it insinuated itself and anxieties into every nook and cranny in the earthly kingdoms that followed. The new polities' secular knowledge of the civilizations on whose bones they rested sharpened their disquiet. They began to ruminate over their mortality. Greed, selfishness, and disregard for the common good; too much democracy and too much despotism; injustice, inequality, and exhaustion of the land; rebellion in the countryside, and foreign invasions; and fears of regression vented as apocalyptic myths and visions mingled with prophecies of messianic and revolutionary figures: all these and other symptoms of mismanagement, complacency, and insecurity niggled and gnawed at the rulers' consciences. They saw how uneasiness slipped imperceptibly into wonted misery and instability. They saw the locus of interests, energies, and ideas initially centered at the juncture of African, European, and Asian land masses, swinging from Mesopotamia to the Mediterranean during the first and second millennia. They witnessed first-hand that locus turn from the Mediterranean to western and northern Europe and its American extension.

By the time the locus wheeled yet again during the late twentieth century, from the North Atlantic Rim to the West Pacific Rim and beyond, fears were sublimated in all manner of secular concerns. The man who once stood alone in the marketplace bewailing 'the end' was drowned out by popular culture's katzenjammer of doomsday bugs, zombie plagues, alien invasions, intelligent and hostile machines, nuclear terrorism, meteor strikes, and catastrophes wrought by climate or geology. Political and social conservatives worried that society today is not as it used to be. Radicals were convinced that yesterday's world must be swept aside and a new one put in its place. Moralists pined for some calamity to assuage the guilt they shouldered on society's behalf for its sins against the earth. Malcontents brewed up resentment and curses against a society they felt was responsible for modern life's monotony or some other ailment. Scholars and publishers came up with a whole genre of literature called declinism.

Yet none of this explained the decline nor the West's unshakeable faith in what it took to be its strengths. Christianity had never been about God's perfection. He was powerful only when treated *as if* absolute - when doubt was retained, and His presence was left to choice. When treated as absolute, God became humankind's plaything. As certainty closed in, Christianity faded and, with it, philosophy, literary culture, art, and music. Western civilization became infatuated with technology and science. Its children became technologists. The question was not whether society might throw up another Allegri, Lotti, or Turner, but why would it want to? There was no memento mori in this purely rational world.

Why did puritanism take hold? Part of the answer is extraordinarily mundane: Europe's geography. It is compact and located at the crossroads between Africa and Asia. These qualities favored intense competition amongst its people. Commerce demanded organization. Organization cultivated an affective mood that, with time and familiarity, slipped into a Puritanical one. Puritanism elevated understandings and stories into absolute truths. Certain knowledge demanded certainty in how knowledge was acquired, and those methods were equated with rationality. Rationality was woven into personal identity: scientific-like thought distinguished the educated from the ignorant, the intelligent from the stupid, the broad mind from rank prejudice, and the civilized from the uncivilized. Left with nowhere to go and nothing to do except follow the intellectual runs laid down, subsequent generations held their faces to the ground, obsessed with the frivolous details perfection demands.

Puritanism worked the most damage through economics. During the last quarter of the twentieth century, the demands of war and welfare - far more so than the fast-waning mystique of monarchy and Church - afforded the state more control over civilian logistics than ever before. Yet the politicians just gave that control away. Predatory businesses turned societies into hunting grounds. A struggle over resources was played out in each country between private corporations and the rest of society. Society enjoined businesses to take on a social role. Businesses insisted that society ought not meddle in economic affairs. In these so-called mixed economies, the privately-owned leviathans' value often exceeded the GDP of the smaller Third World states.

One crisis after another struck the West through the turn of the twenty-first century. Political leaders - determined not to undermine the economies they revered – continued to cede what influence over procurement and distribution they still had and became increasingly ineffective. By 2017, not quite thirty years after Fukuyama[457] trumpeted the final victory of democracy and market, economic growth had 'ceased to benefit most people.'[458] By 2020 it was evident that Britain was slipping toward what was, in the fashionable jargon of the day, the 'outer core' of the 'global political economy.' Social mobility seized up, except for those willing to hustle in whatever way they could. Cities grew flimsier. There are plenty of reports from the time on the declining quality of construction. But one only had to stroll down a street or slip into a building to sense the shabbiness, meanness, banality, and boxiness of the new century's cities. The houses in which most 'ordinary' people lived felt like cartons. Towers of apartments built for the young resembled prisons.

Families shrunk, and so did the population. Only immigration kept numbers up. People were ground down. The old and the sick were thrown to the wolves. Faces, pale and haggard, laid bare souls preoccupied with survival: paying that debt; paying to keep water in the pipes; paying to stay warm; paying to put the next meal on the table; meeting the rent or mortgage. Clothing became mangy, and cleanliness a past luxury. Sales of deodorant, toothpaste, and shampoo fell even as luxury skin creams and scents blossomed. Teachers rummaged about in their own pockets to feed and clean children who turned up at school hungry and dirty. Public organizations, starved of resources, were ordered to focus on the picayune bureaucracy. Petty disputes and flashes of anger on the streets, in shops and supermarkets, and on buses were common occurrences. Intoxicated by drink or drugs or riven by mental illness, desperate minds shouted and bawled, walked around supermarkets, kicked doors, broke whatever could be broken, lashed out at whoever was in reach, and took whatever they pleased, ignored by thuggish policemen, and unchallenged by underpaid security guards trying to hold their own lives together. So much of their world was, like them, uncared for. Roads were worn and pitted. Roadsides were left untended, curbs and signs obscured by wild grass and overgrown hedges and trees. Pavements narrowed and crumbled. Buses and trains became more expensive and uncomfortable. Once-grand airports shriveled inside small, dull, and grimy buildings. Ugly blocks, statements of wannabe grandeur, succeeded only in looking mean, surly, and bitter.

By the early 2020s, the small triangle of roads, buildings, and parks that was Britain's heart could no longer hide its decay. Trafalgar Square, which formed the triangle's northern point, had lost meaning. It was cluttered and appeared to have shrunk. A cherry angioma topped a swirl of ice cream slopped over one of its plinths. On the cherry sat a grotesque 'fly' – a mechanical drone. The sculpture was named 'The End.' The gallery lining the square's northern side was tired, beaten down by satellite dishes, railings, and the roofs of a 'super-boutique' hotel and other buildings that rose behind it in the near distance. Attached to the gallery's eastern flank was a mock neo-classical façade bought and paid for by the supermarket it was named after – Sainsbury's. On its west side, St Martin's, a combo of spire and classical temple front that had always felt awkward, shed any vestige of sincerity and became a stage for shameless showmanship. It 'operated' its music and 'curated' 'sector-leading' 'outputs' and 'concert structures.' Turning south from the Square, past a Tesco Express (another supermarket store), ran Whitehall as it does today but lined with government buildings at that time. Here and there, most noticeably behind the iron bars that block Downing Street and Horse Guard's Parade, men in baseball caps and paramilitary gear swaggered about sporting machine guns. The people who had occupied these buildings in 2020 and over the previous forty years were staggeringly ineffective. The two most prestigious, powerful, and disastrous – the Treasury and the FCO - were little better than exclusive clubs. Their members were interested primarily in the cachet and social accouterments of their jobs and in melding with the roles dictated by popular imagination.

At the end of Whitehall is Parliament, forming the eastern point of the triangle. Whatever this mock gothic-cum-classical assemblage meant to nineteenth-century Londoners, it seemed in 2020 to float on the Thames like a fanciful Victorian cake. To one end of it stands Westminster Abbey which had become a grace and favor bauble of a family whose members were caricatures - waxed dummies stuffed into colorful uniforms.

Buckingham Palace, a dull block of stone, forms the west point of the triangle. The road behind the palace was littered with cheap tourist trinkets, prissy English teas, and expensive and unimaginative royal wares. In front of the palace and between it and Whitehall and Parliament stretched a park of sorts. In late summer, it was still full of dead leaves from the previous year's autumn, rustling in a wind that whipped up dust from bald patches on thin, hay-colored lawns. Deckchairs were scattered about. A desperate wooden cubicle boasted award-winning coffee. And near it, hidden under a bank of soil and unkept bushes, were filthy toilets open only to those with bank cards.

Tourists still trudge this dreary route today. Its features, cowering under brutal hunks of concrete and glass, are still more shrunken than they were in 2020, even more irrelevant and run down. They are not ruins quite yet. Some have even flourished as expensive apartments. But the sense that their twenty-first-century denizens were just going through the motions, insulated from the truth by their own self-importance, has been replaced by emptiness.

Superficiality was a quality of so many aspects of life at that time. A new bevel on a computer screen or watch, a lid that opened more smoothly, a trackpad that ran into the chassis of a laptop, or a mobile screen that curved around the edge of the phone, qualified as instances of creativity. Product design and technology replaced art. Unmade beds or brightly colored steel shaped into glistening balloons deserved pride of place in the most expensive and exclusive galleries. Outside the organization, education, which had brought such vitality and creativity for so long, was extinguished. Some believe the destroyer was 'youth culture.' [459] But transforming education into a process did the real damage. Schools and universities became publishing houses for credentials. Thinking and writing became a bureaucratic exercise, as Sorokin prophesized. [460] So did academic publishing. Forms were devised and filled in and became more important manuscripts. These obeyed the formula of their genre. The finished article - the book - was left on shelves unread. Its puffing and the name of its publishing house stamped on its spine were more significant than its content. The public intellectual plugged and plied like never before. Scientists promised bizarre discoveries and proclaimed extraordinary truths made bizarre and extraordinary not by nature but through lay descriptions intended to glitz up their profession and applications for funding. Historians and social scientists, archaeologists, and classicists, became entertainers. They assumed characters and mannerisms for the screen and declared whatever needed to be declared - from democracy's final triumph to the collapse of civilization - in dramatic tones. New generations of 'classical' music stars performed all kinds of antics and facial contortions until the audience could hardly remember what it had been listening to.

Ordinary social life was degraded. The treatment of relationships as absolute turned them into objects which needed perfecting. Politeness was formalized. One *had* to be civil, not out of habit, nor because civility made society pleasurable, but to sidestep legal sanctions. Dealings with officialdom and wider public interactions that strayed beyond a wooden courteousness were labeled 'abuse' and punished under the law. Over time, relationships became instrumental. People functioned rather than felt. They were too often swamped by disinterest, thoughtlessness, or suspicion. The driver, the pedestrian, the passenger, the shopper, the diner, the cyclist, the poor, the old, the young, and the sick - became sources of inconvenience and anger and targets for ill-concealed hostility. Society became a reason and place for venting frustration of every kind. Autonomy and independence trumped reciprocity, obligation, loyalty, and attachment. By the early 2020s, the West's population had fallen to around 14% of humanity – about half what it had been 72 years earlier. Europe's population had also begun to drop in absolute numbers. By the end of the century, less than 10% of humanity would be found scattered amongst the West's remains.

A further consequence of Puritanism was that the West failed to notice the pace of progress slow. The initial creative wave set in motion by industry, and the billows of redistribution pushed along by war and unrest, had been remarkable. And there was no question that technology and science improve as much by increments as by jumps.[461] So the West flattered itself as sclerosis set in.[462] By 2020, aside from lighter hand-held 'phones and computers, better internet coverage, and the evolution of huge warehouses crammed with brightly packaged food, the material lives of most people had not changed much over the previous fifty years. Nor did it change much in the next fifty years. Indeed, too many saw their private material lives deteriorate along with the public world.

The West also failed to appreciate what was happening in the Third World. China's vision was expanding trans-Eurasian trade and populating Eurasia's vast spaces. So the West hammed it up: China was acting out Mackinder's heartland theory and subjugating Asia. Other commentators took on studied reasonableness: the world is becoming multipolar and politically diverse.[463]

Nor did the West comprehend the revival of trans-Saharan trade linking West Africa to the Levant, Central Asia, the Indian subcontinent, and the West Pacific arc that reaches from Japan in the north to Indonesia in the south and is anchored by

China in the middle. A band encircling the earth between the equator and the 45th parallel, that once contained the poorest of humankind, stretching from West Africa's Atlantic coast to the West Pacific Rim, is now wealthier than the West at its zenith imagined itself to be. Even the once-isolated Pacific Islands – written off until their tiny populations with their digital memories were concentrated in Fiji, the Philippines, and Papua New Guinea – now form a chain of glittering stars in the night ocean draped between Asia and Central America, Mexico, and northern Latin America.

The southern Europeans, already geographically a part of this band, found it easy to merge with it in all other respects. America's southern states took over the baton from the north and became the country's economic heart, beating in rhythm with Mexico and Central America.

Meanwhile, cities in northern Europe and North America ensured the West's dissolution through their determination to retain their identity. Unwilling to form state-private combines and submit to societies' directives, businesses dominated their own run-down territories, even as African and Asian entities eclipsed them. They could not bear to cede control. Each was their own lord and master. Each preferred a small pond. And so they got together and something of the old Hanseatic League returned – a string of defensive cities devoted to trading and the rule of law along northern Europe's coast, across the Atlantic, and as far West as Minneapolis. And the more doggedly they adhered to their ideals, the weaker and more irrelevant they became.

The certainty that something or someone would come to its rescue pervaded the West throughout its decline. But every remedy tried was just more of the same. However modest and temporary, every uptick in fortunes was taken as a sign of recovery. Leaders, parties, and personalities came and went with increasing regularity. When Russia reasserted its dominion over Ukraine at the start of the third decade of the 21st century, the West, nearly fifty countries in all, pulled as one, or so it seemed. Germany's enforced military weakness came to an end and promised to relieve some of America's defense burdens. Japan re-discovered its military confidence. But Putin had their measure, drew the war out, and saw the West's interest in Ukraine gradually fizzle out. His relationship with China was further cemented at a time when the USA feared just such an alliance.[464] Russia was further helped by yet another of the West's economic crises as resources accumulated in the hands of the few. Japan, compelled to follow the West for too long, now decided to throw its lot in with Asia and its erstwhile nemesis, China, as did the Philippines, cutting America out of the western half of the Pacific. Country after country followed suit. The US shrank with its markets, and its southern states felt the growing pull of Mexico and Central America. The cities of the new 'Hanseatic League' became increasingly decrepit - historical curiosities determined to stay *au courant*.

London was amongst the most enthusiastic of these cities. Its hinterland, England, scratched a living as an early industrial theme land. Shabby and dreary nineteenth-century railway arches, warehouses, and factories were renovated and blended with new imitations. Yet the air still reeked of decay. Outside London, the National Trust became the country's biggest employer and landlord, its parks littered with chichi bed-and-breakfasts, dainty potteries, glassmakers, fromageries, cobblers, antique shops, pretentious chocolatiers, perfumeries, bakeries, and all manner of artisans. But most of the country's population was now either living in London - a clutch of dusty and dirty boroughs covering most of southeast England, interspersed with grander areas populated by wealthy merchants - or had emigrated to southern Europe or further afield. Thus, the West gave out in a silence tinged with resentment.

Could it have been saved? Could the West have shaken itself out of its dreams? Could it have taken remedial action? That was always unlikely. The only alternative thought to be realistic[465] during the first half of the twenty-first century was either a 'mixed' economy governed by brawnier democracies or state capitalism the West supposed China exemplified. Either way, capitalism was 'here to stay and has no competition.'[466] Blinkered by certainty, the West could not understand or accept redistribution in command, the private sector as its extension, ductile rules and organization, and direct communication between leadership and people.

There were times when the Third World appeared stymied by its own waves of Puritanism, giving the West false hope. The Islamic world had often felt the clerics' certainty bear down on everyday life. That was before sectarianism became oh-so démodé. From the eastern fringe of southeast Asia to Senegal in the far west, and from Comoros in the south to the 'Land of the Pure' and Kazakhstan in the north, homosexuals, women, atheists, castes, Shia, Sunni, Christian, Hindu, Buddhist, the affable, and the uncommitted had been swept aside by cocksure men. Islam split Africa's north from its sub-Saharan (predominantly Christian) south but did not mark the boundaries of intolerance. Just about every other kind of narrow-mindedness that humans are capable of was to be found in one country or another: from the persecution of dissenting political views in Botswana to the massacre of Congolese migrants hoping for no more than a marginally better life in Angola, to the rejection of illegitimate children in Madagascar. After a long affective period,

Korea drifted silently into a Puritanical mood in the twenty-first century, centered initially on bundles of small churches. Hong Kong fell victim to intolerance and decay in the late twentieth and early twenty-first centuries. It was saved only when integrated with Shenzhen in 2047. China then suffered its own bout of puritanism. This had raised its head many times before, most obviously during Mao's last decade. It showed itself once again during the 2019-2023 pandemic. The Party's actions had saved many lives at the outbreak's start and probably millions by its end. China's politics was rightly characterised as a 'practical arrangement that works for the national good.'[467] Chinese adults were perplexed at the West's insistence that democracy was the ultimate end. Westerners, it seemed, could not become less democratic even if their survival depended on it.[468] But unmoderated rigor could just as easily cripple Chinese society, too, as though by crystal arthropathy. Over the next few years, a weakening of natural immunity in the population left the 'big whites' firefighting covid variants that caused few problems in the rest of the world. At the same time, India, whose population had outgrown China's earlier in the century, experienced another pulse of economic expansion. Only then was China spurred into action: a vast anti-bureaucratic campaign followed by a massive boost to the arts and education.

Even so, as we look back from our vantage point at the start of the twenty-second century, puritanism has not yet seized the Third World to the extent and depth it once did in the West. This doesn't mean it won't happen, especially now that the Third World is synonymous with densely populated, effectively organized, and materially comfortable societies. But if the West, undone by its Puritan urges, serves as a warning to 'the rest' and teaches us that the details of what is thought and done often matter less than the atmosphere in which we live our lives, then it will have done humanity a very great service.

End Notes

Introduction

[1] Vaihinger, H. 2021. *The Philosophy of 'As If.'* Routledge: London and New York.

[2] Sorokin, P. 1970. *Social and Cultural Dynamics.* Porter Sargent Publisher: Boston.

[3] Polanyi, K. 1944. *The Great Transformation.* Beacon Press: Boston.

[4] Holt, J. 1995. *How Children Fail.* De Capo: Boston.

[5] Sumner, A. and Tribe, M. 2008. What could development studies be? *Development in Practice* 18: 755-766.

[6] Kohm, H. 1957. *Is the Liberal West in Decline*? Pall Mall Press: London.

[7] Spengler, O. 1926. *The Decline of the West.* George Allen and Unwin: London. (Translated by Charles Atkinson).

[8] Currie-Alder, B. 2016. The state of development studies. *Canadian Journal of Development Studies* 37: 5-26.

[9] Mohan, B. 2008. The fall and rise of the Third World. *Journal of Comparative Social Welfare* 25: 71-78.

Part 1, Chapters 1-5.

[10] Deodhar, S.Y. 2018. *Indian Antecedents to Modern Economic Thought.* WP 2018-01-02. Indian Institute of Management: Ahmedabad.

[11] *Guanzi.* 2001. Princeton University Press: Princeton. Rickett, W. A. (trans.).

[12]Roncaglia, A. 2017. *A Brief History of Economic Thought.* CUP: Cambridge.

[13] Or, more technically, a sustained rise over time in a nation's production of goods and services. Wolla, S. 2017. Why are some countries rich and others poor? *Page One Economics*. September. Federal Reserve Bank of St Louis.

[14] Smith, A. 1909. *Wealth of Nations.* Collier and Son: New York. See page 335.

[15] Say, J-B., 1971. *A Treatise on Political Economy.* Kelley: New York. (Translated from the French by Prinsep, C.R, 1880). '*When the producer has put the finishing hand to his product, he is most anxious to sell it immediately, lest its value should diminish in his hands. Nor is he less anxious to dispose of the money he may get for it; for the value of money is also perishable. But the only way of getting rid of money is in the purchase of some product or other. Thus, the mere circumstance the creation of one product immediately opens a vent for other products*' (p.134-135).

[16] Mill, J.S. 2009. *Principles of Political Economy.* Project Gutenberg ebook, (page 450). See also: Mill, J.S. 1974. *A System of Logic. Books IV-VI.* Routledge and Kegan Paul and University of Toronto Press: Toronto (p. 949).

[17] Malthus, T. 1998. *An Essay on the Principle of Population.* Electronic Scholarly Publishing Project.

[18] Marshall, A. 2013. *Principle of Economics* (Eighth Edition): Palgrave Macmillan: Basingstoke.

[19] Harrod, R. 1939. An essay in dynamic theory. *Economic Journal*, 49:14-33; Domar, E. 1946. Capital expansion, rate of growth, and employment, *Econometrica*, 14: 137-147.

[20] Kaldor, N. 1957. A model of economic growth. *The Economic Journal*, 67: 591-624.

[21] Schumpeter, J. 1983. *The Theory of Economic Development.* Transaction Publishers: New Brunswick and London.

[22] Kaldor, N. 1954. The relation of economic growth and cyclical fluctuations. *The Economic Journal* 64: 53-71.

[23] See: Kapchan, C. 2012. *No One's World.* OUP: New York.

[24] Bogart, D. and Ricardson, G. 2006. *Parliament, Property Rights, and Public Goods in England.* Department of Economics, University of California: Irvine. Hodgson, G. 2017. 1688 and all that: property rights, the Glorious Revolution and the rise of British capitalism. *Journal of Institutional Economics* 13: 79-107.

[25] Tawney, R. 1954. *Religion and the Rise of Capitalism.* The New American Library: New York. (See page 188).

[26] See, for example, Burns, A. 1969. The Business Cycle in a Changing World. NBER: Cambridge, Mass.; Clark, C. 1940. The Conditions of Economic Progress. OUP: Oxford; Kuznets, S. 1971. Economic Growth of Nations. Harvard: Cambridge, Mass.

[27] Lindert, P. 2004. *Growing Public: social spending and economic growth since the eighteenth century. Volumes I and II.* CUP: Cambridge

Chapters 2.

[28] Allen, G.C. 1958. *Japan's Economic Recovery.* Oxford University Press: London.

[29] Schollhammer, H. 1971. Organization structures of multinational corporations. *The Academy of Management Journal* 14: 345–365, p.349.

[30]World Bank. 1993. *The East Asian Miracle.* OUP: New York.

[31] Crush, J. 1993. Postcoloniality, decolonization and geography. In A. Godlewska & N. Smith (eds). *Geography and Empire*. Oxford: Blackwell.

[32] See, for example, Edwards, M. 1989. The irrelevance of development studies. *Third World Quarterly* 11: 116-135.

[33] Commission on Growth and Development 2008. *The Growth Report.* The World Bank. Washington.

[34] Ghana, for instance, attained middle income status in 2007, and saw growth peak at nearly 15% in 2011. Aryeetey, E. and Baah-Boateng, W. 2016. *Understanding Ghana's Growth Success Story and Job Creation Challenges*. The Brookings Institution: Washington, D.C.

[35] Wagstyl, S. 2010. The rise of the developing world. *Financial Times*. September 28th; Xie, E. *et alia* 2017. Country-specific determinants of cross-border mergers and acquisitions. *Journal of World Business* 52: 127-183.

[36] Pilling, D. 2019. Africa poised to play major role in the world. *Financial Times* August 28th.

[37] Feng, E. and Pilling, D. 2019. The other side of Chinese investment in Africa. *Financial Times*, March 27th.

[38] Lewis, L. and Aglionby, J. 2019. Japan renews African investment push as rivals surge ahead. *Financial Times.* August 28th.

[39] Tartar, A. and Sam, C. 2019. How the rise of developing countries has disrupted global trade. *Bloomberg New Economy*, May 7th.

[40] Davey, S. 2000. *Health. A Key to Prosperity*. World Health Organization: Geneva.

[41] Pilling, D. 2019 *op.cit*.

[42] Chen, S. and Ravallion, M. 2008. *The Developing World Is Poorer Than We Thought, But No Less Successful in the Fight against Poverty*. Policy Research Working Paper 4703. World Bank Development Group: Washington.

[43] Banerjee, A. and Duflo, E. 2020. How poverty ends. *Foreign Affairs*, January/February: 22.

[44] Hamel, K. and Khara, H. 2018. A global tipping point: half the world is now middle class or wealthier. Future Development. September 27. Brookings Institution; Hamel, K. Tong, B., and Hofer, M. 2019. Poverty in Africa is now falling – but not fast enough. *Future Development*. March 28th. Brookings Institution.

[45] Colmer, J. 2014. *Urbanization, Growth, and Development: Evidence from India*. Centre for Economic Performance, London School of Economics, London. Jayanthakumarn, K. *et alia* (eds.) 2019. *Internal Migration, Urbanization, and Poverty in Asia*. Springer-ADB: Singapore.

[46] UN-Habitat 2020 *Urban Indicators Database*.

[47] Carstens, A. and Shin, H.S. 2019. Emerging markets aren't out of the woods yet. *Foreign Affairs*. March 15th. Wheatley, J. 2019. Does investing in emerging markets still make sense? *Financial Times*, July 16th.

[48] United Nations, Department of Economic and Social Affairs. 2019. *World Economic Situation and Prospects No.122*. January 21st. New York.

[49] Bremmer, I. 2010. *The End of the Free Market*. Portfolio: New York.

[50] Radelet, S. 2016. *The Great Surge. The Ascent of the Developing World*. Simon and Schuster: New York.

[51] Kupchan, C. 2012. *No One's World*. OUP: New York.

[52] See, for example, North, D.C. 1995. NIE and Third World. development. In Harriss, T. *et alia* (eds) *The New Institutional Economics and Third World Development*. Routledge: New York, pp.17-26.

[53] Fosu, A. (ed) 2013. *Development Success*. OUP: Oxford.

[54] Fouquet, R. and Broadberry, S. 2015. Seven centuries of European economic growth and decline. *Journal of Economic Perspectives* 29: 227-244.

[55] *Ibid.*

[56] *Maddison Project Database, 2022*. Groningen Growth and Development Center. University of Groningen.

[57] Palat, R. 2010. World Turned Upside Down? Rise of the global South and the contemporary global financial turbulence. *Third World Quarterly* 31: 365-384.

[58] Dargin, J. 2013. *The Rise of the Global South*. World Scientific: Singapore.

[59] King, S. 2014. *Losing Control: the emerging threats to Western prosperity*. Yale University Press: London.

Chapters 3.

[60] Chu, Y.H. and Zheng, Y.N. (eds). 2021. *The Decline of the Western-Centric World and the Emerging New Global Order*. Routledge: Abingdon.

[61] Rowland, B. (ed) 2016. *Is the West in Decline?* Lexington Books: Lanham.

[62] Turner, F. 1992. *Beyond Geography: the western spirit against the wilderness*. Rutgers: New Brunswick.

[63] Stanley, T. 2021. *Whatever Happened To Tradition?* Bloombury: London.

[64] Scruton, R. 2002. *The West and the Rest: globalization and the terrorist threat*. ISI: Wilmington.

[65] Ferguson, N 2011 *Civilization: the West and the Rest*. Penguin: New York.

[66] Ryan, B. 2019. *How the West Was Lost. The decline of a myth and the search for new stories*. Hurst & Company: London.

[67] Berman, M. 2012. *Why America Failed.* John Wiley and Sons: New Jersey.

[68] See, especially, Mann, M. 2012. *Sources of Social Power*. Cambridge University Press: Cambridge. Dahl, R. 1961. *Who Governs?* Yale University Press: New Haven. Truman, D. 1951. *The Governmental Process*. Knopf: New York. Braybrooke, D. and Lindblom, C. 1963. *A Strategy of Decision*. The Free Press: New York.

[69] Samuelson, R. 1997. *The Good Life and Its Discontents: the American Dream in the Age of Entitlement*. Vintage Books: New York. Lasch, C. 1979. *The Culture of Narcissism*. W.W. Norton and Company: New York.

[70] Kennedy, P. 1987. *The Rise and Fall of Great Powers*. Rowland, B., *op. cit.*

[71] Morris, I. 2019. *Why the West Rules – For Now*. Farrar, Strauss, and Giroux: New York.

[72] Friedman, T.L. and Mandelbaum, M. 2011. *That Used to be Us.* Picador: New York. Orhangazi, O. 2008. Financialization and capital accumulation in the non-financial corporate sector. *Cambridge Journal of Economics* 32: 863-886.

[73] Joffe, J. 2013. *The Myth of America's Decline.* W.W. Norton: New York.

[74] Homer-Dixon, T. 2006. *The Upside of Down: catastrophe, creativity and the renewal of civilization.* Vintage: New York. See also: Kenny, C. 2013. *The Upside of Down: why the rise of the rest is good for the west.* Basic Books: New York. Krugman, P. 1994. Does Third World growth hurt first-world prosperity? *Harvard Business Review*, July: 1-16.

[75] Herman, A. 1997. *The Idea of Decline in Western History.* The Free Press: New York.

[76] Diamond, J. 2005. *Collapse: how societies choose to fail or succeed.* Viking: New York.

[77] Gamble, A. 1994. *Britain's Decline*. (Fourth Edition). St Martin's Press: New York.

[78] Tawney, *op.cit.*

[79] Vico, G. 1948. The New Science. Cornell University Press: New York. (Trans. Bergin, T. and Fisch, M.)

[80] Spengler, *op.cit.*

[81] Sorokin, *op.cit.*

Chapters 4-20.

[82] *Guanzi 2001 op.cit.* p.54.

[83] See Kalecki, 1937. A Theory of the business cycle. *Review of Economic Studies* 4: 77-97.

[84] Independent Commission on International Development Issues. 1980. *A Programme for Surival*. The Hague, p.5.

[85] See, for example, Ehrlich, P. 1968. *The Population Bomb*. Ballantine: New York; Peterson, E. 2017. The role of population in economic growth. *Sage Open* October-December: 1-15.

[86] Malthus, T. 1798. *An Essay on the Principle of Population*. Printed for J. Johnson, in St. Paul's Church-Yard: London.

[87] Maltus, *op.cit.*, p.4.

[88] Malthus, *op.cit.*, p.21.

[89] Becker, G. *et alia.* 1999. Population and economic growth. *American Economic Review* 89: 145-149.

[90] Orbeta, A. 2005. *Poverty, Vulnerability and Family Size: evidence from the Philippines.* ADB Institute Research Paper Series No. 68. Tokyo.

[91] Randers, J. 2012. *The State of Sustainability Leadership.* Programme for Sustainability Leadership. University of Cambridge, p.4.

[92] Christiansen, D. 1977. *Ethics and Compulsory Population Control.* The Hastings Center Report 7: 30-33.

[93] *Ibid.*

[94] Cited in: Gulhati, K. 1977. Compulsory Sterilization: The Change in India's Population Policy. *Science* 195: 1300-1305K.

[95]John, A. 1987. Have three, or more if you can afford it. *Straits Times*. March 2, p.1.

[96] See Peterson, *op.cit.* p.12.

[97] Meadows, D. *et alia* 1972. *Limits to Growth.* Universe Books: New York.

[98] Randers, J. 2012. *2052: A global forecast for the next forty years.* Chelsea Green Publishing: Vermont.

[99] Potter, R. and Lloyd-Evans, S. 1998. *The City in the Developing World.* Longman: London, p.13.

[100] Goode, R. 1955. Accelerated depreciation allowances as a stimulus to investment. *The Quarterly Journal of Economics* 69: 191-220.

[101] Brazell, D., Dworin, L. and Walsh, M. 1989. *A History of Federal Tax Depreciation Policy.* OTA Paper 64. Depreciation Analysis Staff, Office of Tax Analysis.

Eisner, E. 1952. Depreciation allowances, replacement requirements and growth. *American Economic Review*, 42: 820-831.

[102] Alchian, A. and Demsetz, H. 1972. Production, information costs, and economic organization. *American Economic Review* 62: 777-795.

[103] Knight, 1921. *Risk, Uncertainty, and Profit.* Houghton Mifflin: Boston.

[104] World Trade Organization 2006. *World Trade Report.* Geneva.

[105] Kalouptsidi, M. 2014. *Detection and Impact of Industrial Subsidies.* National Bureau of Economic Research Working Paper Series 20110: Cambridge, Mass.

[106] Trade Committee, Trade and Agriculture Directorate 2019. *Measuring Distortions in International Markets.* Organization of Economic Co-operation and Development: Paris. McBride, J. and Chatzky, A. 2019. *Is Made in China, 2025 a threat to Global Trade?* Council on Foreign Relations: New York.

[107] Pickard, S. and Makhijani, S. 2014. *Fossil Fuel Exploration Subsidies: China.* Oil Change International: Washington, D.C.

[108] Global Subsidies Initiative. 2014. *Indonesia Energy Subsidy Briefing.* International Institute for Sustainable Development: Winnipeg.

[109] Asian Development Bank. 2015. *Fossil Fuel Subsidies in Thailand.* Manila.

[110] Sovacol, B. 2017. Reviewing, reforming, and rethinking global energy subsidies. *Ecological Economics* 135: 150-163.

[111] International Monetary Fund (Fiscal Affairs Department) 2015. *How Large are Global Energy Subsidies?* (Country-level Subsidy Estimates). Coady, D. *et alia.* 2015. *How Large Are Global Energy Subsidies?* IMF Working Paper WP/15/105. Sovacol, B. *Ibid.*

[112] International Labour Organization (ILO) *World Social Protection Database 2020.*

[113] Midgley, J. and Hosaka, M. 2011. *Grassroots Social Security in Asia.* Routledge: New York.

[114] Dixon, J. 1987. *Social Welfare in Africa.* Croom Helm: London

[115] Sub, K. and Shi, S. 2013. Emergence of new welfare states in east Asia? *International Journal of Social Quality* 3: 106-124.

[116] Chinn, D. 1977. Distribution equality and economic growth: the case of Taiwan. *Economic Development and Cultural Change* 26: 65-79.

[117] Blake, S. 1991. *Shahjahanabad: the sovereign city in Mughal India, 1639-1739.* Cambridge University Press: Cambridge. Kim, T.J. 2003. *Political Economy and Population Growth in Early Modern Japan.* School for Public Policy and Management, Korean Development Institute: Sejong.

[118] Davidson, B. 1978. *A History of West Africa.* Longman: Harlow.

[119] Elvin, M. 1972. The high-level equilibrium trap: the causes of the decline of invention in the traditional Chinese textile industries. In Willmott, W. (ed) *Economic Organization in Chinese Society.* Taipei: SMC Publishing, 137–72, p. 141. Bin Wong, R. 2002. The search for European differences and domination in the early modern world: a view from Asia. *The American Historical Review* 107: 447-469.

[120] Elvin, *op.cit*; Hartwell, R. 1962. A revolution in the Chinese iron and coal industries during the Northern Sung, 960-1127. *Journal of Asian Studies* 21: 153-62. Hartwell, R. 1966. Markets, technology and the structure of enterprise in the development of the eleventh-century Chinese iron and steel industry. *Journal of Economic History* 26: 29-58.

[121] Toshio, F., 1991. The village and agriculture during the Edo period. In Hall, W. (ed) *The Cambridge History of Japan 4.* CUP: New York, pp. 478–518.

[122] Nobukio, N., & McClain, J., 1991. Commercial change and urban growth in early modern Japan. In Hall, W. (ed) *The Cambridge History of Japan 4.* CUP: New York, pp.519-595.

[123] Toshio, *op.cit.*. Saxonhouse, G. 1995. The stability of mega organizations: the Tokugawa state. *Journal of Institutional and Theoretical Economics* 151: 741–747. Fulcher, J. 1988. The bureaucratization of the state and the rise of Japan. *The British Journal of Sociology* 39: 228–254.

[124] Lo, H.L. 1963. *Hong Kong and its External Communications Before 1842.* Institute of Chinese Culture: Hong Kong. Siu, K.K. 1984. The Hong Kong region before and after coastal evacuation in the early Ch'ing dynasty. In D. Faure *et alia* (eds) *From Village to City: studies in the traditional roots of Hong Kong society.* Center for Asian Studies, University of Hong Kong: Hong Kong, pp.1-9. Baker, H. 1966. The five great clans of the New Territories. *Journal of the Hong Kong Branch of the Royal Asiatic Society* 6: 25-47. Wheatley, P. 1964. The land of Zanj: exegetical notes on Chinese knowledge of East Africa prior

to A.D. 1500. In R. Steel and R. Prothero (eds) *Geographers and the Tropics: Liverpool essays*. Longman: London, pp.39-87.

[125] Wood, A. 1940. *A Brief History of Hong Kong.* South China Morning Post: Hong Kong.

[126]Bristow, R. 1987. *Land-use Planning in Hong Kong.* OUP: Hong Kong.

[127] Smith, C. 1984. Shanshuipo: from proprietary village to industrial-urban complex. In D. Faure *et alia* (eds) *op.cit.* pp.73-105. Leeming, F. 1977. *Street Studies in Hong Kong*. OUP: Hong Kong.

[128] Orme, G. 1912. *Report on the New Territories, 1899-1912.* Government Sessional Papers. Hong Kong. Lai, D.C.Y. 1963. *Some Geographical Aspects of the Industrial Development of Hong Kong Since 1841*. MA Thesis (unpublished). The Chinese University of Hong Kong: Hong Kong.

[129] Ofek, H. 2001. *Second Nature: economic origins of human evolution.* Cambridge University Press: Cambridge. Gamble, C. 1999. *The Paleolithic Societies of Europe*. Cambridge University Press: Cambridge. Isaac, G. 1983. Aspects of human evolution. In D. S. Bendall (ed) *Essays on Evolution: a Darwin century volume*. Cambridge University Press: Cambridge. Horan, R., Bulte, E., and Shogren, J. 2008. Coevolution of human speech and trade. *Journal of Economic Growth* 13: 293–313.

[130] Stiner, M., Munro, N., Surovell, T., Tchernov, E., and Bar-Yosef, O. 1999. Paleolithic population growth pulses are evidenced by small animal exploitation. *Science* 283: 190–194.

[131] Zheng, H. X., Yan, S., Qin, Z. D., & Jin, L. 2012. MtDNA analysis of global populations supports that major population expansions began before Neolithic time. *Scientific Reports* 2 745, https://doi.org/10.1038/srep00745. Aimé, C., Laval, G., Patin, E., Verdu, P., Ségurel, L., Chaix, R., *et al.* 2013. Human genetic data reveal contrasting demographic patterns between sedentary and nomadic populations that predate the emergence of farming. *Molecular Biology and Evolution* 30: 2629–2644. Advance Access, September 24, 2013.

[132] Cohen, D. 2011. The beginnings of agriculture in China: A multiregional view. *Current Anthropology* 52: s273–s293p. s288.

[133] Belfer-Cohen, A., & Goring-Morris, A. 2011. Becoming farmers: the inside story. *Current Anthropology* 52: s209–s220.

[134] Hammer, M., Karafet, T., Park, H., Omoto, K., Harihara, S., Stoneking, M., *et al.* 2006. Dual origins of the Japanese: common ground for hunter-gatherer and farmer Y chromosomes. *Journal of Human Genetics* 51: 47–58.

[135] Rose, J. 2004. New evidence for the expansion of Upper Pleistocene population out of East Africa, from the site of Station One, Northern Sudan. *Cambridge Archaeological Journal* 14: 205–216, p.212.

[136] Siebert, S., Haser, J., Nagieb, M., Korn, L., and Buerkert, A. 2005. Agricultural, architectural and archaeological adaptation of a scattered mountain oasis in Oman. *Journal of Arid Environment* 62: 177–197.

[137] Bovil, E. 1922. Jega market. *Journal of the Royal African Society* 22: 50–60.

[138] Fogg, W. 1940. Villages, tribal markets and towns: some considerations concerning urban development in the Spanish and international zones of Morocco. *Sociological Review* 32: 85–107, p.2.

[139] Shiba, Y. 1970. *Commerce and Society in Sung China* (Trans. Elvin, M.) Center for Chinese Studies, Michigan Abstracts of Chinese and Japanese Works on Chinese History, No. 2, Ann Arbor.

Hayashi, K. 1980. *Xu and Shi in Guangdong Province During the Ming and Qing Periods*. International Geographical Union Working Group on Market-Place Exchange Systems, Nagoya, August 27-9. Spencer, J. 1940. The Szechwan village fair. *Economic Geography* 16: 48–58.

[140] Gissing, C. 1884. A journey from Mombasa to Mounts Ndara and Kasigao. *Proceedings of the Royal Geographical Society and Monthly Record of Geography* 6: 551-566, p.551.

[141] Christie, J. 1876. *Cholera Epidemics in East Africa*. Macmillan: London, p.124.

[142] *Ibid.*

[143] Fearon, D. 1966. Notes on the history of Berbera. *Somaliya* 2: 1-14.

[144] De Maret, P. 2002. Urban origins in Central Africa. In Sinclair, P. (ed) *The Development of Urbanism in Africa from a Global Perspective.* Uppsala University, pp.1-15.

[145] Simbao, R. 2006. A crown on the move. *African Arts* Autumn: 26-41. Macola, G. 2016. Luba-Lunda states. In MacKenzie, J. (ed) *The Encyclopaedia of Empire*. John Wiley and Sons: New Jersey.

[146] This was true of towns in general before colonial rule, says Onokerhoraye, A. 1976. The planning implication of the present structure of urban economics in traditional Nigerian cities. *Planning Outlook* 18: 19-34.

[147] Winters, C. 1977. Traditional Urbanism in North Central Sudan. *nnals of the Association of American Geographers* 67: 500-522. Edwards, D. 2007. The archaeology of Sudan and Nubia. *Annual Review of Anthropology* 36: 211-228.

[148] Poncet, M. 1709. *A Voyage to Aethiopia*. Lewis: London.

[149] *Ibid.*

[150] Hovarth, R. 1969. The wandering capitals of Ethiopia. *The Journal of African History* 10: 205-219.

[151] Blake, S. 1991. *Shahjahanabad: the sovereign city in Mughal India, 1639-1739.* Cambridge University Press: Cambridge.

[152] Blake, S. 1991. *Shahjahanabad: the sovereign city in Mughal India, 1639-1739.* Cambridge University Press: Cambridge.

[153] Sinopoli, C. 1994. Monumentality and mobility in Mughal capitals. *Asian Perspectives* 33: 293-308.

[154] Choudhary, M. 2017. 'Migrating banjaras and settling tandas.' *International Journal of History and Cultural Studies* 3: 26-35.

[155] Cattaneo, A. and Robinson, S. 2020. Multiple moves and return migration within developing countries. *Population, Place and Space* e2335: 1-21.

[156] Bell, M., Bernard, A., Charles-Edwards, E., and Zhu, Y. (eds) 2020. *Internal Migration in the Countries of Asia*. Springer: Switzerland. Irudaya Rajan, S. and Bhagat, R.B. 2021. Internal migration in India. *Policy Brief 12.* KNOMAD, World Bank; Munshi, K. and Rosenweig, M. 2018. Why is labor mobility in India so low? *VoxDev* July 16th.

[157] Kim, J. 2016. The current state of South Korea's democracy. *Journal of International and Area Studies* 23: 1-15.

[158] World Bank. 1997. *World Development Report, 1997: the state in a Changing World.* Oxford University Press: New York, p.23.

[159] See, for example, Crook, C. 1992. Third World Economic Development. In *The Concise Encyclopedia of Economics.* Library of Economics and Liberty.

[160] International Monetary Fund 2017. *Regional Economic Outlook: Sub-Saharan Africa*. Washington, D.C.. Toesland, F. 2019 Africa's megacities a magnet for investors. *Africa Renewal* April 9, 1-6.

[161] Lewis, W.A. 1955. *The Theory of Economic Growth.* George Allen and Unwin: London. (See page 172).

[162] Balogh, T. 1966. *The Economics of Poverty*. Weidenfeld and Nicolson: London. Bardhan, P. 2002. Decentralisation of governance and development. *Journal of Economic Perspectives* 16: 185–205. Bauer, P. and Yamey, B. 1963. *The Economics of Underdeveloped Countries.* Cambridge University Press: Cambridge. Olson, M. 1984. *The Rise and Decline of Nations*. Yale University: New Haven. Sobel, J. 2002. Can we trust social capital? *Journal of Economic Literature* 40: 139–154.

[163] Medina, L. and Schneider, F. 2019. Shedding light of the shadow economy. *CESifo Working Paper 7981*: Munich.

[164] African Economic Outlook 2012. *Mauritania 2012.* African Development Bank. Abidjan.

[165] Lall, S., Henderson, J. and Venables, A. 2017. *Africa's Cities: opening doors to the world.* World Bank: Washington D.C.

[166] Toesland, *op.cit.*

[167] Nwaka, G. 2005. The urban informal sector in Nigeria. *Global Urban Development* 1: 1-11.

[168] Bangasser, P. 2000. The ILO and the informal sector. *Employment Paper Number 9.*

[169] *Ibid.*

[170] Zeev Maoz, Johnson, P. *et al.* 2019. The Dyadic Militarized Interstate Disputes (MIDs) Dataset Version 3.0: Logic, Characteristics, and Comparisons to Alternative Datasets, *Journal of Conflict Resolution* 63: 811-835.

[171] Nakata, T. 1978. Corruption in the Thai bureaucracy: who gets what, how, and why in its public expenditures. *Thai Journal of Development Administration* 18: 102-128. Gray, C. 1979. Civil service compensation in Indonesia. *Bulletin of Indonesia Economic Studies*. 15: 85-113. Wade, R. 1982. The system of administrative and political corruption: canal irrigation in south India. *The Journal of Development Studies* 18: 287–328.

[172] Mauro, P. 1995. Corruption and growth. *Quarterly Journal of Economics* 110: 681-712.

[173] Haller, D., & Shore, C. 2005. *Corruption: Anthropological perspectives.* Pluto: London, p.5. Gupta, A. 1995. Blurred boundaries: The discourses of corruption, the culture of politics, and the imagined state. *American Ethnologist* 22: 375–402.

[174] Vivanathan, S., & Sethi, H. 1998. By way of a beginning. In S. Vivanathan & H. Sethi (eds.) *Foul Play: chronicles of corruption 1947–97.* New Delhi: Banyan Books. Yang, M. 1994. *Gifts, Favors and Banquets: the art of social relationships in China.* Ithaca: Cornell University Press.

Yang, M. 2000. Putting global capitalism in its place: Economic hybridism, bataille and ritual expenditure. *Current Anthropology* 41: 477–509. Yang, M. 2002. The resilience of guanxi and its new deployments: a critique of some new guanxi scholarship. *China Quarterly* 170: 459–476.

[175] See De Soto, H. 2000. *The Mystery of Capital: why capitalism triumphs in the West and fails everywhere else.* New York: Basic Books.

[176] Mansoor Marican, Y. 1979. Combating corruption: the Malaysian experience. *Asian Survey* 19: 597-610.

[177] de Zuniga, J., Assistant Governor, *Bangko Sentral Ng Pilipinas*, Manila, September 21, 2007.

[178] de Zuniga, J., Assistant Governor, *Bangko Sentral Ng Pilipinas*, Manila, September 21, 2007.

[179] Inciong, T., Assistant Secretary, Department of Education, Manila, September 25, 2007.

[180] Urquilo, P., Chief of Staff, Senator Honasan, G., The Philippine Senate, Manila, December 12, 2007.

[181] Escudero, F. Senator, The Philippine Senate, Manila, December 19, 2007.

[182] Abad, J., Chief of Staff, Senator Aquino, B., The Philippine Senate, Manila, December 19, 2007.

[183] Joson, L.G., OIC (HRMD, Planning), Department of Education, Manila, September 10, 2007. Interview with the author.

[184] Source (Department of Education) requested anonymity.

[185] Anonymous written allegations circulated among colleagues.

[186] Source (Department of Education) requests anonymity.

[187] Constantino-David, Member, GSIS Board of Trustees, October 8, 2010.

[188] Source, Office of the Vice President, requests anonymity.

[189] Lacson, D., Chairman, Government Service Insurance System, Manila, October 8, 2010.

[190] Ibid.

[191] Source, Office of the Vice President, requests anonymity.

[192] Source, Philippine Senate, requests anonymity.

[193] Soliman, Secretary, DSWD, Manila, September 12, 2010.

[194] Henares, K., Commissioner, Bureau of Internal Revenue, Manila, August 4, 2010.

[195] Soliman, Secretary, DSWD, Manila, September 12, 2010.

[196] Velasco-Allones, M., Executive Director, Career Executive Service Board, Manila, September 2, 2010.

[197] Source, Presidential Management Staff, Malacanang, requests anonymity.

[198] Soliman, Secretary, DSWD, Manila, September 12, 2010.

[199] Sto. Tomas, P., former member of Search Committee, Arroyo administration, and former Secretary and Undersecretary, Department of Labor and Employment, Manila, September 2, 2010. Interview with the author.

[200] Bauer, P. 1991. *The Development Frontier*. London: Harvester Wheatsheaf.

[201] 不需要考虑亲情的问题

[202] Department of International Economic and Social Affairs. 1990. *World Economic Survey, 1990.* United Nations: New York

[203] See, for example, Lea, D. 2002. Are there advantages to maintaining customary land tenure in Papua New Guinea? *Pacific Economic Bulletin* 17: 42-54.

[204] Helpman, E. 2004. *The Mystery of Economic Growth*. Harvard University Press: Cambridge, Mass.

[205] Henley, G. 2013 *Property Rights and Rural Household Welfare*. ODI. Domingo, P. 2013 *Property Rights and Social, Political and Economic Empowerment.* ODI; Mattingly, M. 2013. *Property Rights and Urban Household Welfare*. ODI; Mason, N. and Newborne, P. 2013. *Water Rights and Rural Household Welfare*. ODI; Locke, A. 2013. *Property Rights and Economic Growth* ODI. Leblang, D.

1996. Property rights, democracy, and economic growth. *Political Research Quarterly* 49: 5-26.

[206] Rights and Resources Initiative 2015. *Who Owns the World's Land?* RRI: Washington D.C.

[207] Zarook, R. 2021 Map of the week. *Ubique: American Geographical Society* December 9.

[208] Kay, S. 2016. *Land Grabbing and Land Concentration in Europe*. Transnational Institute: Amsterdam.

[209] Answeeuw, W. and Baldinelli, G. 2020. *Uneven Ground.* International Land Coalition: Rome.

[210] Bayley, D. 1966. The effects of corruption in a developing nation. *Western Political Quarterly* XIX: 719–732.

[211] Evans, P. 1989. Predatory, developmental and other apparatuses: A comparative political economy perspective on the third world state. *Sociological Forum* 4: 233–246. Evans, P. 1995. *Embedded Autonomy: states and industrial transformation.* Princeton University Press: Princeton, NJ.

Weiss, L. 2000. Developmental states in transition: Adapting, dismantling, innovating, not normalizing. *Pacific Review* 13: 21–55.

Wade, R. 1990. *Governing the Market: Economic theory and the role of government in East Asian industrialization.* Princeton University Press: New Jersey. Haggard, S. 2000. *The Political Economy of the Asian Economic Crisis.* Institute of International Economics: Washington, D.C. Jomo, K. S. 2000. Comment: crisis and the developmental state in East Asia. In R. Robinson, M. Beeson, K. Jayasuriya, & H. Kim (eds) *Politics and Markets in the Wake of the Asian Crisis.* Routledge: London.

[212] Nye, J. S. 1967. Corruption and political development: a cost-benefit analysis. *American Political Science Review* LXI: 417–427.

[213] Kelsall, T. 2011. Rethinking the relationship between neo-patrimonialism and economic development in Africa. *IDS Bulletin*, 42: 76-87. Wai, Zubairu, 2012. Neo-patrimonialism and the discourse of state failure in Africa. *Review of African Political Economy* 39: 27-43.

[214] Colombia Accident Investigation Board 2003 *Report Volume I*, Washington DC.

[215] Ito, T. 2015. *The Plaza Agreement and Japan: Reflection on the 30th year Anniversary*. The Baker Institute for Public Policy. Rice University: Houston

[216] Akram, T. 2018. *The Japanese Economy: stagnation, recovery, and challenges*. Thrivent: Minneapolis. Obstfeld, M. 2009. *Time of Troubles: The Yen and Japan's Economy, 1985-2008*. Chicago-Columbia Business School: San Francisco.

[217] Belke, A. and Volz, U. 2020. The yen exchange rate and the hollowing out of the Japanese industry. *Open Economies Review* 31:371–406.

[218] Yoshino, N. and Taghizadeh-Hesary, F. 2015. *Japan's Lost Decade.* ADBI Working Paper 521. Asian Development Bank Institute: Tokyo. McKinsey Global Institute 2000. *Why the Japanese Economy is Not Growing.* Washington.

[219] Baba, N. and Hisada, T. 2002. Japan's financial system. *Monetary and Economic Studies*, April: 43-52. Fukao, M. 2003. *Japan's Lost Decade and its Financial System*. Blackwell: Oxford. Gotoh, F. 2020. *Japanese Resistance to American Financial Hegemony*. Routledge: Abingdon.

[220] Choi, W. *et alia* 2013. *Beyond Korean Style: shaping a new growth formula*. McKinsey Global Institute 2013. San Francisco.

[221] Leiteritz, R. 2015. Capital account policy in South Korea: the informal residues of the developmental state. *Colombia Internacional* 83: 235-265.

[222] Gullick, J. 1958. *Indigenous political systems of Western Malaya.* Monographs on Social Anthropology, No. 17. London School of Economics, Athlone Press: London.

[223] Ahmat, S. 1970. The political structure of the state of Kedah 1879-1905. *Journal of Southeast Asian Studies* 1: 115-128.

[224] *Ibid.*

[225] Andaya, B. and Andaya, L. 1991. *A History of Malaysia.* Macmillan: London.

[226] Allen, J. 1998. History, archaeology, and the question of foreign control in early historic-period Peninsular Malaysia. *International Journal of Historical Archaeology* 2: 261-289; Kheng, C. 1994. Feudalism in pre-colonial Malaya: the past as a colonial discourse. *Journal of Southeast Asian Studies* 25: 243-269.

[227] John, E. *et alia* 2008. Much ado over village heads. *New Sunday Times*. April 6.

[228] Esa, M. 2019. The status of village headmen in the community. *International Journal of Recent Scientific Research* 10: 35915-35917.

[229] Andersen, A. *et alia* 2016. Negotiating development narratives within large-scale oil palm projects on village lands in Sarawak, Malaysia. *The Geographical Journal:* 1-11.

[230] Yaakop, R. 2014. The British legacy and the development of politics in Malaysia. *Global Journal of Human-Social Science D* 14: 1-13.

[231] Wong, C.H. 2018. Constituency delimitation and electoral authoritarianism in Malaysia. *The Roundtable* 107: 67-80.

[232] Kamarrudin, N. and Rogers, R. 2020. Malaysia's democratic and political transformation. *Asian Affairs* 47: 1-23.

[233] Fausto, S. Modernization under democracy (1985-2010). In Fausto, B. (ed) 1999. *A Concise History of Brazil.* CUP: Cambridge.

[234] Afonso, J. 2004. The relations between different level of government in Brazil. *CEPAL Review* 84: 133-155.

[235] Schneider, B. 2015. The developmental state in Brazil. *Revista de Economia Política* 35: 114-132.

[236] Fausto, S. Modernization under democracy (1985-2010). In Fausto, B. (ed) *A Concise History of Brazil.* CUP: Cambridge, pp.324-416.

[237] Lisboa M. and Latif, Z. 2013. Democracy and growth in Brazil. *Instituto de Ensino e Pesquisa Working Paper 311/2013.* São Paulo

[238] Massi, E. and Singh, J. 2018. Industrial policy and state-making in Brazil. *Third World Quarterly* 39: 1133-1150.

[239] Badham-Jones, M. 2014. *Overview of Corruption and Anticorruption in Botswana.* Transparency International. David, A. 1995. Responsiveness in Botswana politics: do elections matter? *Journal of Modern African Studies* 33: 381-402.

[240] Phirinyane, M. (ed) 2013. *Elections and the Management of Diversity in Botswana.* Light Books: Gabarone.

[241] Pitcher, A. *et al.* 2009. Rethinking patrimonialism and neopatrimonialism in Africa, *African Studies Review* 52: 125-156.

[242] Ang Yuen Yuen and Nan Jia 2014. Perverse complementarity: political connections and the use of courts among private firms in China. *The Journal of Politics* 76: 318-332.

[243] Fukuyama, F. 2012. The patterns of history. *Journal of Democracy* 23: 14-26.

[244]Dittmer, L. 1995. Chinese informal politics. *China Journal* 34: 1–39, p.18.

[245] Dittmer, *op. cit.* p.17.

[246] Dittmer, *op. cit.* pp.30-31.

[247] Dittmer, *op. cit.* p.33.

[248] *Ibid.*

[249]Miquel, G. 2007. The control of politicians in divided societies: The politics of fear. *Review of Economic Studies* 74: 1259–1274.

[250] Flinders, M. 2009. The politics of patronage in the United Kingdom: shrinking reach and diluted permeation. *Governance* 22: 547–570, p. 550.

[251] Pearce, J., Branyiczki, I., and Bigley, G. 2000. Insufficient bureaucracy: Trust and commitment in particularistic organizations. *Organization Science* 11: 148–162. Gambetta, D. 1988. Mafia: the price of distrust. In D. Gambetta (ed.) *Trust.* Basil Blackwell: New York.

Putnam, R. 1995. Bowling alone: America's declining social capital. *Journal of Democracy* 6: 65–78. Putnam, R. 1993. Making Democracy Work. Princeton University Press. New Jersey.

[252]Aufrecht, S., & Bun, L. 1995. Reform with Chinese characteristics: the context of Chinese civil service reform. *Public Administration Review* 55: 175–182. Laguna, M. 2011. The challenges of implementing merit-based personnel policies in Latin America: Mexico's civil service reform experience. *Journal of Comparative Policy Analysis: Research and Practice* 13: 51–73. McCourt, *op. cit.* Nunberg, R. and Taliercio, R. 2012. Sabotaging civil service reform in aid-dependent countries: are donors to blame? *World Development* 40: 1970–1981.

[253] Benit-Gbaffou, C., & Piper, L. 2012. Party politics, the poor, and the city: reflections from the South African case. *Geoforum* 43: 173–177.

[254] Das, R. 2004. Social capital and poverty of the wage-labor class: problems with social capital theory. *Transactions, Institute of British Geographers* 29: 27–45.

[255]Reno, W. 2002. The politics of insurgency in collapsing states. *Development and Change* 33: 837–858.

[256] Fukuyama, F. 2011. *The Origins of Political Order*. Farrar, Straus and Ginoux: New York.

[257] Pak, J. and Park, P. Liberal democracy in South Korea. *Foreign Policy*. Brooking.

[258] Guha, S. 2014. Patronage and state-making in early modern empires in India and Britain. In Piliavsky, A. (ed) *The Idea of Patronage in South Asia.* Cambridge University Press: Cambridge.

[259] Iglitzin, L. 1970. Violence and American Democracy. *Social Issues* 26: 165-186.

[260] Muller, E. and Weede, E. 1990. Cross-national variation in political violence. *Journal of Conflict Resolution* 34: 624-651, p. 631.

[261] University of California, Davis. *Correlates of War Project.* (Various data sets)

[262] Helliwell, J. 1994. Empirical linkages between democracy and economic growth. *British Journal of Political Science* 24: 225-248

[263] Drury, C. *et al.* 2006. Corruption, democracy, and economic growth *International Political Science Review* 27: 121-136.

[264] Iverson, T. and Soskice., D. 2019. *Democracy and Prosperity*. Princeton: Oxford.

[265] Moore, B. 1966. *Social Origins of Dictatorship and Democracy: lord and peasant in the making of the modern world.* Penguin Books: London.

[266] Sheehan, J. 2006. The problem of sovereignty in European history. *American Historical Review* 11: 1–15, p.4.

[267] For more recent arguments in this vein, see Huntingdon 1968; and Doucouliagos, H. and Ulubasoglu, M. 2008. Democracy and economic growth: a meta-analysis. *American Journal of Political Science* 53: 61-83.

[268] Mandelbaum, M. 2007. *Democracy's Good Name*. Public Affairs: New York.

[269] Fukuyama, 2011. *op cit.*

[270] See, for instance, Solt, F. 2001. Institutional effects on democratic transitions: neo-patrimonial regimes in Africa, 1989-1994. *Studies in Comparative International Development* 36: 82-91. Rueschemeyer, D. Stephens, E., and Stephens, J. 1992. *Capitalist Development and Democracy.* University of Chicago Press: Chicago.

[271] Cheeseman, N. and Smith, J. 2019. The retreat of African democracy. *Foreign Affairs*. January 17th.

[272] Mounk, Y. 2019. The dictators' last stand. *Foreign Affairs* 98: 138-148. Malik, N. 2019. Feel smug about western democracy? *The Guardian*, June 30th.

Part II, Chapters 21-39.

[273] Brown, P. 1967. The later Roman empire. *The Economic History Review*: 20: 327–343, p.333.

[274] Boyd, W. 1947. *The History of Western Education.* Adam and Charles Black: London.

[275] Stevenson, J. 1989. The beginnings of literacy in Ireland. *Proceedings of the Royal Irish Academy C* 89: 127-165.

[276] Goody, J. 1994. *The Development of Literacy, Family, Culture and the State.* CUP: Cambridge.

[277] Wood, I. 2013. Entrusting Western Europe to the Church. *Transactions of the Royal Historical Society* 23: 37-73.

[278] O Carrigáin, T. 2015. Is there an archaeology of lay people at early Irish monasteries? *Bucema* 8: 1-18.

[279] Hoyt, R. 1967. *Life and Thought in the Early Middle Ages*. Lund: Minneapolis.

[280] Godden, R. Literacy in Anglo-Saxon England. In R. Gameson (ed.) *The Cambridge History of the Book in Britain.* CUP: Cambridge, pp.580-590.

[281] Wormald, C. 1977. The uses of literacy in Anglo-Saxon England and its neighbours. *Transactions of the Royal Historical Society* 27: 95-114.

[282] Turner, C. 1901. The permanent influence of Alfred the Great. *The Sewanee Review* 9: 472-482.

[283] Pratt, D. 2007. *The Political Thought of King Alfred the Great*. CUP: Cambridge.

[284] Pratt, D. 2001. The illnesses of King Alfred the Great, *Anglo Saxon England* 30: 39-90; Smyth, A. 2002. *The Medieval Life of King Alfred the Great.* Palgrave:Houndsmills.

[285] Gwynn, A. 1940. Irish monks and Clunaic reform. *Studies: an Irish quarterly review* 29: 409-430.

[286] Doucette, J. and Møller, J. 2020. The collapse of state power, the Clunaic reform movement, and the origins of urban self-government in medieval Europe. *International Organization* 1-20.

[287]Furniss, D. 1968. The monastic contribution to mediaeval medical care: aspects of an earlier welfare state. *Journal of the Royal College of General Practitioners* 15: 244–250.

[288] Brodman, J. 2009. *Charity and Religion in Medieval Europe.* Catholic University of America Press: Washington D.C.

[289] Russell, J. 1944. The clerical population of medieval England. *Traditio* 2: 177-212.

[290] Brodman, 2009 *op.cit.*

[291] Thorndike, L. 1940. Elementary and secondary education in the Middle Ages. *Speculum* 15: 400-408.

[292]Kunstler, B. 2006. The millennial university, then and now: from late medieval origins to radical transformation. *On the Horizon* 14: 62–69.

[293] Calixtus III held office for just three years before his death.

[294] Dyer, C. 1968. A redistribution of incomes in fifteenth-century England. *Past and Present* 39: 11-33.

[295] Dyer, C. 2012. Poverty and its relief in late medieval England. *Past and Present* 216: 41-78. Clark, E. 1994. Social welfare and mutual aid in the medieval countryside. *Journal of British Studies* 33: 381-406.

[296] Turner R. 1978. The Miles Literatus in twelfth and thirteenth century England. *The American Historical Review* 83: 928-945.

[297]Bebbington, D. 2011. Christian higher education in Europe: a historical analysis. *Christian Higher Education* 10: 10–24.

[298]Martin, B. 2012. Are universities and university research under threat? Towards an evolutionary model of university speciation. *Cambridge Journal of Economics* 36: 543–565. Brockliss, L. 1996. Curricula. In H. de Ridder-Symoens (ed.) *A History of the University in Europe.* Universities in early modern Europe (Vol. 2). CUP: Cambridge.

[299] Trevelynan, G. 1980. *English Social History*. Penguin: London.

[300] Kelly and Grada 2011. The poor law of old England. *Journal of Interdisciplinary History* XLI: 339-366.

[301] Lindert, P.H. 1998. Poor relief before the welfare state. *European Review of Economic History 2*: 101-140.

[302] Daunton, M. 2007. *Wealth and Welfare: an economic and social history of Britain, 1851-1951.*

---

303 Thomas, R. 1965. A quantitative approach to the study of the effects of British imperial policy upon colonial welfare: some preliminary findings. *The Journal of Economic History*, 25: 615-638.

304 Datta, K. 1959. India's trade with Europe and America in the eighteenth century. *Journal of Economic and Social History of the Orient* 2: 313-323.

305 Kanefsky, J. and Robey, J. 1980. Steam Engines in 18th-Century Britain: A Quantitative Assessment *Technology and Culture*, 21: 161-186. Mathias, P. 1975. Skills and the Diffusion of Innovations from Britain in the Eighteenth Century. *Transactions of the Royal Historical Society* 25: 93-113. Musson, A. and Robinson, E. 1959. The Early Growth of Steam Power. *Economic History Review* 11: 418-439. Kanefsky, J. 1979. *The Diffusion of Power in British Industry, 1760-1870*. Ph.D. Thesis. University of Exeter. Redlich, F. 1944. The leaders of the German steam-engine industry during the first hundred years. *Journal of Economic History* 4: 121-148. Robinson, E. 1974. The early diffusion of steam power. *Journal of Economic History* 34: 91-107. Nuvolari, A., Verspagen, B. and von Tunzelmann, N. 2011. The early diffusion of the steam engine in Britain, 1700–1800: a reappraisal. *Cliometrica* 5:291–321. Atack, J., Bateman, F., and Margo, R. 2006. *Steam Power, Establishment Size, and Labor Productivity Growth in Nineteenth-Century American Manufacturing*. Working Paper 11931, National Bureau of Economic Research. Cambridge, MA. Atack, J., Bateman, F., and Margo, R. 2003. *Capital Deepening in American Manufacturing, 1850-1880.* Working Paper 9923, National Bureau of Economic Research. Cambridge, MA. Pursell, C.W. 1969. *Early Stationary Steam Engines in America: a study in the migration of a technology*. Smithsonian Institution Press: Washington. Atack, J., Bateman, F., and Weiss, T. 1980. The regional diffusion and adoption of the steam engine in American manufacturing. *Journal of Economic History* 40: 281 – 308. Broadberry, S. Campbell, B., van Leeuwen, B. 2012. When did Britain industrialize? The sectoral distribution of the labor force and labor productivity in Britain, 1381–1851. *Explorations in Economic History*, doi: 10.1016/j.eeh.2012.08.004.

306 Trevelyan, *op.cit.*, p. 80.

307 Stone, L. 1977. *The Family, Sex, and Marriage in England, 1500-1800.* Weidenfeld and Nicolson: London.

[308] Hunt, L., and Jacob, M. 2001. The affective revolution in 1790s. *Eighteenth-Century Studies* 34: 491–521.

[309] Trevelyan, *op.cit.*

[310] Hunt and Jacob, *op.cit.*

[311] Walker. M. 1998. *German Home Towns. Community, State, and General Estate* 1648-1871. Cornell: Ithaca.

[312] Bochmann, A., Dresler, A., and Tietze, W The city of Chemnitz in Saxony (Germany) building its new economic profile *GeoJournal* 37: 539-556. Friedrichs, R. 1996. German cities in the late early modern era: some problems and prospects. *Urban History* 23: 72 – 85. Poling, K. 2014. Shantytowns and pioneers beyond the city wall: Berlin's urban frontier in the nineteenth century. *Central European History* 47: 245–274. Copeland, M. 1917. *The Cotton Manufacturing Industry of the United States.* Harvard University Press: Cambridge. Walker. M., *op.cit.*

[313] Gibb, G. 1946. The pre-industrial revolution in America. *Bulletin of the Business Historical Society* 20: 103-116.

[314] Mukhopadhyay, A. and Dutt, A. 1994. Population Density Gradient Changes of a Postindustrial City - Cleveland, Ohio (1860-1990) *GeoJournal* 34: 515-518. Kershner, F. 1949. From country town to industrial city: the urban pattern in Indianapolis. *Indiana Magazine of History* XLV: 327-228. Robinson, R. and Briggs, C. 1991. The rise of factories in nineteenth-century Indianapolis. *American Journal of Sociology* 97: 622-56. Department of the Interior, Census Office. 1883. *Report on the Manufactures of the United States at the Tenth Census, 1880.* Government Printing Office: Washington. Fishbein, M. 1973. *The Censuses of Manufactures 1810-1890*. Reference Information Paper No. 50. National Archives and Records Service, General Services Administration: Washington. Atack, J., Bateman, F., and Margo, R. 2008. Steam power, establishment size, and labor productivity growth in nineteenth-century American manufacturing. *Explorations in Economic History* 45: 185–198. Broadberry, S. Campbell, B., van Leeuwen, B. 2012. When did Britain industrialise? The sectoral distribution of the labour force and labour productivity in Britain, 1381–1851. *Explorations in Economic History*, doi: 10.1016/j.eeh.2012.08.004. Atack, J., Margo, R. and Rhode, P. 2015 *The Division of Labor and Economies of Scale in Late Nineteenth-Century American*

Manufacturing: new evidence. National Bureau of Economic Research: Cambridge, MA. Kim, S. 1999. *The Growth of Modern Business Enterprises in the Twentieth Century.* Washington University in St. Louis and National Bureau of Economic Research: Cambridge, MA. Hathaway, I. and Litan, R. 2014. *The Other Aging of America: the increasing dominance of older firms.* Economic Studies, July. The Brookings Institution. Washington, DC. Atack, J. 1986. Firm size and industrial structure in the United States during the nineteenth century. *Journal of Economic History* 46: 463-475. Atack, J., Bateman, F., and Margo, R. 2005. Capital deepening and the rise of the factory: the American experience during the nineteenth century. *Economic History Review* 58: 586-595. Brady, D. (ed) 1966. *Output, Employment, and Productivity in the United States after 1800.* National Bureau of Economic Research: Cambridge, MA.Prude, J. 1996. Capitalism, industrialization, and the factory in post-revolutionary America. *Journal of the Early Republic* 16: 237-255. Goheen, P. 1973. Industrialization and the growth of cities in nineteenth-century America. *American Studies* 14: 49-65. Gibb, G. 1946. The pre-industrial revolution in America: a field for local research *Bulletin of the Business Historical Society* 20: 103-116.Blumin, S. 2006. Driven to the city: urbanization and industrialization in the nineteenth century. *Organization of American Historians Magazine of History* May: 47-53.

[315] Knappen, M. 1939. *Tudor Puritanism: a chapter in the history of idealism.* University of Chicago Press: Chicago. Trinterud, L. 1951. The origins of Puritanism. *Church History* 20: 37–57. Hill, C. (ed.) 1988. *Collected Essays of Christopher Hill (Vol. 2). Religion and Politics in Seventeenth Century England.* Brighton: Harvester. Dickens, A. 1982. Heresy and the origins of English protestantism. In A. Dickens (ed.) *Reformation Studies.* The Hambledon Press: London.

[316]Seed, J. 2005. The spectre of puritanism: forgetting the seventeenth century in David Hume's history of England. *Social History* 30: 444–462, p.451- 452 *passim.*

[317] Hannay, A. and Marino, G. (eds) 1998. *The Cambridge Companion to Kierkegaarde.* Cambridge University Press: Cambridge.

[318] Clark, K. 1969. *Civilization.* BBC: London, p.235.

[319]Howes, F. 1974. *The Music of William Walton.* Oxford University Press: London.

[320] Orwell, G. 2013. *Complete Works of George Orwell.* Delphi Classics: Hastings

[321] Parrish, J. 1967. Rise of economics as an academic discipline: the formative years to 1900. *Southern Economic Journal* XXXIV: 1-16. Mason, E. 1982. The Harvard Department of Economics from the beginning to World War II. *The Quarterly Journal of Economics* XCVII: 383-433.

[322] Rashi, S. 1992. Adam Smith's rise to fame: a re-examination of the evidence. *The Eighteenth Century* 23: 64-85.

[323] Rothschild, E. 1992. Adam Smith and conservative economics. *The Economic History Review* 45: 74-96.

[324] Trachtenberg, A. 2007. *The Incorporation of America.* Hill and Wang: New York.

[325] Clout, H. 2004? *Alexander Maconochie: Britain's First Professor of Geography.* Department of Geography, UCL: London.

[326] Cited in Clout, H. *op. cit.* p.6.

[327] Mackinder, H. 1904. The geographical pivot of history. *The Geographical Journal 23: 421-443.*

[328] Gaddis, J. 1998. History, grand strategy, and NATO enlargement. *Survival* 40: 145–151. Eichler, J. 2021. *NATO's Expansion After the Cold War.* Springer: Cham.

[329] Barker, A. 1982. *Quangos in Britain.* Macmillan: London.

[330] Veggeland, N. 2020. *Democratic Governance in Scandinavia.* Springer: Cham.

[331] Braithwaite, T. 2007. The Regulatory State? In Goodin, R. (ed) *The Oxford Handbook of Political Science.* Oxford University Press: 217-238.

[332] *Ibid.*

[333] See, for instance, Malik, N. 2019. The myth of free speech. *The Guardian* September 3.

[334] Petersen, J. 2017. *The Big Picture: violence and free speech.* Public Books and NYU Institute for Public Knowledge.

[335] Hinsliff, G. 2019. Mob politics is the hateful new norm. *The Guardian* January 8.

[336] Goldstein, R. 1998. Political caricature and international complications in nineteenth-century Europe. *Michigan Academician* 30: 107-122.

[337] Barrell, J. 2004. Coffee house politicians. *Journal of British Studies* 43: 206-232. Fairlie, S. 2009. A short history of enclosure in Britain. *The Land* 7. White, J. 2013. *A Great and Monstrous Thing.* Harvard: Massachusetts.

[338] White, J. *op.cit.*

[339] Shorto, R. 2017. Three eighteenth-century revolutions and why they matter in 2017. *New York Times* May 18. Barrell 2004.

[340] *Charlie Hebdo*, 2020 January 7. Editorial by Riss: new faces of censorship.

[341] *Ibid.*

[342] House of Lords 2007. *Opinions. Judgments – R v. Rogers*. UKHL 8.

[343] *Twitter.* October 18 2015. @ajplus.

[344] Police Service of Northern Ireland, Equality and Diversity Unit 2013. *The Appropriate Language Guide.*

[345] Valogh, E. 2005. Crime-facilitating speech. *Stanford Law Review* 57: 1095-1222.

[346] Benesch, S. 2012. Words as weapons. *World Policy Journal* Spring: 7-12; Haiman, F. 2000. The remedy is more speech, *The American Prospect* December 5.

[347] Farrington, D. 1998. Predictors, causes and correlates of male youth violence. *Crime and Justice* 24: 421-475.

[348] *Ibid.*

[349] Collins, R. 2008. *Violence*. Princeton University Press: New Jersey.

[350] See: Modig, C. 2009. *Never Violence. Thirty Years on from Sweden's Abolition of Corporal Punishment.* Government Offices of Sweden and Save the Children.

[351] See, Shonkoff, J. *et alia*. 2012. The lifelong effects of early childhood adversity and toxic stress. *Pediatrics* 129, e232–e246. Tomoda, A. *et alia* 2009. Reduced prefrontal cortical gray matter volume in young adults exposed to harsh punishment. *NeuroImage*, 47(Suppl. 2), T66–T71.

[352] Larzelere, R. 2000. Weak evidence for a smacking ban. *BMJ* 320:1538. Trumbull, D. 2000. Spanking: a reasonable and necessary option. *BMJ*, 320:1538. Hain R. 2000. Occasional smacking does no harm. *BMJ* 320, 1538. Fry R. 2000. Parents must be in charge of their children. *BMJ* 320, 1538.

[353] Robertson, L. 2017 *Literature Review on Outcomes of Parental Discipline Styles, Evidence on Effective Parenting Styles and the International Experience of Prohibition of Physical Punishment in Law.* The Scottish Centre for Crime and Justice Research. Glasgow.

[354] Lehtinen, V. *et alia* 1990. Prevalence of mental disorders among adults in Finland: basic results from the mini Finland health survey. *Acta Psychiatr Scand* 81: 418-425. OECD/EU 2018. *Health at a Glance: Europe 2018.* State of Health in the EU Cycle, OECD Publishing, Paris/EU.

[355] Zechmeister-Koss, I. and Tüchler, H. 2014. Prevalence of mental disorders an uptake of mental health services in Tyrol. *LBI-HTA Projektbericht Nr:113b.* Wein: Ludwig Boltzmann Institut; Laszewska, A. *et alia.* 2018. Prevalence of mental diseases in Austria. *Wien Klin Wochenschr* 130: 141–150.

[356] Wagner, G. e alia. 2017. Mental health problems in Austrian adolescents: a nationwide, two-stage epidemiological study applying DSM-5 criteria. *European Child Adolescent Psychology* 26: 1483–1499.

[357] Dalsgaard, S. et al. 2020. Incidence rates and cumulative incidences of the full spectrum of diagnosed mental disorders in childhood and adolescence, *JAMA Psychiatry 77:155-164.* The prevalence of major depressive orders among those aged 20-34 in 2000 was around 3.5%. Olsen L. *et alia* 2004. Prevalence of major depressive and stress indicators in the Danish general population. *Acta Psychiatrica Scandinavica* 109: 96-103.

[358] Bijl, R. et al. 2003. The prevalence of treated and untreated mental disorders in five countries. *Health Affairs* 22: 122-133. Robert Kuch Institute 2005. *German Health Survey for Adolescents and Children.* Steffen, A. *et al.* 2020. Trends in prevalence of depression in Germany between 2009 and 2017 based on nationwide ambulatory claims data. *Journal of Affective Disorders* 271: 239-247. Menzies, R., Gluckman, P. and Poulton, R. 2020. *Youth Mental Health in Autearoa, New Zealand.* Centre for Informed Futures, University of Auckland. Sommer, M. 2018. *Mental Health Among Youth in Denmark.* Nordic Centre for Welfare and Social Issues. Andersen, I. et al. 2011. Increasing prevalence of depression from 2000-2006. *Scandinavian Journal of Public Health* 39: 857-863. Grobe, T., Steinmann,n S. and Szecsenyi, J. 2018. *Arztreport 2018.* Barmer: Berlin. Mental Health Foundation 2016. *Fundamental Facts About*

Mental Health. MHF: London. Mental Health Commission 2011. *Child and Youth Mental Health and Addiction*. Wellington.

[359] See, for instance, Bjereld, Y. *et al.* 2020. Measuring the prevalence of peer bullying victimization: a review of studies from Sweden during 1997-2017. *Children and Youth Services Review 119*. Annerbäck, E. *et alia* 2014. A cross-sectional study of victimization and bullying amongst schoolchildren in Sweden: background facts and self-reported health complaints. *Scandinavian Journal of Public Health* 42: 270-277. Wolke D. *et alia*. 2001. Bullying and victimization of primary school children in England and Germany: prevalence and school factors. *British Journal of Psychology* 92: 673-696. Fischer, S. *et al.* 2020. Traditional bullying and cyberbullying among children and adolescents in Germany: cross-sectional results of the 2017/18 HSBC study and trends. *Journal of Health Monitoring* 5: 53-68.

[360] The Sentencing Project. 2014. *Americans with Criminal Records*. Washington, DC. Umez, C. 2018. *Barriers to Work*. National Conference of State Legislatures: Washington, DC.

[361] Dowbiggin, I. 2000. Delusional diagnosis? The history of paranoia as a disease concept in the modern era. *History of Psychiatry* XI: 37-69.

[362] Ruscio, A. *et al.* 2017 Cross-sectional comparison of the epidemiology of DSM-5 Generalized Anxiety Disorder across the globe. *JAMA Psychiatry* March 15. Newman, T. 2018. Anxiety in the west: is it on the rise? *Medical News Today*. September 5th.

[363] Slee, A. *et alia* 2021. Trends in generalized anxiety disorder and symptoms in primary care. *The British Journal of Psychiatry* 218: 158-164.

[364] Sica, C. *et alia*. 2002. Religiousness and obsessive-compulsive cognition and symptoms in an Italian population. *Behaviour Research and Therapy* 40: 813-823. Lewis, C. and Lowenthal, K. 2018. Religion and obsessionality: obsessive actions and religious practices. *Mental Health, Religion and Culture* 21: 117-122.

[365] Schama, S. 2019. Who Speaks for the People? *Financial Times*, October 4.

[366] Milton, J. 1644. *Areopagitica. A Speech of Mr. John Milton for the Libertuy of Unlicenc'd Printing to the Parliament of England.*

[367] See, for instance, Hartland-Swann, J. 1952. On the state of modern philosophy. *Philosophy* 27: 76-769. Burge, T. 1992. Philosophy of Language and Mind, 1950-1990. *The Philosophical Review* 101: 2-51.

[368] 2003, the Fed's Thermostat, *WSJ*, August 19.

[369] *Cf.* McCloud, N. and Kumbhakar, S. 2008. Does subsidy drive productivity? A cross-country analysis of Nordic dairy farms. *Bayesian Econometrics* 23: 245-74.

[370] Felipe, J. (ed) 2015. *Development and Modern Industrial Policy in Practice.* Edward Elgar: Cheltenham.

[371] Gebhardt, G. 2012. Financial instruments in non-financial firms: what do we know? *Accounting and Business Research* 42: 267-289.

[372] These I limit to money-market fund shares, security repurchase agreements, debt securities, loans [mortgages and consumer credit], corporate equities, and mutual fund shares.

[373] United Nations Environment Programme. 2016. *Government Subsidies to the Global Financial System.* Inquiry Working Paper 16/11. Nairobi.

[374] Desilver, D. 2018. For most US workers, real wages have barely budged in decades. *Pew Research Center.* August 7.

[375] Gosling, A., Machin, S. and Meghir, C. 1994. What has happened to men's wages since the mid-1960s?' *Fiscal Studies* 15: 63-87.

[376] Cribb, J. and Johnson, P. 2018. *Ten years on: have we recovered from the financial crisis?* Institute for Fiscal Studies: London; Machin, S. 2015 *Real Wage Trends.* Bank of England: London.

[377] Treasury, The Australian Government 2017. *Analysis of Wage Growth.* Canberra.

[378] Corlett, A. 2019. *The Shifting Shape of UK Tax.* The Resolution Foundation. London.

[379] See: Transparency International. 2011. *Cabs for Hire: fixing the revolving door between government and business.* London.

[380] Competition and Markets Authority. 2022. *Annual Report and Accounts 2021 to 2022.* House of Commons: London.

[381] Syal, R. 2021. Boris Johnson accused of orchestrating Greensill 'cover-up.' *The Guardian*, July 22nd.

[382] Ure, A. 1835. *Philosophy of Manufactures*. Charles Knight: London. Cited in Taylor, A. 1960. Progress and poverty in Britain, 1780-1850. *History*, 45:1-31.

[383] Worstall, T. 2015. There is no Victorian-style poverty in the UK, none at all. *Forbes*, April 10.

[384] Booth, C. 1895. *Life and Labour of the People in London.* Macmillan and Co. London and New York.

[385] Floud, R. et al 2011. *The Changing Body : health nutrition and human development in the Western world since 1700.* CUP: Cambridge. Lindert, P. and Williamson, J. 1983. English workers living standards during the industrial revolution: a new look. *The Economic History Review 36: 1-25.* King, S. and Tomkins, A. (eds). 2003. *The Poor in England, 1700-1850.* Manchester University Press: Manchester. Sokoll, T. 1993. *Household and Family Among the Poor*. Verlaag fur Regionalgeschichte: Bochum.

[386] Alston, P. 2018. Statement on Visit to the United Kingdom, by Professor Philip Alston, United Nations Special Rapporteur on extreme poverty and human rights. *Office of The High Commissioner, United Nations Human Rights.*

[387] Irvine, S. *et alia* 2022. *Food Banks in the UK.* House of Commons Library: London.

[388] Edin, K. and Shaefer, L. 2015. *$2 a Day. Living on Almost Nothing in America.* Houghton Mifflin Harcourt: Boston. Allen, R. 2017. Absolute poverty: when necessity displaces desire. *American Economic Review* 107: 3690-3721.

[389] Donovan, S. and Bradley, D. 2018. *Real Wages Trends, 1979-2017* Congressional Research Service 7-5700. Washington, D.C.

[390] Piketty, T. 2014. *Capital in the Twenty-First Century.*Harvard University Press: Cambridge, Mass. (Translated by Goldhammer, A.)

[391] Smith, G. *et alia* 2002. Health inequalities in Britain. *Journal of Epidemiological Community Health* 56: 434-435. Pamuki, E. 1985. Social class and inequality in mortality from 1921 to 1972 in England and Wales. *Population Studies* 39: 17-31. Jackson, R. 1994. Inequality of incomes and lifespans in England since 1688. *The Economic History Review* 47: 508-524.

[392] Marmot, M. *et alia*. 2020. *Health Equity in England: the Marmot Review 10 years on.* The Health Foundation: London.

[393] Powell, M. 2019. Inquiries in the British National Health Service *The Political Quarterly*, 90: 180-184; Cowie, G. 2021 *Non-Statutory public inquiries*. Commons Library Research Briefing. London; Cowie, G. 2021 *Statutory public inquiries: the Inquiries Act 2005*. Commons Library Research Briefing. London; Elliott, R. A. *et alia*. 2020. Economic analysis of the prevalence and clinical and economic burden of medication error in England *BMJ Qual Saf* 0:1–10; Elliott, R. A. et al. 2018. *Prevalence and economic burden of medication errors in the NHS in England*. Policy Research Unit in Economic Evaluation of Health & Care Interventions. Manchester; Norris, E. and Shepheard, M. 2017. *How Public Inquiries Can Lead To Change*. Institute for Government: London; Kewell, B. and Beck, M. 2010. NHS Inquiries: a time series analysis. *Public Money and Management* 28: 375-382. Goodwin, D. 2019. NHS inquiries and the problem of culture. *The Political Quarterly* 90: 202-209. Carrier, J. and Kendall, I. 2016. *Health and the NHS*. Routledge: Abingdon, New York.

[394] NHS Confederation 2013. *Challenging Bureaucracy*. London.

[395] MacLean, R. 2014. *The Vale of Leven Hospital Inquiry Report*. APS Group: Edinburgh.

[396] Goodwin, *op.cit.* See also: Klein, R. 1978. Normansfield: vacuum of management in the NHS. *BMJ* 2: 1802-1804. *BMJ* 1978. The Normansfield Inquiry 2: 1560-63. Wardhaugh, J. and Wilding, P. 1993. Towards an explanation of the corruption of care. *Critical Social Policy* 37: 4-31.

[397] Francis, R. 2013. *Report of the Mid Staffordshire NHS Foundation Trust Public Inquiry*. The Stationary Office: London.

[398] Dudley and Walsall Mental Health Partnership Trust NHS. (2013). *Winterbourne, Francis, Cavendish, Keogh and Berwick reports—Overview report*. London.

[399] Plymouth University. 2015a. Programme *specification, BSc (Hons) Nursing, Year 1*. Plymouth University: Plymouth.

[400] *Ibid.*

[401] NHS England and NHS Improvement 2020, July 20. *Letter from Amanda Pritchard to Ted Baker, Chief Inspector of Hospitals, Care Quality Commission.*

[402] Berwick, M. 2018. *Dudley Group Foundation Trust Group Emergency Department Mortality Review Summary.*

[403] NHS Digital 2019. *Hospital Accident and Emergency Activity - 2018-19.* London

[404] Lipson, B. 2020. *New Zealand's Education Delusion.* New Zealand Initiative, Wellington.

[405] Dyke, W.H. 1906. *Report of the Consultative Committee Upon Questions Affecting Higher Elementary Schools*. HM Stationary Office: London. p.7.

[406] *Ibid.*

[407] Partridge, R. 2020. New Zealand's great education decline and the future of work. *New Zealand Herald* October 13.

[408] Bolton, P. 2012. *Education: Historical Statistics.* House of Commons Library: London.

[409] Holt, *op.cit.*

[410] *Ibid.*

[411] Busteed, B. 2020. Wake up higher education. The degree is on the decline. *Forbes.* September 25.

[412] Plymouth University. 2015b. *Programme specification, BSc (Hons) Geography.* Plymouth University: Plymouth.

[413] Hopson, C. and Montgomery, N. 2015. *The Foundations of Good Governance: a compendium of best practice.* (Third Edition). DAC Beachcroft and NHS Providers. London.

[414] Her Majesty's Chief Inspector of Constabulary 2019. *State of Policing*. London; Her Majesty's Chief Inspector of Constabulary 2018. *Policing and Mental Health.* London.

[415] See: European Commission Justice and Consumers 2019. *The 2019 EU Justice Scoreboard.* Luxembourg.

[416] Fair Trials 2021. *Disparities and Discrimination in the Europan Union's Criminal Legal System.* Brussels.

[417] King, A. 2008 *The British Constitution.* Oxford; Ringen, S. 2021. Britain is not a well-governed country. March 5. *The Constitution Society.* London; National Audit Office. 2021. *Overview of the UK Government's Response to the COVID-19 Pandemic.* HC 366 Session 2019–2021 21 May.

[418] Seoul Metropolitan Government. Seoul's Fight Against Covid-19. Briefing note on practices and measures in tackling COVID -19. Updated: April 7, 2020.

[419] https:// www.theguardian.com / world / video / 2020/mar/27/i-shook-hands-with-everybody-says-boris-johnson-weeks-before-coronavirus-diagnosis-video

[420] https://www.ft.com/content/920c8356-5d34-11ea-8033-fa40a0d65a98

[421] See the CMO's comments to the Commons Health Committee, reported in the Guardian, March 5, 2020 (https://www.theguardian.com/world/2020/mar/05/corona-virus-minister-hints-u-turn-decision-stop-daily-uk-updates).

[422]https://www.fairobserver.com / region / europe / uk-government-coronavirus-19-respose-measures-public-health-news-77112/amp/

[423] https://coronavirus.data.gov.uk/

[424] https://www.hse.gov.uk/coronavirus/social-distancing/index.htm

[425] See, for instance, http://metro.co.uk/2020/03/01/boris-johnson-meets-scientists-fighting-coronavirus-lab-north-london-12330729/

[426] Jeremy Hunt on the BBC's Today Programme, Radio 4, February 28, 2020

[427] https://www.nytimes.com/2020/03/05/world/europe/coronavirus-united-kingdom-national-health-service.html

[428] See: Report of the WHO-China Joint Mission on Coronavirus Disease 2019 (COVID-19); widely publicized, e.g. Japan Times, March 6, 2020 (https://www.japantimes.co.jp/news/2020/03/06/world/not-drill-urges-world-fight-coronavirus/#.XmSE8C47pfU.mailto

[429] http://www.theguardian.com/world/2020/feb/27/they-have-no-idea-government-failing-on-coronavirus-say-gps

[430] https://youtu.be/o9jJz00szgU

[431] https://www.theguardian.com/commentisfree/2020/mar/17/coronavirus-force-nhs -terrible-choices-covid19?

[432] https://www.theguardian.com/society/2020/mar/18/uk-failures-over-covid-19-will -increase-death-toll-says-leading-doctor?

[433] https://www.theguardian.com/society/2020/mar/04/prof-chris-whitty-the-expert-we-need-in-the-coronavirus-crisis?

[434] *Sky News*, March 16.

[435] https://www.bbc.com/news/science-environment-51892402.

[436] Kramer, S. *et alia*. 2019 *Religion and Living Arrangements Around the World.* Pew Research Center: Washington, D.C.

[437] National Audit Office 2021 *Initial Learning from the Government's Response to the COVID-19 Pandemic*. Session 2021-22 19 May, HC 66. London.

[438] Wellhofer, E.S. 1996. *Democracy, Capitalism and Empire in Late Victorian Britain.* Macmillan: Basingstoke.

[439] *Hansard C.* Deb 20 March 1911 Vol 23 column 70.

[440] *Hansard C.* Deb 31 August 1914 Vol 66 column 468.

[441] *Hansard, C.* Deb 23 June 1915 Vol 72 cc1256-1257.

[442] *Hansard C.* Deb 13 February 1918 Vol 103 cc148-233.

[443] *Hansard C.* Deb 8 August 1918 Vol 109 cc1578-636.

[444] *Hansard C.* 24 August 1939 Vol 351 cc2-63.

[445] *Hansard C.* 6 September 1990 Vol 177 cc735-736.

[446] Lebow, R.N. 2011. Aggressive democracies. *St Antony's International Review* 6: 120-133.

[447] See, for instance, Hobson, C. 2017. Democratic peace: progress and crisis. *Perspective on Politics* 15: 697-710.

[448] Campbell, K. and Sullivan, J. 2019. Competition without catastrophe. *Foreign Affairs* 98: 96-110.

[449] See, for instance, Issacharoff, S. 2018. Democracy's deficits. *The University of Chicago Law Review* 85: 485-519. Saunders, R. 2019 The rise and fall of British democracy. *New Statesman*. September 27th.

[450] Berman, S. 2019. *Democracy and Dictatorship in Europe*. OUP: New York. Wolf, T. 2018. Saving liberal democracy from the extremes. *Financial Times*, September 25th. Mounk, Y. 2018. *The People vs. Democracy.* Harvard University Press: Cambridge. Münchau, W. 2018. Italy illustrates the way to liberal democracy's demise. *Financial Times* May 20th. Stiglitz, J., Tucker, T. and Zucman, G. 2020. The starving state. *Foreign Affairs*. January/February.

[451] Calhoun, C. 1988. Populist politics, communications media, and large-scale societal integration. *Sociological Theory* 6: 219-241.

[452] Weisberg, J. 2019. Can democracy survive if the media fail? *Foreign Affairs* September/October 204-209.

[453] Runciman, D. 2018. *How Democracy Ends.* Profile: London

[454] Widfeldt, A. 2015. *Extreme Right-Wing Parties in Scandinavia.* Routledge: London. Selle, P. and Østerud, Ø. 2006. The eroding of representative democracy in Norway. *Journal of European Public Policy* 13: 551-568.

[455] Ispahani, L. and Knight, S. 2017. Shoring up a democracy under siege. *Journal of International Affairs* 71: 51-69. *Journal of International Affairs.* 2018. Interview with Sheri Berman. Democracy in Europe is being reconsidered from top to bottom. Berman, S. *op. cit.*

[456]Zitelmann, R. 2019. State capitalism? *Forbes*. November 1st.

[457] Fukuyama, F. 1992. *The End of History.* Free Press: New York.

[458] Fahnbulleh, M. 2020. The Neoliberal Collapse: markets are not the answer.' *Foreign Affairs.* January/February 38-43.

[459] Rose, J. 2001. *The Intellectual Life of the British Working Classes*. Yale: New Haven.

[460] Sorokin, *op.cit.*

[461] See Rostow, W.W. 1990. *Theorists of Economic Growth from David Hume to the Present. With a Perspective on the Next Century.* OUP: New York.

[462] Gordon, R. 2016. *The Rise and Fall of American Growth.* Princeton University Press: New Jersey. Clark, G. 2016. Winter is coming. *American Economic Review: Papers and Proceeding* 106: 68-71.

[463] Kupchan, *op. cit.*

[464] See, for instance: Westad, O.A. 2019. The sources of Chinese conduct. *Foreign Affairs*, September/October: 86-95.

[465] See, for instance: Gerstle, G. 2022. *The Rise and Fall of the Neoliberal Order.* OUP: New York. Banerjee, A. and Duflo, E. 2012. *Poor Economics*. Hatchette: London.

[466] Milanovic, B. 2020. The clash of capitalisms. *Foreign Affairs*, January/February.

[467] Li, E.X. 2012. Why China's political model is superior. *New York Times.* February 16th.

[468] *Ibid.*

Selected Acronyms

A&E	Accident and Emergency
ABPI	Association of the British Pharmaceutical Industry
ADB	Asian Development Bank
ASDA	Associated Dairies
ASEC	Assistant Secretary
BDP	Botswana Democratic Party
BP	Before Present
BP	British Petroleum
CESO	Career Executive Service Officer
CMA	Competition and Markets Authority
CQC	Care Quality Commission
CSN	Companhia Siderúrgica Nacional
DHSS	Department of Health and Social Security
DPWH	Department of Public Works and Highways
ERAP	Pare or 'Buddy' (President Estrada's nickname)
FTSE	Financial Times Stock Exchange Group
GATT	General Agreement on Tariffs and Trade
GDP	Gross Domestic Product
GMA	Gloria Macapagal Arroyo
GNP	Gross National Product
GP	General Practitioner
GPA	Agreement on Public Procurement
HDI	Human Development Index
ICIS	Independent Commodity Intelligence Services
ICLEI	International Council for Local Environmental Initiatives
ICT	Information Communication Technology
IMF	International Monetary Fund

KAMPI	Kalibat ng Malayang Pilipino
KPMG	Klynveld Peat Marwick Goerdeler
LGU	Local Government Unit
MOD	Ministry of Defense
MP	Member of Parliament
NGO	Non-Governmental Organization
NHS	National Health Service
NMC	Nursing and Midwifery Council
NPA	New People's Army
NPC	National People's Congress
NUCD	National Union of Christian Democrats
OECD	Organization for Economic Cooperation and Development
OFSTED	Office for Standards in Education, Children's Services and Skills
PEA	Public Estates Authority (now Philippine Reclamation Authority)
PMS	Presidential Management Staff
PNB	Philippine National Bank
PNOC	Philippine National Oil Company
QAA	Quality Assurance Agency
SME	Small and Medium Enterprises
UMNO	United Malays National Organization
UNCTAD	United Nations Conference on Trade and Development
UNDP	United National Development Programme
USEC	Undersecretary
WHO	World Health Organization
WTO	World Trade Organization
ZTE	Zhongxing Telecommunication Equipment

Index

B

C

D

E

O

P

U

V

W

www.ingramcontent.com/pod-product-compliance
Lightning Source LLC
LaVergne TN
LVHW010718210926
848485LV00008B/1438/J
* 9 7 8 1 6 8 0 5 3 7 2 3 9 *